CONTEMPORARY AMERICAN BIOGRAPHY

CONTEMPORARY
AMERICAN
BIOGRAPHY

Edited by
JOHN A. BECKWITH
and
GEOFFREY COOPE

Essay Index Reprint Series

BOOKS FOR LIBRARIES PRESS
FREEPORT, NEW YORK

Library of Congress Cataloging in Publication Data

Beckwith, John A   ed.
   Contemporary American biography.
   (Essay index reprint series)
   Includes bibliographical references.
   1. U. S.--Biography. 2. Biography (as a
literary form) I. Coope, Geoffrey, joint ed.
II. Title.
CT214.B4 1971   920.073   77-142607
ISBN 0-8369-2483-5

PRINTED IN THE UNITED STATES OF AMERICA
BY
NEW WORLD BOOK MANUFACTURING CO., INC.
HALLANDALE, FLORIDA 33009

CONTENTS

CONTENTS

Profile and Portrait

Autobiography

PREFACE

Preferring to interpret the term "biography" in its widest sense, the editors have not hesitated to present selections of the greatest variety of both form and content, with the hope that the book will appeal to the interests of whatever reader. The inclusion of "portraits," "profiles," and "close-ups" from recent periodicals, along with the more conventionally literary types of biography, is intended to foster an interest in the lives and personalities of living men and women. The selections from radio literature, news accounts, and even a book of verse are intended not only to indicate the diversity of contemporary biography as to form, but to encourage curiosity about, and analysis of, the forms themselves as matters of general literary interest.

Because biographers often write of the same figure and must frequently make use of identical facts, it is felt that their writings provide a most satisfactory opportunity for making comparisons of literary method—selection of materials, mode of treatment, choice of form, and many other problems connected with the craft of literature. The inclusion of biographies of the same people will, it is hoped, provide such an opportunity. The study aids at the end of the volume are intended not to dictate a pedagogical method, but merely to suggest some organized plan of study for those who wish one. It was also felt that the related and comparative method of presenting further readings might be more effective than the more usual formal list. In any case, formal lists are easily available in most libraries. Further, no apology is made for the inclusion of rather simple words in the lists suggested for vocabulary study; experience has taught the editors that taking them for granted is no courtesy to the student.

The customary acknowledgments to authors and publishers are made elsewhere in this volume; but the editors desire to give special thanks, for their generosity and help, to Patience, Richard, and John Abbe; to Mr. Ted Malone, Miss Alice Leone Moats,

Mr. Beverly Smith, Mr. Frederic Sondern, Jr., Mr. Sigmund Spaeth; to the publishers of *The American Magazine*, *The Forum*, *Life*, *Time*, and *The Reader's Digest*; and to Mr. W. T. Couch and the University of North Carolina Press.

CONTEMPORARY AMERICAN BIOGRAPHY

INTRODUCTION

The Biographical Element in Literature

Biography can perhaps be most inclusively defined as that element in literature which narrates the lives of real people. Some critics may prefer to regard it as a distinct *type* of literature; and this, indeed, is allowable if one is not required to regard a type as too rigid and inflexible a category. Perhaps even so it is less clearly defined than some other types better established and more easily determined. The biographical element can be found in many kinds of books; it is only when it is the dominant element in a work that we can speak of such a work as a biography. The ancients made no real distinction between history and biography, and many modern historians have written biographically in their historical works. Thomas Carlyle went so far as to say that "history is the essence of innumerable biographies." Even a sub-variety of the biographical type—the so-called *portrait* or *profile* —is to be found in historical works, as, for instance, the portraits of Elizabeth and Cromwell and others in John Richard Green's *History of the English People.*

In addition to works of an historical nature, books of a general expository character frequently contain biographical elements, as also do books of travel and adventure, articles on world affairs, and such miscellaneous books by journalists on contemporary history as those by Gunther, Sheean, Adamic, and others. Thus, although we may safely allow the more or less formal biography as a distinct type of literature, we must not forget that biography as a literary element is frequently to be found in books not primarily biographical.

In the chemical laboratory a student is often taught to produce some element in its free state by means of chemical action. He then studies this element, say the gas hydrogen, until he becomes familiar with its properties. All this is very proper and useful; but the student must not then suppose that he can go outside of the laboratory and expect to find hydrogen in a free and unmixed state in the actual world of nature. He will instead find water and

1

air, both of which contain the element he is looking for. But he will never be able accurately to refer to either of those natural occurrences as hydrogen. At most he can call them hydrogenous substances. Correspondingly, any discussion of types is to be understood as a laboratory procedure by which a reader of literature may quantitatively and qualitatively analyze actual books for the biographical element they contain.

Biography versus Fiction

A biography and a novel, or at least that kind of novel which uses the name of a character for its title (*Tom Jones, Henry Esmond, Madame Bovary*), have this much in common—both narrate the life of a person. The novelist, however, invents or creates his character, and, even when he bases it upon an actual person, feels no obligation to remain true to all the facts. More frequently his hero, or protagonist, is an essentialized human being drawn from experiences of many persons and even created out of imagination and fancy. A biographer cannot trim the subject of his work to fit his ideas of what the person should or would have been, and remain a true biographer. He is committed, just as an historian is, to the actual facts. Of course, a biographer must usually interpret the facts or generalize from them, in order to present the person more clearly or more vividly, or for some other reason. But unless his interpretation is in the nature of a scientific synthesis, he is apt merely to present a highly subjective impression of reality rather than reality itself.

This is the debatable ground of biography. Precisely where does biography merge into biographical fiction? That there is such a thing as biographical fiction is not only allowable but proper, just as it is also proper to speak of historical fiction as a type. Actually there is no danger in admitting both the existence and the value of such works, provided they are called neither biography nor history, but are referred to as containing a biographical or historical element. There is undoubtedly some part of a narrative of the life of a real person in such widely different works of literature as André Maurois' *Ariel* (Shelley) and Gertrude Atherton's *The Conqueror* (Alexander Hamilton) even though the characters they present are not wholly, sometimes not even proportionately, factual. In the former much if not most of the dialogue is invented; in the latter, even scenes and events. Nevertheless, it may be said that wherever the reader encounters any demonstrable attempt to narrate the lives of real persons in a work of whatever character, he is dealing with biography.

HISTORY OF BIOGRAPHY

Biography has a long and distinguished history; many of the great books of literature fall within its limits as a type. To name only a few, the four synoptic Gospels of *The New Testament*, the *Lives* by Plutarch, those of the Caesars by Suetonius, of Sir Thomas More by William Roper, of John Donne by Izaak Walton, of the English poets by Samuel Johnson, of Johnson himself by Boswell, of Lord Nelson by Southey, and so on down to the life of Lincoln by Carl Sandburg—here are classics of many ages and countries. However, the historical study of the type is in no way essential to an enjoyment of such examples as appear in this volume, and it may properly be postponed until such introductory reading experiences have interested the reader sufficiently to arouse curiosity and motivate study. Lack of space here prevents an adequate history; and since a brief and inconclusive account is likely to be of almost no value, the reader is referred to the excellent and easily available accounts in the two latest editions of the *Encyclopedia Britannica*. The one by Edmund Gosse (*Ency. Brit.*, 11th ed.), himself a biographer, is especially complete and accurate.

Some recent tendencies may be noted, however. Dissatisfied with the earlier biographical tendency to suppress damaging or unflattering events and traits of character, more recent writers, led by Lytton Strachey at the beginning of the present century, instituted a highly self-conscious rebellion against the eulogistic element in biography. The extremists of this group popularized the recent and fashionable "debunking" *life*, which all too frequently overcorrected the previous weakness and fell into the opposite one. However, it has been pointed out with considerable accuracy that Strachey's method, instead of being entirely original, is only an extension of a method used by Samuel Johnson in dealing with the lives of seventeenth- and eighteenth-century poets. Even if this is only partly true, so much danger attaches to the categorical definition of what the tendencies of recent biography really are, that it is wise to think of biography as continuous, even if developing, and not differing generically enough in any period to warrant division into a "modern type" and an "earlier type."

However, one development, gradual—not momentary and cataclysmic—is worth attention. This is the increasing occurrence of biographies of rather obscure and little-known individuals, the biographical manifestation of a growing democratic spirit which no longer restricts itself to aristocratic chronicle, to the lives of the famous, but prefers instead to write of the obscure and mediocre success, of the equally obscure and mediocre failure. Such lives as those told in *These Are Our Lives* would hardly have commanded the pen of a Johnson or his Boswell; but in a more modern day they couple, with an inherent literary satisfaction to the reader, whatever democratic implications the reader is able to draw from them.

Finally, attention can profitably be called to the improvement of biographical tools—especially psychology as an instrumentation of character analysis. True, the older biographers were lay psychologists of no mean order; and the poet Browning, without benefit of behavioristic psychology, succeeded in penetrating deeply into the minds of his characters. Nevertheless, communication of ideas about the motivation of human actions has been immeasurably helped by the fact that readers and writers alike are today informed on the subject of psychological terminology and procedure. The more extreme psychological method, that of the psychiatrist and pathologist, is still perhaps more tempting and dangerous than it is useful; nearly all such new literary tools have been both badly and unrestrainedly used in the first flush of enthusiasm, especially by writers not of the first rank. Yet it would be unintelligent to deny to biography, or to any other form of literary expression, the use of the tools produced by the age, and thus prevent it from taking its rightful place in the history of cultural development.

PURPOSES AND METHOD IN BIOGRAPHY

Several purposes are recognized as motivating the writing of biography. Some historical critics regard one of these, the desire to commemorate a person after death, as the probable origin of biographical literature. Closely allied to this purpose is the didactic, hortatory, or moral. Lives of great men, it was found, could be used as models of proper conduct for the young. Still another purpose, perhaps more purely artistic than the preceding, is the natural human desire to break the narrow prison of one's own life, to share vicariously in the lives of others. Added to this curiosity about other individual ways of life is a deeper curiosity for the meaning of life itself. At the present time, although biography in the form of commemorative obituary and moral example survives—the former especially in fraternal and institutional literature, and the latter in popular magazines and religious literature—natural human curiosity about lives in particular and life in general, rather than commemoration or didacticism, probably accounts for most of the tremendous output of contemporary biography.

In addition to purposes there are also methods or techniques of writing biography. First deciding on a purpose, the biographer will choose a method—commonly in this order, because purpose to some extent determines method. If a writer is moved by the didactic or hortatory impulse, he will most likely select facts that are favorable to his subject; and even though he may in all honesty desire to record his subject's defects, and may actually do so, he will nevertheless lay greater stress on good qualities rather than bad. His method will be to subject facts, first to a rigorous selection, or at least a selective emphasis, then to a eulogistic interpretation. Even if he uses the life of a bad man for moral purposes, the method is comparable. He will emphasize the subject's bad qualities to strengthen the lesson of the ultimate tragedy and moral defeat. The first method gives us the hagiography or "saint's life" in all its forms, the second the story which teaches that "crime does not pay."

Finally, there is the matter of form. But since a biographer, although he may use prose almost as a matter of course, is not prohibited from using verse, and within these two forms all manner of specific subforms, the choice is practically the same as for any other type of writer. The reader will find various literary forms in this volume, with all manner of typographical aids in addition.

Short Biography

The short biography—from one to twenty thousand words—is historically as old as biography itself. In fact, in older literature it was the rule rather than the exception. Like its fictional relative, the short story, it is easily adapted to the requirements of publication in a single issue of a magazine. Many leading periodicals carry a biographical article in each issue; others include it in a book review or news account, where it serves a secondary but important purpose. Not all short biographies appear in periodicals, however; some are incorporated in books by journalists on contemporary or historical matters, such as Gunther's *Inside Europe* or Sheean's *Personal History*. Finally, complete books—collections of short biographies—are both numerous and popular. These frequently develop some special and unifying theme, or otherwise use some logical method of grouping, as the following titles indicate: *Eminent Victorians, Twelve Bad Men, Crusaders of Chemistry, Earth Conquerors, Microbe Hunters,* etc.

All that has been said about biography as a whole can be said equally of the short biography. It is inspired by the same motives and can assume the same forms. There are, however, some minor and specific differences of technique. Because of its limited space, short biography demands a sure artistic sense; and although the preparatory research need not be so exhaustive as that required for, say, such a biography as that of Lincoln by Sandburg, it must be thorough, or the resulting work will give the impression of shallowness. The biographer selects the short form, not because he lacks material, but because he wants to achieve a single, dominant impression with an economy of means. Thus, the selection of proper details makes great demands on the author. He cannot use all the available details, because there is no space for an impressive marshaling of facts. Indeed, he may decide to list them, as Gamaliel Bradford lists them with appended dates, at the beginning of the biography, and thus leave himself free for analysis and interpretation in the biography itself. Limited space also tempts the writer to select only a few character traits, and this is another challenge to the biographer's skill. For if certain peculiar traits receive too strong an emphasis, oversimplification of character is likely to result, even caricature. To select the proper details, to present them proportionately and in correct perspective requires a discrimination and vision which is at once the opportunity and the pitfall of the writer of short biographies. Yet in spite of the difficulties of the form, many contemporary short biographies succeed in giving surprisingly accurate appraisals of life and character.

The Comparative Study of Biography

There can be but a single autobiography of any one man, one selection of facts, one choice of method, one interpretation— those of the man himself. He may, as not infrequently happens, write more than one autobiographical book, but no one else may write them for him. It is otherwise with biography. There is hardly one figure of first rank in any field whose life has not been written at least several times by several writers. As new facts concerning a man's life become available and new methods of interpretation become popular, the hitherto standard "lives" become inadequately revealing, and a new biography must be written, although not always a better one. Sometimes, however, several biographies of a man appear almost simultaneously, differing from each other in many ways, and written for a variety of purposes. For instance, William Dean Howells, the novelist, once wrote a campaign life of Lincoln. Perhaps it helped to elect him. At any rate it was written with a single purpose in mind—to enhance the vote-getting value of a political candidate. Obviously, such a life must present facts selected so as best to achieve its purpose. Another kind of life may be written for a biographical dictionary; here facts are more important than interpretations of character. Or a life may be written by a friend or colleague and deal only with a small part of the subject's experiences and perhaps cover only a fraction of his life span. Such partial lives are not only interesting to read on their own account, but also useful to a subsequent writer of a "whole" biography.

Whatever the purpose or length or method, biographies differ as widely as any other form of writing. Any more than a casual interest in a man is likely to send the student to as many different biographies of the subject as he can obtain. He is then faced with the problem of comparing, weighing, and sifting the evidence and the method of presenting it. He is faced with the problem of interpretative additions—with, in fact, the whole fascinating matter of biography. Thus each of the three sets of comparative biographies printed in this text presents a problem in the critical and appreciative reading of biographical writing, and the opportunity to study such differences (and others) of approach, method, and interpretation as have been mentioned above.

PROFILE AND PORTRAIT

Some biographies, especially short ones, do not attempt to cover the subject's entire life span, to appraise the significance of his whole life, or to estimate his total achievement. The reader is made to see the subject only at a certain time (or times) and under special conditions. Such partial biographies are frequently called portraits because, although they may be accurate at the time of their writing, at another time or under other circumstances the figure they portray may be utterly different. The partial biography that results from an attempt to write of living figures is by its very nature likely to be a portrait. For instance,

Vincent Sheean's picture, in *Personal History*, of General Chiang Kai-shek in the nineteen-twenties is not the Chiang Kai-shek of today; neither is Gunther's Hitler of 1940 likely to be the Hitler of 1950, and it certainly will not be the Hitler of a biography written fifty years after his death. In short, to pronounce judgment with any degree of finality upon a living character is impossible—even if the subject is already an old man, as he is in "Dewey at Eighty." It is safer to classify biographies of living men as portraits, although for further qualifications of this statement the reader is referred to the notes on the selection by John Gunther at the end of the volume. Incidentally, it does not follow that all so-called portraits must deal with living subjects. The posthumous biographer may attempt to narrate only a moment of his subject's life, at a particular time and under particular circumstances, as the title "Lincoln at Gettysburg" might illustrate. But it must be remembered that such a biographer has the facts of the entire life at his disposal, so that although his account is only of a moment, a knowledge of the whole life underlies and supports it. This is a very different matter from presenting a biographical moment in the light only of the moment itself and what has preceded it in the life of the subject. A dramatic critic can, and sometimes does, judge a new play by witnessing only the second of three acts, but he might do a far better job of criticism by coming to the theatre early enough to see the first act and staying for the third as well.

AUTOBIOGRAPHY

Autobiography is a form of biography possessing the distinguishing characteristic of having been written by the subject himself. As a division of literature, its boundaries are so loosely defined as to include memoirs, diaries or journals, even letters, as well as the more formal chronicle of one's life. In fact, many books of travel, exploration, and adventure are highly autobiographical.

The writer of autobiography, as of biography, seeks to perpetuate his subject's memory—in this case his own. He may try to justify, even magnify, himself, and so become self-laudatory. He may submit his life as a model that aspirants to success may follow, or sensationalize it from exhibitionist motives. Classic examples of this last are the confessions of Rousseau and the memoirs of Casanova. Although it is difficult to remain detached or objective about matters of self, many writers have had no other purpose than to give a conscientious and truthfully proportionate account of their lives and achievements.

As autobiography has no set form, so also it has no special technique. The writer is free to approach and limit his subject as he likes, to select any method he sees fit. His freedom, however, is not absolute. If he expects the reader to judge his autobiography favorably, he must avoid self-praise and, on the other hand, all obvious self-depreciation which will invite the charge of insincerity

Offhand one would judge a man himself to be the best qualified to tell the story of his life. Here at last one would expect an authentic account—the ultimate truth. Such is by no means the case. Unconsciously a writer may leave out significant details simply because he has forgotten them. Consciously he may leave them out because they do not contribute to the unity of his plan; because they show him in a way which, for reasons of shame or pride, he does not wish to be revealed; because they may offend someone still alive or whose memory is still alive. Further, he may unintentionally misinterpret even the demonstrable facts of his own life. He may think he is making the correct generalization, the substantiable synthesis; yet he may only be rationalizing, and thus be guilty of distortion. Reflection on the autobiographic process forces one to conclude that truth is as illusive in an autobiography as in a biography, in the self-portrait as in the portrait done by another hand. In spite of this, autobiography has always been, and always will be, a most satisfactory kind of reading, for it often happens that the very attempt to conceal facts and to misinterpret them neither conceals nor misinterprets. The reader may arrive at truth of character as much by what an author does not reveal as by what he does. It is the psychological analyst in each of us that keeps us fascinated with autobiography.

COMPARATIVE READINGS IN BIOGRAPHY

BRAINS WIN AND LOSE: WOODROW WILSON

GAMALIEL BRADFORD

‎‎ШЛЛЛЛЛЛЛЛЛЛЛЛЛЛЛЛЛЛЛЛЛЛЛ

CHRONOLOGY

THOMAS WOODROW WILSON.
Born, Staunton, Virginia, December 28, 1856.
Graduated Princeton, 1879.
Married Ellen Axson, June 24, 1885.
Ph.D., Johns Hopkins, 1886.
Professor at Bryn Mawr, 1885-88.
Professor at Wesleyan, 1888-90.
Professor at Princeton, 1890-1902.
President Princeton, 1902-10.
Governor of New Jersey, 1911-13.
President, 1913-21.
Married Edith Bolling Galt, December 18, 1915.
Signed Treaty of Versailles, June 28, 1919.
Died, February 3, 1924.

I

It would not be just to speak of Wilson as all brains. There was plenty of emotional life also. Yet you feel always that the intellect was the driving, the controlling force, and the defects of brains are as obvious in him as the excellences. For brains can do the greatest things in the world, they can develop ideals, they can build up states and civilizations, but they can also mislead and ruin and shatter an individual who puts a too blind trust in them.

Thomas Woodrow Wilson was born in Staunton, Virginia, in 1856. He came of that Scotch-Irish stock which gave America Andrew and Stonewall Jackson and so many other stubborn workers and fighters. His ancestors were teachers and ministers and the hereditary taint was in his blood, but always he wanted to manage men as well as to instruct them. He did not shine in his early education nor in the attempted practice of law. But

From Gamaliel Bradford, *The Quick and the Dead*, 1931, by permission of Houghton Mifflin Company, publishers.

when he began to teach at Bryn Mawr, at Wesleyan, and at Princeton, he showed the stuff that was in him. His success as a teacher and his evident energy and initiative made him President of Princeton, and his efforts to democratize education in that ancient university made him a conspicuous figure to the whole country, though circumstances prevented him from achieving his ideals. What he had done—and said—at Princeton brought him the governorship of New Jersey in 1910 and this was merely a stepping-stone in his sudden and astonishing passage to the Presidency in 1912, when the split in the Republican Party gave the Democrats an easy victory. Wilson was first interested in domestic reforms, the re-shaping of the tariff and the universally lauded establishment of the Federal Reserve System, though these were more or less interrupted by disturbed conditions in Mexico. Then in 1914 came the Great War and Wilson was faced with heavier burdens than had come to any president since Lincoln, while the burden was made much more severe by the loss of his wife who for years had been his beloved companion and most intimate adviser. After struggling vainly to remain a force for peace rather than an agency of destruction, the President was finally compelled to join the Allies, and victory was achieved largely by American brains, money, and valor. Wilson then went to Paris to make over the world by the League of Nations. After a gigantic struggle with all sorts of contending passions and selfishnesses he returned with the world imperfectly made over in the shape of a League and a Treaty which the Senate refused to accept. In a passionate effort to persuade the American people to reverse the Senate's verdict, Wilson shattered his health completely, and the last year of his Presidency was passed under a tragic cloud of physical feebleness and political failure. He died of a brain disease in 1924.

To begin with, it is interesting and curious to gather some of Wilson's comments on the general subject of brains, for it is evident that he had an immense, instinctive esteem for them, felt that they were the greatest agency for moving the world, at any rate his agency. And to this end he wanted them positive, sweeping with swift efficiency to conclusions which should make themselves felt as well as accepted. "Tolerance," he says, "is an admirable intellectual gift; but it is of little worth in politics. Politics is a war of causes, a joust of principles." And further, "In this grand contestation of warring principles he who doubts is a laggard and an impotent." The play of brain, the activity of brain, energetic, exhaustless intellectual labor, seems to him the thing in life that is really worth while: "There is a sort of grim satisfaction in tiring one's mind out, if it be only to prove one's mastery over natural disinclinations." And the lack of brain, which is for the most part a mere indolent unwillingness to use it, always merits his infinite contempt: "I overheard two men one day talking about a third man and one of them referred to his head. 'Head,' the other said, 'head! that isn't a head, that's just a knot. The Almighty put that there to keep him from raveling out!' And we have to admit that there are such persons."

As Wilson appreciates the power of brains, so he fully understands their dangers, at any rate as he perceives them in others. There is the danger of mistaking a head-load of facts for the power of using them: "Some of the best informed men I ever met could not reason at all. You know what you mean by an extraordinarily well informed man. You mean a man who always has some fact at his command to trip you up." There is the even more serious danger of mistaking theories for facts and so endeavoring to impose them upon the world: "Life is a very complex thing. No theory that I ever heard propounded will match its varied pattern; and the men who are dangerous are the men who are not content with understanding but go on to propound theories, things that will make a new pattern for the universe. Those are the men who are not to be trusted."

Yet to the Scotch-Irish Wilson brains in the abstract, theorizing for the curiosity and pleasure of it, seemed a vain and futile affair. When people try to relegate him and confine him to the academic cloister, he rebels and protests: "It has always seemed to me an odd thing and a thing against nature that the literary man, the man whose citizenship and freedom are of the world of thought, should ever have been deemed an unsafe man in affairs." What are thoughts for if they are not transmuted into deeds? What are brains for if not for an illumination and a guide in making a better world to live in? And thoughts, if they are good for anything, are so great and so real that the man who prizes and cherishes them properly will be ready to go out and do battle for them at any time: "If I was not ready to fight for anything I believe in, I would think it my duty to go back and take a back seat."

So much for brains in general, and Wilson on his own mind is even more interesting. When he is cool and detached, he is aware of the limitations and defects of the intellect, no man more so. It is apt to lead to subtle and ingenious insincerity, as he suggests in a comment on Jefferson, "the sort of insincerity which subtle natures yield to without loss of essential integrity." It is apt to lead to pride and wilfulness, as when he says of himself, "I am proud and wilful beyond measure," and as is intimated in the remark of Professor Perry, "I used to think that his only rea' fault of character was his impatience with the slower processes of other men's minds." And in Wilson's case at any rate it is apt to lead to intense concentration in one field of view to the exclusion of other solutions and important considerations, which is what he meant by the widely quoted description of his "single-track mind."

On the other hand, it requires but little acquaintance with Wilson's life and words and work to appreciate his immense enjoyment of intellectual power and his constant and implicit reliance upon it: "It is not men that interest or disturb me primarily: it is ideas. Ideas live; men die." This reliance upon the intellect was much enhanced by the fact that he did not suffer from the evil that it draws upon some of its followers, that of dissolving, disillusioning, bringing scepticism and consequent cynicism in its train. Wilson had his moments of doubt, perhaps; but in the main the Scotch assurance in his blood made him magnificently confident in the conclusions to which his reason led him. Observer after observer insists upon his absolute conviction of the truth after he had once arrived at it. When that state of mind was reached, all that remained was to hand the conviction on to others.

One evil of the intellectual life Wilson was fully aware of and stated and reiterated with the peculiar clarity of self-revelation in which he was so often a master, that is the isolation of it. The mass of mankind do not want to think for thinking's sake, perhaps they cannot. Hence the habitual, turbulent thinker is left to himself and he cannot but feel it: "The intellectual life is sometimes a fearfully solitary one. . . . The man devoted to that life is more than all other men liable to suffer from isolation, to feel utterly alone." And even finer is the passage in which he enlarges on this condition in regard to Lincoln: "There is a very holy and very terrible isolation for the conscience of every man who seeks to readjust the destiny in affairs for others as well as for himself, for a nation as well as for individuals. That privacy no man can intrude upon. That lonely search of the spirit for the right no man can assist."

II

Thus, having emphasized the importance of brains in general in Wilson's case, it becomes of interest to make a more detailed study of the swift and brilliant instrument which wrought so largely for good and evil in the world.

How much did he owe to education? Apparently not much in the ordinary sense. Like so many other men who have done great things, he educated himself: "The rule for every man is, not to depend on the education which other men prepare for him—not even to consent to it; but to strive to see things as they are, and to be himself as he is." Hence in his various schools and colleges he was not conspicuous, and would not condescend to busy himself too much with concerns which he felt not to be his. This temper sometimes fretted his scholarly relatives. "Tommy," cried his uncle James, "you can learn if you will. Then, for Heaven's sake, boy, get some of this. At least, if you have no ambition to be a scholar, you might wish to be a gentleman." The boy quietly went his own personal way, learned what he wanted and needed, and stored it up where it would do the most good when the call for it should come.

As to the special elements of intellectual activity, it does not appear that he set the highest store by mere accuracy or thoroughness. When it was necessary to go to the bottom of things, he went, with secure, unwearied probing. But he was always justly accused of a certain impatience with detail. What appealed to him far more than scholarly drudgery was the instinct of system, or order, or arrangement. This was a cardinal principle of his life, not only in intellectual matters but in daily and practical, and it enabled him to accomplish so much, in spite of physical and spiritual handicaps. See where you are going and map out your course, then you will get somewhere. And in his teaching and in his own studies the love of clarity and lucidity was everpresent. No doubt this passion for orderliness sometimes degenerated into a plague. The teaching caste has its special defects like others. A drift towards pedantry, towards the intrusion of academic method in the wrong place, is one of them. And Wilson was not free from it. In him there was sometimes a tendency to treat men of the world like unruly and inattentive students who needed to be made to see things as they are. But unquestionably the strong instinct of lucid arrangement, in thoughts and words and deeds, was one of the agents that carried him furthest.

What saved him more than anything else from the excesses of intellect and pedantry was the play of the imagination. You could not tie him down to dull research because his mind was always soaring, always keeping an outlet into the region of splendid dreams and many-colored ideals. He himself was inclined to attribute the imaginative side of his nature to an Irish element in his origin, meaning I suppose a Celtic element, and many of his biographers lay a good deal of emphasis on this. Just where the Celtic strain came into the solid Scotch-Irish ancestry is not clearly indicated. But in any case the imagination came in and the benefits of it were beyond question.

The play of it showed above all in the infinite ability and facility with words. This love for words and their exact and delicate uses was inborn, and constant practice and exercise brought it to perfection. Wilson's father was a close and thoughtful student of style, and the son early imbibed his father's tendency. He studied style as an instrument in writing, he studied it even more in vocal expression and he always looked upon oratory as the most effective means of influencing and controlling men. As Mr. Baker said of him: "He delights in words: in exact expression. Words are beautiful to him; and he is fond of new words which more clearly express the content of his ideas."

At the same time Wilson was careful to avoid the errors and the attitude of the mere rhetorician. What counted above all was thoughts. Words were merely the vehicle and of little or no account without the profound and powerful working of the mind beneath them. Or rather, the words and the thoughts were so inextricably and beautifully mingled that in using the one you were naturally and almost inevitably developing the other: "You must immerse your phrase in your thought, your thought in your phrase, till each became saturated with the other." And it is probable that in this connection Wilson would have liked to think that his admirable characterization of Burke was appropriate to himself: "His powers are all of a piece; his heart is mixed up with his mind; his opinions are immediately transmuted into convictions; he does not talk for distinction, because he does not use his mind for the mere intellectual pleasure of it, but because he also deeply feels what he thinks."

On this literary basis Wilson produced a very considerable

amount of printed matter which hardly receives enough attention in view of his greater political prominence. His American History and his Washington are rather in the nature of pot-boiling, but the earlier critical and biographical essays and the political writing of all periods are notable and original work. It is true that William Bayard Hale, who was first Wilson's enthusiastic biographer and later, after the development of war bitterness, his harshest critic, has little trouble in pointing out and ridiculing defects of style. But as Professor Perry justly remarks, no author could stand against such minute and malignant scrutiny. One smiles to think what would be left of Shakespeare if subjected to it. And the fact remains that Wilson was a master of the English language, both written and spoken.

To return to some further elements of his intellectual equipment. One asks oneself how far he was subject to prejudice, to those unreasoning movements of the spirit which are always the greatest enemies of intellectual power. He admits that he was not free from such things. But he at least believed that he was willing and anxious to subject such prejudices to the test of argument, and it seemed to him that he kept an open mind and welcomed objection and clear-cut presentation of an opposing point of view. Others do not always agree with him about this: "In argument he was fluent and resourceful, though not always logical. The rough and tumble of a give and take discussion annoyed and easily disconcerted him." On the other hand, one of his closest friends, Robert Bridges, insists that he got immense fun out of discussion as a pure game: "He always wanted to put his mind alongside of yours; the exercise of the faculty of intelligent debate and discussion was of infinite variety and joy to him. I never knew but one other man who got so much fun out of the exercise of his faculties."

However his convictions were arrived at, there is universal agreement that, once set, they were extraordinarily fixed and unchangeable. Having gone through his intellectual processes to the end, the man was certain he was right and all his physical and spiritual energy must be directed to carrying his conclusions into effect. It is true that at times he emphasizes the necessity of adapting oneself to changing circumstances. But the rock-like persistence of the convictions seems to be the thing that stands out with most of his associates and will be likely to stand out in history.

As to the special manifestations of the intellect in varied forms of application, what mainly strikes one, at any rate if one comes as I do from the minute study of Roosevelt, is the lack of versatility. Wilson's intellectual world was narrow from the beginning to the end. He had little command of languages, was strangely ignorant of the general great literature of the world. To science, which interested Roosevelt so immensely, he was quite indifferent, and indeed resented its intrusion into the more speculative and emotional fields. For abstract philosophy he cared little and his knowledge of it was slight. Even in religion his interest was not intellectual but practical. He imbibed and retained a vivid and animating orthodoxy, carrying it into a sure practical belief in divine interposition in the affairs of this world and an individual survival in the future. He maintained and proclaimed these beliefs at all times. He even had such queer minor quirks of superstition as his whimsical clinging to the number thirteen, which he thought peculiarly propitious to himself. But in all these matters he rather avoided discussion and intellectual probing and was satisfied with the practical application.

Even in the fields which might be thought peculiarly his own his information was singularly limited. He by no means kept up with the modern movement of political economy. His acquaintance with history in no way approached the broad familiarity with different epochs and nations which is so notable in Roosevelt. Only in the detailed analysis of the working of government was Wilson thoroughly and minutely at home. This was his natural field. This seemed to him the proper, the predominant, the engrossing preoccupation for human powers. At any rate he gave to it all the powers he possessed. Yet even here his thinking seems to me greater in extension than in intension. He did not go to the very bottom of things in the science of government any more than in the science of mind. His intellect was not profoundly penetrative or creative. Nor did he have what I call the passion of thought. Mental processes did not tear him and wrench him as they did Lucretius or Spinoza. What did characterize him as a creature of brains was an enormous and constant intellectual activity. He was always thinking, always fertilely, ingeniously designing and contriving new mental processes leading to new practical ends. It was the working of this activity which distinguished Wilson among contemporary statesmen and which makes the study of him so interesting.

But all this emphasis on brains must not be understood to imply that Wilson was lacking in nerves and sensibility. On the contrary, he was quite as well provided with these things as the average person. It was only that the brain activity was in excess and produces the greater impression. He himself repeatedly insists that after all it is the emotions that count: "I want to remind you that we are governed by our emotions very much more than we are governed by our reason." He was sometimes annoyed and exasperated by the charge of emotional deficiency: "So far as I can make it out, I was expected to be a perfect bloodless thinking machine; whereas I am perfectly aware that I have in me all the insurgent elements of the human race. I am sometimes by reason of long Scotch tradition able to keep those instincts in restraint." And he goes out of his way to proclaim the fires of emotional experience that burn him up: "If I were to interpret myself, I would say that my constant embarrassment is to restrain the emotions that are inside of me. You may not believe it, but I sometimes feel like a fire from a far from extinct volcano, and if the lava does not seem to spill over it is because you are not high enough to see the caldron boil." Yet all the time note just the suggestion of intellectual arrogance which the last sentence implies.

If the nerves appeared in no other way, the constant strain of ill health would tend to foster and develop them. Wilson was all his life physically delicate. There are hints of unrevealed maladies which persecuted him. At any rate, he had repeated nervous breakdowns and at all times he was more or less a martyr to indigestion and to the remedies he employed to meet it. Nerves so stretched and tormented would be expected to be frequently unstrung. It does not seem, however, that the general melancholy and depression, so often associated with such physical conditions, were especially present in this case. There was sometimes definite discouragement. There was often the burning discontent which is the greatest spur to progress. There does not seem to have been the vague sense of the hollowness of life and the worthlessness of effort which are apt to be the plague of nerves and brain working together. Perhaps the absence of these things was partly due to a superb and watchfully cultivated intellectual control, which shows in the ability to put aside the most colossal cares in the world and sleep whenever the chance came: "I am not often subject to the dominion of my nerves, and it requires only a very little prudence to enable me to maintain that mastery over myself and that free spirit of courageous, light-hearted work in which I pride myself."

It is of course with any individual impossible to measure exactly the nice balance of nerves and intellect in the great emotional experiences, but still it seems to me that in the two greatest of all, love and religion, the overswaying element in Wilson's case was intellectual. He loved intensely, he felt the power and the presence of God intensely. Yet the feeling is always interpenetrated with an intellectual, analytical clarity, as appears in the following passage: "You have loved some person very dearly. You have tried to merge your individuality with that person and you have never succeeded. There is no person linked spiritually so close to you that you can share his individuality and he can share yours." Doubtless this is the experience of all love, but only the preponderating intelligence dissects it so remorselessly.

Take the minor aspect of nerves, temper. Wilson had a quick, fierce temper. Read Mr. Thompson's account of the outbreak against an impudent camera man in Bermuda. But the temper was restrained and held down with an almost superhuman control, and there is constant testimony to his gentleness and courtesy even when worn out by public and private distress. Take again the aspect of pity and sympathy and sensitiveness to suffering. Among many illustrations there is the story of the woman who appealed to the President of Princeton to reinstate her erring son. She was on the eve of an operation, she said, and her life might depend on the President's clemency. "Madam," was the quiet answer, "as between your life and that of Princeton —the institution—it is better that you should die; for Princeton must live." And he refused, but he was almost prostrated afterwards. The nerves and the intellect also appeared in the same nice adjustment in money matters. It would seem that Wilson was always generous by impulse and ready to give where he had anything to give. But he had a Scotch canniness and thrift and the pestilent plague of his early career was the clinging bane of poverty. This shows in Mrs. Wilson's gentle, half-humorous complaint: "How I hope all this 'limelight' will make that new edition sell enormously. It is very inconvenient for a public man to be penniless." The strain of narrow circumstances came hardest on the wife, however. For Wilson himself was helped by his stoical indifference to luxury. He did not care for costly food, and if he did, he had not the stomach to eat it. Elaborate dressing and expensive, elegant appointments meant little to him: he could do without them.

So with amusements. In early life he took a certain interest in sports, but it was the brain interest not the hand, and when he is connected with baseball or football, it is rather as the manager or the coach than as a star player. He liked to plan and organize and let others act. In later life he played golf—for his health.

Again, with all æsthetic concerns. Mrs. Wilson practiced and loved painting and tried to initiate her husband, but his mind turned in other directions and he deplores it: "It has been one of the few grave misfortunes of my life that I have hitherto known least of the two things that move me most, poetry and painting. My sensibilities in those directions seem to me like a musical instrument seldom touched, like a harp disused." And so they largely remained to the end. He liked the outdoor world but mainly as exercise and diversion. He read certain poets over and over and especially enjoyed reading them to his friends; but his equipment in this line was astonishingly limited for a man who loved words and praised the benefits of literature so highly. He did like to sing and sang well, but even with music I find no indications of large acquaintance with the classical composers. He immensely enjoyed the theatre, in the earlier days more serious Shakespearean acting, Booth and others, but in later time he turned more to the frivolous, the movies and vaudeville shows, to which he was devoted to the end. Very characteristic is his own analysis of the use of such things: "There are blessed intervals when I forget by one means or another that I am President of the United States. One means by which I forget is to get a rattling good detective story, get after some imaginary offender and chase him all over—preferably over any continent but this, because the various parts of this continent are becoming painfully suggestive to me." And here obviously we have brains seeking oblivion by the most immediate and swiftly efficient means.

IV

The most important aspect of nerves is in relation to men and women. When it comes to politics, the tangle of brains and nerves is apt to be conspicuous in Wilson's case, but in ordinary life his human relations mainly involved ordinary feeling. As regards human beings at large and taken in the mass he had at any rate an unfailing curiosity and interest, though it does not seem as if he ever quite touched them or quite loved them. With his remarkable gift of elucidation he makes the curiosity and interest singularly effective. There is the striking passage of the railroad station: "I cannot sit in a railroad station comfortably because men will come in whom I want to kick out and persons will come in whom I want to go up and speak to and make friends with and I am restrained because when I was small I was told that was not good form and I would not for the world be unlike my fellow-men." And again there is his yearning complaint of the irksome limitations of his exalted position: "I like human beings. It is a pretty poor crowd that does not interest you . . . a crowd picked up off the street is just a jolly lot—a job lot of human beings, pulsating with life, with all kinds of passions and desires. It would be a great pleasure if unobserved and unattended I could be knocked around as I have been accustomed to being knocked around all my life. . . . I have sometimes thought of going to some costumers . . . and buying an assortment of beards, rouge, and coloring and all the known means of disguising myself, if it were not against the law."

In ordinary social intercourse Wilson was shy, remote, and difficult. He himself admits it and others agree. Something of how extreme this was is suggested in Hale's anecdote of the attempted visit to a foreigner of distinction: "The President of Princeton (as he was then) carried a letter of introduction to the foreign savant and went to his house to present it. Mr. Wilson's courage failed and he passed and repassed the house several times, and finally paused before it, but with trepidation so great that he could not ring the bell; the call was never made. It was not an exceptional case. 'This,' Mr. Wilson is quoted as saying reflectively, 'is why I know so few people I should like to have known.'" On the other hand, when the ice was once broken and the barriers down, the President's charm was unusual and almost unfailing. The ungraciousness of the harsh features and stiff manner were forgotten in the winning, sympathetic smile and especially in the vivid ease and insinuating grace of the varied and piquant speech. As Colonel House says: "When one gets access to him there is no more charming man in all the world than Woodrow Wilson. I have never seen any one who did not leave his presence impressed. He could use this charm to enormous personal and public advantage if he would."

And under circumstances that were at all intimate the charm flowered into an astonishing and spontaneous gayety. There were jests of all sorts, there was an inexhaustible fund of entertaining stories, the Celtic strain asserting itself in all its magic freedom. Wilson was at one with Roosevelt in his love of Lewis Carroll. He was always quoting Alice in Wonderland and he relished nonsense verses and limericks, himself perpetrating many of them, as the sparkling

> "For beauty I am not a star.
> There are others more handsome by far.
> But my face I don't mind it,
> For I am behind it:
> The man who's in front gets the jar."

When, as Governor of New Jersey, he attended a senatorial dinner, he astonished the legislators by singing darkey songs and joining Senator Frelinghuysen in a riotous Virginia reel.

When it comes to intimate friendships with men, Wilson once more is delightfully human, though perhaps Mr. Baker in emphasizing this protests a little too much. Such relations as that with Robert Bridges were by no means unusual and where there was no question of politics they endured to the end. It appears that men who had once been near to him and appreciated him clung to him with an almost blind devotion and confidence. What is impressive in these matters of affection is Wilson's own almost desperate longing to have people love him. He resented being thought of and treated as inhuman: "It is no compliment to me to have it said that I am a 'great intellectual machine.' Good Heavens, is there no more in me than that? I want people to love me—but I suppose they never will." Yet what strikes me most is that all the emphasis is on being loved not on loving. The truth is that these great people who do great things are too absorbed to waste much life on loving. And always there is the subtle disillusioning play of brain as Mr. Baker himself depicts it: "He wanted love, but must do his own thinking. All his life he was trying to keep his emotions apart from his thoughts—his friendships apart from his convictions. He would love without reservations; he must think coldly. Few men can do that or understand it in others: much tragedy is likely to flow from the attempt." Assuredly it did in Wilson's case.

As to minor yet immensely significant aspects of affection, for example the love of children and the love of animals, I find little evidence. Yet again there is the strange power of his penetrative analysis making you think he had affinities which perhaps he had not: "There are two beings who assess character instinctively by looking into the eyes—dogs and children. If a dog not naturally possessed of the devil will not come to you after he has looked you in the face, you ought to go home and examine your conscience; and if a little child from any other reason than mere timidity will not come to your knee, go home and look deeper yet into your conscience."

But in this matter of human relations Wilson is most interesting in his dealings with women, though naturally one cannot probe them to the very bottom. He took to women, liked them socially and intellectually, poured out his heart to them, tried to think they understood him. For there is no more subtle and exquisite flattery than that of being—apparently—understood, even if all the while the cool brain stands by and assures you that no one has ever understood you or will ever understand you. The purring, sympathetic adulation of good and brilliant women was irresistible. There is nothing more bewitching than to have an agreeable woman discover that you are a genius—especially when you have already surmised it yourself. Therefore Wilson wrote endless self-revealing letters to all sorts of ladies and this not unnaturally got him into trouble and filled Washington and the United States with utterly baseless scandal. Those of the letters to Mrs. Peck that have been published are as innocuous as they are intellectual and we are assured that the unpublished are no different.

Anyway, against these illicit complications Wilson was protected by his unswerving devotion to the wife whose incomparable tenderness and clear insight had gone so far to make him what he was. The reading of the letters printed by Mr. Baker shows how deep and lofty the devotion was and how persistent, and the testimony of Mrs. Wilson's brother and innumerable others proves the enduring beauty of the conjugal relation. Yet all the time, as in friendship, I am struck with a certain one-sidedness of that relation: "It isn't pleasant or convenient to have strong passions. . . . I have the uncomfortable feeling that I am carrying a volcano about with me. My salvation is in being loved. . . . There surely never lived a man with whom love was a more critical matter than it is with me." Still, still being loved, not loving! Oh, the egotism of men—almost equal to the egotism of women! But loving or loved, the women, the first wife and the second wife, played an enormous part in Wilson's career, both the private and the political.

v

And politics, the government of men, for Wilson as for Roosevelt, was all that seriously counted in life. When he was sixteen, looking at the portrait of Gladstone, he said: "That is Gladstone, the greatest statesman that ever lived. I intend to be a statesman too." Looking back from a later time, he said of his boyhood: "I was born a politician and must be at the task for which by means of my historical writing I have all these years been in training." Even when it seemed that circumstances had cut him off from a political career, he looked to it with bitter regret: "I do feel a very real regret that I have been shut out from my heart's first—primary—ambition and purpose, which was, to take an active, if possible a leading part in public life, and strike out for myself, if I had the ability, a *statesman's* career." And he proclaimed to his Princeton students: "We are not put into this world to sit still and know; we are put into it to act."

Then when he was fifty-three years old and actual politics seemed completely out of his range, he was thrust into the thick of them partly by his success at Princeton and partly by his failure. It was his original, independent grasp of the educational problem that attracted the attention of the country, and if he had been able to carry through his educational and social program at Princeton, it is doubtful whether he would have risked such prospects for the extremely dubious venture of the governorship of New Jersey in 1910. But from that turning-point politics was the whole of him.

And first it is necessary to establish squarely the lofty ideal aims of Wilson's political life. To any one who has followed him at all closely the slurs of Roosevelt, "he is astute and conscienceless," "his lack of all convictions and willingness to follow every opinion," are merely ridiculous. Wilson's aims may often have been unrealizable, but if so, it was because of their loftiness. He wanted to govern, but it was because he saw the superb possibilities of government and fully appreciated the lamentable defects which had hitherto kept those possibilities unattained. He was not mad enough to say that he could remedy the defects, but he was man enough to say that he would give his brain and his whole soul and his very life to trying. Men had claimed too much for Democracy. They had dallied with Democracy and professed to have put it to the proof and found it a failure and they were beginning to laugh at it and throw it aside. He believed that Democracy, for all its failures and defects, held the future of the world, as Lincoln believed it. He believed that Democracy, rightly guided and interpreted, even perhaps through the dazzling conception of a world unity, held the only possible hope of the future, and he was ready to give all that was in him in every way to the attempt to realize that hope.

Nor was Wilson by any means a mere dreaming idealist. He had fixed and definite and largely elaborated theories as to how the ideal should become a reality. Even as a boy he was an organizer and all through his career he was inclined to make systematic plans and frame constitutions of one kind or another. His first and perhaps his best book, *Congressional Government*, was an analytical study of the shortcomings of legislative administration in the United States, and from that point to the conception of the Covenant of the League he was always busy with governmental ideas, the weakness being that he was inclined to leap at once to larger outlines and to some extent disregard the patient working out of details. But always the theory of government was his passion.

Also, it is interesting to see how with all his intellectual preoccupations, he did not have the intellectual's dread of decision and responsibility. When he had made up his mind and saw his way, he wanted to go right ahead and act, or thought he did and insisted that he did. When he had made a critical decision, he never wasted time sighing over the consequences, but accepted the burden and forgot it, except as it affected the future. In theory he abhorred a moral coward, one who hesitates and palters and shifts in the face of sudden emergency. When the moment of trial comes, intellectual caution should be flung to the winds; and he spurns men "who are dried up at the source by the enemy of mankind which we call Caution. God save a free country from cautious men. . . . Caution is the confidential agent of selfishness."

Yet in spite of all this free vigor of theory, the old lurking, critical, hesitating intellect could not be altogether escaped and as you follow Wilson's political course, you cannot help feeling the defects as well as the qualities of brains. How they stand out in a confession like the following. To think of all who are looking to him, he says "makes me tremble not only with a sense of my own inadequacy and weakness, but as if I were shaken by the very things that are shaking them and if I seem circumspect, it is because I am so diligently trying not to make colossal blunders. If you just calculate the number of blunders a fellow can make in twenty-four hours if he is not careful and if he does not listen more than he talks, you would see something of the feeling I have." Cannot you watch the brains working, working through it all? It was this that caused the delay and the apparent uncertainty in the dealing with Mexico and in the even more critical dealing with the Great War. It may have been wise policy, it may have been debating inefficiency. It unquestionably was the action of intellect rather than will, and it not only irritated his enemies but provoked dubious comment from his faithful supporters, so that even Colonel House murmurs, "The trouble with the President is that he does not move, at times, with sufficient celerity," and one of the most judicious members of the Cabinet, Franklin K. Lane, cries, almost in despair, "We have had to push and push and push to get him to take any forward step. . . . He comes out right, but he is slower than a glacier and things are mighty disagreeable when anything has to be done."

Which brings us to the supreme problem of politics, at any rate for a temperament like Wilson's, the problem of dealing with human beings. He wanted to rule men, to work for their good, to manage them, but somehow he never had quite the tact or the touch to enable him to do it. As regards the general mass of mankind, taken individually, we have already seen something of his attitude in his social relations. He was intensely curious about men and women, he wanted to understand their motives, their tastes, their habits, their traditions: "The whole problem of life is to understand one another." Yet something held him off from them. It was partly perhaps the nice distinction that he makes in speaking of Jefferson: "Mr. Jefferson was only a patron of the people; appealed to the rank and file, believed in them, but shared neither their tastes nor their passions." And elsewhere he admits that Jefferson's attitude was largely his own. Also there was something of the intellectualist's contempt for the ignorant prejudice and offhand bravado of the crowd. As one not unfriendly observer says of him: "He mostly saw man the individual in his littleness and was intolerant, impatient, and disgusted with him. . . . He wanted to speak for the common crowd, but in private he frequently found it difficult to tolerate them. 'He has a bungalow mind,' was a favorite description. 'I sometimes wish they were not so damned honest and just had a little brains.' "

On the other hand, when it came to the masses collectively, he had immense, magnificent power over them by his gift of eloquence, could sway them hither and thither as he chose. Here also, as I pass from his earlier speeches, with their simple, sincere, scholarly earnestness, to the later political oratory, I feel a certain descent, as of a man who was striving to put his thoughts into a dialect unfamiliar and somewhat distasteful. But in spite of this, he got magnificent effects and effect. From his boyhood he loved oratory and practiced it, appreciated its defects and dangers but also its incomparable magic.

And the outcome of his pains and study was the crystallizing of those tremendous phrases, some of which, like the "too proud to fight," went far to ruin him, while others, like "making the world safe for Democracy," echoed and resounded with a strange animating glory in the ears of millions of weary and war-torn men and women. Somebody has said that Wilson's phrases did more to win the war than anything else. At any rate, borne on the swelling tide of them and the superb ideals they embodied, he went to Europe against the advice of his wisest counsellors, and achieved a triumphal progress such as has perhaps never come to any one man before. Alas, that it should have been possible to say, even with rhetorical exaggeration, that when he went to Europe he was the greatest man that ever lived, and when he returned he did not have a friend.

For when it came to handling men as individual co-workers, Wilson's weaknesses became apparent. He wanted to get near them, to conciliate them, to work with them, above all to understand them. But something in his make-up made the contact difficult, if not impossible. His heart was approachable, his head was not. As a group of indignant Democratic followers said to a curious, inquiring Republican, "we never get near him—no more than you—he holds us at arm's length." Still, still there was the cold, solitary intellect, shrinking into itself and bent upon working out its own processes in its own way.

The most striking element in this matter of Wilson's dealing with individuals is the long, profoundly tragic series of wrecked friendships that he left scattered behind him in his political career—West and Hibben at Princeton, Harvey, Garrison, Page, Lansing, and finally even the long-suffering Tumulty and Colonel House. In every single case no doubt Wilson had his good reasons. In every single case no doubt he had to choose between a principle and a friend, and the friend had to go. But it makes a record that is not pleasant to look over and one is reminded of the harsh criticism on Sainte-Beuve, that he deserted all his friends in the name of truth and in the end truth deserted him. Wilson would certainly never have admitted anything of the kind for himself, but at any rate he did not conform to the saying of a very wise person, that the law of love is higher than the law of truth.

Another significant and closely connected point in Wilson's human political relations is the constant drift to inferiors. His apologists deny this. They say that he readily consulted experts. He did, in their special lines, as in his admirable turning over of the entire military management to Pershing. Moreover, he sought information from many sources until his mind was made up. But the fact remains, that he instinctively surrounded himself with men who were his intellectual inferiors, who looked up to him and flattered him. It is true, he insisted that he was not under the influence of any one. But all men are influenced, and when your inferiors are closest to you, it is they who do the influencing. If you read Tumulty's book, you see what Tumulty was, and you also see how Wilson turned to him. The same is true of Lansing and of Daniels, and the Commission that Wilson took with him to Paris forms the harshest of all comments on him in this regard. To be sure, there is Colonel House, perhaps the most extraordinary figure in all the extraordinary aggregation, and who will venture to call Colonel House, that curious, subtle, flexible, insinuating, dominating spirit, inferior to any one? Yet in his extreme submission and loving devotion to his chief, Colonel House's influence was perhaps much of the same nature in its working as that of the others.

Then when Wilson emerged from this unwholesome atmosphere of comparative inferiority, when he came into bitter life and death conflict with those who were his equals or superiors, not perhaps in character, certainly not in ideals, but in energy, in resource, above all in political experience and political unscrupulousness, with the Wests at Princeton, with Lloyd George and Clemenceau at Paris, with Cabot Lodge at Washington, he was beaten, not in his ideals, but in his effort to put the ideals into effect.

VI

So we have considered the man's political career externally. Now let us turn to the lining of it, as it were, to his own view of that career and of himself. It is evident that there was a clear, persistent force of ambition guiding him from the beginning, and as to the nature and extent of such ambition he has words as illuminating as his words always are. Of the significance of ambition in general, of its larger purport, he says: "It is for this reason that men are in love with power and greatness: it affords them so pleasurable an expansion of faculty, so large a run for their minds, an exercise of spirit so varied and refreshing." And even in early years he analyzed clearly and subtly the working of this passion in himself: "Those indistinct plans of which we used to talk grow on me daily, until a sort of calm confidence of great things to be accomplished has come over me which I am puzzled to analyze the nature of. I can't tell whether it is a mere figment of my own inordinate vanity, or a deep-rooted determination which it will be within my power to act up to."

In the formative period the ambition was naturally vaguer and more indeterminate in its character. It never seems to have taken any legal aspect, though law was his chosen profession. But before he came to controlling men directly, he cherished the desire to influence them by written words, gave the closest attention to all the secrets of style and the use of them to make an enduring impression on the world: "I wish I could believe that I had inherited that rarest gift of making great truths attractive in the telling and of inspiring with great purposes by sheer force of eloquence or by gentle stress of persuasion." Yet it does not appear that the ambition was ever purely literary in form, there was no mastering desire to produce imaginative beauty for its own satisfying excellence.

To the literary ambition succeeded the academic, or the two went hand in hand. But here again the passion was not for pure scholarship, but rather to use learning as well as literary gift to arouse and stimulate his fellow-men: "I have no patience for the tedious toil of what is known as 'research'; I should be complete if I could inspire a great movement of opinion, if I could read the experiences of the past into the practical life of the men of to-day and communicate the thought to the minds of the great mass of the people so as to impel them to great political achievements."

Yet neither in writing books nor in teaching lay the real field of this eager, ardent spirit. Almost from childhood, as we have already seen, he burned to have a hand in the ruling of men, as he early wrote to a friend, "to mould the world as our hands might please." As the years ran on, he became more secure, more hopeful of the possibilities in this line: "I seem to myself to have become . . . more confident, steady, serene— enjoying in a certain degree a sense of power—as if I had gotten some way upon the road I used so to burn to travel—and yet fairly restless and impatient with ambition, as of old." And in his discontent with the academic routine he murmured to his brother-in-law: "I am so tired of a merely talking profession. I want to do something."

Then he got the chance to do something with a vengeance. What man in the world ever had a bigger? And can it be doubted that he thoroughly enjoyed it, enjoyed the prominence, enjoyed the distinction, enjoyed the publicity? Mr. Baker says, no doubt justly, that he had never the habit, so marked in Roosevelt, of dramatizing his own doings. Yet over and over and over you have the sense of his rich appreciation of standing where he did: "From the messages I get I realize that I am regarded as the foremost leader of liberal thought in the world." Do you suppose that the obscure writer, the humble teacher, did not relish that position to the full?

The relish was all the keener from his perfect understanding and vivid memory of the struggles he had had to go through, of the difficulties he had encountered in getting where he was. Take such moments as that when he seemed to have lost the nomination in 1912 and said to his sympathizing wife: "My dear, of course I am disappointed, but we must not complain. We must be sportsmen." Crises like that bring out the burning essence of a whole life. The same alternations of triumph and failure appear in his confession to Colonel House: "I spoke of his success, and he said his Princeton experience hung over him sometimes like a nightmare; that he had wonderful success there, and all at once conditions changed and the troubles, of which every one knew, were brought about. He seemed to fear that such a dénouement might occur again."

Yet with all the ups and downs there seems to be less of discouragement and depression than might have been expected. Such moments will come, in one form or another: "Complete success, such as I have had at the Hopkins, has the odd effect upon me of humiliating rather than exalting me; for I can't help knowing how much less worthy and capable I am than I am thought to be." But in the main there is the stern, firm, unshakable persistence which comes with a gaze forever fixed upon a remote object that must and will be attained.

Something the same grit and vigor show in the attitude towards criticism. Wilson did not like it, but he endured it grimly. The curious point in this regard is the working of the intellectual temperament. His friends insist that he did not bring in the personal side, was thinking only and always of the truth and the right. But precisely because he was so absolutely convinced that he was right, it came to seem to him that those who criticized and opposed him were actuated not by conviction but by malevolence, and the very loftiness and earnestness of his ideals infused a peculiar element of bitterness into his personal animosities.

Thus out of such a strange tangle of ambitions and ideals sprang this extraordinary and almost unparalleled career, a career in which triumph after triumph seemed only to lead in the end to tragic defeat, so that one realizes the direct significance of Wilson's words: "A man may be defeated by his own secondary successes." But through the dreamlike quality of it all and through the complicated web of seething passions and thwarted aspirations there runs that lofty sweep of noble idealism which must never be forgotten and which shines in Wilson's own words of the very last years: "I would rather fail in a cause that I know some day will triumph than to win in a cause that I know some day will fail." Yet even here how eminently characteristic is the reiterated *I know*. He knew, he knew, he always knew, for he was a creature of brains.

MEESTER VEELSON

John Dos Passos

ᴸᴸᴸᴸᴸᴸᴸᴸᴸᴸᴸᴸᴸᴸᴸᴸᴸᴸᴸᴸᴸᴸᴸᴸᴸᴸᴸᴸᴸᴸᴸᴸᴸᴸᴸᴸ

The year that Buchanan was elected president Thomas Woodrow Wilson
  was born to a presbyterian minister's daughter
  in the manse at Staunton in the valley of Virginia;
it was the old Scotch-Irish stock; the father was a presbyterian
minister too and a teacher of rhetoric in theological seminaries;
the Wilsons lived in a universe of words linked into an incontrovertible firmament by two centuries of calvinist divines,
  God was the Word
  and the Word was God.
Dr. Wilson was a man of standing who loved his home and
his children and good books and his wife and correct syntax and
talked to God every day at family prayers;
  he brought his sons up
  between the bible and the dictionary.

The years of the Civil War
  the years of fife and drum and platoonfire and proclamations
  the Wilsons lived in Augusta, Georgia; Tommy was a backward child, didn't learn his letters till he was nine, but when he
learned to read his favorite reading was Parson Weems'
  Life of Washington.

In 1870 Dr. Wilson was called to the Theological Seminary
at Columbia, South Carolina; Tommy attended Davidson college,
  where he developed a good tenor voice;
  then he went to Princeton and became a debater and editor
of the *Princetonian.* His first published article in the Nassau
Literary Magazine was an appreciation of Bismarck.

Afterwards he studied law at the University of Virginia; young

From *U. S. A.*, copyright, 1930, 1933, 1934, 1935, 1936, 1937 by
John Dos Passos.

Wilson wanted to be a Great Man, like Gladstone and the eighteenth century English parliamentarians; he wanted to hold the packed benches spellbound in the cause of Truth; but lawpractice irked him; he was more at home in the booky air of libraries, lecturerooms, college chapel, it was a relief to leave his lawpractice at Atlanta and take a Historical Fellowship at Johns Hopkins; there he wrote *Congressional Government*.

At twentynine he married a girl with a taste for painting (while he was courting her he coached her in how to use the broad "a") and got a job at Bryn Mawr teaching the girls History and Political Economy. When he got his Ph. D. from Johns Hopkins he moved to a professorship at Wesleyan, wrote articles, started a History of the United States,

spoke out for Truth Reform Responsible Government Democracy from the lecture platform, climbed all the steps of a brilliant university career; in 1901 the trustees of Princeton offered him the presidency;

he plunged into reforming the university, made violent friends and enemies, set the campus by the ears,

and the American people began to find on the front pages the name of Woodrow Wilson.

In 1909 he made addresses on Lincoln and Robert E. Lee and in 1910

the democratic bosses of New Jersey, hardpressed by muckrakers and reformers, got the bright idea of offering the nomination for governor to the stainless college president who attracted such large audiences

by publicly championing Right.

When Mr. Wilson addressed the Trenton convention that nominated him for governor he confessed his belief in the common man (the smalltown bosses and the wardheelers looked at each other and scratched their heads); he went on, his voice growing firmer:

that is the man by whose judgment I for one wish to be guided, so that as the tasks multiply, and as the days come when all will feel confusion and dismay, we may lift up our eyes to the hills out of these dark valleys where the crags of special privilege overshadow and darken our path, to where the sun gleams through the great passage in the broken cliffs, the sun of God,

the sun meant to regenerate men,
the sun meant to liberate them from their passion and despair
and lift us to those uplands which are the promised land of every
man who desires liberty and achievement.

The smalltown bosses and the wardheelers looked at each other
and scratched their heads; then they cheered; Wilson fooled the
wiseacres and doublecrossed the bosses, was elected by a huge
plurality;

so he left Princeton only half reformed to be Governor of
New Jersey,
and became reconciled with Bryan
at the Jackson Day dinner: when Bryan remarked, "I of
course knew that you were not with me in my position on the
currency," Mr. Wilson replied, "All I can say, Mr. Bryan, is
that you are a great big man."

He was introduced to Colonel House,
that amateur Merlin of politics who was spinning his webs
at the Hotel Gotham
and at the convention in Baltimore the next July the upshot
of the puppetshow staged for sweating delegates by Hearst and
House behind the scenes, and Bryan booming in the corridors
with a handkerchief over his wilted collar, was that Woodrow
Wilson was nominated for the presidency.

The bolt of the Progressives in Chicago from Taft to T.R.
made his election sure;
so he left the State of New Jersey halfreformed
(pitiless publicity was the slogan of the Shadow Lawn Campaign)
and went to the White House
our twentyeighth president.

While Woodrow Wilson drove up Pennsylvania Avenue beside Taft the great buttertub, who as president had been genially
undoing T.R.'s reactionary efforts to put business under the
control of the government,

J. Pierpont Morgan sat playing solitaire in his back office on
Wall Street, smoking twenty black cigars a day, cursing the
follies of democracy.

Wilson flayed the interests and branded privilege refused to
recognize Huerta and sent the militia to the Rio Grande
to assume a policy of watchful waiting. He published *The
New Freedom* and delivered his messages to Congress in per-

son, like a college president addressing the faculty and students. At Mobile he said:

I wish to take this occasion to say that the United States will never again seek one additional foot of territory by conquest; and he landed the marines at Vera Cruz.

We are witnessing a renaissance of public spirit, a reawakening of sober public opinion, a revival of the power of the people, the beginning of an age of thoughtful reconstruction . . .
but the world had started spinning round Sarajevo.

First it was *neutrality in thought and deed*, then *too proud to fight* when the *Lusitania* sinking and the danger to the Morgan loans and the stories of the British and French propagandists set all the financial centers in the East bawling for war, but the suction of the drumbeat and the guns was too strong; the best people took their fashions from Paris and their broad "a's" from London, and T.R. and the House of Morgan.

Five months after his reelection on the slogan *He kept us out of war*, Wilson pushed the Armed Ship Bill through congress and declared that a state of war existed between the United States and the Central Powers:
Force without stint or limit, force to the utmost.

Wilson became the state (war is the health of the state), Washington his Versailles, manned the socialized government with dollar a year men out of the great corporations and ran the big parade
of men munitions groceries mules and trucks to France. Five million men stood at attention outside of their tarpaper barracks every sundown while they played *The Star Spangled Banner.*

War brought the eight hour day, women's votes, prohibition, compulsory arbitration, high wages, high rates of interest, cost plus contracts and the luxury of being a Gold Star Mother.

If you objected to making the world safe for cost plus democracy you went to jail with Debs.

Almost too soon the show was over, Prince Max of Baden was pleading for the Fourteen Points, Foch was occupying the bridgeheads on the Rhine and the Kaiser out of breath ran for the train down the platform at Potsdam wearing a silk hat and some say false whiskers.

With the help of *Almighty God, Right, Truth, Justice, Freedom, Democracy, the Selfdetermination of Nations, No indemnities no annexations,*

and Cuban sugar and Caucasian manganese and Northwestern wheat and Dixie cotton, the British blockade, General Pershing, the taxicabs of Paris and the seventyfive gun
we won the war.

On December 4th, 1918, Woodrow Wilson, the first president
to leave the territory of the United States during his presidency,
sailed for France on board the *George Washington,*
the most powerful man in the world.

In Europe they knew what gas smelt like and the sweet sick
stench of bodies buried too shallow and the grey look of the
skin of starved children; they read in the papers that Meester
Veelson was for peace and freedom and canned goods and butter and sugar;
he landed at Brest with his staff of experts and publicists
after a rough trip on the *George Washington.*
La France héroïque was there with the speeches, the singing
schoolchildren, the mayors in their red sashes. (Did Meester
Veelson see the gendarmes at Brest beating back the demon-
stration of dockyard workers who came to meet him with red
flags?)
At the station in Paris he stepped from the train onto a wide
red carpet that lead him, between rows of potted palms, silk
hats, legions of honor, decorated busts of uniforms, frockcoats,
rosettes, boutonnières, to a Rolls Royce. (Did Meester Veelson
see the women in black, the cripples in their little carts, the
pale anxious faces along the streets, did he hear the terrible
anguish of the cheers as they hurried him and his new wife to
the hôtel de Mûrat, where in rooms full of brocade, gilt clocks,
Buhl cabinets and ormolu cupids the presidential suite had been
prepared?)
While the experts were organizing the procedure of the peace
conference, spreading green baize on the tables, arranging the
protocols,
the Wilsons took a tour to see for themselves: the day after
Christmas they were entertained at Buckingham Palace; at New-
years they called on the pope and on the microscopic Italian king
at the Quirinal. (Did Meester Veelson know that in the peas-
ants' war-grimed houses along the Brenta and the Piave they
were burning candles in front of his picture cut out of the illustrated papers?) (Did Meester Veelson know that the people of

Europe spelled a challenge to oppression out of the Fourteen Points as centuries before they had spelled a challenge to oppression out of the ninety-five articles Martin Luther nailed to the churchdoor in Wittenberg?)

January 18, 1919, in the midst of serried uniforms, cocked hats and gold braid, decorations, epaulettes, orders of merit and knighthood, the High Contracting Parties, the allied and associated powers met in the Salon de l'Horloge at the quai d'Orsay to dictate the peace,

but the grand assembly of the peace conference was too public a place to make peace in

so the High Contracting Parties

formed the Council of Ten, went into the Gobelin Room and, surrounded by Rubens's History of Marie de Medici,

began to dictate the peace.

But the Council of Ten was too public a place to make peace in

so they formed the Council of Four.

Orlando went home in a huff

and then there were three:

Clemenceau,

Lloyd George,

Woodrow Wilson.

Three old men shuffling the pack,

dealing out the cards:

the Rhineland, Danzig, the Polish corridor, the Ruhr, self determination of small nations, the Saar, League of Nations, mandates, the Mespot, Freedom of the Seas, Transjordania, Shantung, Fiume and the Island of Yap:

machine gun fire and arson,

starvation, lice, cholera, typhus;

oil was trumps.

Woodrow Wilson believed in his father's God

so he told the parishioners in the little Lowther Street Congregational church where his grandfather had preached in Carlisle in Scotland, a day so chilly that the newspaper men sitting in the old pews all had to keep their overcoats on.

On April 7th he ordered the *George Washington* to be held

at Brest with steam up ready to take the American delegation
home;

but he didn't go.

On April 19 sharper Clemenceau and sharper Lloyd George
got him into their little cosy threecardgame they called the
Council of Four.

On June 28th the Treaty of Versailles was ready
and Wilson had to go back home to explain to the politicians
who'd been ganging up on him meanwhile in the Senate and
House and to sober public opinion and to his father's God how
he'd let himself be trimmed and how far he'd made the world
safe
for democracy and the New Freedom.

From the day he landed in Hoboken he had his back to the
wall of the White House, talking to save his faith in words,
talking to save his faith in the League of Nations, talking to
save his faith in himself, in his father's God.

He strained every nerve of his body and brain, every agency
of the government he had under his control; (if anybody disagreed he was a crook or a red; no pardon for Debs).

In Seattle the wobblies whose leaders were in jail, in Seattle
the wobblies whose leaders had been lynched, who'd been shot
down like dogs, in Seattle the wobblies lined four blocks as Wilson passed, stood silent with their arms folded staring at the
great liberal as he was hurried past in his car, huddled in his
overcoat, haggard with fatigue, one side of his face twitching.
The men in overalls, the workingstiffs let him pass in silence
after all the other blocks of handclapping and patriotic cheers.

In Pueblo, Colorado, he was a grey man hardly able to stand,
one side of his face twitching:

Now that the mists of this great question have cleared away,
I believe that men will see the Truth, eye for eye and face to
face. There is one thing the American People always rise to and
extend their hand to, that is, the truth of justice and of liberty
and of peace. We have accepted that truth and we are going
to be led by it, and it is going to lead us, and through us the
world, out into pastures of quietness and peace such as the
world never dreamed of before.

That was his last speech;
on the train to Wichita he had a stroke. He gave up the
speaking tour that was to sweep the country for the League of

Nations. After that he was a ruined paralysed man barely able to speak;

the day he gave up the presidency to Harding the joint committee of the Senate and House appointed Henry Cabot Lodge, his lifelong enemy, to make the formal call at the executive office in the Capitol and ask the formal question whether the president had any message for the congress assembled in joint session;

Wilson managed to get to his feet, lifting himself painfully by the two arms of the chair. "Senator Lodge, I have no further communication to make, thank you . . . Good morning," he said.

In 1924 on February 3rd he died.

JUSTICE HOLMES

BEVERLY SMITH

∟⅃

When Justice Oliver Wendell Holmes resigned last winter, at the age of ninety-one, after thirty years as a member of the United States Supreme Court, President Hoover said:

"I know of no American retiring from public life with such a sense of affection and devotion of the whole people."

For strict accuracy, however, the words of the President must, with deference, be amended to read "affection and devotion of those who know him." The people as a whole know surprisingly little about Justice Holmes. Jurists all over the world honor him. They know that his book, *The Common Law*, still stands as a classic after fifty years; that his name will be linked in American Constitutional history with that of John Marshall, and that he has given to legal thinking a new realism and vitality which will be increasingly felt in the years to come. But to most of us he remains little more than a name. Lawyers find this hard to believe. A lawyer friend of mine said to me:

"But Holmes is the greatest living American. Of course everybody knows about him."

The conclusion does not necessarily follow. We Americans regard the Supreme Court with reverence. We rise up in anger when any reflection is cast upon it. But we have, generally, only the vaguest notion of its membership and powers. And that vagueness extends even to Holmes, its most brilliant member for thirty years past. I have talked with that abused citizen, "the man in the street." I have asked all kinds of people, in casual conversation, what they could tell me about Justice Holmes.

Here are some of the answers:

From a policeman: "Maybe he's over at General Sessions. Supreme Court? No, I never heard of him." From an aisle manager in a department store: "Gee, I don't know. Why don't you

From *The American Magazine*, February, 1933, by permission of the author and publishers.

43

ask the manager up in the office?" From a poorly dressed man on a park bench: "What are you trying to do, kid me? Holmes is the judge who just retired from the Supreme Court." From a delicatessen dealer: "Never heard of him. What you want to know for? Write an article? Why don't you write about my store—it's the cleanest in town." And from a bright young mechanic a reply that might have pleased Holmes himself: "Sure, he's on the Supreme Court. He's one of the young judges that always disagrees with the old birds."

Of all the replies, more than four fifths were the brief "Never heard of him." Possibly I struck an exceptionally rich vein of ignorance. I don't think so. They seemed to be the usual run of people. Certainly all could have answered correctly in a split second on Jimmy Walker, Greta Garbo, Al Capone, or Babe Ruth.

Justice Holmes would not wish it otherwise. He has no desire to be a popular idol. At the very prospect, I imagine, he would express his dissent in Civil War language which would sear the printed page and cause the sound apparatus of a news reel camera to burst into flame. He does not give interviews. He is not interested in publicity. It is inconceivable to him that anyone should be interested in his life apart from his legal writings. When biographers ask him for details he says, "Since 1865 there have been no biographical details."

Yet it seems a pity that we should not know a little more about this man while he still lives among us. He has lived a grand life. As a soldier—in the Civil War he was often wounded, twice seriously—as a thinker, and as a judge, his courage has never faltered. He has kept bright the American ideal of freedom of thought and speech, and labored to make the Constitution a living instrument of guidance rather than a dead hand to hold us back. And, with all the weight of his learning, he is one of the gayest, wittiest, most charming men alive.

Americans, busy with the conquest of a continent, have during the last century honored their men of action rather than their thinkers. From this, perhaps, has grown up the idea that doing much thinking is tiresome and unprofitable. Thought is a bore, and the thinker, we suspect, is a dull dog, a grind, an impractical theorist. This tradition, it seems to me, has diverted many of the best young American minds into so-called "practical" pursuits. Nowadays we are beginning to believe that we should be better off if some of our leaders had devoted less energy to action and more to thought. A glance at the life of Holmes ought to dispel the foolish idea that thought is "dull." Thinking can be the hardest work in the world. But Holmes has shown that it can also be a glorious and exciting adventure.

And when he, who knows so well the heroism of the battle-field, says that thinking may be heroic, we believe him.

"To think great thoughts you must be heroes as well as idealists," he writes. "Only when you have worked alone—when you have felt around you a black gulf of solitude more isolating than that which surrounds the dying man, and in hope and in despair have trusted to your own unshaken will—then only will you have achieved. Thus only can you gain the secret, isolated joy of the thinker, who knows that, a hundred years after he is dead and forgotten, men who never heard of him will be moving to the measure of his thought—the subtile rapture of a postponed power, which the world knows not because it has no external trappings, but which to his prophetic vision is more real than that which commands an army."

Holmes's influence upon all who have known him cannot be explained by his ideas alone, nor by the vigor and flash of the prose in which he clothes his philosophy. There is about him a personal charm as strong as magic.

It resides partly in his fine physical presence. The tall, soldierly figure, only recently a little stooped with age. The snowy whiteness of his hair, his bushy eyebrows, his jauntily flowing mustaches. The aquiline features, the gray-blue eyes, now stern, now snapping with inner laughter. And with this is his manner, the courtliness of a vanished day. There is a flattering assumption, even to the very young, that you are his equal, man to man.

The magic works upon all kinds of men. It has been felt by statesmen—Theodore Roosevelt, Lord Bryce, Viscount Morley, Jusserand; by judges—Charles Evans Hughes and Louis D. Brandeis; by philosophers and professors, by students who have served as his secretaries. The intellectuals vie with one another in their eulogies, each feeling that he understands Holmes a little better than the others.

And when you talk with his neighbors in the little village of Beverly Farms, Mass., where Holmes has passed his summers since he was a boy, you find that they feel the same way about him. They are proud of the eminent visitors who come to see the justice, but somehow he has gracefully made them feel that he likes his old neighbors just a little bit better than he does all the statesmen and professors and diplomats.

One day I was talking with James Emo, watchman at the railroad crossing near Justice Holmes's summer home. He was telling me of how the justice, taking his morning constitutional, stopped every day to chat with him. He did not speak of the justice as a celebrity, but as a friend whom it had been great good luck to know.

"The justice was interested in Rex, my Newfoundland dog, which used to be with me here at the crossing," Mr. Emo explained. "He would always ask me about Rex's health and habits. Wanted to know whether Rex could tell from the whistle which way the train was coming from, and talked about how Rex, when the train was coming on the near track, would get up and move over about twenty feet."

From the way Mr. Emo's face lighted up, I could see that Holmes's inquiries had given him a new and special interest in Rex. Just so I have seen a professor's face light up when Holmes showed an interest in an essay on the nature of certain points in the Constitution. Just so, throughout his long years, the vividness of Holmes's interest in life has kindled the interest of other men. . . .

On March 9, 1841, Dr. Oliver Wendell Holmes, a young Boston physician later to be noted as the author of *The Autocrat of the Breakfast Table*, wrote to his sister to announce the birth on the preceding day of his first son. The child, he suggested, might some day be a member of Congress or President, but at the moment was "scratching his face and sucking his right forefinger."

Think for a moment of the changes which that child, now our Justice Holmes, has witnessed in his lifetime. In 1841 America was a sparsely populated rural nation of twenty millions, its cities scattered chiefly along the Atlantic seaboard. Chicago was a village and the West was a wilderness. Texas was an independent state, and the gold rush which opened up California was in the undreamed-of future.

But Boston was already coming into its golden age. Emerson, Longfellow, Hawthorne, Whittier, and Lowell walked its streets and hobnobbed with Holmes, Sr., at the Parker House. It was in such a tradition, and under the influence especially of Emerson, that young Holmes grew up.

He graduated from Harvard in 1861, and that summer

marched away for Virginia with the 20th Massachusetts—the regiment which was to stand among the first half dozen in the North in percentage of losses.

Holmes saw his share. Wounded twice at Ball's Bluff, the second bullet missing the heart by half an inch. The surgeons guessed the wound as mortal, but he recovered and was invalided home. Back again for the mud, rain, scurvy, dysentery, and heartbreaking reverses of the Peninsular campaign. Wounded again at Antietam. Shot through the neck and left for dead on the battlefield. Picked up at night by some farmer boys, nursed back to life, and invalided home again. Back once more with his company in the fall, and in the spring, at Chancellorsville, his foot shattered by shrapnel. There was talk of amputation, but the foot healed, and still again he returned to the front.

He was not wounded again. Apparently the Confederate marksmen gave him up as a bad job. What was the good of wasting bullets on him? He always came back, anyway.

Never did life open up more pleasantly and temptingly for a young man than for Holmes after the war. He was the young hero, an officer, tall, dashing, and debonair. Good looks, social position, son of a famous author. The ladies doted on him; the men sought him out as a drinking companion. And Holmes liked it. No man enjoyed a good drink, a good dinner, a good play, and the conversation of charming women more than he. But life meant more to him than this.

The war had given Holmes something which he could never have found in the genteel Brahmin tradition. Battle had brought him up with a jolt against the realities which no pretty literature can express. He himself has said it best:

"In our youth our hearts were touched with fire. It was given us to learn at the outset that life is a profound and passionate thing."

And it was with passion that he flung himself into the study of the law. He knew well that its study can be dry and technical, its practice a sordid scramble for clients, a winning of cases which were better lost. But he knew too, as he has said, that "Every calling is great when greatly pursued." This idea is central in his philosophy. He recurs to it again and again. Whatever you do, do it with all your might: "The joy of life is to put out one's power in some natural and useful or harmless way. There is no other. And the real misery is not to do this."

During the next fifteen years, as student, practicing lawyer, and contributor to the reviews, Holmes went after the law with all his might. His friends were afraid that he was working himself to death. He wasn't content to learn the rules; he tracked down the history of the rules to find how they originated, and why, and whether they had outlived their usefulness. Grappling with the endless perplexities of the law, he fought to see clearly its purpose and meaning in the lives of men.

The mighty judges and scholars of England, who had always been rather sniffish toward American efforts at legal learning, sat up one day in 1881, pushed aside their port, and rubbed their eyes. Here was a book, *The Common Law*, by an American, a young fellow named Holmes, who actually had something to say. Here was a new view of the common law. The law was not a set of sacred and eternal principles magically drawn by the judges from a mass of dead precedents. The law was a body of rules based on experience, living and growing to serve man's changing destiny.

In this book Holmes anticipated the modern teachings of the law by a generation. He brought the law down to earth, carved it to human proportions, gave it a new vitality to serve man's needs.

The book was as good as a passport to membership in any court in the world, and in the following year, 1882, his own state honored him for it. Holmes was appointed justice of the Supreme Judicial Court of Massachusetts. He was then forty-one years old. "To *think* of it," his father commented. "My little boy a judge and able to send me to jail if I don't behave myself." Holmes remained a member of the court for twenty years, the last three years of the period as chief justice.

Conventional Boston was just a trifle puzzled by the new justice. Unquestionably an aristocrat, they agreed, but with queer democratic leanings. He consorted with all kinds of people. Why, he seemed to consider the individual more important than his social position! He believed the rights of labor were as important as the rights of property!

He was invariably courteous to the members of the bar, but sometimes the courtesy only half concealed a biting impatience with pomposity, verbosity, and pretense. He once advised a long-winded attorney to take a course of reading in risqué French novels, and thus learn the value of innuendo. The bar was also scandalized to learn that the justice sometimes went to a burlesque show. On one such occasion, it was reported, after a joke from the stage calculated to bring a blush to the cheek of a top sergeant, Justice Holmes was heard to say devoutly to himself:

"Thank God I am a man of low tastes."

But the bar knew, and everyone knew, that there was no chink in the bright armor of Holmes's personal integrity. And the wiser minds knew that the highest court of Massachusetts was honored by the presence of one of the great legal thinkers of the ages.

On December 2, 1902, President Theodore Roosevelt appointed Chief Justice Holmes of Massachusetts a member of the United States Supreme Court. In a speech of farewell to members of the Boston Bar, after mentioning the difficulties of the task that lay before him, Holmes expressed his faith, as so often, in a military figure of speech:

"But, gentlemen, it is a great adventure, and that thought brings with it a mighty joy. To have one's chance to do one's share in shaping the laws of the whole country, spreads over one the hush that one used to feel when awaiting the beginning of a battle. . . .

"We will not falter. We will not fail. We will reach the earthworks if we live, and if we fail we will leave our spirit in those who follow, and they will not turn back. All is ready. Bugler, blow the charge."

How nobly he has fulfilled that high resolve only those who understand the nature of the judicial process can appreciate. Judges do little that can be described in the headlines. Abrupt and obvious changes in the laws are made only by the legislatures. The judges can only fill the gaps in the clear meaning of statute and precedent.

This much can be said: Holmes's influence has always been on the side of individual freedom of thought and speech—"not free thought for those who agree with us, but freedom for the thought we hate"—and in favor of allowing legislatures a considerable freedom of experiment in legislation. To him the Constitution is not a straitjacket. "To rest upon a formula is a slumber that, prolonged, means death." Only by trial and error can mankind learn on this earth.

Because of the brilliance of some of his dissenting opinions there is a popular belief that Justice Holmes has almost always disagreed with his colleagues. He has even been called the Great Dissenter. As a matter of fact he dissented in only about one tenth of the cases that came before the Supreme Court in his thirty years of service. In nine tenths of his opinions he agreed with the majority.

Another mistaken belief is that Holmes is a radical. "He's not a radical; he's not a conservative," one of his friends told me. "He's just an honest, intelligent man." The conservative wants to change nothing; the radical wants to change everything; Holmes sees change as the law of life and growth and wants only to see that it comes about in an orderly fashion and "according to the rules."

His greatest service of all perhaps has been to give judges everywhere a new *method of approach* to the law. The law is not man's master but his servant. It must grow and change to fit his ever-changing needs. "It is revolting," he has written, "to have no better reason for a rule of law than that so it was laid down in the time of Henry IV. It is still more revolting if the grounds upon which it was laid down have vanished long since, and the rule simply persists from blind imitation of the past."

Judges must not be enslaved by words and formulas, he finds. They must "think *things*."

Nor does Holmes allow formulas to interfere with his way of life. If he had followed a conventional social life he could never have accomplished so much work or ranged so widely in his reading. The routine glitter of Washington official life does not appeal to him.

He would rather play solitaire, or ride out to Rock Creek Park to note the changing colors of the flowers, or go to the Smithsonian Institution with Justice Brandeis to study the new biological specimens, or stroll about the National Zoo, watching the bears get fat and roaring with laughter as he listens to Dr. William M. Mann, director of the Zoo, who tells what he says are the best animal stories in the world.

He does not let social convention dictate his friendships. He does not like every Tom, Dick, and Harry. In fact, he is extremely discriminating. But the discrimination is not based on wealth or social class or race or education. He looks straight through all these things for the quality in the man himself. Honesty, naturalness, straightforwardness, courtesy, common sense—these always appeal to him. And when he likes a man, that man likes him. His servants fairly worship the ground he walks on—which is a pretty good endorsement for any man.

One of Holmes's favorites used to be John Mallow, a barber who had a shop above the Old Corner Bookstore in Boston. The justice, before leaving Washington to go north for his summer vacation, would let his hair grow quite long so that he could have the pleasure of John's ministrations and conversation. The learned Justice of the Supreme Court, who had been bored during his life by so many eminent and pretentious men, would sometimes linger in the chair for more than an hour chuckling at John's talk.

One day Holmes asked John where he would like to go on his vacation. John named a little place in Vermont which he and his wife had longed to revisit.

"Then that is just where you are going," Holmes said. "Let me know all that it costs."

To talk with Justice Holmes is an adventure. "He is today, as ever, the best company in Washington," said Chief Justice Charles E. Hughes recently. His talk carries a special exhilaration. "If this man, so brave and wise, so old and yet so youthful, finds life so good," you think to yourself, "it must be good."

One great piece of good luck Justice Holmes has had in his life. He found in Miss Fanny Dixwell, whom he married in 1872, his match and true companion. Her wit and high spirit were the equal of his own. She died in 1929, after fifty-seven years of a marriage which their friends said was like a honeymoon to the end.

They began their marriage living in a flat over a drug store in Boston, Mrs. Holmes cooking the breakfast. Later she was hostess at the most brilliant and entertaining dinner parties in Washington. Never did she let the dignity of the Supreme Court put a damper on her spirits. She liked to go to fires. In their early days in Washington, when a fire engine came past the house, she would say, "Come on, Wendell, let's go." And she and the Justice of the Supreme Court would race hand in hand after the engines.

She kept her husband amused and guessing to the last. She did not hesitate to call him sharply to account occasionally, especially about his clothes and his health. All his suits, she declared, had been purchased before the Civil War. As for his health, he did not seem interested. Today, when he is asked to what he attributes his extraordinary age and vigor, he replies, "To bad air and lack of exercise." But when Mrs. Holmes insisted on some point affecting his welfare, he would always obey, except in one thing: He would not eat tapioca pudding. He had had too much of it as a child, apparently. He still refers to it scornfully as "stick-jaw."

Holmes's wit is not easily reproduced on paper. It is spontaneous and flows from the circumstances of the moment. Justice William R. Day, one of Holmes's colleagues, was a frail, tiny mite of a man. One day his son, a big six-footer, appeared before the Supreme Court and argued his case ably. Holmes scribbled a note and passed it along to his fellow judges: "A block off the old chip."

One day a burglar was arrested in the home of a Washington woman. The next evening she was telling Holmes about it. "I went right down to the jail and talked to that burglar," she said earnestly. "I told him how evil his way of life was. I told him how much happier he would be if he reformed. I talked to him for two hours."

"Poor man," murmured Holmes. "Poor man!"

As befits a student of words and an old soldier of the Army of the Potomac, he has a striking artistry in the use of profanity, when he is among intimates. But he yields the palm here to his old friendly enemies, the Confederates. "Young feller," he said one day to a friend, "you will never appreciate the potentialities of the English language until you have heard a Southern mule driver search the soul of a mule."

He is intensely American. Nothing so exasperates him as the man who praises everything European as superior to everything American. He has a deep feeling for the romance, power, and spirit which carved this nation out of the wilderness. He wants this country to be, truly, the land of the free and the home of the brave. But there is nothing of the jingo or the narrow nationalist about his attitude. He appreciates the greatness in the traditions of other lands, and is deeply read in their literatures.

The extent of his reading is almost incredible. He has been at it since boyhood. When you read voraciously every day for eighty years you cover a lot of territory. He has absorbed the literature of the Greeks and the Romans, sometimes in translations but "the purple passages in the original"; Dante and Rabelais, and Shakespeare, Montesquieu and Darwin—the list is endless, and it stretches straight down to the present day. Ernest Hemingway, Milt Gross, Anita Loos, the light verse of James Montague and Samuel Hoffenstein, share his interest with heavy tomes of philosophy, psychology, and the law.

He likes young people and refreshes himself from their youth.

Each year he has a new secretary, a young man selected from the honor graduates of the Harvard Law School. A year with him is a liberal education, eagerly sought after. And Holmes, indeed, seems to learn as much from these young men as they do from him. They are his liaison with the future. And he is demanding of their best energies. The young men, while they are his secretaries, must not become engaged to marry. "But I," he says, "reserve the right to die or resign."

He is not much inclined to give advice to the youngsters. He rather doubts its value, holding that every man must work out his own philosophy. "The advice of the elders to young men," he once said, "is very apt to be as unreal as a list of the one hundred best books." A very eminent American told me, "Holmes's greatest influence is by his example. He is a gentleman and a civilized man. That is something very rare in the world. He is a thinker, and thinkers are more needed in America today than ever before in our history."

Holmes has never been interested in wealth or power. He has said, "Happiness, I am sure from having known many successful men, cannot be won simply by being counsel for great corporations and having an income of $50,000 a year. . . . To an imagination of any scope the most far-reaching form of power is not money; it is the command of ideas."

Holmes's retirement from the bench has not greatly altered his way of life. He still passes his winters in Washington and his summers at Beverly Farms on the Massachusetts coast. His reading, his adventures among new ideas, his talks which are so rich for his old friends, continue as before.

On his ninetieth birthday, March 8, 1931, Justice Holmes was presented with a symposium of essays written by his friends. A microphone was brought into his study and he was persuaded to speak briefly in reply.

"In this symposium," he said, "my part is only to sit in silence. To express one's feelings as the end draws near is too intimate a task.

"But I may mention one thought that comes to me as a listener-in. The riders in a race do not stop short when they reach the goal. There is a little finishing canter before coming to a standstill. There is time to hear the kind voices of friends and to say to oneself, 'The work is done.'

"But just as one says that, the answer comes: 'The race is

over, but the work is never done while the power to work remains.'

"The canter that brings you to a standstill need not be only a coming to rest; it cannot be, while you still live. For to live is to function. That is all there is in living.

"And so I end with a line from a Latin poet who uttered the message more than fifteen hundred years ago: 'Death plucks my ear and says, "Live, I am coming." ' "

OLIVER WENDELL HOLMES

Justice Touched with Fire

Elizabeth Shepley Sergeant

Here is a Yankee, strayed from Olympus. Olympians are reputed at ease in the universe; they know truth in flashes of fire, and reveal its immortal essence in cryptic phrase. How disturbing to the solemnities of average mortals, average lawyers, average judges even, is the swift, searching, epigrammatic thought of Mr. Justice Holmes. Even the wise-cracks he loves to fling out are keyed to profundity and wit. He has lived through the most restless periods of American history since the American Revolution itself, yet his early divinations of the law, outlined nearly half a century ago, and his Supreme Court opinions, which have together recast American legal thinking, seem to have been formulated in the elegant leisure that we associate with the classics.

Oliver Wendell Holmes's tall and erect figure, which a ripe and white old age has scarcely stooped; his grand manner, at once noble and dazzling—those have never asked quarter of time. Watch his snowy head for a moment among his younger peers on the bench. Note the set of the shoulders in the gown, the oval contour of the face with its fine, angular New England features, the flow of the level white brows into the thin distinction of the nose, the martial mustachios, with their heavy guardsman's droop and their curved ends of punctilio. The eyes, the most striking feature, give off sparkles of scintillating grey-blue, and have more scepticism and gentle malice than mercy in their depths. Though at bottom Holmes is and looks a simple American gentleman of aristocratic rectitude, he has a spice of the

Reprinted from *Fire Under the Andes* by Elizabeth Shepley Sergeant, by permission and special arrangement with Alfred A. Knopf, Inc., authorized publishers.

Mephistophelean quality which he himself has recommended to the naïveté of judges.

The Justice is listening to a complex argument—listening till his mind, hovering and intent, like the wasp that paralyses the caterpillar, has driven straight to its heart. Then, while the other judges still patiently listen, he reads over the briefs, calls the pages to bring reports containing opinions relied on by counsel, and is ready, by the time counsel is rising to his peroration, to draft an opinion that will not fail to "strike the jugular."

The jurist who, at fourscore years and five, can command this penetration of essentials, this intense focusing of mental powers, has some rare elixir in his veins. Is it not the true elixir of youth? The youth offered by a young Bostonian to his country in the most heroic of her wars, and thrice wounded, at Ball's Bluff, Antietam, and Fredericksburg? Judge Holmes's clearest genius— the sharp and supple functioning of his mind—in some nameless fashion draws its strength from his curiosity and awe in the face of the mystery of existence. It seems that the near presence of death in those three stern and shadowed years fused his intellect and his emotion in a single shaft of will. It made sceptical philosophy a necessity, but gave to fundamental doubt a practical idealism. It affirmed man's destiny on earth as battle, his chances those of war. But it discovered to him that the root of joy as of duty and the worth of life itself is to put out all one's powers to the full, though the end be dim and the plan of campaign little understood. "Men carry their signatures upon their persons," he has written, "although they may not always be visible at the first glance." The friends of the Justice all know the signature that the Civil War inscribed. It is that of a youthful fighter who somehow inspired the fate of the lonely thinker with the faith of the soldier.

The son of Dr. Oliver Wendell Holmes was a fortunate youth. Born in the flower of New England's cultural dominance, and at the dawn of the Darwinian age into a family at once brahminical, literary, and scientific, brought up at that "autocratic" breakfast-table where a bright saying gave a child a double help of marmalade, he must early have acquired the rich flavour of belles-lettres which in him has ever mellowed the scientific habit. Celebrated men were familiars at his father's house, and from the greatest among them—Emerson—he drew a priceless intellectual ferment. Yet, with his glancing wit and his worldly charm, he might have been tempted away from the isolated path of the original thinker but for the war of secession. It was, in his own view, his greatest good fortune to graduate from Harvard in the class of '61, at the age of twenty, just as this war was beginning, and to learn one day, as he was walking down Beacon Hill, with Hobbes's *Leviathan* in his hand, that he had a commission in the Twentieth Massachusetts Volunteers; a regiment commemorated at last in the Boston Public Library by one of the lions of St. Gaudens that guard the entrance stairway. So the young officer, whom we may see in his uniform at Langdell Hall, at the Harvard Law School, with his visored cap on his knee, in one of those touching little faded photographs which were a sop to parental love—a mere lad, trusting and vulnerable, like all lads who have fought all the great wars—went forth to a baptism that he has never forgotten.

It came at Ball's Bluff: an engagement where the Twentieth Massachusetts got its first crucial trial. There were tactical errors which cost dear. The blues, defeated but "too proud to surrender," as the greys declared, were driven down the cliff on the Virginia shore into the Potomac, where, dying, swimming, drowning in numbers, they yet struggled to transport the survivors and the wounded in the few sinking boats to the island in mid-stream, and then to the Maryland shore, while the river was whipped into a foam of bullets, and darkness fell. Lieutenant Holmes, apparently mortally wounded in the breast, was laid in a boat with dying men and ferried through the night. As he recovered consciousness, he heard the man next him groan and—thinking he probably had his own dose—said to himself:

"I suppose Sir Philip Sidney would say: 'Put that man ashore first.' I think I will let events take their course."

A story written down by the elder Holmes in the *Atlantic Monthly* (not altogether to the pleasure of the younger?) is indicative of another side of the Justice's character. This relates how, after the battle of Antietam, Dr. Holmes started out to search for a wounded son. But the doctor could not find his young hero, though he followed this clue and that. At last, in despair, he was taking a train for the north at Hagerstown, Maryland, when, "in the first car, on the fourth seat to the right, I saw my captain."

"Hullo, my boy!"

"Boy, nothing!" (The original tale does not run quite this

way.) The "boy" had been spending a week much to his taste.
"As he walked languidly along [in Hagerstown], some ladies saw
him across the street and, seeing, were moved with pity and,
pitying, spoke such soft words that he was tempted to accept
their invitation to rest awhile beneath their hospitable roof. The
mansion was old, as the dwellings of gentlefolk should be; the
ladies were some of them young, and all were full of kindness;
there were gentle cares and unasked luxuries and pleasant talk,
and music sprinklings for the piano, with a sweet voice to keep
them company."

The words call up, along with other images of an America
gone for ever, a quaint photograph found in a portfolio in the
memorial Alcove at the Boston Library: a bevy of devout young
ladies in bustles and tight waists and long, flowing skirts, sewing
together on a flag. Such a flag was presented, after Ball's Bluff,
to Company E "by the sisters of Lieutenants Lowell and Putnam," with a polished letter from Charles Eliot Norton about
the honour of the Bay State. The Colonel of the Twentieth, by
the way, on first reaching head-quarters, and asked by the commanding officer if he had arms, uniforms, and accoutrements,
replied proudly: "My regiment, sir, came from Massachusetts."

Back to Massachusetts, then, came young Holmes, to the soil
for whose outcropping rocks and barberry bushes and sand dunes
and old towns built of brick and shingle he has confessed a
rooted affection. He had no path to blaze unless he chose: the
natural Puritan aristocracy from which he sprang awaited him
with its pleasant securities. But there burned in this young man,
as there burns in the Holmes of to-day, a sense of the valuable
brevity of existence. Life was a rich but a responsible adventure,
and he had a simple democratic conviction, denied to some who
are born under the shadow of Beacon Hill, that "the deepest
cause we have to love our country" is "that instinct, that spark,
that makes the American unable to meet his fellow man otherwise than simply as a man, eye to eye, hand to hand, and foot to
foot, wrestling naked on the sand." Holmes was recognizing fiery
energies which later claimed mountain climbing as an outlet. A
stern intellectual ambition, worthy substitute for the primitive
and heroic, was taking shape. A sentence of his own conjures him
up for me, standing apart even in his tested group: "In our youth
our hearts were touched with fire. It was given to us to learn at
the outset that life is a profound and passionate thing."

It is hinted that among those young ladies of the best families who—Boston being truly a village in the sixties—"knew every carriage in town," the return of a handsome wounded soldier (also the class poet of the decimated '61) made a stir. "That lanky talker of a Wendell Holmes" was an old maid-servant's dictum. Holmes has always loved talking by a fire with a clever and gracious woman, and these ghostly maidens, if they yet lived, could probably tell us why a young man of varied and brilliant parts chose from several possible destinies to enter the Harvard Law School.

For there was also literature, there was above all philosophy. Holmes was not the man to follow in his father's footsteps, or even in Emerson's, though he had in fact qualities as a literary stylist far superior to the doctor's, and gifts as a philosopher which gave a universal impress to his legal thinking. The winds and waves of eternity beat through his writings. "Nerve and dagger," said Emerson, are lacking in the American genius. Holmes the writer has nerve and dagger, as he has in moral and intellectual issues a blade-like courage. But he did not dream, in those tormented days, of being named among great American writers and philosophers. In his twenties this profession of the law which he had elected seemed barren enough. Did he choose it, by a quirk common to New Englanders, for that very reason? Because it was hard, male, undesired? The law enforced more than thought: an activity in the world of men, a reality which the soldier felt bound to espouse, if only that it was so alien to his intuitive bent for inward brooding thought. "It cost me some years of doubt and unhappiness," the Justice has avowed, "before I could say to myself: 'The law is part of the universe—if the universe can be thought about, one part must reveal it as much as another to one who can see that part. It is only a question if you have the eyes.'"

The study of philosophy helped Holmes to find his legal eyes. He likes to tell how he began to read Plato, as an undergraduate at Harvard, and was admonished by Emerson: "Hold him at arm's length. You must say to yourself: 'Plato, you have pleased the world for two thousand years: let us see if you can please me.'" The sequel is pertinent. Young Holmes not only read, but turned off a critical essay which he showed expectantly to his mentor. "I have read your piece. When you strike at a king, you must *kill* him." That shaft went straight to the bull's eye. When

Holmes graduated from the Law School he approached his profession in the spirit of scientific and philosophic inquiry. Not as do the practitioners "to whom the law is a rag-bag from which they pick out the piece and the colour that they want." Holmes had no consuming interest in practice, considered as winning cases and making money. But he had the hope, as yet scarce conscious, of shooting with true aim at some great intellectual marks. "I suppose the law is worthy of the interest of an intelligent man," he once hazarded, in his anguish of doubt whether it was, to Charles Francis Adams, the Minister to England.

That a philosopher could be, must be, a man of intelligence Holmes was morally certain. Was he not "twisting the tail of the cosmos" with his friend Bill James? One gets from the early letters of William James a fine series of images of two golden and impetuous youths, whetting thought on thought, doubt on doubt, in an upper chamber. In the year 1866 when "Bill" was twenty-four and studying medicine, and "Wendell" twenty-five and studying law, they exchanged acute argument on materialism. A year later, when James had gone to Germany to pursue philosophy, and Holmes had been admitted to the bar, discussions of "our dilapidated old friend the Kosmos" continued by letter— interspersed by affectionate reminiscence from James, of "your whitely lit-up room, drinking in your profound wisdom, your golden jibes, your costly imagery, listening to your shuddering laughter." "Why don't you join the Society for Psychical Research?" James is said to have inquired. To which Holmes: "Why don't you investigate Mohammedanism? There are millions of men who think you will be damned without it. Life is like an artichoke, you pull out a leaf, only a tip is edible. You pull out a day, only an hour or two is available for spiritual thoughts."

Holmes was looking, though he may not have realized it, for a personal philosophy that he could use as a raft from which to take the long, deep plunge into his legal-scholarly pursuits. It is typical—for his power of choice and exclusion, his economy of time and means are facets of his greatness—that he did not continue to flounder about in the philosophic waters, trying this system and that, cursing Jehovah and calling on his angels to save, but grasped the planks that he found near at hand and skilfully fitted them together into the aforementioned raft. *Raft* is too perishable a word. Holmes's philosophy was a tidy boat, formed, for all its pointed nails of scepticism, of sturdy Puritan oak, a shipshape bark, in which he could cruise safely about the cosmos among the other worlds and the stars.

Every speech, every personal letter, every opinion of Oliver Wendell Holmes rests on this hardy and lucid doctrine. Divergent though it was from the philosophy of James—who continued his search for a solution that would fit the fate of Man in general, and for himself tended toward those supernatural revelations and consolations which Holmes's scepticism impatiently repudiated,—the affectionate relation continued through life. And every distant interchange made the old philosophic quarrel flare up. The following statement of Holmes's "platform," —happily preserved in the James files—though written from the Supreme Court in 1901, "after reading your two pieces about Pragmatism (pedantic name)" might as well have been written in 1875, or, if William James had lived, in 1926.

"It is as absurd" (the Justice remarks, with familiar humility, before an expert) "for me to be spearing my old commonplaces at you as it would be for an outsider to instruct me in the theory of legal responsibility— but you see, *mon vieux*, although it is years since we have had any real talk together, I am rather obstinate in my adherence to ancient sympathies and enjoy letting out a little slack to you."

"I have been in the habit of saying that all I mean by truth is what I can't help thinking. The assumption of the validity of the thinking process seems to mean no more than that. But I have learned to surmise that my *can't helps* are not necessarily cosmic . . . philosophy seems to me generally speaking to sin through arrogance . . . I can't help preferring champagne to ditch water, but I doubt if the universe does . . . The great act of faith is when a man decides that he is not God . . . If I did come out of it [the universe] or rather if I am in it, I see no wonder that I can't swallow it. If it fixed my bounds, as it gives me my powers, I have nothing to say about its possibilities or characteristics, except that it is the kind of a thing (using this phraseology sceptically and under protest) that has me in its belly and so is bigger than I. It seems to me that my only promising activity is to make my universe coherent and livable, not to babble about *the* universe."

These passages define a consistent character. Judge Holmes has, at eighty-five, an intellectual youth that most men of forty cannot boast. He lives greatly in the brilliant young legal minds of to-day; believes that there are more men of promise in the present than in his own youth; receives their ideas with the courtesy, admiration, and speculative curiosity accorded to honoured guests. One of his favorite aphorisms is that the average life of an idea is fifteen years; another, that the literature of the past is a bore. Yet it is to be noted (since the laity persist in labelling him a radical) that, though he admires Proust and finds *Nize Baby* richly droll, he is more often to be seen, in that dignified Washington study of his, with a volume of eighteenth-century memoirs in his hand than with a daily newspaper. His own universe, material, spiritual, or intellectual, is not subject to perpetual revision. His economics, like his philosophy and his literary tastes, were pretty well settled in the twenties. The foundations of his legal thinking were laid in the thirties. His domestic happiness, which continues unbroken to this day, was established at the age of thirty-one—fifty-four years ago.

Meanwhile he was taking his plunge into the deep waters of the law. In 1869 James comments that "Wendell" is working too hard, taking no vacation. In 1870 he assumes the editorship of the *American Law Review*. In 1873 appears his important edition of Kent's *Commentaries*, and in the same year he becomes a member of the firm of Shattuck, Holmes and Munroe. But he cannot have given much time to practice, for the years from thirty to forty were a period of intensive research: a time of lonely and original productivity, often hinted at in his speeches, when he learned "to lay his course by a star which he has never seen"; and, feeling around him "a black gulf of solitude more isolating than that which surrounds the dying man," learned also to trust his "own unshaken will." During these years he offered his life to the law as completely as he had offered it to his country; and, losing it, found it again in his classic *Common Law*, which dates an epoch in American legal history.

The chapters were written first, as a Boston classic should be, in the form of "Lowell Lectures," and delivered in 1880. Published as a learned volume in 1881, the book was hailed by those competent to judge, both in America and in England, as a great and even a prophetic work. "The law embodies the story of a nation's development through the centuries," we read at the outset, "and it cannot be dealt with as if it contained only the axioms and corollaries of a book of mathematics." "The life of the law has not been logic; it has been experience." Together with the legal essays published before and after in the journals of the period, the book established, as Dean Pound has pointed out, that "functional" and relative view of the law now generally accepted as replacing the anatomical and morphological. Jurisprudence had been considered a self-sufficient science, with traditions all but God-given. Holmes discovered, by following a "right" or some other legal symbol to its early source, that the tradition was based often on some unreasoned survival that had lost all meaning. "The common law"—the phrase, from a later opinion, is famous—"is not a brooding omnipresence in the sky." Holmes emphasized the need of "thinking things rather than words." Pound says that he anticipated the teachers of to-day by thirty years or more. "The Epigoni could easily forget whose armour they were wearing and whose weapons they were wielding."

Justice Holmes's career as a jurist covers eras of rapid and organic social change and his eminence owes much to the insight—an insight very different from the piling of fact on fact—with which he has held the balance between history, experience, and timely necessity. He scrutinized the historical texts not for antiquarian reasons, not to discover an absolute—for in law, as in philosophy, he knew that he was not God—but for a concrete revelation of "man's destiny upon this earth." And looking back, he began to see the law at last as his constant and all-inclusive mistress: "A princess mightier than she who once wrought at Bayeux, eternally weaving into her web dim figures out of the ever lengthening past . . . disclosing every painful step and every world-shaking contest by which mankind has worked and fought its way from savage isolation to organic social life."

The fame that resulted from The Common Law led to a professorship at the Harvard Law School, and before the same year, 1882, was out, to an appointment to the Massachusetts Supreme Bench—"a stroke of lightning which changed all the course of my life." On this bench Holmes spent twenty fertile years, Associate Justice till 1899, Chief Justice till 1902. He managed his court with a practised hand. But through these Boston years, as now, he wore an air of detachment which marked him, in his native town, with a kind of uncommonness, and so, in certain quarters, with a kind of suspicion. The "village" never queries its failures: Tom Blank is a queer duck, but he is the son of John Blank, the banker. Now Oliver Wendell Holmes, Jr., was never the son of the doctor. He was a peacock with shining plumage; he flew afield and consorted with famous English jurists, like Bryce and Sir Frederick Pollock. He climbed Alps with Leslie Stephen. He enjoyed free spirits, whether Back Bay brahmins, or Jews, or Roman Catholic priests. He invited a labour leader to his home. (Said the man: "You have changed my feeling. I used to see an enemy in every house.") With women he had the ease and gaiety of a Parisian or a Viennese, and sought their company. He was impatient with dullness and long-windedness, suggesting, when Chief Justice, that the lawyers of the state would greatly oblige him by taking a course in risqué French novels and so learn to speak in innuendo rather than at length. Yet, all the while, he was more absorbed by the discoveries of his own mind than by the privileges or limitations of the world about him. The mind accompanied his tall and elegant figure in Boston as elsewhere, a pervasive and sceptical presence at every feast.

At a dinner given by the Boston Bar Association two years before the nomination of Oliver Wendell Holmes by Roosevelt to the Supreme Bench of the United States, the Chief Justice, in his responsive speech, asked himself what he had to show for this half lifetime that had passed—"I look into my book, in which I keep a docket of the decisions . . . which fall to me to write, and find about a thousand cases, many of them upon trifling or transitory matters . . . a thousand cases, when one would have liked to study to the bottom and to say his say on every question which the law ever presented. . . . We are lucky enough if we can give a sample of our best and if in our hearts we can feel it has been nobly done."

This reads like a peroration: it was a prelude to the richest maturity of Holmes's life. Twenty-five more years on the Supreme Bench, a thousand more cases, and the Justice still on the firing line. Nearly half a century altogether that Holmes has been "living through," as judge, the wisdom whose foundations were laid before forty. The phrase is his partner, Shattuck's, spoken in a moment when it seemed to Holmes, after many honours, that he had tasted the full feast of the law: "Now you must live it through." One may relate the words to a comment of Dean Wigmore that Justice Holmes is the only one of the long list of judges of the American Supreme Courts who framed for himself a system of legal truths and general truths of life, and composed his opinions in harmony with the system.

The system was flexible because at bottom it was an attitude of tolerance based on insight into the complexity of human affairs. It has done more than any system of orthodoxies to make the Supreme Court a tribunal, as Professor Felix Frankfurter has said, where inevitable frictions between the individual and society, between the expanding powers of the states and nation could be fought out, instead of a deistic chamber operating by scholastic formulae. Holmes's wish has been ever to harmonize conflicting interests; to see where man's social desires come from, and where they are tending. (He maintains that the "little decisions" frequently reveal more of interstitial change in the tissue of the law than famous disputes about a telephone company.) Though he proceeds from the general to the particular, he repudiates finalities. Behind his generalizations are intuitions of reality.

Minority decisions have probably made Mr. Justice Holmes's reputation with the rank and file. Yet his famous dissents as well as his majority decisions have frequently run counter to his personal prejudice. "The decision of a gentleman," says a Boston friend. The decision of a poet would be equally true. For to Holmes a fire smoulders at the core of things which makes them for ever plastic and mobile. *Plus ça change, plus c'est la même chose*, says the French sceptic. Holmes feels that the universe may be "too great a swell to condescend to have a meaning," but he is bound to accept the temporary pattern. "The best test of truth is the power of the thought to get itself accepted in the competition of the market. . . . Every year, if not every day, we have to wager our salvation upon some prophecy based upon imperfect knowledge." The Justice never refuses such a wager, but, taking it up, he uses his mind as guide rather than as dictator. His conservative critics cannot point to a single self-interested opinion. His best friends cannot boast that he has ever decided things their way. Indeed, President Roosevelt, who appointed him because he imagined Holmes had "the right ideas"—i.e., T. R.'s—soon was taught a lesson in true judicial-mindedness by Holmes's dissent in Roosevelt's pet case against the Northern Securities merger.

Roosevelt used to urge young men to fight for *their* ideas. So did President Eliot, whose prejudices were the defect of his passion. Holmes the sceptic thinks one idea very like another, but Holmes the New Englander knows well the difference between one aim and another. So his counsel to young lawyers is: Do the handsome thing, young feller! Don't be content to be a lawyer, be a lawyer in the grand manner. If you are sailing an intellectual bark, prepare for rigours, and head for the Pole. Forget subjectivities, be a willing instrument. Wreak yourself upon life. "If you want to hit a bird on the wing, you must have all your will in a focus. . . . Every achievement is a bird on the wing." Key sentences which reveal a freedom from passion that has made the ideal judicial temper.

A judge of the Federal bench tells of driving with Justice Holmes to the Capitol one morning some years ago, in that neat brougham drawn by a fat cob, with a highly respectable coloured coachman on the box, in which Holmes used to be recognized on the Washington streets. The Justice had got out of the carriage and was striding off, vigorous and loose-limbed, toward the dome when the younger man called out humorously: "Do justice, sir!" Holmes wheeled: "Come here, young feller!" and then, "I am not here to do justice. I am here to play the game according to the rules. When I was at the bar and Lowell used to beat, I'd say to him: 'Judge, your result may be good, but it's another game I undertook to play. I gave you a thrust in tierce and you countered with a bag of potatoes over my head.'"

When in some summer hour of ease in his home at Beverly Farms on the Massachusetts shore—an unpretentious Victorian house, with a gravel drive and formal flower-beds set with cannas and geraniums—he turns to Pepys' *Diary*—"this and Walpole's *Letters* are the two books if you don't want ideas, and don't want to waste your time"—he looks misty at the duel of two friends who fought for love. When he finds himself in the dentist's chair he recalls that fear of pain and rattling musketry which only the brave admit preceded the attack. His intimate talk still breaks into Civil War slang—"Shut your trap!"—his speeches and letters are full of war metaphors and allusions to this past which he says he "cannot bear to read about," perhaps because his remembered picture is too final to bear the intervention of historians, who describe how Sherman kept Lincoln waiting, and why great battles failed. Writing to Henry James, he is "firing away at high pressure with breech-loading speed." In a speech: "When once the dead fifers of thirty years since begin to play in my head, the laws are silent." In another: "Life is a roar of bargain and battle, but in the very heart of it there rises a mystical spiritual tone. . . . It transmutes the dull details into romance. It reminds us that our only but wholly adequate significance is as parts of the unimaginable whole."

This seasoned judge, this gallant gentleman of the old New England, is the most romantic of contemporary Americans. He starts off for the court every morning at 11:30 as if on an errand for the gods—whereas he is to listen to argument from 12:00 to

2:00; lunch from 2:00 to 2:30; sit again from 2:30 to 4:30. Judge Cardozo has used, of his sentences, the word *phosphorescence*. Always Holmes gives out light. When he returns from the court to the sober dignity of his old house on I Street—formerly it was on foot; now the Chief Justice is likely to drive him a part of the distance; but who can be sure that, disdaining his elevator, he will not still take his stairs two steps at a time?—he will be able, with the young secretary who guards the book-lined antechamber of his library, with the visitor, to search thought and make it glow. The secretary—a new jewel of the Harvard Law School every year—wears an exalted air. He must promise not to get engaged during the period. "But I reserve the right," says the Justice with a twinkle, "to die or resign." With this young mind the Justice twists the tail of the still recalcitrant cosmos, engaged in legal disputation, reads his opinions for criticism as modestly as if he were a novice. Sometimes, but rarely, there is a point of law to look up. For Holmes carries the law in his head, as a prophet the words of the Lord. And the Justice, in his own fine and ornamental script, answers every personal letter scrupulously, almost within the hour. "My messenger is waiting." Off it goes. The eye that falls upon the delicate missive in the cheap plethora of the morning mail has found treasure. Every page has some metaphysical touchstone, some literary epigram or casual heresy. "I must read *Twelfth Night* once more—a little girl tells me Shakespere is long in getting to the point. I think we take ourselves too seriously."

Mr. Justice Holmes, who has permanently enriched our law, our literature, our philosophy—of whom another distinguished judge has said: "There is Holmes—and there are all the other judges"—takes himself far less seriously than any good Rotarian. The blithe nonchalance, that true humbleness in the face of acknowledged human vanities, seems to his friends a part of his unerring taste. But it provokes distrust in those who need the support of the rolling platitudes of the Fathers. Holmes bears his critics no grudge. His courtesy to his fellows, like his generosity, is basic, and he has an innocent heart. When one sees his gracious figure outlined against his bookshelves full of classics, with their spaces for the books the Lord will omit mentioning, and their gaps for the books of the future, one is struck by its unquenchable youth. The face has a fine fresh colour, the voice, with its humorous vain echo of hesitation—mmm—that seems to set off the sparks in the eyes, has clarity and fervour. Maliciously it expunges the name of a popular New England poet from the slate of time, honestly it admits that gentlemen prefer blondes. But it will never allow our modern American idol, publicity, a niche in this hospitable library. If glory is here, she is hidden, diffused into a clear sérenity, a scent of tender memory, a vital intellectual replenishment.

Yet do not think of Oliver Wendell Holmes as meagrely recompensed. He has found it well, he says, to have philosophy "the main wind of his life blowing from the side, instead of from behind." He has had his reward in the inspired performance of a daily task, in the constant siege of the eternal verities. Holmes was an infantry officer, at Ball's Bluff, but in the field of ideas he belongs to an arm more mobile. I see him as a light horseman, a fabulous skirmisher, a cavalier for all his "cold Puritan passion," who carries a pennon as well as a lance, and with it "that little flutter which means ideals."

STEVE FOSTER OF "TIN PAN ALLEY"

Sigmund Spaeth

America's most famous composer is usually thought of either as a hopeless drunkard, who might have done great things in music if he had had any real character, or as an angel of sweetness and light moving through a world that did not appreciate or understand him.

Both of these conceptions are, of course, absurdly exaggerated. Stripped of mystery, reverential awe, and downright bunkum, Stephen Collins Foster emerges as a typical tunesmith of his day, with a career startling by parallel to those of our contemporary Tin Pan Alley. Compositions now enshrined as immortal inspirations were in their day treated with the same patronizing hauteur that to-day's highbrow bestows on popular hits. When a concert artist sang one of his numbers as an encore, a New York critic wrote: "Anna Zerr (shame to say) stooped to sing *Old Folks at Home*. One would as soon think of picking up an apple-core on the street." *Dwight's Journal of Music* remarked: "We wish to say that such tunes are erroneously supposed to have a deep hold of the popular mind; that the charm is only skin deep; that they are hummed *without musical emotion*, whistled 'for lack of thought'; that they persecute and haunt the morbidly sensitive nerves of deeply musical persons; that such melodies become catching, idle habits, and are not popular in the sense of musically inspiring, but that such and such a melody *breaks out* every now and then, like a morbid irritation of the skin."

Your modern composer of popular hits is as a rule a "natural musician," and in that category Stephen Foster surely belongs. Irving Berlin still picks out his melodies on the black keys of a piano which, with the help of modern science, automatically transposes them into the right key at the touch of a lever. Few

From *The Etude*, November, 1938, by permission of the author and *The Reader's Digest*.

if any of our "hit" writers are able to make a practical orchestration, and most of them leave even the simplest of piano arrangements to workers in the cubby-holes of the publishers.

These composers all started playing "by ear," and many continue to do so by choice. They are generally infant prodigies, like the majority of serious musicians, delighted to find in time that their talents have commercial value.

A Born Wonder Child

Foster had a similar background, musically, and although he went further than the average song writer of to-day, he never arrived at anything approaching the technic of a Gershwin or a Victor Herbert. A "Yankee Doodle boy," he was born on the Fourth of July, 1826, the same day that Thomas Jefferson and John Adams died. At the tender age of two he picked out chords on a guitar on the floor, calling it his "ittly pizani." At seven he surprised a Pittsburgh music dealer by experimenting briefly with a flageolet and almost immediately playing *Hail, Columbia* without a mistake.

Later he became a more than adequate performer on the flute, piano and violin, with some skill on the banjo and guitar, for the most part self-taught. He could write out his melodies without the help of an instrument, and could harmonize them in the form of a simple piano accompaniment, but he never attempted a more elaborate instrumentation or a development of his impromptu themes into the larger forms of music.

The Foster family, respectable business people, living on the outskirts of Pittsburgh, must have been aware of Stephen's gifts, but seem to have done little to encourage them. At nine he was allowed to sing *Jim Crow* and other Negro ditties in an informal stock company, with an actual cash return of a few cents a week. His first composition, written at the age of thirteen, was the faintly saccharine *Tioga Waltz*, for four flutes. At sixteen he wrote his first song, *Open Thy Lattice, Love*, musically far better.

There are accounts of his playing variations on the flute while others sang his songs, which would make Foster a rather dignified pioneer of modern swing. His brother Morrison, naturally inclined to sentimentalize the family genius, credits Stephen with studying the scores of Handel, Mozart and Weber, and adds that he would "improvise by the hour beautiful strains and harmonies which he did not preserve, but let them float away like fragrant flowers cast upon flowing water." From contemporaries come fleeting descriptions of the composer "swaying rhythmically" and sometimes weeping as he played the piano. His mature voice has been called a pleasant baritone, and he was evidently unrivaled in the singing of his own songs.

He was a sensitive, emotional boy, easily moved to tears. There is much emphasis on his physical courage, proved in rough and tumble fights with street rowdies. Contemporary portraits dwell upon his brilliant, deep brown eyes, his thick, black hair, and the appealing expression of his hook-nosed, rather lantern-jawed face. Some Italian blood on his mother's side may have accounted for these characteristics, as well as for the gift for music.

Like most musicians, past and present, young Steve had to try his hand at something "useful" before he was allowed to devote himself to the thing he did best. He acted as bookkeeper for his brother Dunning in Cincinnati, and it was there that he made his first attempts to break into the field of the professional showman.

The modern song writer has the greatest difficulty in emerging from the amateur class. He is constantly told to "get a reputation," or, more directly, "get someone to sing your songs." Stephen Foster had the same problem in 1840. But at least there were companies of "Ethiopian Singers" traveling about the country, and if one hung around the stage door, it might be possible to persuade some minor artist to accept a manuscript for trial.

AN UNPRINCIPLED MUSICAL THEFT

It was thus that M. J. Tichenor, of the Sable Harmonists, acquired the first copy of *Oh! Susanna*, when the composer was only twenty-one. But Stevie also gave a copy to George N. Christy, "Professor of the Bone Castanets," who calmly turned it over to a New York publisher, with his own name on the cover and no mention of the real composer.

A Louisville publisher named Peters brought out both *Oh! Susanna* and *Old Uncle Ned* "as a favor." Foster never got a cent from these popular hits, but they made over ten thousand dollars for Peters and set him up permanently in the music business. Similarly Firth, Pond & Company, who became Foster's regular publishers in time, acquired *Nellie Was a Lady* and *My Brudder Gum* by merely giving the composer fifty copies of each song.

Foster had that inherent naïveté that marks most of our popular composers, evidently essential to the production of terrific hits, but equally likely to produce terrific absurdities. Like the leaders of to-day's hit parade, Foster contributed his full share of both. He drew upon his own experience for subject matter, sometimes even permitting himself that artificial nostalgia which has produced so many songs about places which their creators had never seen and probably never wanted to see.

Old Folks at Home is itself an example of the unnatural geography that has at various times glorified Dixie, New Hampshire, California, Michigan and other places innumerable. Foster's original manuscript shows the name of the Pedee River, which obviously invited ridicule. His brother suggested Yazoo, which was even worse. Finally they took out a map of Florida, and a roving finger eventually stopped at the name of Swanee, an insignificant and by no means glamorous stream. "That's it," cried Steve, "that's it exactly"; and so the Swanee River became immortal. But the difference between Old Folks at Home (one of the world's most popular songs of all time) and the nostalgic outbursts of Tin Pan Alley is that Foster actually loved his own home to the point of adoration, and could express that love sincerely and convincingly, regardless of names or places.

Some Interesting Origins

It has been proved that he did not write My Old Kentucky Home at Federal Hill, in Bardstown, although he definitely visited it during his youth and must have had it in mind when the title came to him; nor is it true that his relative, Judge Rowan, the master of Federal Hill, was the object of Negro grief in Massa's in de Cold, Cold Ground. These stories are preserved for the edification of tourists, and there is no harm in them.

But the many feminine names that adorn the Foster songs all have a biographical significance, headed by Jeannie with the Light Brown Hair, who also appears several times as Jennie, and is unquestionably Jane McDowell, daughter of a Pittsburgh physician, and responsible for one of Stephen's tenderest and most personal songs. He married Jane in July 1850, but the marriage cannot be called a happy one. The following April they had a daughter named Marion, and then drifted more and more apart. They tried living in New York, unsuccessfully, then boarded with the Foster family back at home, borrowing money from various members. Unsuited they may have been to each other, but it was during one of their temporary estrangements, when Stephen was living in New York, that he wrote *Jeannie with the Light Brown Hair*, perhaps more nearly an art song than any of his others.

Old Black Joe was an actual Negro slave in the McDowell household, and other characters in the Foster songs can be similarly identified. Even *Old Dog Tray* had a living model in a rather worthless hound presented to Stephen by a friend.

A COMFORTABLE INCOME

It is a mistake to suppose that Stephen Foster was unable to make a living by his song writing, or that poverty drove him to drink. By 1849 Firth, Pond & Company agreed to pay him two cents a copy on all his songs, and for the next ten years or more his income averaged at least fifteen hundred dollars annually, a respectable sufficiency in those days. Unfortunately, however, financial security made him lazy and careless. Only when he did not know where he would earn his next dollar could he work effectively.

His publishers were good-natured, and Foster constantly drew royalties in advance. When he fell too far behind, he would sell out all future rights in a group of songs for a flat sum.

Once launched as a professional composer, Stephen continued to follow lines that run remarkably parallel to those of modern tunesmiths. But where modern song writers and publishers indulge in the frankest bribery of performers and band leaders to secure "plugs" for their works, Foster was lucky in usually having at least a singer in readiness to pay for a "first performance." For the miserable sum of fifteen dollars he permitted E. P. Christy to have his name published as the composer of his finest song, *Old Folks at Home*. The falsehood was corrected as soon as Foster found what an enormous hit he had produced, but as late as ten years after the real composer's death, the name of Christy still appeared unchallenged on some publications of *Old Folks at Home*. All too often to-day credit is given to a "plugger" instead of to the actual creator of a song.

AN ORIGINAL CREATOR

Foster's method of composing was modern. The question is often asked, "Which comes first, the words or the music?" With songs of the widest and most immediate appeal, the two seem as a rule to have come simultaneously. But where the composers and lyricists of Tin Pan Alley work best in collaboration, Foster himself supplied both words and music. He would start with a phrase or a title, fully clothed in tones, as Berlin arrived at such musical slogans as *What'll I Do?* or *All Alone*. He is described as writing down words and music together, phrase by phrase, whistling as he worked, and thus arriving gradually at "one harmonious whole."

Attempts have been made to prove that Foster borrowed his best melodies. Will Hays, a rival, claimed that he had a whole book full of German tunes, which he used freely. This is a ridiculous charge, although as a boy Stephen frequently heard Negroes singing in church, and later used some of the strains that he remembered. The tune of *Camptown Races* is practically identical with a folk song called *Hoodah day*, but it is not certain which came first. On the other hand, Foster always insisted that his own *Ellen Bayne* had been stolen for the tune of *John Brown's Body*. When a man writes in such universal patterns of melody, the question of originality is not important.

The Lights Grow Dim

The amazingly consistent record of Stephen Foster as a popular song writer is completed by the manner and the mystery of his death. Little is known of the details of his later life in New York. He seems to have buried himself in the big city in a desperate effort to regain a foothold in the world of music. Tradition has long decreed that popular song writers die in obscurity. The men who wrote *Sidewalks of New York*, *Ta-ra-ra-boom-deay* and *A Hot Time in the Old Town Tonight*, Blake, Sayers and Metz, were unknown to the American public, even by name, when they passed from the picture not long ago.

Nobody seems to have paid much attention to the man, still in his middle thirties, who walked the streets of New York between 1860 and 1864, peddling his songs where he could, and spending most of his earnings on drink. Foster had gradually lost control of his best sellers through the habit of selling out for a lump sum when he needed ready cash. His publishers no longer were willing to advance him money, and his creative gift had sunk to a low ebb.

Old Black Joe, the last of Foster's really successful songs, was copyrighted two days after Lincoln's election in 1860. From then on he seemed unable to produce anything above the average, and most of his attempts were pitifully weak. Wracked by the fever and ague of malaria, he found his only bodily and mental comfort in drink, and he drank as heavily as his income would permit.

Like many a modern composer whose inspiration has left him, Foster tried to revive a waning interest by the musical treatment of current events. But even his war songs were mostly conventional. There is no evidence that he made any attempt to get into active service during the Civil War, but his sympathies were with the North, in spite of the definitely southern atmosphere of so many of his songs.

The painful record of those final years can be read only in his songs. His once fine and straightforward sentiment turned into mawkish sentimentality. He no longer trusted his old power to weld the words and the music together, but allowed others to write his texts for him. Perhaps the most tragic failures were his attempts at comedy, so far removed from the effervescent absurdity of his youthful *Oh! Susanna*.

In the last three years of his life Foster turned out nearly a hundred compositions, all created in the most wretched surroundings. The utter collapse of his inspiration seemed to make him all the more prolific. Most of these songs were sold outright for whatever he could get.

George Cooper, later well known as a writer of song texts, who collaborated with Foster in some of these declining efforts, tells of one of their quick sales. They had just finished *Willie Has Gone to the War*. Stephen "rolled it up and tucking it under his arm, said, 'Well, what shall we do with this one?' " It was a cold winter day, with snow falling and the streets covered with slush. Stephen's shoes had holes in them, but he did not seem to notice it. They walked up Broadway together, and as they passed Wood's Music Hall the proprietor hailed them from the lobby. "What have you got there, Steve?" The song was immediately sold for twenty-five dollars—ten dollars in cash and fifteen dollars more at the box office that night.

It was in a run down grocery store at the corner of Hester and Christie Streets that Foster passed most of his last days. The back room was fitted up as a saloon, and there he spent what money he had on liquor, generally a cheap French rum mixed with sugar. Several visitors to the store speak of meeting him in the same spot. He wore "an old glazed cap," and his face "might have been that of a man of fifty instead of one in his middle thirties." They mention his "anxious, startled expression" and the "soft brown eyes, somewhat dimmed by dissipation." But Cooper insists that Stephen was never really intoxicated, although he drank steadily as long as his money held out.

THE CURTAIN FALLS

From a Bowery lodging house, Cooper received a message on January 12, 1864, that "his friend" had "met with an accident." (Foster was ill and undernourished and fell over the washbasin in a sudden fit of dizziness.) "I found him lying on the floor in the hall," says Cooper, "blood oozing from a cut in his throat, and with a bad bruise on his forehead. Steve never wore any night clothes, and he lay there on the floor, naked, and suffering horribly. He had wonderful big brown eyes, and they looked up at me with an appeal that I can never forget. He whispered, 'I'm done for'; and begged for a drink; but, before I could get it for him, the doctor who had been sent for arrived and forbade it. He started to sew up the gash in Steve's throat, and I was horrified to observe that he was using black thread. 'Haven't you any white thread?' I asked, and he said no, he had picked up the first thing he could find. I decided the doctor was not much good, and I went downstairs and got Steve a big drink of rum, which seemed to help him a lot. We put his clothes on him and took him to the hospital. In addition to the cut on his throat and the bruise on his forehead, he was suffering from a bad burn on his thigh, caused by the overturning of the spirit lamp he used to boil water. This had happened several days before, and he had said nothing about it, nor done anything for it. All the time we were caring for him, he seemed terribly weak, and his eyelids kept fluttering.

"I went back again that day to the hospital to see him, and he said nothing had been done for him and he couldn't eat the food they brought him. When I went back again the next day they said 'Your friend is dead.' His body had been sent down into the morgue, among the nameless dead. . . . I went around peering into the coffins until I found Steve's body."

It was Cooper who notified Foster's family. The newspapers seem to have carried no notice of the composer's death. In his pocketbook they found thirty-eight cents and a slip of paper bearing the words "Dear Friends and Gentle Hearts." Was it perhaps the germ of a song that would have brought him the sympathy and support he so greatly needed?

Stephen Foster remains a typical popular song writer, regardless of time or changing conditions. But, unlike most of Tin Pan Alley's output, his music is as alive to-day, and as universal in its appeal, as though his simple spirit had not been snuffed out at the age of thirty-seven. A popular composer becomes classic through the test of time, and by that test the songs of Stephen Foster are established as unquestioned classics of their kind.

STEPHEN FOSTER

TED MALONE

LⲢⲢⲢⲢⲢⲢⲢⲢⲢⲢⲢⲢⲢⲢⲢⲢⲢⲢⲢⲢⲢⲢ

NBC—WJZ   PILGRIMAGE OF POETRY

1:00-1:15 P.M.   February 25, 1940   SUNDAY

Hello there
This is Ted Malone
speaking to you from a beautiful old Southern mansion
On Federal Hill near Bardstown, Kentucky.
Judge John Rowan built this home here back in 1795
when Thomas Jefferson was president of this young republic.
Old Family portraits
still hang along the hallway in the high ceilinged rooms
Tastefully furnished with
rosewood . . . walnut . . . mahogany . . . and wild cherry.
I can see the old Springhouse halfway down the hill
where the crystal cool water
chilled the great stone jars of milk and butter
And bubbled over to tumble on down
A laughing stream
bordered by watercress and fragrant beds of mint.

Back in 1850,
so one of the old legends goes . . .
A young man and his bride came here on their honeymoon . . .
And they stood by this same window
and looked out across the rolling lawn . . .
She was Jeanie of the light brown hair . . .
and he was Stephen Collins Foster. . . .

Today the spirit of our visit is expressed
in a telegram just received from

From Ted Malone, *Pilgrimage of Poetry*, National Broadcasting Company, 1939-1940, by permission of the author.

Keen Johnson, Governor of the Commonwealth of
Kentucky. . . .[1]

The life of Stephen Foster
is filtered through with legends. .
Fact and fiction weave in and out until that which is easiest to
believe seems least based on truth
and that which no one will accept most likely did occur.
It begins with his birthday in 1826
when nearly all the family trooped off to a picnic celebration.
It was July fourth.
The fiftieth Anniversary of the Signing of the Declaration of
Independence.
And as if that weren't enough
to divert the attention of his patriotic father
news came that John Adams and Thomas Jefferson had both died.
And that was the day Stephen Foster was born.

His childhood is wrapped in legend . . .
like the day he couldn't remember his alphabet
and howling like a Comanche Indian ran out of the school room
and raced a mile down the road before he stopped.
He is said to have shown a strange faculty for music
at a most early age . . .
and it's true that he composed a trio for flutes when he was
only thirteen. . . .
But the first really successful composition of Stephen Foster
was the rollicking nonsensical song
"Oh Susanna" . . .
Some say Susanna was written for a club of fellows
Foster used to write for.
Others claim it was written for the minstrel shows
his prolific pen was to serve for years to come. . . .
But it surely was not written to be introduced
in Andrews' Eagle Ice Cream Saloon in Pittsburgh
nor made famous by the hoarse voices of thousands of pioneers
headed for the California gold fields. . . .
And yet that is just what happened to it . . .
And still today who doesn't recall the absurd lyrics of
"Oh Susanna"

[1] A short memorial telegram from Governor Johnson was read at this
point in the program.

"OH SUSANNA"

I come from Alabama with my banjo on my knee;
    I'se guine to Lou'siana my true lub for to see.
It rain'd all night de day I left
    De wedder it was dry;
The sun so hot I froze to def,
    Susanna, don't you cry.

Oh! Susanna,
    Do not cry for me;
I come from Alabama,
    Wid my banjo on my knee.

I had a dream de udder night
    When ebry ting was still;
I thought I saw Susanna dear
    A coming down de hill,
De buckwheat cake was in her mouf,
    De tear was in her eye,
I says, I'se coming from de souf,
    Susanna don't you cry.

Oh! Susanna,
    Do not cry for me;
I come from Alabama,
    Wid my banjo on my knee.

(PAUSE)

But this isn't the kind of music
for which Stephen Foster is remembered.
And this laughing rollicking style is not typical of his life. . . .

Stephen Collins Foster
was forever lonely.
His family tried to help him.
Urging him to give up writing for some more profitable
profession.
They didn't understand he couldn't throw his pen away . . .
it was the only escape for his loneliness. . . .
They tried to arouse him with practical problems of a livelihood
but Stephen was not impressed.
There was a hunger in his heart more fearful than they threatened.

This was the hunger for companionship and understanding.
This is the secret of Stephen Collins Foster.

When he wrote Nellie was a Lady . . .
There was no girl . . . no dark Virginny bride
no specific occasion he was mourning . . .
but he tolled the bell . . . that forever rang its hollow note
across the world about him.
He understood the sorrow of parting . . .
The pain of loss . . .
and smothered by his feeling of loneliness
he half wrote half sung of an imaginary girl he never knew
and the simple words and plaintive melody echoed in all hearts.

> Nelly was a lady
> Last night she died
> Toll the bell for lovely Nell
> My dark Virginny bride . . .

(PAUSE)

One of the colorful legends in the life of Stephen Foster
is the story of his proposal to Jane Denny McDowell. . . .
Stephen was twenty-four . . .
And had been calling on Jane for some time . . .
when one night the young lady accidentally or deliberately
mixed her engagements and discovered two gentlemen knocking
at her door.
Stephen and a handsome competitor named Cowan.
Neither offered to retire . . .
And so Jane invited them in . . .
And then Stephen went on into another room
To spend the evening with old Joe the darkie servant
Until when the clock struck ten,
Mister Cowan like a perfect gentleman arose and departed.
Then Stephen in his impetuous way
Abruptly asked Jane for her answer Yes or No. . . .
Maybe she paused a moment wondering what life would hold
for them . . .
but if she hesitated
Knowing of his weakness for writing songs
maybe she felt the added responsibility would make him settle
down or maybe she saw the loneliness in his eyes . . .
And her girlish heart pitied him. . . .

Or maybe she was so excited she didn't think of anything
And just closed her eyes and said "yes." . . .
Anyway on July 22nd, 1850
Stephen Collins Foster and Jane Denny McDowell were married.

Then legend and history all get tangled up again
And letters say they went east on their honeymoon
While friends remember they came to Bardstown . . .
but it doesn't really matter . . .
Stephen had come here as a boy—
And Charlotte Foster, his sister, had visited the Rowans often.
No, it doesn't really matter where the honeymoon was spent,
the important thing is that for a little while
Stephen found happiness. . . .
And among the songs he wrote
during the first years of their married life
Was the gay and brilliant Camptown Races . . .

But even Jane could not dispel his loneliness for long
And this time it found expression in the song
for which he is most widely known,
Swanee River . . . or Old Folks at Home . . .

Many story tellers delight in pointing out
that the original version read
"Way down upon the Peedee River"
and relate
Stephen's brother's account of their selection of a better name
    for the river . . .
of the time Stephen considered Yazoo River . . .
And finally took Swanee although he didn't even know
where it was and never did see it in his life . . .
But that only shows they have missed the secret of Stephen
    Foster.
He was writing not for himself alone
but for all people,
lonely for an old home by a road or river . . .
for everyone the world over "far from the old folks at home."

> Way down upon de Swanee ribber,
>   Far, far away,
> Dere's wha my heart is turning ebber,
>   Dere's wha de old folks stay.

All up and down de whole creation,
  Sadly I roam,
Still longing for de old plantation,
  And for de old folks at home.

All de world am sad and dreary,
  Ebrywhere I roam,
Oh! darkeys, how my heart grows weary,
  Far from de old folks at home.

(PAUSE)

One of the most colorful legends of all
is the story of Stephen Foster's song "My Old Kentucky Home."
It was this old mansion of Judge Rowan's Stephen wrote about.
And sitting here today by the desk Stephen Foster used in this
Old Kentucky Home
I like to believe
Stephen Foster wrote his song about this big house on the hill.
And that it was his yearning for the happiness of days gone by
  that made him write.

The sun shines bright in the old Kentucky home,
  'Tis summer, the darkies are gay,
The corn-top's ripe and the meadow's in the bloom,
  While the birds make music all the day.
The young folks roll on the little cabin floor,
  All merry, all happy and bright;
By'n by Hard Times comes a-knocking at the door,
  Then my old Kentucky Home, Good-night!

Weep no more my lady,
  Oh! Weep no more today!
We will sing one song for the old Kentucky Home
  For the old Kentucky Home, far away.

They hunt no more for the possum and the coon
  On the meadow, the hill and the shore,
They sing no more by the glimmer of the moon,
  On the bench by the old cabin door.
The day goes by like a shadow o'er the heart,
  With sorrow where all was delight;
The time has come when the darkies have to part,
  Then my old Kentucky Home, good-night!

Weep no more my lady,
  Oh! Weep no more today!

We will sing one song for the old Kentucky Home,
For the old Kentucky Home, far away.

(PAUSE)

Yes, I like to believe the legend that Stephen and Jane
came here to this old Kentucky home at Bardstown
on their honeymoon.
I like to think it was a memory of his young bride
on a summer's day here beneath the tall, tall trees
that prompted him years later
to sing to her when they had slipped away from each other
and the loneliness had crept back in . . .
A loneliness that couldn't drown . . .
His dream. . . .

JEANIE WITH THE LIGHT BROWN HAIR

I dream of Jeanie with the light brown hair
    Borne, like a vapor, on the summer air;
I see her tripping where the bright streams play,
    Happy as the daisies that dance on her way.
Many were the wild notes her merry voice would pour,
    Many were the blithe birds that warbled them o'er;
Oh! I dream of Jeanie with the light brown hair
    Floating, like a vapor on the soft summer air.

I long for Jeanie with the day dawn smile,
    Radiant in gladness, warm with winning guile!
I hear her melodies, like joys gone by,
    Sighing 'round my heart o'er the fond hopes that die;
Sighing like the night wind and sobbing like the rain,
    Wailing for the lost one that comes not again;
Oh! I long for Jeanie and my heart bows low,
    Nevermore to find her where the bright waters flow.

(PAUSE)

Our legend of loneliness comes to an end
down in a bleak bare room in the Bowery in New York.
Stephen Foster
was living there alone in poverty.
He was sick . . .
All his life all the lyrics of his songs
show his wistful hunger for the illusive dream
he could see and sing about but never seize upon
And there at the end . . .

He was alone . . . all, all alone . . . in his last long loneliness.
Weak with hunger or illness he was found on the board floor
of the dark tenement in the Bowery in New York
and taken to Bellevue hospital where he died
before any of his family arrived.
In his pockets they found a ragged purse
with thirty-eight cents and a scrap of paper
bearing the pencilled phrase . . . "Kind friends and Gentle
hearts . . ."

"Kind friends and Gentle hearts"
maybe that phrase contains the secret of Stephen Foster's
life. . . .
maybe the world loves Stephen Foster's songs
because they sing of the infinite happiness of
"Kind friends and Gentle hearts,"
CUE: G'bye . . .

12:13:50
ANNOUNCER: Ted Malone has been speaking to you from the
Old Kentucky Home on Federal Hill near Bardstown . . . Kentucky's own shrine to Stephen Collins Foster.
    Next Sunday at this same time Ted Malone will
speak to you from the home of Paul Lawrence
Dunbar in Dayton, Ohio. This has been a special
feature of the Blue Network of the National
Broadcasting Company.

STEPHEN FOSTER

HANIEL LONG

ⵑⵑⵑⵑⵑⵑⵑⵑⵑⵑⵑⵑⵑⵑⵑⵑⵑⵑⵑⵑⵑⵑⵑⵑ

Another Pittsburgher, another life, another way of life: thirtieth anniversary of Stephen Foster's death, January 13, 1894.

"No other single individual," wrote Milligan, "produced so many of those songs . . . called folk-songs. . . . All things must have a beginning . . . every folk-song is first born in the heart of some one person, whose spirit is so finely attuned to the inward struggle which is the history of the soul of man, that when he seeks for his self-expression, he at the same time gives voice to that 'vast multitude who die and give no sign.' . . ."

A life "sadly out of harmony with its environment"; and yet "if I make the songs of a people," I care not.

The boy was born on a fourth of July—"not the fourth of Gettysburg and Vicksburg, nor the fourth of Santiago, but the fourth of 1826 when Jefferson died at high noon and Adams at sunset."

Harmony, Pa., May 4, 1832: Mrs. Foster to her son William: ". . . the little children go to school with quite as happy faces as though the world had no thorns in it, and I confess there would be but few if we would all follow the scriptures, in which we would be made strong. . . . Stephen has a drum and marches about after the old way with a feather in his hat and a girdle round his waist, whistling *Auld Lang Syne*. . . . There still remains something perfectly original about him."

Something perfectly original, which was to give him trouble when he went to school and afterwards.

Youngstown, January 14, 1837: "dear Father: I wish you to

From Haniel Long, *Pittsburgh Memoranda*, 1935, Writers' Editions, by permission of the author.

send me a commic songster for you promised to. If I had my pensyl I could rule my paper or if I had the money to buy black ink—but if I had my whistle I w'd be so taken with it I do not think I w'd write a tall. . . . Stephen."

His "little pizano" was his sister's guitar. "Not until twenty years later was the first upright piano brought across the mountains."

Senator Kingsbury of Minnesota: "Stephen and I often played truant together, going barefoot, gathering wild strawberries by shady streams. It shocked me to see him cast away his fine hose when spoiled by perspiration or muddy water. . . . His execution on the flute was the genius of melody."

Youngstown, August 7, 1840: Mrs. Foster to her son William: ". . . as to Stephen, I leave everything regarding the future to your own judgment, West Point or the Navy, I have no choice; you are not only his Brother, but his Father; and I trust all his feelings will ascend to you as his Patron. . . ."

"Dear William, there is a good fire place in my room and if you will just say the word I will have a fire in it at nights and learn something. Don't forget my waistcoat at the tailor's. Your affectionate brother, Stephen."

". . . people liked to hear the boy sing Zip Coon and Longtail Blue . . . but such music as he came in contact with was so associated with idleness and dissipation as to be regarded at best only as an amiable weakness."

And the boy himself began to write songs. He wrote one about a good time coming:
> "Little children shall not toil under or above the soil,
>   But shall play in healthful fields,
>   In the good time coming . . ."

Peters and Field published it in Cincinnati in 1846.

And he attended a Pittsburgh theatre on Fifth street, "an unpretentious structure rudely built of boards but sufficient to secure the comfort of the few who dared to face the consequences and lend their patronage to an establishment under the ban of the Scotch-Irish Calvinists." (Nevin)

And he wrote more songs, and kept on writing songs: "*Nelly Bly, Nelly was a Lady, Dolcy Jones, etc., Aethiopian Melodies by the Author of Uncle Ned and O Susanna. Firth, Pond & Co., New York, 1850.*"

So that at twenty-three he had set his country singing.

Allegheny City, June 21, 1853, sister Henrietta to brother Morrison: "How sorry I feel for poor Stephy, though when I read your letter I was not at all surprised at the news in regard to him and —— (name scratched out). Last winter I felt convinced —— (three lines scratched out, ending in the word "mistake"). . . . May God lead him in the ways of peace, fill his heart with that love which alone is satisfying."

Stephen had left home, stayed in various places, finally settled in New York, where he wrote fourteen more songs, among them *Sewanee River*. "Aside from one or two national airs born out of great historical crises, probably the most widely known song ever written . . . translated into every language, sung by millions . . . in some subtle and instinctive way it expresses the homesick yearning over the past and far away which is the common emotional heritage of the race. . . ." (Milligan)

Pittsburgh, March 3, 1854: brother Dunning to brother William: "Have you heard anything from Stephen lately? It is a subject of much anxiety to me; notwithstanding his foolish and unaccountable course, I hope he will continue to make a comfortable living for himself. . . ."

"The mother of the celebrated song writer" died in January, 1855. In the obituaries Stephen's name is mentioned before that of his father, twice mayor of Allegheny City, or that of his brother, builder of the Pennsylvania Railroad.

"Herz, Sivori, Ole Bull and Thalberg were ready to approve his genius, and chose his melodies about which to weave their witcheries."

And no one knows much more about Stephen except when he came to die.

"N. Y. City, January 12, 1864, Morrison Foster, Esq., Your brother Stephen is lying in Bellevue Hospital . . . very sick. . . . He desires me to ask you to send him some pecuniary assistance. . . . If possible he would like to see you in person. . . . George Cooper."

Cleveland, January 14, 1864 (by telegraph from New York): "To Morrison Foster, Stephen is dead. Come on. George Cooper."

And George Cooper's account was: "I received a message saying my friend had met with an accident. . . . I dressed hurriedly and went to 15 Bowery . . . found him lying on the floor in the hall, blood oozing from a cut in his throat and with a bad bruise on his forehead. . . . Steve never wore night clothes . . . lay there naked suffering horribly. . . . The doctor arrived . . . started to sew up Steve's throat with black thread. 'Haven't you any white thread?' I asked, and he said 'no.' . . . I decided the doctor was not much good . . . went downstairs and got Steve a big drink of rum, which seemed to help him. . . . We put his clothes on him and took him to the hospital. . . . He seemed terribly weak and his eyelids kept fluttering. . . . I went back to the hospital to see him next day. . . . He said nothing had been done for him, and he couldn't eat the food. . . . Next day they said, 'Your friend is dead.' Steve's body had been sent down to the morgue. There was an old man sitting there smoking a pipe. I told him what I wanted and he said, 'Go look for him.' I went around peering into the coffins until I found Steve's body. . . . Next day, his brother Morrison and Steve's widow arrived."

"Bellevue Hospital, Ward 11, Stephen Foster, Died Jan 13th: Coat, pants, vest, hat, shoes, overcoat Jan 10th 1864. Rec'd of Mr Foster ten shillings charge for Stephen C. Foster while in hospital. Wm. E. White, warden."

Died and went naked into the next world, as all men must.

"There was a tendency of habit grown insidiously upon him

. . . against which, as no one better than this writer knows"
(this writer being Nevin), "he wrestled with earnestness inde-
scribable."

And Morrison Foster, thus to an editor: ". . . the public knew
not *him*, but only *of* him, his poetry and music being the only
visible sign that such a person really existed at all. Reference to
certain peculiarities is not only out of place but a cruel tearing
open of wounds, which the grave should close forever."

And yet, Morrison Foster, your brother being in a certain sense
not only Pittsburgh's greatest but America's . . . Coat, pants,
vest, these do not concern us, but what of the wounds and
what caused them?

"Who can say what would have been the sum of Franz Schu-
bert's achievements had he been born in Pittsburgh in 1826?"

What in fact would have been the sum of anybody's achievements who couldn't be a farmer or a manufacturer or a trader
or a politician or a doctor or a lawyer—couldn't help materially
in the young city's life?

What is the sum of their achievements to-day, these unfor-
tunates?

.   .   .   .   .

Up from his blood and entrails through years of blackness
came the ghosts. He did not give a little charity,
gave himself, rendered back to us the old ghosts,
kept himself a gateway for songs
of homelessness, despair and tears,
agonies of a foundling crying for the harmony
out of which he was born.

Thirty-eight years it took his world to kill him,
the fragile masculine nature fighting
not only the enemies outside him, but those inside,
fear, and a sense of guilt—
his love for his good mother, whose love of him
wavered at his gift, seeing the gift as a hindrance
to a useful life ending in comfort and money—

his love for his sister,
who thought the love of God would work out better
for Stephen than a human love,
putting this confusion between the Door
and the Temple the Door opens into—
and the magnificent brother, builder of the P.R.R.—
and the father, twice mayor of Allegheny City—
and the other brothers, fine fellows
marching along content in the regiment,
Stephen at their side, wistful, out of step,
needing support in a nature that amounted to rebellion,
finding support in no one near him where it might count,
but always vague—his country's love of his songs
being like a surf that breaks a long distance off.
Doubtless real women lived then, as ever,
who would have seen him as a gateway for the ghosts,
freed his limbs and heart, intoxicated him and not with whiskey
but he did not find such women, looked for them no doubt,
but did not find them. And so there was a habit
grown insidiously upon him—
so that he would not need to ask himself if it was right
to listen to the murmur of blood and bone within him,
to try to catch what he could of a melody
very strange and disturbing, brain-throttled, fear-stifled,
yet going all through him.

"Mine, O thou lord of life, send my roots rain."

Orange leaf of a moon, holding on to the horizon,
what do you see in the last hours of night?

If you know what dreaming means,
                    says one of Strauss's love songs,
If you knew it, you would come to me.
                    But when you do not come
not you, nor I, more than a sparrow or than twigs in twilight
shall leave on earth a token of our presence.
"If I had my pensyl I could rule my paper
but if I had my whistle I w'd be so taken with it
I do not think I w'd write a tall."
I w'd only whistle, all day long I w'd whistle;

but if I were still unhappy and my heart ached—
                    then, as it is writ in Proverbs,
"Give strong drink unto him that is ready to perish,
and wine unto those that be of heavy hearts;
let him drink and forget his poverty,
and remember his misery no more."

West Point or the Navy, his mother had no choice;
but cursed with a something perfectly original
he pursued his foolish and unaccountable course,
this our beloved, O Pittsburghers,
till he died and went naked into the next world
                    as all men must,
along with Carnegie, Frick, Henry Phipps,
                    Gladstone, Robert A. Pinkerton,
                    and Grover Cleveland—

the next world where, it is said, the soul of a man matters.

This our beloved . . .
                    the day he died
". . . horrors, portioned to a giant nerve,
Oft made Hyperion ache."

BIOGRAPHY

MARY LINCOLN

Wife and Widow

CARL SANDBURG

꘠

This was the beginning of the twenty-two years of married life for this oddly matched couple. They were "the long and the short of it," as Lincoln said more than once. The wife was sensitive about the picture they made standing alongside each other; she never allowed a photograph to be made of them as a couple. They were opposite in more than height. She was chubby; he was lean. She was swift of tongue and vehement in phrase; he was reserved and drawling. While he was rated as coming from the lower working class, "scrubs," she considered herself as indubitably of the well-bred upper class, patrician, and according to one of her sisters, she was in a vexed mood for a moment on the night of her wedding and made a reference to the difficulties in being involved with "plebeians."

The contrast between them which grew in the years was in temper or control. She grew more explosive; her outbursts came at more frequent intervals, were more desperate exhibitions, enacted in the presence of more important persons. Her physical resources and mental ability took on such added pathos from year to year that in a wide variety of ways many who met her referred to her as "a sad case." This while her husband's patience developed, his self-discipline deepened, and in the matter of self-control, knowing what he was doing while he was doing it, he was increasingly noted as a marvel.

The houses they lived in marked their pilgrimage together, (1) the Globe Tavern in Springfield where they lived cheaply and made plans, (2) the one and a half story Eighth Street house where they set up housekeeping, (3) Mrs. Spriggs' modest boarding house in Washington, D. C., (4) the Eighth Street house in Springfield with a full second story added, (5) the White House in Washington, D. C., also known as the Executive Mansion.

Nearly always between these two there was a moving under-tow of their mutual ambitions. Though his hope of achievement and performance was sometimes smothered and obliterated in melancholy, it was there, burning and questing, most of the time. And with Mary Todd Lincoln the deep desire for high place, eminence, distinction, seemed never to leave her. And between these mutual ambitions of theirs might be the difference that while he cared much for what history would say of him, her anxiety was occupied with what society, the approved social leaders of the upper classes, would let her have.

As a newly elected Congressman's wife in 1846, she had gay pulses; she had predicted her husband would go up the ladder and she with him. On his trip to Washington to sit in Congress, she took him by a detour to Lexington, Kentucky, to meet her relatives and the playmates of her youth. She joined him later in Washington where they lived at a plain boarding house and where he saved enough of his salary to pay off the last of the store-keeping debts he got loaded with about twelve years earlier when he learned that as a merchant he was a total loss.

Then her gay pulses as a Congressman's wife went down as her husband lost his seat in the national body. The hope then came that he would be appointed Land Office Commissioner of the United States by the newly elected Whig President, Zachary Taylor. They would live in Washington. Lincoln wrote letters, pulled wires, used connections, traveled to Washington, went the limit as an office seeker. The job was landed by another man. It was not cheerful news at the Lincoln home in Springfield. Lincoln took up mathematics for its mental discipline and sunk himself deep in law study and practice.

Four babies were borne by Mary Todd Lincoln in ten years, all boys, Robert Todd (1843), Edward Baker (1846), William Wallace (1850), Thomas (1853). They made a houseful. Their mother had maids for housework but until the family went to the White House to live she usually sewed her own dresses, did much of the sewing for the children and took on herself many of the thousand and one little cares and daily chores that ac-company the feeding and clothing of babies and upbringing of lusty and mischievous boys. She had hours, days, years of washing and nursing these little ones, tending their garments, overseeing their school studies, watching their behavior, instructing them as to the manners of gentlemen, keeping an eye on their health, working and worrying over them when they were sick. Even those who could not see her as pleasant company, even the ones who believed her a vixen and a shrew, gave testimony that she was an exceptional mother, brooding over her offspring with a touch of the tigress.

Her little Eddy died in 1850, not quite four years old; that was a grief. Thomas, nicknamed Tad, had a misshapen palate and lisped; he had brightness, whimsical bold humor; he was a precious burden to his mother and father.

Mrs. Lincoln knew that her husband understood her faults. She believed she knew his failings and instructed him. Across their twenty-two years of married life there were times when she was a help. Often too she knew she presumed on his patience and good nature knowing that when calm settled down on the household he would regard it as "a little explosion" that had done her good.

She terrorized housemaids, icemen, storekeepers, delivery boys, with her tongue-lashings. He knew these tempers of hers connected directly with the violent headaches of which she complained for many years. He knew they traced back to a deep-seated physical disorder, sudden disturbances that arose and shook her controls till she raved and was as helpless as a child that has spent itself in a tantrum. Sentences of letters she wrote show that she felt guilty and ashamed over her outbreaks of hysteria. If Lincoln ever suspected that these habitual brainstorms were the result of a cerebral disease eating deeper into the tissues from year to year, it is not revealed in any letter or spoken comment in the known record.

In the courting days and in the earlier years of marriage his nickname for her was "Molly." After the children came he called her "mother." When complaints were raised against her he tried to smooth out the trouble, telling one man who had been tongue-lashed that he ought to be able to stand for fifteen minutes what he (Lincoln) had stood for fifteen years.

Though the talk and the testimony blame the woman chiefly there seems to have been one time that the man too lost his control. Lincoln was at the office one morning before Herndon arrived. His hat over his eyes, he gave a short answer to Herndon's "Good morning," sat slumped till noon and then made a meal of crackers and cheese. On the day before, on a Sunday morning, Mrs. Lincoln was in a bad mood, one thing led to another and after repeated naggings Lincoln took hold of her and pushed her toward an open door facing Jackson Street, calling in his peculiar high-pitched voice, "You make the house intolerable, damn you, get out of it!" Churchgoers coming up Jackson Street might have seen and heard all. How would they know it was the first and only time in his life he had laid rough hands on his wife and cursed her? Even letting it pass that people had seen and heard what happened how could he blame himself enough for letting himself go in such cheap behavior? So Sunday had been a day of shameful thoughts. The night had brought no sleep. And at daybreak he had come to the law office, without breakfast, without hope.

The marriage contract is complex. "Live and let live," is one of its terms. It travels on a series of readjustments to the changes recurring in the party of the first part and the party of the second part. Geared to incessant ecstasy of passion, the arrangement goes smash. Mutual ambitions, a round of simple and necessary duties, occasional or frequent separations as the case may be, relieved by interludes of warm affection—these are the conditions on which many a long-time marriage has been negotiated. The mood and color of this normal married life permeates the letters that passed between Lincoln and his wife when he was in Congress. Their household talk across the twenty-two years must have run along many a day and hour in the mood of these letters; exchanges of news, little anxieties about the children and the home, the journeyings of each reported to the other. When he hurried home from the law office during a thunderstorm, knowing that she was a terrorstruck and sick woman during a thunderstorm, it was an act of accommodation by one partner for another. Likewise when a man appeared at the office saying the wife wanted a tree in their home yard cut down, it was accommodation again in his saying, "Then for God's sake let it be cut down!"

We can be sure too that for much of the time Lincoln and his wife went about their concerns peacefully and with quiet affection for each other. Domestic flare-ups, nerve-snappings come to all couples; perhaps to these two they simply came more frequently and more violently. Authentic records—letters written without any thought of future readers—contain many glimpses of placid relations. One can read nothing but calm contentment into Lincoln's sentence about a novel he had received from a friend: "My wife got hold of the volume I took home, read it half through last night and is greatly interested in it." Only the comradeship that comes to those who understand each other can be inferred from Mrs. Lincoln's comment on a trip east: "When I saw the large steamers at the New York landings I felt in my heart inclined to sigh that poverty was my portion. How I long to go to Europe. I often laugh and tell Mr. Lincoln that I am determined my next husband shall be rich."

Together the two shared in the social life of Springfield, entertained and went to parties. The diary of Orville H. Browning, who spent weeks every year in the capital, refers often to parties which Mr. and Mrs. Lincoln gave or attended. Mrs. Lincoln's letters show the extent of these diversions. "Within the last three weeks," she wrote in 1857, "there has been a party almost every night and some two or three grand fêtes are coming off this week." Most pretentious of these, but typical of many others, was Governor Bissell's reception where "a fine brass and string band discoursed most delicious music, and the dancers kept the cotillions filled until a late hour."

As the years passed and Lincoln's fame grew, there came occasional happy outings, brief escapes for Mrs. Lincoln from the routine of keeping house and managing children. There was a trip, with other lawyers, state officers and their wives, over the lines of the Illinois Central Railroad in the summer of 1859.

There was another trip the same year when Lincoln went to Ohio to make Republican speeches, taking Mrs. Lincoln and one of the boys with him. The first audience, at Columbus, was small, but as the trip progressed enthusiasm mounted and ever-larger crowds were present to warm Mrs. Lincoln's pride in her husband's reputation. At Cincinnati marchers with bands met them at the station and escorted them to the Burnet House with cannon booming a salute. They stayed two days, spending several pleasant hours with one of Mrs. Lincoln's cousins.

Lincoln's health, his work, his political aims, are told about in a letter which he wrote to his wife in 1860 on the eastern trip that took him to New York for the Cooper Union speech and nine other speeches. This platform work came hard for him and he made clear to Mrs. Lincoln that he was a troubled man and why.

While visiting their son Robert at Exeter, New Hampshire,

he wrote her a letter on March fourth saying, "I have been unable to escape this toil. If I had foreseen it, I think I would not have come east at all. The speech at New York, being within my calculation before I started, went off passably well and gave me no trouble whatever. The difficulty was to make nine others, before audiences who had already seen all my ideas in print." Thus he let her know that if his nine other speeches seemed rather poor there was a reason.

Neither he nor she knew at that hour how powerful a factor the Cooper Union address would prove in bringing him the nomination for President a few months later. Nor could they guess that a year from the day he wrote this letter he would be taking oath as President at Washington, and again he would be saying in but slightly different words, "I have been unable to escape this toil."

Communications like this have a color not found in the progress of a man and wife whose days are a succession of uninterrupted quarrels. Nevertheless we know there were terrible interludes. Under the progression of her malady, the hammering wear and tear of the repeated periods of hysteria and hallucinations, there was a fading of a brightness seen in her younger years. Compliments came less often. More than twenty years after her query, "Why is it that married folks always become so serious?" she wrote querulously, "The weather is so beautiful, why is it that we cannot feel well?" The days in which she was neither feeling well nor looking well increased. Her sudden angers interrupting a smoothly moving breakfast, her swift wailings in the dark quiet of night-time when fears came to possess her—these brought long thoughts to her husband. Did she become to him a manner of symbol—a miniature of the Sea of Life, smooth and shining with promises and then suddenly treacherous and hateful with devastation? We do not know. It may be so. We cannot be sure in such a realm of the deeper undertows that move people into words and acts.

We do know that from year to year there was a growing control in her husband, a strange and more mystic tinting of his spirit. Under the bonds and leashes that wove and tied his life with that of Mary Todd he saw a self-development that became a mystery to his friends. The outstanding trait of him, according to Herndon, was that he was a "learner," raising the question whether he was indeed such a learner that he could apply to the benefit of his own growth the maxim he quoted to Speed from his father, "If you make a bad bargain, hug it all the tighter."

He was a man in whom the stream of motive ran sluggish. Herndon's theory was that Mary Todd often roused him out of sluggishness, out of vague dreams, into definite actions. When his melancholy weighed down and oversloughed his ambition, Mary Todd with her tongue, arguments, reminders, was a "whiplash." This of course is speculation, an attempt to read secrets in development of human personality. Under the patient exterior of Abraham Lincoln lay a turmoil, a vast crisscross of volcanic currents of which he himself might have had difficulty to tell had he ever tried to unbosom and make clear the play of motives that operated between him and Mary Todd in their twenty-two years of married life.

Pride ran deep in Mary Todd Lincoln, pride of a depth and consuming intensity that might ally it with the pride which the Puritans named aş the first of the seven deadly sins.

When Lincoln was defeated for United States Senator from Illinois in 1855, his wife was in the gallery watching the balloting. Lyman Trumbull, a rival of the same party, won. And though Julia Jayne, the wife of Trumbull, had been a bridesmaid at Mary Todd's wedding, and they had joined in writing poetry and letters to the Sangamo *Journal*, it is said that always after Trumbull's election there was coolness between her and her old-time chum.

Her anxiety matched that of her husband when he ran for the United States Senate against Douglas in 1858. She was not one of those wives who wish their husbands to quit the troublous arena of politics. She had a belief in her own skill at politics and found the role of adviser fascinating.

Months of exaltation, of life intensified, followed Lincoln's nomination at Chicago. Mary Lincoln was no longer the wife of a small-town lawyer; like her husband, she was a public character. The transformation thrilled her. The newspaper correspondents who thronged to Springfield gave her space in their dispatches. There was keen delight in reading in the New York *Herald* that she was "especially gracious and entertaining," and able to inject "brilliant flashes of wit and good nature" into a political conversation.

With the election, life for Mary Lincoln was pitched to an even higher key. "She is in fine spirits!" wrote one of her friends a few days after the result was known.

With Lincoln's inauguration as President of the United States in 1861 she hugged to her heart the gratification of being the First Lady of the Land. Her fond dream had come true, yet for her it was not merely a signal that she was to comfort, cherish the new President and help him carry the load. She took it she was also an adviser and ex-officio cabinet officer, an auxiliary First Magistrate. From the first she suggested appointments and was vehement as to who should fill this or that place.

Was there need for her to blaze forth with hot comments on important men whom Lincoln had chosen for heavy work? Why in the presence of visitors refer to William H. Seward, named to be Secretary of State, as a "dirty abolition sneak"?

Henry Villard, correspondent of the New York *Herald*, told of a story he had from a man who went to bring Lincoln to the railroad train which was waiting to carry the President-elect to Washington for inauguration. And the man said Lincoln's wife was lying on the floor of their room in the Chenery House raging and convulsive, her apparel disordered, moaning she would not go to Washington until her husband promised to make a certain federal appointment. It was a story—possibly nothing to it—and possibly true. In any case it was told by Villard as probably true. That Villard at this time was writing little character sketches of Lincoln and his wife for the New York *Herald*, entirely favorable, filled with well-measured praise and affection, lends to the story. That Mrs. Lincoln changed her plans and itinerary, and did not leave Springfield on the same train with her husband, may or may not be a circumstance in the incident. That Lincoln made one of the most poignantly moving and melancholy speeches of his career that morning just before the train carried him away from Springfield forever may also be no circumstance at all.

Was it a woman's jealousy of her husband or a selfish personal pride or both that brought her decree regarding White House promenades? The established custom followed by Presidents and Presidents' wives up till her time was that the President should lead the grand march with another woman on his arm while the second couple was the President's wife on the arm of another man. Mary Todd Lincoln decreed that she and she only should be the woman on the President's arm when he led the promenade. No woman but herself should be in the First Couple. And it was so ordered and maintained from then on.

She is credited with pluck for staying at the White House

with her husband and children through the spring days of 1861 when it seemed as though Washington would be captured, when the Confederates could easily have taken the Capitol and White House. She refused to travel north to Philadelphia and safety. She had resources of courage; not stamina particularly but a brilliant audacity.

The Washington tumult wore heavily on her in the summer of 1861. She went to Long Branch, the ocean resort near New York City. There she conducted herself quietly, trying to rest, keeping away from the social whirl. The New York *Herald*, however, had sent a clever special writer to the scene; he scribbled columns of gush as though the President's wife were an American queen, maintaining a royal seclusion, wearing a haughty manner. The keen thrusts and malicious manipulations of this writer were reprinted in newspapers fighting the administration. The ridicule went beyond her and struck at her husband in the White House. She learned what curious twists of viewpoint can be put upon a distracted woman seeking a place to look at the ocean in peace and meditation; it couldn't be done.

A steady parade of items about her three "brothers" in the Confederate armies were published in southern and northern newspapers. They were in fact half-brothers, sons of Mary Todd's father by his second wife.

The talk grew and spread that in the White House was a woman traitor and spy, the President's wife, sending information south. On one occasion the President appeared of his own volition before a congressional investigating committee to give them his solemn assurance that his wife was loyal to the Union cause.

One by one the Todd brothers in the Confederate army were killed. And little by little the talk died down that their half-sister in the White House was an informer in sympathy with the southern side.

It was war.

"Lizzie, I have just heard that one of my brothers has been killed," said Mrs. Lincoln one day to her Negro dressmaker, Elizabeth Keckley. And she went on: "Of course it is but natural that I should feel for one so nearly related to me, but not to the extent that you suppose. He made his choice long ago. He decided against my husband, and through him against me. He has been fighting against us; and since he chose to be our deadly enemy, I see no special reason why I should bitterly mourn his death."

The tension of being a Kentuckian at war with the South was in her plea, "Why should I sympathize with the rebels? They would hang my husband tomorrow if it was in their power, and perhaps gibbet me with him. How then can I sympathize with a people at war with me and mine?"

Broken aristocrats, southern sympathizers, disgruntled office-seekers, gossips shaken with war brain storms, employed their tongues on the new social leader of the capital, the new First Lady. And she gave them too many chances to strike at her. More than rumor and passing chatter lay back of Charles Francis Adams, Jr.'s recording of a function he attended at Mrs. Eames': "If the President caught it at dinner, his wife caught it at the reception. All manner of stories about her were flying around; she wanted to do the right thing, but, not knowing how, was too weak and proud to ask; she was going to put the White House on an economical basis and, to that end, was about to dismiss 'the help,' as she called the servants; some of whom, it was asserted, had already left because 'they must live with gentlefolks'; she had got hold of newspaper reporters and railroad conductors, as the best persons to go to for advice and direction. Numberless stories of this sort were current; and Mrs. Lincoln was in a stew."

In the White House she was sometimes designated as "Mrs. President." She took an interest in the case of a soldier who was sentenced to face a firing squad for going to sleep on picket duty. When Lincoln mentioned the case to General George B. McClellan, commanding, he said "the Lady President" was anxious that the boy be pardoned. McClellan in writing to his wife told her it had pleased him to grant a request from "the Lady President."

In her own eyes she was more than "the Lady President"; she conceived of her position as carrying with it prerogatives and privileges akin to those of royalty. She was fond of referring to those who frequented the White House as the "Court," and at times, she made requests, forced exactions, as one who ruled by monarchic decree and whim rather than as the wife of an elected President.

She intervened constantly in the matter of offices—for postmasterships, West Point cadetships—even the reorganization of the cabinet. She wrote from the Soldiers' Home, Washington, D. C., to James Gordon Bennett, publisher and editor of the New York *Herald*, in the fall of 1862, telling him she favored cabinet changes and would do what she could to bring them about. "From all parties the cry for a 'change of cabinet' comes. I hold a letter, just received from Governor Sprague, in my hand, who is quite as earnest as you have been on the subject. Doubtless if my good patient husband were here instead of being with the Army of the Potomac, both of these missives would be placed before him, accompanied by my womanly suggestions, proceeding from a heart so deeply interested for our distracted country. I have a great terror of strong-minded ladies, yet if a word fitly spoken and in due season can be urged in a time like this, we should not withhold it."

One evening Mrs. Keckley had arranged Mrs. Lincoln's hair and helped her into a dress of white satin trimmed in black lace, with a surprise of a long train in the height of daring fashion. She entered the Guests' Room where Willie Lincoln lay abed with a cold and fever. And as Elizabeth Keckley wrote of it, "As she swept through the room, Mr. Lincoln was standing with his back to the fire, his hands behind him, and his eyes on the carpet. His face wore a thoughtful, solemn look. The rustling of the satin dress attracted his attention. He looked at it a few moments; then, in his quaint quiet way remarked:

" 'Whew! Our cat has a long tail tonight!'

"Mrs. Lincoln did not reply. The President added:

" 'Mother, it is my opinion, if some of that tail was nearer the head, it would be in better style'; and he glanced at her bare arms and neck. She had a beautiful neck and arm and low dresses were becoming to her. She turned away with a look of offended dignity, and presently took the President's arm, and both went downstairs to their guests, leaving me alone with the sick boy."

The cup of happiness ran over for Mary Todd Lincoln at times when she realized to the full her ambition to be a great lady and publicly approved as such. Praise was showered on her and lavish compliments bestrewn over her after the White House party which she gave on February 5, 1862. *Leslie's Weekly* made this social function the topic of a leading article, elaborately illustrated. "There has been a social innovation at the White House," the article began, "and the experiment has been a brilliant success." Until this event came off there had been "a false deference to the false notion of democratic equality." Except for state dinners to foreign ministers and cabinet members the parties previously had consisted of public receptions where the Execu-

tive Mansion was thrown open, as *Leslie's Weekly* noted, "to
every one, high or low, gentle or ungentle, washed or unwashed,"
resulting in a "horrible jam" endurable only "by people of sharp
elbows, and destitute of corns, who don't object to a faint odor
of whisky." Now, however, Mrs. Lincoln had inaugurated the
practice of "respectable people in private life" by inviting five
hundred of the "distinguished, beautiful, brilliant" people representing "intellect, attainment, position, elegance." Whether the
writer in *Leslie's* was lit up with genuine enthusiasm or was just
a plain snob, he or she wrote as though conveying glad tidings.
"Indeed, no European court or capital can compare with the
Presidential circle and the society at Washington this winter,
in the freshness and beauty of its women. The North, while it
has confessedly been possessed of even more than its numerical
proportion of beautiful and accomplished women, has never
before been in a social supremacy. The power which controlled
the Government has been altogether Southern, and society has
always taken the same hue. But all that is changed now, and the
dingy, sprawling city on the Potomac is bright with the blue
of Northern eyes, and the fresh, rosy glow of Northern com-
plexions." Early in the evening the windows of the White House
were lighted for gayety, and by half-past nine the entrances were
crowded with guests, and carriages lined the White House yard
to the avenue. Invitation cards were presented at the door. The
ladies in swishing, crinkling crinoline and their escorts in silk
top hats and cutaway coats passed to the second-story dressing-
rooms. They returned to the grand entrance, were shown into
the Blue Room, then conducted to the grand saloon or East
Room where the President and his wife greeted them while the
Marine Band played soft music in a side room. At half-past
eleven doors were thrown open to an apartment where sand-
wiches were served with drinks from a Japanese punchbowl. The
regular supper came afterward, served by Maillard of New York
in the dining-room.

Many were named as present and set off with distinction.
But the lavish comment was reserved for Mrs. Lincoln. "Primarily, we must remark the exquisite taste with which the White
House has been refitted under Mrs. Lincoln's directions is in no
respect more remarkable than in the character of the hangings of
the various rooms, which relieve and set off the figures and
dresses of lady guests to the greatest advantage. First, as hostess,
and second in no respect, Mrs. Lincoln. She was attired in a

lustrous white satin robe, with a train of a yard in length, trimmed with one deep flounce of the richest black Chantilly lace, put on in festoons and surmounted by a quilling of white satin ribbon, edged with narrow black lace. The dress was, of course, décolleté and with short sleeves, displaying the exquisitely molded shoulders and arms of our fair 'Republican Queen,' the whiteness of which was absolutely dazzling. Her headdress was a coronet wreath of black and white crêpe myrtle, which was in perfect keeping with her regal style of beauty. Let us here add, *en passant*, that Mrs. Lincoln possesses that rare beauty which has rendered the Empress of the French so celebrated as a handsome woman, and which our transatlantic cousins call *la tête bien plantée*. Her ornaments were pearls."

Such was the presentation of Mrs. Lincoln to the wide national audience of a popular illustrated weekly newspaper. She had wanted this recognition. It slaked a thirst she had. Later that same year, in November, New York newspapers gave many paragraphs to her visit there. But it was not so pleasant a visit. For the Lincoln administration at Washington had been losing ground and the end of the war seemed far off. *Harper's Weekly* published a large engraving from a photograph portrait of Mrs. Lincoln, with the news: "Mrs. Lincoln has lately been spending some time in this city, and has been serenaded and visited by many of our leading citizens." Along with this was the information that one of her brothers, killed in battle, had been the jailer of Union prisoners at Richmond. "His brutality and cruelty were such, however, that Jefferson Davis finally removed him from the post, and sent him to join his regiment. Mrs. Lincoln's sisters are understood to sympathize rather with the rebels than with the Government. It is probably this division of sentiment which has given rise to the gossip and scandal respecting the views of the lady who presides over the White House."

At one time newspapers and common talk were filled with accusations and suspicions that she was getting military secrets from her husband and White House callers, and sending the information to Southern commanders. She told the White House clerk who handled mail, William O. Stoddard, that she would prefer he opened all her mail as it came. "Don't let a thing come to me that you've not read first yourself and that you are not sure I would wish to see. I do not wish to open a letter, nor even a parcel of any kind, until after you have examined it. Never!"

Stoddard took it on himself to throw into the wastebasket and
the fireplace many accusing and threatening letters addressed to
her, written by persons Stoddard considered "insane and
depraved."

In all the representations of the gossips, however, there was
never an intimation during war time that she mistreated her
children. A story that she had whipped Tad came later, and
was on the face of it a malicious fabrication. She was fond of
her young ones and, if anything, overindulged them. And something of this mother heart was stirred into action as the train-
loads of broken and battered soldiers were unloaded at Washington fresh from the battlefields. Much that she did was worthy of
her place and her own best impulses. Day after day she visited
the wounded in the Washington hospitals, talked with them,
took them fruit and delicacies, wine and liquors that admirers
had sent for the use of the White House table. In her own
way she tried to lighten the burden her husband was carrying.
She invited old Illinois friends to breakfast at the White House
so that he might forget himself for a few moments in talk of
old times. She made him ride with her on bright afternoons in
the hope that an hour or two of fresh air would blot some of
the fatigue from his face.

A different reputation might have been built up for her, W. O.
Stoddard, the mail clerk, believed, if she had taken pains now
and then to have the newspaper correspondents know of her
hospital visits, her donations of supplies, and other good works.
Yet even to Stoddard, who wanted to overlook her faults, she
was difficult. "It was not easy at first," he wrote, "to understand
why a lady who could be one day so kindly, so considerate, so
generous, so thoughtful and so hopeful, could upon another day
appear so unreasonable, so irritable, so dependent, so even nig-
gardly, and so prone to see the dark, the wrong side of men and
women and events."

On a chilly day in February, 1862, Willie Lincoln had gone
riding on his pony and taken a cold that passed into fever. He
was twelve years old, a blue-eyed boy, not strong, liked his books,
sometimes curled up in a chair with pencil and paper and tried
his hand at writing poems. One verse of his piece titled Lines
on the Death of Colonel Edward Baker read:

> There was no patriot like Baker,
> So noble and so true;

He fell as a soldier on the field,
His face to the sky of blue.

As he lay that night breathing rather hard there drifted up to the room the fragments of music from the Marine Band playing in the ballroom below. Though the doctor had said there was no reason for alarm about the patient the President had ordered no dancing for that evening. Several times Mrs. Lincoln left the party below and came upstairs to stand over Willie's bed and see how he was.

A few days later the mystic and inevitable messenger came for the boy. Elizabeth Keckley wrote: "The light faded from his eyes, and the death-dew gathered on his brow." She had been on watch but did not see the end, telling of it, "I was worn out with watching, and was not in the room when Willie died, but was immediately sent for. I assisted in washing him and dressing him, and then laid him on the bed, when Mr. Lincoln came in." He lifted the cover from the face of his child, gazed at it long, and murmured, "It is hard, hard to have him die."

The mother wept for hours, and at moments moaned in convulsions of grief.

They closed down the lids over the blue eyes of the boy, parted his brown hair, put flowers from his mother in his pale crossed hands, and soldiers, senators, the cabinet officers, ambassadors, came to the funeral. The mother couldn't come. She was too far spent.

The body was sent west to Illinois for burial. The mother clutched at his memory and if his name was mentioned her voice shook and the tears came. "She could not bear to look upon his picture," said Mrs. Keckley. "And after his death she never crossed the threshold of the Guest's Room in which he died, or the Green Room in which he was embalmed."

The death of Willie gave impetus to the malady gnawing at her brain. Noah Brooks told how a charlatan named Colchester posed as a spiritualistic medium, induced her to receive him at the Soldier's Home and in a darkened room pretended to receive messages from the dead boy. Brooks revealed the fraud. She turned to others for revelations. In amazement Orville H. Browning recorded in his diary: "Mrs. Lincoln told me she had been, the night before, with old Isaac Newton, out to Georgetown, to see a Mrs. Laury, a spiritualist, and she had made wonderful revelations to her about her little son Willie who died last

winter, and also about things on the earth. Among other things
she revealed that the cabinet were all enemies of the President,
working for themselves, and that they would have to be dis-
missed, and others called to his aid before he had success."

The war years pounded on. McClellan, whom Mrs. Lincoln
epitomized as a "humbug," was eventually replaced by Ulysses
S. Grant. "He is a butcher," she told her husband as Grant was
moving slowly and at terrible cost toward Richmond. "But he has
been very successful in the field," argued the President, as Mrs.
Keckley heard it. Mrs. Lincoln responded, "Yes, he generally
manages to claim a victory, but such a victory! He loses two men
to the enemy's one. He has no management, no regard for life.
If the war should continue four years longer, and he should
remain in power, he would depopulate the North. I could fight
an army as well myself. Grant, I repeat, is an obstinate fool and
a butcher."

"Well, Mother," came the President's slow and ironical voice,
"supposing that we give you command of the army. No doubt
you would do much better than any general that has been tried."

In the spring of 1864 the President and Mrs. Lincoln went to
City Point for a visit with Grant's army. Adam Badeau of Grant's
staff was riding in an ambulance with Mrs. Lincoln and Mrs.
Grant and happened in the course of talk to say that the wives
of army officers at the front had been ordered to the rear. This
indicated that lively fighting was soon to begin, a sure sign,
Badeau remarked, for not a lady had been allowed to stay at the
front except Mrs. Griffin, the wife of General Charles Griffin,
who had a special permit from the President.

"What do you mean by that, sir?" came the cry from Mrs.
Lincoln. "Do you mean to say that she saw the President alone?
Do you know that I never allow the President to see any woman
alone?"

Badeau tried to tone down what he had said. "I tried to palliate my remark," he noted later. And in doing so he smiled some
sort of smile which brought from the raging woman the reply,
"That's a very equivocal smile, sir. Let me out of this carriage
at once. I will ask the President if he saw that woman alone."
She told Badeau in the front seat to have the driver of the ambulance stop. He hesitated. She thrust her arms past Badeau and
took hold of the driver. Mrs. Grant at that point managed to
quiet Mrs. Lincoln enough to have the whole party set out on
the ground. General George G. Meade now came up and paid

his respects to the President's wife. She went off on the arm of the Gettysburg commander before Badeau could give Meade the word that he mustn't mention Mrs. Griffin's getting a special permit from the President to stay at the front. Later, however, Badeau saluted Meade as a diplomat for when Meade and Mrs. Lincoln returned she said to Badeau, "General Meade is a gentleman, sir. He says it was not the President who gave Mrs. Griffin the permit, but the Secretary of War." And when Badeau and Mrs. Grant talked over the day's events they agreed it was all so mixed up and disgraceful they would neither of them ever mention to anybody what had happened, except that she would tell her husband.

The next day was worse. For it happened that the wife of General Ord, commander of the Army of the James, was not subject to the order retiring wives to the rear, and mounted on a horse suddenly found herself riding alongside President Lincoln, with Mrs. Lincoln and Mrs. Grant in an ambulance just behind them. Mrs. Lincoln caught sight of them and raged. "What does this woman mean by riding by the side of the President? And ahead of me? Does she suppose that *he* wants *her* by the side of him?"

Mrs. Grant did her best to quiet the frenzied woman. Then she came in for a tongue lashing, in the midst of which Mrs. Lincoln flashed out, "I suppose you think you'll get to the White House yourself, don't you?" Mrs. Grant replied she was satisfied where she was; she had greater honor than she had ever expected to reach. "Oh!" was the reply. "You had better take it if you can get it. 'Tis very nice."

The trip ended. Mrs. Ord came to the ambulance and suddenly found herself facing a storm of insults, epithets and dirty names before a crowd of army officers. What did she mean by following the President? And Badeau wrote, "The poor woman burst into tears and inquired what she had done, but Mrs. Lincoln refused to be appeased, and stormed till she was tired. Mrs. Grant still tried to stand by her friend, and everybody was shocked and horrified."

And the evening of that day was worse yet. On a steamer in the James River at a dinner given by President and Mrs. Lincoln to General and Mrs. Grant and the General's staff, Mrs. Lincoln openly and baldly before all suggested that General Ord should be removed from command. He was unfit for his place, to say nothing of his wife. General Grant, of course, had to reply that so far as he could see General Ord was a good commander.

During this City Point visit these outbreaks of Mary Todd Lincoln kept on. And according to Badeau, "Mrs. Lincoln repeatedly attacked her husband in the presence of officers because of Mrs. Griffin and Mrs. Ord. He bore it as Christ might have done, with an expression of pain and sadness that cut one to the heart, but with supreme calmness and dignity. He called her 'Mother,' with his old-time plainness; he pleaded with eyes and tones, and endeavored to explain or palliate the offenses of others, till she turned on him like a tigress; and then he walked away, hiding that noble, ugly face that we might not catch the full expression of its misery."

Her speech included frequent use of the word "sir." Men recalled her overuse of "sir." Mrs. Keckley several times noted the expression, "God, no!" when Mrs. Lincoln wished to be emphatic in denial.

She spoke to Mrs. Keckley of an "unprincipled set" of politicians with whom she was having dealings in 1864 toward the reëlection of the President in the coming campaign. "Does Mr. Lincoln know what your purpose is?" asked Mrs. Keckley.

"God, no! He would never sanction such proceedings, so I keep him in the dark, and will tell him of it when it is all over. He is too honest to take the proper care of his own interests, so I feel it my duty to electioneer for him."

Henry Villard made note of the "common set of men and women" in whose company she was too often seen. Out of them he singled, for an example of both type and method, the so-called "Chevalier" Wikoff, a handsome, well-mannered, well-educated pretender who was in reality merely a salaried social spy of the New York *Herald*. "Wikoff showed the utmost assurance in his appeals to the vanity of the mistress of the White House," Villard wrote. "I myself heard him compliment her upon her looks and dress in so fulsome a way that she ought to have blushed and banished the impertinent fellow from her presence. She accepted Wikoff as a majordomo in general and in special, as a guide in matters of social etiquette, domestic arrangements, and personal requirements, including her toilette, and as always welcome company for visitors in her salon and on her drives."

Mrs. Keckley told of her impression of the White House couple. "I believe that he loved the mother of his children very tenderly. He asked nothing but affection from her, but did not always receive it. When in one of her wayward, impulsive moods, she was apt to do and say things that wounded him deeply. If he had not loved her, she would have been powerless to cloud his thoughtful face. She often wounded him in unguarded moments, but calm reflection never failed to bring regret." Thus ran the observation of this remarkable mulatto woman who as friend and helper of Mary Todd Lincoln was more notable than any other who tried to smooth her pathway.

One day in 1864 she told Mrs. Keckley that the reëlection of Mr. Lincoln was important to her. "Somehow I have learned to fear that he will be defeated. If he should be defeated, I do not know what would become of us all. To me, to him, there is more at stake in this election than he dreams of."

"What can you mean, Mrs. Lincoln?"

"Simply this. I have contracted large debts, of which he knows nothing, and which he will be unable to pay if he is defeated."

"What are your debts, Mrs. Lincoln?"

"They consist chiefly of store bills. I owe altogether about twenty-seven thousand dollars, the principal portion at Stewart's in New York. You understand, 'Lizabeth, that Mr. Lincoln has but little idea of the expenses of a woman's wardrobe. He glances at my rich dresses, and is happy in the belief that the few hundred dollars I obtain from him supply all my wants. I must dress in costly materials. The people scrutinize every article that I wear with critical curiosity. The very fact of having grown up in the West subjects me to more searching observation. To keep up appearances I must have money—more than Mr. Lincoln can spare for me. I had, and still have, no alternative but to run in debt."

"And Mr. Lincoln does not even suspect how much you owe?"

"God, no! And I would not have him suspect. The knowledge would drive him mad. He does not know a thing about my debts, and I value his happiness, not to speak of my own, too much to allow him to know anything. This is what troubles me so much. If he is reëlected, I can keep him in ignorance of my affairs; but if he is defeated, then the bills will be sent in and he will know all." And having told this, "something like a hysterical sob escaped her."

Meantime, outside the White House and over the country the discussion, the talk, the gossip, of four years about the First

Lady of the Land had gathered headway. Her reputation had become the sinister creation of thousands of personal impressions spoken by people who had seen her or talked with her; of thousands of newspaper items about her comings and goings to Long Branch, Saratoga Springs, Boston, New York, for rest, for parties and receptions, for shopping; of hundreds of items about gifts presented to her, her house, her boys; of hundreds of items of public prints and private gossip about her gowns and coiffures, her jewels and adornments; of private information held by scores of persons in high office who knew of her caprices, tempers, jealousies. The journalist, biographer and novelist Mary Clemmer Ames set forth a viewpoint common to a large and possibly overwhelming majority of the men and women of the country who held any definite viewpoint at all: "Wives, mothers and daughters, in ten thousand homes, were looking into the faces of husbands, sons and fathers, with trembling and with tears, and yet with sacrificial patriotism. They knew, they felt the best-beloved were to be slain on the country's battlefields. It was the hour for self-forgetting. Personal vanity and elation, excusable in a more peaceful time, seemed unpardonable in this. Yet, in reviewing the character of Presidents' wives, we shall see that there was never one who entered the White House with such a feeling of self-satisfaction, which amounted to personal exultation, as did Mary Lincoln. To her it was the fulfillment of a lifelong ambition, and she made her journey to Washington a triumphal passage."

Mary Clemmer Ames wrote what was partly overstatement, partly and in degree a harsh judgment, yet she also reported what was in the heart of numbers of women. "In the distant farmhouse women waited, breathless, the latest story of battle. In the crowded cities they gathered by thousands, crying only, 'Let me work for my brother; he dies for me.' With the record of the march and the fight, and of the unseemly defeat, the newspapers teemed with gossip concerning the lady in the White House. While her sister-women scraped lint, sewed bandages and put on nurses' caps, and gave their all to country and to death, the wife of the President spent her time in rolling to and fro between Washington and New York, intent on extravagant purchases for herself and the White House. Mrs. Lincoln seemed to have nothing to do but to 'shop,' and the reports of her lavish bargains, in the newspapers, were vulgar and sensational in the extreme. The wives and daughters of other Presidents had managed to dress as elegant women without the process of so doing becoming prominent or public. But not a new dress or jewel was bought by Mrs. Lincoln that did not find its way into the newspapers."

In the White House Mrs. Ames saw "a lonely man, sorrowful at heart, weighed down by mighty burdens"; toiling and suffering alone. Washington had become one vast hospital. "The reluctant river laid at the feet of the city its priceless freight of lacerated men. The wharves were lined with the dying and the dead. One ceaseless procession of ambulances moved to and fro. . . . Our streets resounded with the shrieks of the sufferers. Churches, halls and houses were turned into hospitals. . . . Through it all Mrs. Lincoln 'shopped.' . . . The nation seemed goaded at last to exasperation. Letters of rebuke, of expostulation, of anathema even, addressed to her personally came in to her from every direction. Not a day that did not bring her many such communications, denouncing her mode of life. . . . To no other American woman had ever come an equal chance to set a lofty example of self-abnegation to her countrywomen. But just as if there were no national peril, no monstrous national debt, no rivers of blood flowing, she seemed chiefly intent upon pleasure, personal flattery and adulation; upon extravagant dress and ceaseless self-gratification.

The politicians with whom Mrs. Lincoln held interviews and had dealings regarding appointments and nominations, also her extreme household economy, were discussed by thousands in somewhat the words of Mary Clemmer Ames. "Vain, seeking admiration, the men who fed her weakness for their own political ends were sure of her favor. Thus, while daily disgracing the State by her own example she still sought to meddle in its affairs. Woe to Mr. Lincoln if he did not appoint her favorites. Prodigal in personal expenditures, she brought shame upon the President's House by petty economies, which had never disgraced it before. Had the milk of its dairy been sent to the hospitals, she would have received golden praise. But the whole city felt scandalized to have it haggled over and peddled from the back door of the White House. State dinners could have been dispensed with, without a word of blame, had their cost been consecrated to the soldiers' service; but when it was made apparent that they were omitted from personal penuriousness and a desire to devote their cost to personal gratification, the public censure knew no bounds."

Mary Clemmer Ames reports what happened as a result of the letters that poured in on the Lady President. "From the moment Mrs. Lincoln began to receive recriminating letters, she considered herself an injured individual, the honored object of envy, jealousy and spite, and a martyr to her high position. No doubt some of them were unjust, and many more unkind; but it never dawned upon her consciousness that any part of the provocation was on her side, and after a few tastes of their bitter draughts she ceased to open them."

There came the reëlection of the President in the fall of 1864. There came the night of April 14, 1865, when she was alongside her husband in a box at Ford's Theater. She sat close to him, leaned on him, as she afterward told it to her friend, Dr. Anson G. Henry. And she was a little afraid her behavior might be embarrassing to the daughter of Senator Harris of Rhode Island sitting near by. She said to the President, "What will Miss Harris think of my hanging on to you so?" He replied, "She won't think about it." And those were his last words. There came the assassin's bullet. And soon Abraham Lincoln lay on a bed in the back room of the Peterson house across from Ford's Theater, breathing hard all night long and trying to struggle back to consciousness. His wife sat in the front room weeping, "uttering heartbroken exclamations all night long," leaving the house with the moan, "Oh, my God, and I have given my husband to die." There came to her such dumb despair as made all pain in her life till then seem easy in comparison. The bitterness of the hour was that so few friends could come to speak a word or touch her hand or sit in quiet with her and give her comfort by silent presence. The nearest to a great friend that came then was Elizabeth Keckley, the mulatto woman who carried solace and ministering hands, and who was given trust and confidence that no others received.

Mary Clemmer Ames fathomed some of the bitterness of the hour. "Mrs. Lincoln bewept her husband. There is no doubt but that, in that black hour, she suffered great injustice. She loved her husband, with the intensity of a nature, deep and strong, within a narrow channel. The shock of his untimely taking-off might have excused a woman of loftier nature than hers for any accompanying paralysis."

This was nearly the word, "paralysis." She lay physically helpless for days and wandered mentally and called for death to take her, crying she had lost all worth living for. It was five weeks before she was able to leave the White House. It was not strange she stayed five weeks, wrote Mary Clemmer Ames. "It would have been stranger had she been able to have left it sooner. It was her misfortune that she had so armed public sympathy against her, by years of indifference to the sorrow of others, that when her own hour of supreme anguish came, there were few to comfort her, and many to assail. She had made many unpopular innovations upon the old serene and stately régime of the President's House. Never a reign of concord in her best day, in her hour of affliction it degenerated into absolute anarchy. The long-time steward (overseer and caretaker) had been dethroned that Mrs. Lincoln might manage according to her own will. While she was shut in with her woe, the White House was left without a responsible protector. The rabble ranged through it at will. Silver and dining-ware were carried off, and have never been recovered. It was plundered, not only of ornaments, but of heavy articles of furniture. Costly sofas and chairs were cut and injured. Exquisite lace curtains were torn into rags, and carried off in pieces."

While all of this was going on downstairs, Mrs. Lincoln in her apartments upstairs refused to see anyone but servants, while day after day immense boxes containing her personal effects were leaving the White House for the West. "The size and number of these boxes," noted Mrs. Ames, "with the fact of the pillaged aspect of the White House, led to the accusation, which so roused public feeling against her, that she was robbing the national house and carrying the national property with her into retirement. This accusation which clings to her to this day (1871) was probably unjust. Her personal effects, in all likeliness, amounted to as much as that of nearly all other Presidents' wives together, and the vandals who roamed at large through the length and breadth of the White House were quite sufficient to account for all its missing treasures."

ELINOR WYLIE

CARL VAN DOREN

Let me tell the story of Elinor Wylie, that pure yet troubled genius, as truly as I can. It is several stories. She was a legend before she was a fact, and the legend came to New York ahead of her. Sometimes she seemed to be living up to it, with little mystifications about herself. At other times she would feel transient compunctions and tell her closer friends things they would not have thought of asking for. It was hard, knowing her, to disentangle fact from legend, and either from the roles, romantic or realistic, which she alternately played. I am not too sure that I have disentangled the four stories, though she often confided in me and though I have since her death tried, so far as research at this distance can go, to make one clear story out of them.

Because the legend said she came from Philadelphia, she let most people believe she had been born there, or in suburban Rosemont. When the Hall-Mills murder case made Somerville, New Jersey, conspicuous, she told me as an amusing secret that that was where she had actually been born. She let it be thought too that she had been born in 1887. But one evening at a party she drew me into a corner and asked me what day in September was my birthday. I told her the 10th. She knew the year was 1885.

"Then I'm really three days older than you. I was born on the 7th. Nobody knows but Bill. You won't tell, will you? Do you think I'm an awful liar?"

I did not consider it a lie for any woman to misrepresent her age, but I said only that I did not think this was a lie, and of course I would not tell. I had a policy for her confidences. Whatever she told me as a secret I kept to myself till I had

From Carl Van Doren, *Three Worlds*, Harper & Brothers.

heard the same thing from three other persons to whom she
had told it.

A single confidence did not bind her. She told me that she
had been married at eighteen, when she should have said twenty
to agree with what I already knew about her age. And because
I had written a life of Peacock, Shelley's friend, and because
she not only loved Shelley but identified herself with him, she
identified me with Peacock, and at times dramatically assumed
that I was seven years older than she, as Peacock was older than
Shelley. She knew better, but it was a pleasant fiction. When I
game her my *Nightmare Abbey*, in which Peacock had laughed
at Shelley, she took it almost as a gift from the satirist to his
subject.

Shelley so obsessed her in her final years that she liked to
think he had been her earliest and only hero; but in 1924 she
told me that her first hero was Darcy in *Pride and Prejudice*.
She admired him for his pride, for his refusal to be hoodwinked
by his love for Elizabeth into overlooking the disadvantages of
marrying into her family, and for the delicacy with which his
love in the end showed how strong it was. Gerald Poynyard in
Jennifer Lorn is partly Darcy. Though Elinor Wylie respected
the passions, she respected minds and manners too.

She had grown up among minds and manners. The eldest of
the five children of Henry Martyn Hoyt and Anne McMichael
of Philadelphia, she was a great-granddaughter of Morton McMichael, who had been mayor of the city, and a granddaughter of
another Henry Martyn Hoyt who had been governor of Pennsylvania, and a daughter of the Solicitor-General of the United
States. Taken at two from Somerville to her Philadelphia sub-
urb, she lived there till she was twelve, and then in Washington
till she was twenty-five. She went to Miss Baldwin's School in
Bryn Mawr and to Mrs. Flint's School in Washington, and she
studied drawing in a class at the Corcoran Museum of Art.
Before her marriage she spent the summers with her family at
Northeast Harbor, Mount Desert, Maine. When she was
eighteen (but she told me sixteen) she and her sister Constance
went with their grandfather, Morton McMichael, for the season
in Paris and London. He introduced them to his friends Sir
Henry Irving and Ellen Terry, and to Bram Stoker, who dedi-
cated *The Jewel of Seven Stars* to the two girls. Elinor Wylie
never mentioned Ellen Terry or Irving or Stoker to me, but she
said that her grandfather, that year and other years, had been

a good part of her education. The rest of it, she said, came mostly from her father. She had as a girl been both taught and petted by older men.

She missed this after her marriage to Philip Hichborn, son of Admiral Philip Hichborn, in Washington in 1905. William Rose Benét, then at Yale with her younger brother Henry, says he saw her in Washington while she was a bride, and thought her happy. Later she believed she had not been. "I didn't know what love and marriage meant," she told me. "The other girls talked about such things, but I would never listen. My marriage was a prison. I felt stifled. There was no room for my mind at all. I had to get away. While my father was alive I had him to turn to. But after he died I was desperate, and I ran away with Horace. He was twenty years older than I, and father as well as husband to me." (Wylie was only fifteen years older.)

She told me this, sitting beside me while I drove her and Benét from Cornwall to Waterbury. "I left my baby when I ran away," she went on. "That was the one thing I have ever done that I think was bad. Other things, no. I would do all of them over again. But that was utterly bad. I was a bad woman. And now I would rather have a child that I could think of as really my own than anything else I shall ever have. I tried to have children after I married Horace, but not one of them lived. I have had a miscarriage since I married Bill. The doctors say that anything like that again would be the same as putting a gun to my head." I think all this seemed the truth to her, but I know now that before her last miscarriage she was sometimes hysterical with fear and resentment.

The Hoyts, the McMichaels, the Hichborns, and the Wylies were so well known in Philadelphia and Washington that the elopement of Elinor Hoyt Hichborn and Horace Wylie in December 1910 raised an enormous scandal. Newspapers did their worst. As Horace Wylie's wife would not divorce him, the lovers had to leave the country, to live quietly as Mr. and Mrs. Waring in England near the New Forest. The papers invented stories of a wild residence in Corsica, which neither of them ever saw, though they went now and then to France. After two years Philip Hichborn killed himself. "Of course," Elinor Wylie said, "if Philip had killed himself over me he could not have waited two years to do it." But the scandal had another episode of melodrama to increase it. Scandal followed her all her life, ready to lift its head from old files of news at every step she took: when she and Horace Wylie came back to Boston in July, 1915, and after his divorce were married the next year, and when they lived two summers in Mount Desert and a winter in Augusta, Georgia, and when in 1919 they returned to Washington where he obtained a minor post in a Government bureau.

No newspaper, so far as I know, ever noticed a literary coincidence of the year 1912, when Philip Hichborn's stories were collected and published as *Hoof Beats* in Boston, and Elinor Wylie's (really Hichborn's) *Incidental Numbers* was privately printed in London. Some one more inquisitive than I will have to ask those who know what the coincidence means, which of the books was issued first and which of them led to the other, if either did, and what motives were involved in this sad rivalry the year Philip Hichborn died.

The poems of *Incidental Numbers* had little of Elinor Wylie's magic. She was not precocious, and in a sense she was still at school, with Horace Wylie and rural England for her teachers. The fashionable world is full of women who write bad poems with good intentions, and Elinor Wylie at twenty-seven had only begun to outgrow her world, though she had run away from it. Eight years later she had outgrown it. Even if Washington had forgiven her, I think she could not have gone back to it, as she sometimes thought she could have. In any case, she was not forgiven, and she had few friends outside her family. Then in 1919-20 she renewed her acquaintance with Benét, and met Sinclair Lewis, who was in Washington writing *Main Street*.

Through them she learned of a world which would not hold her past against her, and in 1921 she left Washington for New York. It meant a separation, and two years later a divorce from Horace Wylie. A love which was almost a classic had passed like any other. The story of it was not a few pages long, as here, but a dozen years. (Pinch a story too tight, and the life goes out of it.) Much as Elinor Wylie told me about herself, she never told me about the end of this chapter, only about her respect and affection for Horace Wylie, whose name she kept for herself as poet. Servants and strangers might call her Mrs. Benét, but I never heard the words Elinor Benét, and now I see them for the first time and realize that they were her name.

She made her way at once into the literary society of Manhattan. What in Washington had seemed shocking, in New York seemed dramatic. Almost nobody knew exactly what her story was, but everybody knew she had a story and thought of her as some kind of heroine. Her poems began to be noticed and applauded. The first one I saw was "The Eagle and the Mole" in the *New Republic*, and I read it over and over, excited as I had been at Edna Millay's "Renascence" in the *Lyric Year* in 1912. I think now, as Benét thought then, that Elinor Wylie should have had the *Nation's* poetry prize for 1921; but her crisp notes were lost in the clamor. Benét told me about her poems, self-consciously, and I guessed she was more to him than a new poet. I knew nothing else about her, except the vaguest legend, till I first met her late in 1922.

II

Mary Colum and Jean Wright planned a meeting at the Mac-Dowell Club where many poets were to read their work to a large audience, and I was to be chairman and introduce the poets. Elinor Wylie was one of them. She looked like the white queen of a white country. White-faced in white satin, she had no color but in her lustrous eyes and her bronze hair. She seemed restless and remote. Introducing her, I said her poems were like bronze bells. This delighted her. She read with a shy fire, but her voice was actually higher in pitch then her verses. Clear and fresh, it was not sweet, and in heightened moments it might be shrill. Shelley's voice was sometimes shrill.

I did not happen to see her again for another year, at a dinner just after she and Benét came back to town from a short honeymoon. That evening she was neither queen nor poet, but a laughing woman. On the way home in a taxi she and Mary Colum made fun, with such lively and inventive malice, of a dull Englishman who had been at the dinner that I felt insensitive for having noticed only that he was another dull Englishman.

The summer following Elinor Wylie and Benét came from the Canbys' House at Yelping Hill to Wickwire. That day the Puritan marrow of her bones was in her mind. It was raw and windy after a hot week, but she refused to wear a coat and walked about with bare arms, deliberately cold. At heart she was New England, she declared, like the first Hoyts in Massachusetts. At the lake she insisted on swimming all the way to the float, though it was too far for her, and she reached it breathless. In swimming clothes she had an angularity which did not appear when she wore her usual dress and looked stately.

She was immensely pleased when I told her that my daughter Anne had asked me if that was the lady who had written "My Love Came Up From Barnegat."

The *Century* published as much of her work as she would let me have, including *The Venetian Glass Nephew*, which was to furnish her some money she needed for the house she had bought in New Canaan, Connecticut.

"Can *The Venetian Glass Nephew* help me at all as yet?" she wrote from New Canaan, October 3, 1924. "I find I have unexpectedly to pay the *interest*, as well as the *paying off*, on the mortgage. There *is* a difference, though it takes an expert to understand.

"What a pity that these sordid things exist in a world where we are going into the 18th century next week-end! Both Bill & I are longing to see the lovely house [Wickwire] again— and it was so nice seeing you & Irita last Monday.

"P. S. Of course I hope you can manage this advance, but if you can't, don't picture me as suicidal in consequence. It is my reprehensible nature to welcome excitement & change, & the idea of being melodramatically foreclosed & forced to find another—& of course a better—place to live is in itself attractive to my mind. But one must do one's duty, hence this letter."

Without telling the treasurer of the *Century* all the facts in the case, I managed the advance for the whole novel when only a third of it was written. At Wickwire that week-end she gave me the first part, and I left the others to read it in the library. She was in more suspense than I realized, for her sharp ears overheard me laughing aloud as I read, and she called out in such glee that I had to go back to tell her how brilliant I thought it was.

She wrote the rest of the book in New Canaan, working after the three Benét children had left for school and before they came home. Elinor Wylie was not one of those spawning writers who pour out loose first drafts and then trim and tighten them. She began a sentence on her typewriter only when it was finished in her mind and needed no corrections. In the entire manuscript there was hardly a change, even of a syllable, to the page. And she made only one copy, which she sent to me, and which I sent to the *Century's* printers in New Hampshire. She liked the risk. There was the further risk that the serial began in the magazine before the book was done. It had to be done, and of course it was. I never trusted another writer so far as that.

III

She had often talked about a novel dealing with the Salem witches, one of whom was an ancestor of hers. "But it isn't about the witches," she said, "so much as about the witch-hunters. They were the evil ones. They found what they were looking for because they created it out of themselves. You know who the real Man in Black was. Why, it was Cotton Mather." She had suffered from witch-hunters herself, I imagined she was thinking. But that must be put off for something still closer to her. She could hardly bear to put it into words, and she pledged me to total secrecy. There had never been such an idea for a novel. Suppose Shelley had not been drowned in the Gulf of Spezia, but had been picked up by an American boat, and had decided to go incognito to America, not back to his wife, whom Elinor Wylie hated. To write the book would be almost to have Shelley for a visitor and to show him America, which Elinor Wylie loved.

I sent her books, for *The Orphan Angel*, about the America of the early nineteenth century. There were no pains to which she would not go to be accurate. After all, she was setting the stage and preparing her house for Shelley.

"Thank you," she wrote from Peterboro on August 12th, "ten thousand times for the noble collection of Americana, which has saved my life & Shelley's. . . .

"I was really much impeded for lack of proper material, & these books are a happy release. I am working myself deaf dumb blind & lumbagoishly lame, but am otherwise well & contented."

"My darling lovely novel can't be finished, after all," she wrote in September, "because Mrs. MacDowell is closing the colony on the 22nd, & the children are returning the 26th. I know, I know, how infinitely sweeter & more valuable real people are than the products of one's fancy, but in this case I am prejudiced. My hero is not entirely the product of my own fancy. Some god became imaginative indeed at his creation, & went aside from the beaten track of button-molding in making him. Which is true, if metaphorically mixed

"You will perceive perhaps that I am depressed. I believe

that it is a mistake to work throughout one's vacation. I don't *see the necessity*. West Cornwall was a bright oasis, as I told Irita.

"Every day I am reminded of you by the invaluable books. I could have done nothing without them. When—do you happen to know, since you know so much—did they first have steamboats on the Ohio? In 1822 do you think? . . ."

"Your review," she wrote without a date but with a New Canaan postmark of the 5th of October, "appeared just after my weeping eyes were looking their last on Peterboro, & though it served to stanch my tears it was impossible to write to you in mid-air, as it were. Three days with Grace Conkling, another three with the dear old Commodore in New York, & a week in New Canaan without servants have not advanced my correspondence, & it is with a stiff & enervated hand that I now seize a very bad pen & indite you these few lines. . . .

"I am heartily disgusted with the—really you must forgive me, it is the only possible term—gutless Virginio now that I have him between dull commonplace blue cloth covers, & if I did not believe that Shiloh & David were more alive & kicking I should be sad indeed. Thus it is to write a book under bad conditions & when one is tired—the lack of vitality is all too apparent in the tale. But what is one to do—sell matches? I have three little stepchildren, kind lady, & a mortgage on my house, & extreme astigmatism, & I feel as if I had a shawl over my head & chilblains. I suppose in addressing you I should rather say 'kind sir' but I was thinking of some sort of district visitor.

"You see I am writing out of a purple thundercloud of gloom, which your review has lit with lovely flashes. The trouble is—a book half done & a steep impassable prospect of finishing it this winter. All my plans were changed for us at the eleventh hour by the rich & powerful people who mold our lives.

"I'm sorry that I'm beginning to imitate Shelley in this melancholy fashion. Poor darling Shelley, I have not his other virtues to make my dejection forgivable! Nevertheless, please forgive me. And accept my thanks for the lovely gift of the review."

She wrote again the 6th:

"I've just heard that you are in town after all. I'm so sorry that I didn't know it Saturday, for I sent you a fairly long letter

to Cornwall, & we all know what the Connecticut mails are.
Perhaps it may reach you in time for Christmas.

"It thanked you for your brilliant and benevolent review of
my immortal works, & it contained certain stanzas written in
dejection by an unfinished novel.

"I hear—from another of your devoted admirers—that you
are looking tired. There is nothing so restful—or so distressingly
dull—as a regular bread & butter job. Your present way of life,
while far more remunerative than mine for example, probably
resembles it in discovering that it is harder, while pleasanter &
more exciting, to do your own work than the other man's. Yet
that—my own work—is precisely what I am fervently pining for
at present. To do no work at all—except the other woman's,
the dear classic dishwashing, dinner-cooking woman—is incom-
parably the hardest.

"Did we not make a mistake in our youth—which was so
very nearly contemporaneous—in becoming what Miss Sinclair
& the Peterboro servants call creators? What a noble shoemaker
—to choose a trade at random, or because shoemakers are
always liberals—would not you have made, & I know how
excellent at contriving artificial flowers or the peep-show scenes
inside Easter eggs! You will say that these also savor of creation,
but our present trouble—if indeed your impeccable admirable-
ness will accept the word—springs from our stubborn attempt
to utilize our wretched minds, to make unpleasant grayish con-
volutions work for us instead of trained & agile fingertips & the
beautiful rhythmic strength of habit. 'How lovely is benign
stupidity!' as no one really ever wrote.

"Two years ago the New Republic would have had a poem
from me on this subject; now you must put up with a dull letter.
It is hard on you, dear Carl, & I hope it is hard on the New
Republic."

The Benét children went to California to live with their aunt
Kathleen Norris, and Elinor Wylie finished The Orphan Angel,
sitting up all night to write the last words in a flat in Bank
Street and the next day sailing for Europe. Her novel, selected
by the Book-of-the-Month Club, brought her more money than
she could have expected to earn by her precise and delicate art.
She spent what she was afraid was a guilty share of it for Shelley
letters. This was paper his hand had touched. This was ink that
had come from his sacred pen. She loved Shelley. He would
have loved her if he had known her. They loved each other.

She fiercely defended him once when I said I sometimes found his self-pity tiresome. She wrote her sonnets "A Red Carpet for Shelley." She wrote essays about him and a short story, "A Birthday Cake for Lionel"—Lionel who is in effect Shiloh ten years older. Returning to England in 1925, ten years after she had left it, she thought of herself as almost Shelley, perhaps a friend of Shelley, returning to England ten or so years after Shelley's death in Italy. From this came Mr. Hodge and Mr. Hazard, her fourth novel. It had its origin, she told me, in two words spoken by a stupid man from Oxford, who, hearing she was writing sonnets to Shelley, muttered "Poor Shelley." She heard him. Her revenge was to pillory him as Mr. Hodge, who in the novel hears that Mr. Hazard is writing a sonnet to Milton, and says "Poor Milton."

IV

During her last three years Elinor Wylie lived—with summers in England—in a flat in Ninth Street, her drawing-room dominated by its memorable silver mirror and her study at the back as austere as her style. Nobody worked harder than she. Four novels and four books of verse in seven years are proof enough. But her evenings were free, and she had countless friends. There were of course many Elinor Wylies. I can claim to know only one of them.

My Elinor Wylie had as sure and strong an intelligence as I have ever known. It was impossible to bring up an idea that she had not had or did not instantly understand. It was impossible to bring out a fact that did not fit into something she already knew. No formal scholar, she had a scholar's instinct for exactness. She could not be comfortable imagining steamboats on the Ohio in 1822 unless she knew they had been there, or imagining a volume of Plato into Mr. Hazard's pocket in 1833 unless she could find out that such pocket volumes then existed. She asked me the minutest questions. Had I ever come across any account of a frontier blue-stocking who might be a model for one of the women who courted Shiloh on his travels? I had, in A New Home—Who'll Follow? She was sorry that the book was about Michigan and a time later than 1822, but she used it, transforming what she used.

This young lady (Caroline Matilda Stansbury Kirkland had written

of Eloise Fidler) was not as handsome as she fain would have been, if
I may judge by the cataracts of ash-coloured ringlets which shaded her
cheeks, and the exceeding straitness of the stays which restrained her
somewhat exuberant proportions . . . Her dress was in the height of
fashion, and all her accoutrements *point device*. A gold pencil-case of
the most delicate proportions was suspended by a kindred chain around
a neck which might be called whity-brown; and a note-book of cor-
responding lady-likeness was peeping from the pocket of her highly-
useful apron of blue silk—ever ready to secure a passing thought or an
elegant quotation. Her album—she was just the person to have an
album—was resplendent in gold and satin, and the verses which meandered over its emblazoned pages were of the most unexceptional quality,
overlaid with flowers and gems—love and despair. . . .

Miss Fidler wrote her own poetry, so that she had ample employment
for her time while with us in the woods. It was unfortunate that she
could not walk out much on account of her shoes. She was obliged to
make out with diluted inspiration. The nearest approach she usually
made to the study of Nature, was to sit on the wood pile, under a
girdled tree, and there, with her gold pencil in hand, and her "eyne,
gray as glas," rolled upwards, poefy by the hour.

And, standing marvel of Montacute, no guest at morning or night
ever found the fair Eloise ungloved. Think of it! In the very wilds to be
always like a cat in nutshells, alone useless where all were so busy. . . .
And then her shoes! "Saint Crispin Crispianus" never had so self-sacri-
ficing a votary. No shoemaker this side of New York could make a sole
papery enough; no tannery out of France could produce materials for
this piece of exquisite feminine foppery.

Now Elinor Wylie's version in *The Orphan Angel*:

Miss Rosalie Lillie was seated upon the woodpile in an attitude of
negligent grace; her fine eyes were fixed above the distant tamarack-trees
in contemplation of some winged chimæra of the mind. A gold pencil-
case was suspended by a delicate chain around the lady's creamy throat;
a notebook peeped out from the pocket of her blue satin apron, and a
gilded album lay within reach. Under a furred cloak her attire was frail
and silken; she wore thin-soled bronze slippers, and her hands were
encased in gloves of primrose kidskin.

Miss Lillie was a singularly lovely girl; her features were regular and
her figure tall and classically formed. She had a rich abundance of chest-
nut hair and her velvet eyes were the color of purple-brown pansies. She
looked very expensive and unsuitable against a background of enormous
forest trees and ragged rail fences; the smoky November sun picked out
the Italian cameo upon her bosom and increased the splendid damask
of her cheek.

The document wanders, the work of art marches. One stroke,

and the lady is mounted upon her woodpile. Another, and she
is contemplating some winged chimæra of the mind, not
merely rolling her eyes. Stroke by stroke, the portrait is laugh-
ingly perfected. Kind epithets increase the lady's beauty. Her
useless shoes become thin-soled bronze slippers. Her nonde-
script gloves appear as primrose kidskin. Her merely gray eyes
turn to the color of purple-brown pansies. She is no longer the
object of homespun ridicule. If she looks very expensive and
unsuitable against her background of trees and fences, that may
not be, the overtones imply, entirely her fault, but partly the
fault of nature for being so vast and of the works of man for
being so small and mean.

What Elinor Wylie did with Eloise Fidler in making her
over into Miss Rosalie Lillie she did with all the subjects of her
art, and, for that matter, with her life. She both wrote and
spoke with a lovely, amused formality which baffled the downright. But life had two or three times got out of hand with her
and had been tragic. She could never forget that. It kept alive
the perpetual contradictions of her nature. She was a woman
who had beauty and genius. Beauty compelled her and genius
compelled her, both of them without always giving her simple
motives for her compulsions. Doubly driven, she was doubly
sensitive. Two careers side by side in one woman. No wonder
she often seemed ruthless, often hysterical, habitually bewildering. Within a few moments she could be suspicious and ingen-
uous, insolent and tender, capricious and steadfast, desperate and
hilarious, stirringly profound and exquisitely superficial.

And there was her vanity, which might have been unendurable
if she had not so freely admitted it and laughed about it. Before
her sister Nancy Hoyt came from Washington Elinor Wylie
made me promise—and everybody else, I suppose—that I would
faithfully tell her if I thought Nancy more beautiful than she.
Once when Jacqueline Embry of Kentucky was visiting in New
York I took her to call. Elinor Wylie could hardly wait to ask
her guest to show her bronze hair and let it be compared with
Elinor Wylie's own. At a large dinner a strange and tactless
Russian woman said, "Mrs. Benét, I have heard you were not
really beautiful, but I think you are." Elinor Wylie, disregarding
the present compliment, wept that anybody could ever have
said that she was not beautiful. One evening at a large party
at Dreiser's studio she felt herself neglected. She could not bear
being less than first in any company. Nothing on earth would

do but that a few of her close friends should join her in another
room and hear her read some poems—say some poems, as she
always put it. Her friends humored her in such tantrums of
vanity and went to all lengths in flattering her. She liked flattery
as a lizard likes the sun. "How can she take it," Jacqueline
Embry asked me, "in such spoonfuls? Even if it is the very
best butter?" Perhaps the friends who humored and flattered
her the most were sometimes bored by her vain tantrums. I
know I was, though I admired and adored her.

v

In June, 1928, when I arrived in London, Elinor Wylie was
already there, living in her tiny house in Chelsea. She had asked
me to meet her the first evening at Osbert Sitwell's, where she
was to be. Barely off the boat, I misjudged the occasion, which
was for Sunday evening, and did not dress. The whole evening
was spoiled for her by my improper tweeds—or so it seemed.
"But you did bring evening clothes, didn't you? I am giving
you a party this week, and I've already asked everybody to meet
you, and I can't bear to have you come in this brown coat." I
told her I should not think of wearing it, but she would not be
reassured, as she did not listen. "Please don't wear the brown
coat to my party." She made me think of an anxious young girl
who had planned something that was to be very grown-up and
correct and was afraid that one of her guests might treat it as
if it were for children.

Her house in Chelsea when I got there was in a headless confusion over water streaming from a broken pipe. She had writers
not plumbers for dinner. After I had telephoned the water
company for an emergency repairman, she forgave me my mistake
of Sunday evening. "Nobody but an American," she announced
with fantastic extravagance, "would have known what to do.
And no American but Carl would have known how to do it in
London." I felt like a disconcerted elder brother in the face of his
sister's bragging.

When the others left she asked me to stay behind to hear
her say some new poems she had written. They were sonnets,
she told me. So, sitting in her Chelsea drawing-room, I heard
a dozen or so of the nineteen sonnets which she later called
"One Person," and which belong to the supreme love poetry in
English or in any language. I heard them, and I read them,

too much moved to notice that one of them lacked a line. In her passion she had lost count. It was as strange in her, most accurate poet, as if she had forgotten to tend her hair or hands.

At first reticent and watchful while I heard and read, she was quickly warmed by my excitement over the poems, threw off her secrecy, and—then at a later dinner in Soho—told me the story behind them. I must know the whole story, she said. There was a man—she told me his name—whom at last she loved absolutely. To me she did not make him sound glorious, though she tried. All the glory was in her. She had never been in love before, she was sure. She had only been loved.

> I have believed me obdurate and blind
> To those sharp ecstasies the pulses give:
> The clever body five times sensitive
> I never have discovered to be kind.

This is one of her sonnets. In her speech, the same thing in troubled yet exultant prose. Now at last the pulses had wakened in her blood and her senses leapt. Little enough had actually come of it. Jealous circumstances had kept the lovers apart, and they had been alone only in a forest. Three trysts: "And afterward," she said, "you won't believe it, but we realized that we had met under an oak, an ash, and a thorn." Little could ever come of it. She would not disrupt her life again. This must remain a radiant experience of the mind. But it did not belong solely to her mind. It was flesh too, and it tore at her. She cried out against the cruel separation. "I don't want much. I don't expect it. I could be satisfied if I could know that sometime, maybe when we are very old, we could spend the same night under one roof. It would not have to be together. Only under the same roof, peacefully. Is that too much to expect? Don't you think I could dare to hope for that?" I soothed her as well as I could, but she was overwhelmed by the most shaking emotion I ever saw in her. Even Shelley could not help her:

> A woman by an archangel befriended.
> Now must I end the knightly servitude
> Which made him my preserver, and renounce
> That heavenly aid forever and at once. . . .

Love is what it means to the lover, not to the bystander, and I could not question the reality of the tempest which racked her. All that she had written in the sonnets she said, in rushing sentences. "And am I not your child who has come home? And am

I not your hound for faithfulness?" At last, she said, she had
learned to feel humble and obedient.

> O dear my lord, believe me that I know
> How far your virtues have outnumbered mine.

She herself was nothing beside him, who had borne everything.
"The little beauty that I was allowed,"—what was that to his
"degree of noble and of fair"? How could she deserve, how
comfort him?

> How is it possible that this hand of clay,
> Though white as porcelain, can contrive a touch
> So delicate it shall not hurt too much?
> What voice can my invention find to say
> So soft, precise, and scrupulous a word
> You shall not take it for another sword?

"To educate me fitly for your bride" an eternity might be
enough. In the meantime let him be patient with her. Let him
make what use of her he could, though he only set her like a
timber in his house to "bear a little more than I can bear." Her
words rushed and tumbled, and her eyes were wild. She was as
pale as a priestess at the mercy of her oracle, flaming through
her.

I never saw her alive again, and I remember her best for
these perfect sonnets and her broken commentary. What she
and the sonnets together said was that this final love had come
to her like first love, and had dissolved her to her youngest
elements, but that she was no less a poet than before, and she
could instinctively find ripe, skilful words for emotions which
ordinarily go no farther than sighs and tears, timid raptures and
pitiful despairs. For once in the world, youth knew and age
could. The heart of sixteen spoke with the tongue of forty.

I went to Paris and Cannes for a summer among the expatriates. I heard mysteriously about her that she had had a fall and
had hurt herself, but could get no definite news about her.
Back in New York, I still heard only uncertain rumors. She
had had a stroke, the rumors said, and one side of her face was
paralyzed. Her friends could not believe she would ever survive disfigurement. When in December she came home I did
not go at once to see her, but telephoned her and asked when
I might. This would allow her to choose the time or to put it
off indefinitely. She said she was not well and very busy but

that she must see me early in the coming week. She died that Sunday night, as swiftly as the curtain falls after a tragedy.

Tragedy and triumph. Now she would have to drag out no long old age, beauty fading, strength fraying. Her end was as neat as her art. Perhaps she had been beaten in that early career from which she had turned, at thirty-five, to poetry, but she had outlived her defeats. No poet of her time would be longer remembered, and no woman. In her last scene the poet and the woman in her had shared a triumph beyond which neither could hope to go. Lift the trumpets upon this peroration. Let the black curtain fall.

Her dead face was lovely and serene and proud. Those who were to miss her most took their tone from her, as they had when she was alive, and bore themselves gracefully as well as seriously at her funeral. Death became her, and they could not wish for her life which she might not herself desire. The lives of the immortals are not measured by their fevered years.

A young man was speaking softly. He was Philip Hichborn, he said, her son. He had been brought up to think she was evil, a mother who had wantonly left her child. Two years ago, in England, he had gone to see her. (She had told me about that. He had come to see her, and had been silent, and had hated her, she thought.) Now he was saying that when he had seen her he had believed her beautiful and magical, and had not known what to say or how to say it. He was sure she had thought he did not love her. But he did, at sight. He had since then read her books and had found out all he could about her, and he had determined that this Christmas he would visit her again. At last they would be mother and son. "And now it is like this." There is no death quite complete. However it ties its ultimate knot, some loose strand dangles in the wind of life.

NELLIE BLY

It was Nellie Bly who first made America conscious of the woman reporter. She burst like a comet on New York, a dynamic figure, five feet three, with mournful gray eyes and persistent manners. She dramatized herself in a new form of journalism, going down in a diving bell and up in a balloon, posing as a lunatic, a beggar, a factory hand, a shop girl and a Salvation Army lass.

But Nellie's great coup, which neither she nor any other newspaper woman equaled again, was her trip around the world in 72 days, 6 hours, 11 minutes, outdoing the dream of Jules Verne's Phileas Fogg and creating no end of an international stir.

She sailed from New York on November 14, 1889, and came home in triumph on January 25, 1890, the *World* bringing her across the country from San Francisco by special train and greeting her with the smash headline leading the paper, "Father Time Outdone!"

With two small satchels, two frocks, a toothbrush, some flannel underwear, a bank book, a ghillie cap and a sturdy plaid ulster, Nellie galloped and ran, roasted and froze, sped from ship to train, to burro, to jinrickshaw, to sampan, to barouche, until she reached the terrific climax of outdoing Father Time for Joseph Pulitzer. It was exhilarating journalism, good for the *World*, superb for Nellie, entertaining for the public, and it did no one any harm.

One had only to follow her career from its beginnings in Cochrane Mills, Pennsylvania, to know that Nellie was destined for front-page notice. She was born on May 5, 1867, in the small town founded by her father, who was a judge. Her name was Elizabeth Cochrane. She had enterprising blood in her

From Ishbel Ross, *Ladies of the Press*, Harper & Brothers.

veins. Her granduncle, Thomas Kennedy, went around the
world before she was born but it took him three years and he
came back with wrecked health. He intended to write the history
of his trip but never did. However, Nellie carried on.

Her father, a scholarly man, took charge of her early education. She was an imaginative child, fond of books and given to
scrawling fantastic fables on their fly-leaves. She went to a
boarding school in Indiana at thirteen but was brought home
within a year because of her delicate health. When her father
died and his estate was settled there was no money, although he
had been regarded as a man of wealth.

With the enterprise that was to mark her entire career, Nellie
left home and sought her fortune in Pittsburgh. Almost at once
she got in touch with the newspaper world by answering an
article in the Pittsburgh *Dispatch* entitled "What Girls Are
Good For." Her letter was not published but she was asked to
write a piece for the Sunday paper on girls and their sphere in
life. Without any hesitancy she put her views on paper, received
a check for her efforts and was asked to write more.

Nellie's newspaper sense was alert from the start. Having
landed on the springboard, she plunged boldly into the sea
with a piece entitled "Divorce." She signed it Nellie Bly, a
pseudonym suggested to her by George A. Madden, managing
editor of the *Dispatch*. He had taken it from Stephen C. Foster's
song, popular at the moment.

Nellie started her newspaper career with an original idea.
She went through factories and workshops in Pittsburgh, her
crusading spirit already in full flower. Her articles were emotional and spat their indignation. They all had the personal
quality which gave her a steady and constant following in later
years. At first she made $5 a week. Eventually she was to make
$25,000 from her writings in a single year.

She covered society, the theater and art for her paper. She
was young and looked it. She had only just put up her hair, and
she seemed shy and sensitive. Her large gray eyes were honest
and questing. Her manners were meek. This quality stayed with
Nellie to the time of her death. It concealed some of the
terrific driving force that made her dauntless in the pursuit of
her object. It fooled many of her unwitting victims.

She set out on her travels early. She had not been in Pittsburgh long before she decided to see the world. She took her
mother and they went to Mexico and journeyed everywhere

that the train would take them. Nellie sent back rather trite
letters to her paper. The smart newspaper girls who had preceded
her had all done travel correspondence. Why not Nellie?

When she returned to Pittsburgh her salary was raised to
$15 a week, but she had seen a larger world and she was no
longer satisfied, so she decided to try New York. The walls of
Jericho didn't crumble at the first blast of the trumpet. She
tramped the hot streets in the summer of 1887 and wondered
what she could do to make the metropolitan publishers know
that she had arrived. Then, as now, they were singularly incredu-
lous of the merits of a woman reporter.

Nellie reached her lowest ebb when she lost her purse with
nearly $100, practically all the money she had in the world.
Feeling desperate, she made another assault on the gold-domed
World building. She had been beseeching Mr. Pulitzer by letter
to allow her to go up in the balloon which he was sponsoring
at St. Louis, but her pleas had been ignored.

She had no introductions but she was determined to crash
the inner sanctum. She badgered the custodian of the gate for
three hours until she got to John A. Cockerill and finally to Mr.
Pulitzer himself. She was not particularly good-looking, nor was
she smart. But she was a human dynamo and almost at once
she enlisted the interest of her shrewd and experienced audience.
She laid before the two editors a list of suggestions for stories—
all of the stunt order. They looked them over and were favorably
impressed.

Nellie then told them the tale of the lost purse. They felt
sorry for the poor little creature in New York without a bean.
In her soft, persistent way she could always wheedle people into
doing what she wished. Mr. Pulitzer gave her $25 to keep her
going until he and Mr. Cockerill had had time to come to some
decision on her suggestions.

Nellie went back to her furnished room, sure that the battle
was won. And indeed, from that moment on, all gates opened
automatically for the small tornado, and nothing stayed her
course. The World decided to let her work up one of her own
ideas—that she should feign insanity and investigate the treatment of the insane on Blackwell's Island. There had been complaints about the way in which patients were treated there.

This was not the easiest assignment for a reporter on trial,
but Nellie was a gifted actress. She practised her part before a
mirror. She tore down her heavy brown hair and made faces at

herself. She read ghost stories so as to create a morbid state of mind. She laughed wildly at her own reflection. Then, when she felt in the proper mood, she dressed in old clothes and went to a temporary home for women, where she feigned madness so successfully that she was committed to Blackwell's Island without any difficulty. Four physicians pronounced her insane. And to her horror she found that the more sanely she behaved, the crazier they believed her to be, with the exception of one doctor who apparently was not taken in by her histrionics.

As soon as she was out she wrote two sensational stories in which she described her experiences. This was her formal introduction to the New York public. The World was in its crusading heyday and was widely read, so that many thousands were aware that Nellie Bly had come to town. She told of the cold, the poor food and the cruelty to which the patients were exposed. She found the asylum a "human rat trap, easy to get into, impossible to get out of." She charged the nurses with goading their patients. She saw demented and gray-haired women dragged shrieking to hidden closets, their cries being stifled by force as they were hustled out of sight.

The headlines on Nellie's first-person stories announced that she had deceived judges, reporters and medical experts. The revelations created considerable stir in official circles. She was summoned to appear before the Grand Jury. She accompanied the jurors on a visit to Blackwell's Island. But, somehow, many of the abuses of which she had written so graphically seemed to have been toned down by the time they got there. Nellie ascribed this anticlimax to the fact that the official visit was expected. There had been time to clean up the halls, improve the look of the beds and move some of the patients to remote spots where their constant complaints could not be heard. Practically none of the patients she had described by name were to be found for questioning and the nurses contradicted Nellie on every point.

However, the Grand Jury sustained her findings, $3,000,000 was voted for improvements and changes were made in the management of the asylum. The World was pleased with Nellie and Nellie was pleased with herself. She was taken on the regular staff and was told to go to work on her ideas.

She went in for reform and one of her first attacks was leveled with deadly effect against Edward R. Phelps, whom she exposed as the lobby king of Albany. Her glee is apparent in her story which appeared on April 1, 1888:

For I'm a Pirate King!
I'm in the Lobby Ring!
Oh! what an uproarious,
Jolly and glorious
Biz for a Pirate King!

I was a lobbyist last week. I went up to Albany to catch a professional briber in the act. I did so. The briber, lobbyist and boodler whom I caught was Mr. Ed Phelps. I pretended I wanted to have him help me kill a certain bill. Mr. Phelps was cautious at first and looked carefully into my record. He satisfied himself that I was honest and talked very freely for a king. . . .

From this point on, Nellie practically became the town reformer. Dr. Charles H. Parkhurst gave her credit for being of great aid to him. She visited the city prisons and turned out stories which resulted in the appointment of matrons to handle women prisoners. In order to write authoritatively she had herself arrested and went through the regular procedure. She visited the free dispensaries as an invalid to see what sort of medical care the poor were getting from the city. She spent a day in a diet kitchen and visited old women's homes. She sought employment as a servant through a number of agencies. She worked behind the glove counter of a large shop. She made paper boxes in a factory and found that more men wanted to flirt with her at this job than at anything else she tried. She put on a campaign against the handsome bucks who sauntered through the park when the grass was verdant and the dogwood bloomed. She rounded up the scoundrels one by one but the master technician eluded her. He appeared only on Wednesdays, drove a dashing pair of bays at a smart clip through the park, ogled the girls and usually made off with a brace of beauties to an unknown destination.

It took Nellie half a dozen Wednesdays to snare him. She spotted him at last by his whiskers. They were a rippling bronze and swept his four-in-hand. At the first glitter of his percipient eye she stepped into his carriage, arranged a rendezvous, lured him on to his undoing, and then unmasked the villain, sparing him nothing. He was a bartender from downtown who attended to his business six days a week and on the seventh put on his cutaway, pomaded a curl over his forehead, waxed his whiskers, plunged a sparkling horseshoe deep into his tie and drove his equipage through the park, casting the glad eye on the bell-sleeved beauties.

Nellie went back to her desk under the gold dome of the *World* building and wrote her exposé in finicky longhand. She ran the masher off his beat. His magnificent whiskers were seen no more in Central Park. Meanwhile, she went complacently on her way, the darling of the reading public.

So pervasive was she that the officials of public institutions began to look at every beggar woman's face with the suspicion that the deadly Bly girl might be lurking behind some disguise. Readers of the *World* watched eagerly to see what Nellie would be up to next. Mr. Pulitzer was not blind to the value of her services. In the winter of 1889 he decided to sponsor her trip around the world. He had rejected the same idea a year before. She received four days' notice to start and all her transportation was bought for her in New York.

It was still a ladylike age. There was little talk of the vote. The woman's page in the *World* was headed "Fair Woman's World." It had flower garnitures, music notes, a lady with a fan and a bustle. *The Master of Ballantrae* was running serially when Nellie got her orders to run a race with Father Time.

Thousands had been entranced by the dream of Phileas Fogg, who went around the world in eighty days. If the mythical Phileas could do it in a dream in eighty days, why not the enterprising Nellie in less?

She decided that luggage would hamper her movements, because of customs and porters, so she chose her wardrobe with care. She had a "blue plaid in ladies' cloth" made up in twelve hours at Ghormleys'. By noon the tailor had it boned and fitted, and at five o'clock on the same day it was ready for the final try-on. Miss Wheelwright, her own dressmaker, made her a tropical costume of camel's hair cloth. She selected a heavy Scotch plaid ulster and a gossamer waterproof for downpours. So enterprising was Nellie that she set off without an umbrella, a dashing piece of business for 1889. She had two satchels—one a substantial gripsack, sixteen by seven inches, the other a light contraption which she slung over her shoulder. She had a toothbrush, a bank book, a pair of "easy-fitting shoes" and some changes of flannel underwear. She wore a thumb ring on the left hand as a talisman. She had worn it the day she sought work on the *World* and so considered it lucky.

One of her masculine colleagues on the paper interviewed

Nellie the day she sailed. "And what will you do for a medicine chest, Miss Bly?" he asked solicitously. Miss Bly laughed heartily. There would be chemists everywhere along the line in such a modern and well-ordered world, she pointed out.

Her send-off was quieter than her return. Her paper announced:

> On four days' notice Miss Bly starts out with a gripsack for the longest journey known to mankind—she knows no such word as fail, and will add another to her list of triumphs—circumnavigation of the globe. The World today undertakes the task of turning a dream into a reality.
>
> With all the millions now invested in methods and modes of communication, interstate and international, the story of Miss Bly will give a valuable pointer in enabling the reader to appreciate these avenues of intercourse at their full value, to see their merits and their defects and note the present advanced state of invention in these lines of human effort.

Nellie sailed on the *Augusta Victoria* and pushed on according to the itinerary which had been carefully prepared for her. She carried a twenty-four-hour watch with her, so that she could keep track of the time in New York. She was to take her chance along the line. No chartered trains or extra fast ships were to speed her on her way.

Viewed at this distance, her feat scarcely seems as breathtaking as it did at the time, since all she had to do was to stick to her schedule and make her well-ordered connections. It was a bit difficult to keep the excitement going at first. Cable communication was not what it is today. However, the *World* staff worked hard. Attention was drawn to the hazards of fog, the monsoon and vagrant storms. A circular chart was published every day, showing Nellie's stops. The public followed the game with checkers or pennies or dice, betting when she would reach each point.

Her stories came through as often as possible. They bubbled over with gay comment on the odd ways of foreigners, the food she had to eat, the cold she suffered on sea and land. Nellie had her own particular way of making it seem cataclysmic if her coffee was cold. She managed to make even the carriage of an English train somewhat enthralling.

Her rapid survey of London forced her to the conclusion that it was a foggy city. She crossed to Boulogne and went to Amiens to visit Jules Verne. This was a romantic gesture she had thought of herself. She found him living a leisurely life in an old stone house where she made a breathless call. Jules looked with Gallic amazement at this enterprising girl who had grown so serious over a dream.

He wished her luck but told her frankly that he did not think she could do better than Phileas. She rejoined her ship and went on to Brindisi, sending her messages by special code. By November 27th she had reached Port Said. From there she proceeded to Aden and then to Colombo, where she had to wait five days for a ship. This gave her time to write about the elephants, the Cinnamon Gardens and the beauties of Kandy. Her travelogue was warming up. The stay-at-homes were beginning to feel that perhaps Nellie Bly had a good idea.

The ballyhoo was built up with cunning that would have done Barnum credit. When the cablegrams were sparse, columns were written by scornful whiskered scribes in the World office on "Some of the Queer Things Nellie Bly Will See During Her Stay in Japan." But never had the Japs seen anything more extraordinary than Nellie with her ghillie cap, her plaid ulster, her two knapsacks and her stop watch.

By this time the whole English-speaking world was more or less racing with Nellie, and reporters met her at every stop. She basked in this attention and wrote home graphically about it. A free trip to Europe was offered by the World for the person who most closely estimated the time she would take to complete her tour, down to seconds. It took considerable ingenuity on the part of the copy readers to think up new heads for the stories. "Nellie Bly's Rush" and "Nelly Bly on the Fly" were more or less typical. The excitement was intense.

Nellie sailed from Colombo on the Oriental and by December 18th was at Singapore. From there she went on to Hongkong, encountering a monsoon, the first genuine excitement of the trip. This gave her imagination full play. Nevertheless, she reached port two days ahead of her itinerary and had to wait five days before she could push on to Yokohama. These stops were trying to Nellie's ardent spirit. She preferred to be on the run.

She spent Christmas Day in Canton, eating her lunch in the Temple of the Dead. On December 28th she started for Yokohama on the Oceanic and spent New Year's Eve on shipboard. She had a stormy trip through the Yellow Sea and reached Yokohama on January 3rd. She went to Tokyo and saw the sights.

Four days later she set off again and had a rough trip across the Pacific. The World had a special train waiting to rush her across the country. Nellie traveled in state, flags flying along the route, crowds greeting her at every stop. It was a triumphal trip, although she didn't linger for welcoming speeches. Not until she reached New York did she learn that the train had nearly been derailed at one point along the route. Thus she was cheated of all the extravagant emotions that undoubtedly would have found their way into print had she known that danger lurked anywhere in her vicinity.

Ten guns boomed from the Battery and Brooklyn to welcome her home on January 25th. She had covered 24,899 miles. The World gave her its entire front page and most of the paper besides, the maximum publicity that any newspaper woman has ever received. An exclamatory two-column head led the paper.

FATHER TIME OUTDONE!

Even Imagination's Record Pales Before the Performance of "The World's" Globe-Circler

Her time: 72 days., 6 hrs., 11 mins., — sec.

Thousands Cheer Themselves Hoarse at Nellie Bly's Arrival

Welcome Salutes in New York and Brooklyn

The Whole Country Aglow with Intense Enthusiasm

Nellie Bly Tells Her Story

Nellie got off the train in Jersey City, bands playing, crowds cheering her. Again the unfortunate young man on the World, who had to see that Nellie's race was properly chronicled in her own paper, wrote—no doubt with the consciousness of Mr. Pulitzer's eye on him:

It is finished.
Sullen echoes of cannon across the gray waters of the bay and over the roofs and spires of three cities.

People look at their watches. It is only 4 o'clock. Those cannot be the sunset guns.

Is some one dead?

Only an old era. And the booming yonder at the Battery and Fort Greene tolls its passing away. The stage-coach days are ended, and the new age of lightning travel begun.

And amid all the tumult walks the little lady, with just a foot of space between her and that madly joyous mob. She is carrying a little walking-stick in one hand and with the other waves her checkered little fore-and-aft travelling cap, and laughs merrily as her name is hoarsely shouted from innumerable throats. Tense faces stare from the long galleries that bend ominously beneath their awful load of humanity. The tops of passenger coaches lying upon the side tracks are black with men and boys. . . .

But the little girl trips gaily along. The circuit of the globe is behind her. Time is put to blush. She has brushed away distance as if it were down. Oceans and continents she has traversed.

Cablegrams and telegrams poured in to the *World*. One of the first came from Jules Verne, who cabled handsomely: "I never doubted the success of Nellie Bly. She has proved her intrepidity and courage. Hurrah for her and for the director of the *World*. Hurrah! Hurrah!" The welcoming committee threw the final bouquet at her head: "Miss Bly has done for American journalism what Stanley did for it in 1873."

No wonder the little girl was set apart for the rest of her life and heard strange echoes of this welcome even to her dying day. After the tumult had died down she told her story in four detailed chapters, which were read by thousands of admirers. A race-horse was named after her. Her picture was distributed with the *Sunday World*. Games bore her name. Songs were sung about her.

Almost anything that happened to her after this was bound to be anticlimax. She lay low so as not to mitigate her triumph, and also because she needed a rest. After a breathing spell she returned to her desk and her racy stories again enlivened the news-stands.

Everything by Nellie was written in the first person. Her style had many airs and graces, comments and interpolations. Yet it was clear, readable and somewhat cunningly devised, although

the sentiment often seemed forced and her desire to right the
wrongs of the world was overpowering. She made an emotional
play in a peculiar style that has not been duplicated by any
woman in journalism. Much of it might seem like drivel in
to-day's paper, yet it fitted the contemporary frame and no one
could question her right to front-page attention. She thought up
nearly all of her own stories, although her paper backed the
crusades.

What Nellie's own opinions were no one ever knew, for she
had stock sentiments which she trotted out to suit any occasion
that might arise. She was strongly moralistic. Her stories evoked
much money for charity, particularly her ten-column account
in 1893 of the work of the Salvation Army after she had dressed
as a Salvation Army lass and worked at the Front Street headquarters.

She interviewed murderers, passed a night in a haunted house
hoping to meet a ghost, and described her own sensations in
great detail. She wrote a biting piece about society women whom
she discovered in pool rooms betting on the races. She exposed
a famous woman mind-reader and described the misery of starv-
ing tenement dwellers. Little went on in the social order, in fact,
that did not call for one of Nellie's smug sermons. The evildoer
had reason to draw blinds when she was about. This was all
good for the World, which was then riding high as an instrument of reform.

In 1895 she married Robert L. Seaman, a wealthy Brooklyn
manufacturer whom she met at a banquet in Chicago. He was
seventy-two. She was not quite thirty. Her more envious colleagues called her a gold digger. She lived in state at 15 West
Thirty-seventh Street until her husband's death in 1910. She
became slightly social for a time, having Sunday evening gather-
ings, but this was not the sort of thing for which she cared.
She was one of Hetty Green's few intimates and used to go and
visit her when the old lady of Wall Street felt she could tolerate
company.

After her husband's death things went to pieces in remarkably
short order. She was not so keen at business as at journalism,
although her lawyers never were able to persuade her of this
fact. She became involved in endless litigation. Her factory made
steel barrels, tanks, cans and tubs. A series of forgeries by em-
ployees, disputes of various sorts, and a mass of vexatious

squabbles swallowed up the millions that Nellie's husband had
left her. She was reduced to a penniless state. When her company
went bankrupt she formed another; when it, too, went bankrupt she formed a third. Meanwhile her creditors charged her
with fraud.

Nellie packed up and went to Austria, but her troubles followed her. She transferred her property to an Austrian friend,
which brought further complications during wartime under the
Alien Custodians' Act. She came back bitter against her brother,
charging him with having mishandled her affairs during her
absence. In place of front-page stories signed by Nellie, obscure
paragraphs now appeared in the papers dealing with Mrs. Seaman's battles in court.

She developed into a professional litigant. Her disposition
had suffered and she had become shrewish, another Becky
Sharp. It had always been Nellie's habit to win. She was stunned
to find the world against her. She thought she was in the right.
She was a bundle of contradictions. One moment she was tight-
fisted; the next, generous to an excessive degree. She rarely
referred to her brilliant past, so obsessed was she by her business
troubles. She could not quite believe that her fortune had
melted away so unreasonably.

Shortly after her return from Austria, Arthur Brisbane took
her on the *Journal* and again Nellie Bly's name appeared above
news stories. But in the meantime journalism had changed. It
was no longer startling or even novel to do stunts. New Yorkers
did not get excited when she started picking up stray children
and finding homes for them—even taking them under her own
wing in the two-roomed suite she shared with a woman friend at
the Hotel McAlpin.

Nellie's last splash was a sensational one, yet it passed almost
unnoticed. On January 30, 1920, she witnessed the execution of
Gordon Hamby at Sing Sing, the first woman in twenty-nine
years to see an execution in New York State.

Hamby was a spectacular young murderer, of the Gerald
Chapman order. Just before he died he sent Nellie his ouija
board with the note: "A slight remembrance (all I have at this
time) for your infinite kindness and friendship."

Nellie saw the execution under the pretext of campaigning
against capital punishment. She sat in the seat farthest away
at her own request. Hamby smoked a cigarette she had given

him as he walked jauntily to the chair. Nellie shut her eyes when the current was turned on. Her story in the *Journal* next day began:

Horrible! Horrible! Horrible!
Hamby is dead. The law has been carried out—presumably the law is satisfied.
Thou Shalt Not Kill.
Was that Commandment meant alone for Hamby? Or did it mean all of us?
I only know that I kept repeating "Thou Shalt Not Kill! Thou Shalt not Kill." . . .
The horribleness of life and death. Through my mind flitted the thought that one time this young boy going to the death chair had been welcomed by some fond mother. He had been a babe, lo, loved and cherished. And this is the end. . . .

But journalism had changed to such a degree that the new crop of women reporters scarcely noticed that Nellie had put over another tremendous scoop, and if they did, it no longer seemed to matter, for the day for such antics was over and newspaper work was on a different basis.

Nellie Bly was now little more than a legend. If this was bitter to her, on one knew it. She had never cared for the opinion of her colleagues. Her eyes had always been fastened on the larger audience. In any event, she was tired and ill, and her main preoccupation was with her abandoned children.

She had a private office at the *Journal*. Few of her fellow workers ever saw her. She had never lounged about the city room, or been one of them, for she was usually acting a part or was bent on secret missions. When she did appear, she wore a large hat and a veil with chenille dots. True to form, she carried herself with an air of mystery.

On January 28, 1922, the *World* ran a half column on an inside page announcing the death of Nellie Bly, the most spectacular star the paper had ever had. She had died of pneumonia on the previous day in St. Mark's Hospital at the age of fifty-six, lonely, friendless and worn out. Funeral services were held for her at The Little Church Around the Corner.

Those who knew Nellie Bly in her youth mistakenly recall her as a tall and rather stunning figure—one of the newspaper beauties, like Winifred Black, Polly Pry and "Pinky" Wayne. But this was an impression created largely by Nellie's own manner. Actually she was small and demure, with rather large ears, a courageous mouth and calculating eyes. As time went on she grew more massive and carried herself with dignity. She had occasional outbursts of temper but was never really aggressive. She was simply a woman of indomitable will.

HORATIO ALGER, JR.

Frederick Lewis Allen

ⅬⅬⅬⅬⅬⅬⅬⅬⅬⅬⅬⅬⅬⅬⅬⅬⅬⅬⅬⅬⅬⅬⅬⅬ

If you relish paradoxes, consider the career of Horatio Alger, Jr. He made his fame writing books in which boys rose "from rags to riches"—yet he himself did not begin life in rags and did not die rich. The boys in his books got ahead by outwitting thieves and sharpers—yet he himself, a mild and generous little man who gave freely of his earnings to newsboys and bootblacks on the New York streets (the sort of boys who were his favorite heroes), was an easy mark for impostors. His books were, and are, generally regarded by the critical as trash—yet their sales mounted into the millions, he was one of the most popular of all American authors, if not of all authors of all time; and there can be little doubt that he had a far-reaching influence upon the economic and social thought of America—an influence all the greater, perhaps, because it was innocently and naïvely and undogmatically exerted.

Alger wrote always about boys who were on their own, making their way for themselves, usually in the big city. His own boyhood was quite different. It was highly protected and regimented. He was born in 1832 in Revere, Massachusetts, a town which has become one of the northern suburbs of Boston; Horatio Alger, senior, his father, a Unitarian minister, was a bleak, God-fearing man who fought the sins of the flesh and wanted to rear up young Horatio to join him in the spiritual leadership of America. Young Horatio was kept away from all playmates who might prove naughty influences; was put through such a strict course of study that by the time he was eight years old he could explain the Revolutionary War, add fractions in his head, and write the synopsis of a sermon; and became such a little prig that the neighbors' children called him Holy Horatio. When he

From *The Saturday Review of Literature*, September 17, 1938, by permission of the author and publishers.

was fourteen he was sent away to school and learned for the first time the joys of natural play and of mischief; but even after he reached Harvard his primness remained. He fell in love with Patience Stires of Cambridge when he was nineteen, and wanted to marry her, but gave her up—to his lasting regret—when his father told him that marriage would prevent him from continuing his preparation for the church. And later he left a boarding-house at college because, seeing his landlady scantily dressed in the doorway of her room, he resolved to "move to where there is greater respect for decency." Yet, earnest puritan though young Alger was, he did not want to follow his father into the ministry. He wanted to write.

After he left Harvard College he went through a long period of false starts and indecision and frustration. He tried to write but failed miserably. He completed a long theological course but hated it. He went to Paris, tasted the Bohemian life, tasted briefly also the delights of the flesh (because, as he wrote in his diary, genius had prerogatives and he would have prerogatives too), but went through agonies of shame over his affair with Elise Monselet—and produced in Paris nothing of any literary moment. He returned to America and became a minister at Brewster, Massachusetts. But still he was so obsessed by his literary ambition that he would sketch out plots on the margins of his sermons; and in 1866—when the Civil War had ended and he was thirty-four years old—he gave up the church once and for all and went to New York to write boys' books.

There he remained most of the rest of his life. He never married; there was a period when he was pathetically in love with a married woman, but even then he did not apparently hope to win her from her husband, though he so adored her that when she tired of him he went into a mental breakdown. One of his closest attachments was to a Chinese boy whom he befriended and fathered for three years, until the boy was tragically killed in a street accident. Another close attachment was to Charles O'Connor, who ran the Newsboys' Lodging House in New York. It was at this Lodging House that he spent most of his time, for he was devoted to the ragged boys who frequented it, and found in them a constant gold-mine of the sort of literary material that he could use. And year by year he turned out Horatio Alger books in profusion—always wanting to write important books for adults, always dreaming of the novel (to be called "Tomorrow") that he would some day produce, but always unable to make a go of anything but the boys' stories which flowed from his pen in a torrent.

The truth seems to be that Horatio Alger never fully grew up to adult life, that he shunned its passions and battles and hard realities. Always, deep down in his heart, he wanted a boy's life—not a boy dominated by a stern father and dressed up in neat and proper clothes, but rather a boy free from parental supervision, free to soil and rumple his clothes, free to make a living for himself and test his budding self-reliance. Alger wanted also to be a man of letters, but could not achieve this ambition because his mind, while clear and logical, was childishly naïve, unimaginative, and bewildered by the complexities of mature life. After his books had become widely known, and people began to turn to him as an authority on slum conditions in New York, he was asked to serve on charitable and civic committees, but though he was happy to be treated as a person of importance he usually sat silent at board meetings; either he was too self-distrustful to speak or the problems discussed there took him beyond his depth.

Once, to be sure, he briefly plunged into city affairs with ardor and courage. Having learned how the Italian *padrones* in New York kept little Italian immigrant boys in virtual slavery, lived on their earnings, and thrashed them cruelly, Alger not only wrote a book exposing the *padrone* system (*Phil the Fiddler*), but conducted a campaign of public protest, made speech after speech, and was instrumental in ending the abuse, though more than once he was beaten up by irate *padrones* or their hired thugs. But most of the time, what Alger most enjoyed was to shun adult society and play with the Lodging House boys: to go dashing off with them to fires, to beat the drum in their children's band, to ride on the open horse-cars, to go to Barnum's Museum, to work at organizing a children's theater. One excited entry in his diary, about an especially splendid fire, ended with the triumphant words, "Rode back on engine." As he made money with his books he would spend it on the boys— giving them presents, setting up a bootblack in business, helping a newsboy's mother with the rent payments. He died in 1899, at the age of sixty-seven—still a nice boy, hard-working, generous, friendly, innocent of heart.

It was this perpetual youth's singular fortune to have just that simplicity, that elementary directness of approach to fiction-writing, which would make his books a joy to immature minds.

From the moment when William T. Adams, the author of the "Oliver Optic" books, encouraged him, in 1865, to write *Ragged Dick*, the way was clear for him. *Ragged Dick* was followed by over a hundred other volumes—exactly how many, it would take an indefatigable bibliographer to discover. (Herbert R. Mayes, writing Alger's biography, ran the total up to 119, and later found that he had left out several.) Some of the titles, such as *Bound to Rise, Luck and Pluck, Sink or Swim, Do and Dare, Strive and Succeed*, will evoke nostalgic memories in many an older reader today. And almost all of the books were essentially the same—variations upon an invariable theme.

The standard Horatio Alger hero was a fatherless boy of fifteen or thereabouts who had to earn his way, usually in New York City. Sometimes he had to help support a widowed mother with his bootblacking or peddling; sometimes his parentage was unknown and he lived with an aged and eccentric miser, or with a strange hermit who claimed to be his uncle. It might even be that his father was living, but was having trouble with the mortgage on the old farm. Always, however, the boy had to stand on his own feet and face the practical problem of getting on.

This problem was set before the reader in exact financial detail. On the very first page of *Do and Dare*, for example, it was disclosed that the young hero's mother, as postmistress at Wayneboro, had made during the preceding year just $398.50. Whenever "our hero" had to deal with a mortgage, the reader was told the precise amount, the rate of interest, and all other details. When our hero took a job, the reader could figure for himself exactly how much progress he was making by getting $5 a week in wages at the jewelry store and another $5 a week tutoring Mrs. Mason's son in Latin. Our hero was always a good boy, honest, abstemious (in fact, sometimes unduly disposed to preach to drinkers and smokers), prudent, well-mannered (except perhaps for the preaching), and frugal. The excitement of each book lay in his progress toward wealth.

Always there were villains who stood in his way—crooks who would rob him of his earnings, sharpers who would prey upon his supposed innocence. His battles with these villains furnished plenty of melodrama. They tried to sell him worthless gold watches on railroad trains, held him up as he was buggy-driving home with his employer's funds, kidnaped him and held him prisoner in a New York hide-out, chloroformed him in a Philadelphia hotel room, slugged him in a Chicago alley-tenement. But always he overcame them—with the aid of their invariable cowardice. (There must be many men now living who remember the shock of outraged surprise with which they discovered that the village bully did not, as in the Alger books, invariably run whimpering away at the first show of manly opposition, but sometimes packed a nasty right.) The end of the book—or series of books, for often several volumes were devoted to the varied adventures of a single boy—found our hero well on his way toward wealth: a fortune which might reach to more than a hundred thousand dollars, which, to the average boy reader of the seventies and eighties, was an astronomical sum.

The Alger style was incredibly simple, matter-of-fact, and unoriginal. Whenever Alger turned aside from plain literal fact for a bit of analysis or description, he became a fountain-head of eighth-grade clichés. Nothing whatever was left to the reader's imagination. The dialogue, though it had little relation to the confusing way in which people speak in real life, had at least the merit of transparency. When young Rufus wanted to take Miss Manning and his little sister Rosie out for an evening's diversion, for instance, there would be no beating about the bush:—

"Miss Manning," he said, "have you any engagement this evening?"

"It is hardly necessary to ask, Rufus," she replied; "my company is not in very great demand."

"You have heard of the Japanese jugglers at the Academy of Music?"

"Yes; Mrs. Florence was speaking of them this morning. She and her husband went last evening."

"And we are going this evening. Wouldn't you like to go, Rosie?"

"Ever so much, Rufie. Will you take me?"

"Yes, I have got tickets; see here"; and Rufus drew out the three tickets which he had purchased in the morning.

"Thank you, Rufus," said Miss Manning. "I shall like very much to go. It is long since I went to any place of amusement. How much did the tickets cost?"

"A dollar and a half apiece."

"Isn't that rather extravagant?"

"It would be if we went every week; but now and then we can afford it."

The reader, you will see, always knew just where he was. No frills, no literary antics; always the story moved with elementary clarity.

Nor did any subtleties of character-drawing prevent one from determining immediately who were the good characters and who were the bad ones. They were labeled plainly. When Andy Grant, the poor farmer's son, met Conrad Carter, the rich squire's son, and said to him, "That's a new bicycle, isn't it?" Conrad replied,

"Yes; I got tired of the old one. This is a very expensive one. Wouldn't you like to own a bicycle?"
"Yes."
"Of course, you never will."

From that moment on, the reader could feel sure that Conrad would never say a decent word or do a decent thing; that Andy would outdistance Conrad in the boat race and Conrad would whine excuses for his defeat; that Conrad would try to burn up Andy's boat and burn his own by mistake; and that when Andy's hard work in New York at last enabled him to pay off Squire Carter's mortgage on the Grant farm, Conrad would go into a dreadful rage, as all thwarted villains do. Similarly, the good characters were always definitely noble and uttered splendid sentiments. And always virtue triumphed. Thus the reading of an Alger story was like watching a football game in which you knew the names and numbers of all the players, and the home team made all the touchdowns.

Any writer who in thirty-three years turned out well over a hundred such books and whose memory (especially as he got on in life) was often faulty, must have been expected to make mistakes. Alger made them. Frequently he got his characters mixed, to the dismay of his publishers, who had to rearrange the names. But he had talent for improvisation. When his hero was to be taken out for a ride on the savage horse Bucephalus— which the villain hoped would run away and kill him—it would suddenly be divulged that the boy had been taking riding lessons the preceding year and had won a reputation as a rider of surpassing skill. Nothing had been said in preceding pages about this course of instruction, but Alger didn't bother to go back and insert a reference on page 45; the accomplishment was sprung upon the delighted reader, Bucephalus was mastered, and the story roared right ahead, to the triumph of the young Jehu and the downfall of the villain.

When one considers that the period in which these books were the delight of millions of American boys was that very period when the economic expansion of the United States was going on full tilt, to the accompaniment of every sort of financial knavery and speculative excess; and when one realizes that to most of these millions of young readers the Alger books provided their first intelligible picture of economic life and the making of an individual fortune, one looks again, with an analytical eye, to see how the Alger hero's fortune was achieved. And one notes, not without amusement, that the boy never got rich from the direct fruits of his industrious labor. How could he, starting in at $5 a week, even with rapid increases in pay? No; he got his hands on capital.

Sometimes this capital was inherited: the supposed orphan, ragged though he was, proved to be the son of a man whose supposedly worthless mining stock was good for $100,000. Sometimes the capital was a gift: rich Mr. Vanderpool was so impressed with the boy's pluck that he made over to him the $50,000 that the boy had helped him to save from the robbers. Or the boy was out in Tacoma, buying lots as a real-estate agent (on his boss's inside information that the Northern Pacific was to be extended to the Coast), and in a Tacoma hotel he befriended an invalid gentleman, who out of gratitude gave him a part interest in some lots that promptly soared in value and put him on Easy Street. The method varied; but when the time came for our hero to get into the money, it was a transaction in capital which won the day for him.

Yet always he was so good, and husbanded so prudently the $175 in his savings account (though he was generous, too, to the poor washerwoman and to the other bootblacks), that to the casual reader the lesson of these stories was not that hard work brings in but a pittance, or that the way to succeed is to stand in with the men who have the capital, but something quite different. The lesson was that capital comes as a reward from heaven to him who labors mightily and uses his head all the time. Work, save, be a good boy, shun the fleshpots, and presently the mining stock will fall into your lap and all will be well.

Possibly this explains something about the Gilded Age—when Americans worked furiously, and opened up the West, and accomplished wonders in invention and manufacturing; when the average American of moderate means was hard-headed, diligent, and on the whole fairly scrupulous; but when the ethical level of the big operations in capital was often well-nigh barbaric. Once capital began to fall into a man's lap, he did not inquire unduly whence it came. He had labored meritoriously; merit was always rewarded—was it not?—and now his reward was at hand; obviously it must come from heaven. One remembers Rockefeller saying, "God gave me my money," and one knows that other men of millions felt as he did. Who knows but that to some of them—and to some of their successors in more recent times—this conviction grew, in part at least, out of early lessons in economics from *Andy Grant's Pluck* or *Tom the Bootblack* —lessons learned when the man of millions had been a farm boy reading in the shade of the barn, or a grocer's clerk hiding under the counter the latest enthralling volume in the "Brave and Bold" series?

The total sale of the Alger books will probably never be known, for he had numerous publishers, many of the publishing firms were short-lived, and the books went through many editions—in cloth at $1 or $1.25, in paper at 40 or 25 or 10 cents. But one can get at least a clue from the fact that M. A. Donahue & Company of Chicago, who did not begin publishing them till after Alger's death, estimate their own total, very roughly, at close to ten million copies; and that Street & Smith's estimated total, likewise very roughly computed, would be above two million. The John C. Winston Co. estimate their total sales at five million. Probably it is safe to guess that the grand total must have been well beyond twenty million copies, and may have been far greater. One seldom sees an Alger book nowadays; when the Children's Aid Society questioned seven thousand boys in 1932 (on the hundredth anniversary of Alger's birth), it found that less than twenty per cent of them had ever heard of Alger, only fourteen per cent of them had ever read an Alger book, and not a single boy owned one. But during the Alger heyday, from about 1870 to about the time of the World War, the results of any such inquiry would have been far different. Parents who were people of cultivation generally frowned on the books as rubbish of a low intellectual order; some parents frowned on them as likely to tempt boys to run away from home (a charge that so distressed Alger that he inserted in many of his later volumes an explicit warning that boys in happy homes had better stay there); but other parents welcomed them as valuable incentives to thrift and ambition. And boys of all ages and conditions ate them up.

As they read, they must have dreamed of success—which included wealth, of course, and power, and the thrill of being on the way up, of being prominent, being envied—and also, presumably, a chance to marry happily, and live in a fine house, and enjoy the good things of this earth. What would they have thought, one wonders, had they been able to see, through those dreams of theirs, the man Alger himself—scribbling away in his room in the bare, dour-looking building of the Newsboys' Home in a dingy part of downtown New York; leaving his labors to play with the little newsboys and bootblacks, and perhaps to take a group of them to the circus; a man disappointed in the defeat of his real literary ambitions, disappointed in love, awkward in the society of mature men and women, and apparently almost unaware, as he went innocently and obscurely about the city, that his influence was reaching into millions of families and helping to determine the trend and tradition of American business life?

PROFILE AND PORTRAIT

PAST MASTER

STAFF OF *Time*

ᒐᒥᒐ

The creative spirit dwells celibate and solitary. All history yields hardly a famous poem representing a marriage of two minds, and only a few famous works of fiction—the novels of Erckmann-Chatrian, the fairy stories of the brothers Grimm. But in the theatre, which is always the product of many hands, collaboration has long and royally flourished, producing such well-known partnerships as the Elizabethan Beaumont & Fletcher, the Victorian Gilbert & Sullivan, the contemporary Hecht & MacArthur.

But only once in the history of the English-speaking theatre has one man been a partner in two firms that have both become household names. In the 1920s, the best-known playwrighting partnership in the U. S. was that of Kaufman & Connelly. In the 1930s it has been that of Kaufman & Hart.

Amazing as the success of these two comedy-writing firms has been, more amazing still is the fact that, in addition to serving as a full-time partner in each, George S. (for nothing) Kaufman has also set up in the play business with at least 22 other people, once conducting a thriving emporium with the late Ring Lardner, a going concern with Morrie Ryskind, four swanky shops with Edna Ferber, two small hamburger stands with Alexander Woollcott, a pushcart with Howard Dietz, and a sidewalk trade out of a suitcase with Herman J. Mankiewicz.

This week, while celebrating his 50th birthday, the greatest collaborator of his time can look back on a career in the theatre that would be spectacular in a man of 100. Kaufman's current collaboration with Moss Hart, *The Man Who Came to Dinner* (*Time*, Oct. 30), is one of the biggest smash hits of the last ten years. Kaufman's unequaled record: at least one show on Broadway every year since 1921. Fifteen of those shows Burns Mantle has included in various annual volumes of the *Best Plays*.

From *Time*, November 20, 1939, by permission of *Time*, Inc., publishers.

One of them (*You Can't Take It With You*) had the fifth longest run (837 performances) in the history of Broadway; 14 others ran close to 200 performances or better. Two won the Pulitzer Prize. Twenty were sold to the movies for a total of over $1,500,000. Further, Kaufman ranks as one of the best directors in show business, and off the stage as well as on, as one of Manhattan's greatest wits. Once, just for the hell of it, he wrote a play all by himself—and that was a hit.

Such a career argues more than a brilliant writer of comedy. It proclaims a past master of show business, who has learned every trick of the trade and invented many a new one. It proclaims an amazing foresight in always taking the pulse of Broadway as the clue to its heart, a habit of always writing fashionable plays and never revolutionary ones. It proclaims a playwright who has made sport of everything while never giving offense to anybody. It proclaims a really great practical theatre mind, with no philosophy except that the theatre is entertainment, and that good entertainment pays.

Not that Kaufman's record is devoid of flops. Of 34 productions, eleven lost money, five others would have, except for movie sales. But a record which includes *Dulcy, Merton of the Movies, Beggar on Horseback, The Butter and Egg Man, The Royal Family, June Moon, Once in a Lifetime, Of Thee I Sing, Dinner at Eight, You Can't Take It With You* and *The Man Who Came to Dinner* implies as great a knowledge of what the public will laugh at as of how to keep it laughing. Kaufman beat all his rivals at comedy and satire because what really concerned him was never the nature of the target, but only the location of the bull's-eye.

TEAMWORK

Probably this lack of passionate convictions has helped make Kaufman the ideal collaborator. His adaptable, accommodating mind is geared to avoid collisions. It is also geared to let the other fellow's personality, rather than Kaufman's, permeate the play. What colors *Beggar on Horseback*, for example, is the pleasantly house-broken imaginativeness of Marc Connelly; what colors *The Royal Family* is the romantic bustle of Edna Ferber. The plays Kaufman has written with Moss Hart are better fused because, as comic playwrights, the two men are cut to much the same pattern.

Kaufman's own reason for constantly collaborating is simply that he needs collaborators, that he doesn't think his plays would be very good if he worked alone. Every collaboration is an evenly shared two-man job, with long preliminary stretches for working out every detail of plot, until suddenly "a bell rings" and the collaborators start their "star-chamber sessions" of writing. Every line of dialogue is written together. From start to finish, a play takes anything from five weeks (*You Can't Take It With You*) to seven months (*The Royal Family*), depending on the trouble it causes and the make-up of Kaufman's collaborator. Kaufman & Hart usually work much faster than Kaufman & Ferber.

Kaufman & Connelly separated, amicably, long ago. Connelly, Broadway has always intimated, was too "sot" in his ideas to work smoothly in harness. Of Hart, 15 years his junior, Kaufman says: "I have been smart enough as I grew older to attach to myself the most promising lad that came along in the theatre."

Working with Kaufman means working with a perfectionist. Hart called their first job together "The Days of the Terror." The daily schedule was from 10 A.M. "until exhausted," which meant until starved as well, since Kaufman cares nothing for food. They would spend two hours shaping one short sentence, a whole day discussing an exit. Kaufman's working habits are notorious. "In the throes of composition," Collaborator Alexander Woollcott once said, "he seems to crawl up the walls of the apartment in the manner of the late Count Dracula."

It was perfectionism which also turned Kaufman into a director. He used to be driven half-crazy seeing other directors maul his lines, twist their meanings, spot a laugh where there was none. He first took over direction in 1925, on the only play he has written by himself, *The Butter and Egg Man*. He lacked confidence to finish the job, or even his next two or three, but since then he has directed almost all his own shows.

He loves directing, though he belittles it as "a lot of overrated goings-on." His ability to keep things moving and get every last chuckle out of a funny line is based on pounding away tirelessly at details, and on an infallible ear for the rhythm of conversation. He will rehearse a play for 15 minutes without looking at the stage, only listening to the dialogue. Suddenly he will call a halt, take out one word which interrupts the flow. No actor has ever managed to ad-lib even a syllable into his lines without Kaufman's spotting it.

TAKE

As a playwright, Kaufman has been the biggest money-maker in the contemporary U. S. theatre. His share in his movie sales alone comes close to $400,000. His biggest hit, *You Can't Take It With You*, grossed around $2,000,000 in Manhattan and on tour, showed almost $1,000,000 clear profit. Since Kaufman has a cut in his shows as well as royalties from them, he has made a small fortune on hit after hit. There have been lean seasons, even bad ones. But in a big year he makes easily $250,000.

Broadway is a gold mine for Kaufman, but he never rests on his ores. He is just as apt to start thinking up a new play when he has a smash hit as when he has a flop. A friend has said that if Kaufman isn't a millionaire, he'll do until one comes along; but Kaufman may not be altogether fooling when he insists that constant work is something of a financial necessity. A generous man, he has never worshipped at the shrine of Compound Interest. "All I know," he once said, "is that I have earned a great deal of money and I haven't got any of it. If I don't get a hit each year I am in a damned bad way."

TRAVELS

Kaufman was born in Pittsburgh of a middle-class Jewish family who "managed to get in on every business as it was finishing, and made a total of $4 among them." After leaving high school, George started studying law because it seemed a good way to put off working for several years. But after three months he quit, because he couldn't make heads or tails of it all.

Then the family moved to Paterson, N. J. Having no idea where Paterson was, Kaufman was delighted to find it within commuting distance of New York. He was soon commuting regularly—to work in a hatband factory. He also began contributing to F.P.A.'s column in the old *Evening Mail*. Eventually F.P.A. invited him to lunch, disillusioned him as to what writers looked like, but found a job for him on the Washington *Times*. When he lost that, Adams got him another on the New York *Tribune*. Later he became a dramatic reporter on the *Tribune*, when Heywood Broun was dramatic critic. Broun—who wanted to work at something else—in "a burst of bad judgment" lent his job to Kaufman. After reading Kaufman's reviews, Broun took the job back.

Kaufman traveled to the *Times*, where for the next 13 years
—years that made him wealthy and famous—he remained, at a
very unimportant salary, as dramatic editor. To a worrisome man
who never felt secure, the job was a backlog; to an easily bored
one, it was an excuse for leaving dull dinner-parties early. As dramatic editor, Kaufman left his mark. Before his time, Manhattan's
dramatic pages were stodgy affairs, choked with publicity handouts. Kaufman tabooed these "dog stories," brought a light touch
—which has become standard—to the writing of copy. When
an underling became ponderous by introducing into his stories
fancy footnotes requiring asterisks, daggers and signs of the
zodiac, Kaufman cured him by throwing in a footnote of his
own, reading: "Does not carry dining car."

THANATOPSIS

When Kaufman & Connelly hit the limelight with *Dulcy* in
1921, it was as more than rising young playwrights. They were
part of a group which, by virtue of talent, wit and hobnobbing
together, was coming to dominate the sophisticated Manhattan
scene. Their lunch club, the Algonquin Hotel, had waked up
one morning to find itself famous, and celebrity-chasers flocked
there, as to a play, to observe Kaufman, Connelly, Broun, Woollcott, Benchley, Dorothy Parker, F.P.A. & Co. at lunch, and to
hear their laughter, though not what gave rise to it. The male
members enhanced their glamour by forming the Thanatopsis
Literary and Inside Straight Club, whose legendary sessions, devoted to poker and wisecracks, F.P.A. reported in his column.

The Algonquin's Round Table perished years ago, but it be-
queathed Kaufman, Benchley and Dorothy Parker as the town's
great wits. Kaufman has proved almost as much of a spout offstage as on. His puns are endless: "One man's Mede is another
man's Persian" or (of a college girl who eloped) "She put the
heart before the course." So are his retorts discourteous. When
Adolph Zukor, then president of Paramount, offered Kaufman
$30,000 for movie rights on a play, Kaufman, who thought the
rights worth much more, replied: "I guess not. But I'll tell you
what I'll do—I'll give you $40,000 for Paramount." So are his
crazy cracks. A high-pressure salesman trying to sell Kaufman
some goldmine stock spieled dramatically: "You can shovel the
gold right off the ground into wheelbarrows." "What!" exclaimed Kaufman. "You have to stoop for it?"

Twists

Like most wits, Kaufman cracks his jokes with a dead pan, goes through life with a mournful one. Rangy and restless, hard to know, harder to understand, always blunt, often brusque, occasionally brutal, he is completely free from affectations but bulging with quirks. He is frightened of growing old, or being considered rich, or losing his hair. He forms friendships slowly, feels he has few friends. He talks to himself, makes strange faces, nods his head—a woman who sat opposite his desk at the *Times* for a long time wondered why he was always graciously bowing to her.

Lacking the courage to stay away, he goes to all his openings (arriving with the ushers) and suffers through them. He hates first-night audiences—the swishiest and toughest gang in the world—and usually hangs backstage, "so I don't have to look at all those bastards out front." He is in a constant dither that his show will flop. After one opening that had the audience rolling in the aisles, the leading man found Kaufman crushed against a wall "looking a little like the late Marie Antoinette in the tumbril."

Social rigmarole bores him stiff: he detests dinner-parties, loathes travel, has never been to the opera, took his first drink at 30 and has taken few since. He fights innovation, was almost the last person to adopt soft collars and a wrist watch, was once told by his wife "It's a good thing you were not the world's first baby, or you'd still be crawling."

He is completely unathletic. "Ring Lardner once told me that the only exercise he got was when he took the links out of one shirt and put them in another. That goes for me too." He does play croquet, however—with a fierce desire to win, as he plays parlor games and bridge. Called by Ely Culbertson "the best amateur bridge player in the U. S.," he hates playing with his dub friends, tackles the experts without getting hurt, peppers the game with such comments as "I'd like a review of the bidding, with the original inflections."

With his wife and 14-year-old daughter, he lives part of the time in a big Manhattan town house, part of the time on a 50-acre estate in Pennsylvania's literary-minded Bucks County. Dark-eyed, grey-haired Beatrice Kaufman, whom he married in 1917, is gay, sociable, hostessy, keeps her husband in touch with such friends as Woollcott, Harpo Marx, the Robert Sherwoods, the Irving Berlins. To Woollcott, whom Kaufman has hilariously scalped in *The Man Who Came to Dinner*, and who has been at different times his collaborator, brief biographer and boss, he is devoted. Talking to him, he says, "is like holding your face before an open drain," but Woollcott is "an entrancing companion."

The most successful comedy writer of his generation, Kaufman talks, half-vaguely, half-excitedly, of writing a really serious play— a play about Jews which he and Edna Ferber have been turning over in their minds for the past five years. Then, distinctly as an after-thought, he maintains that he has written two serious plays already—*Merrily We Roll Along*, in 1934, and last season's *The American Way*.

EXCELLENCY IN A RICKSHA

STAFF OF *Time*

ⅬⅬⅬⅬⅬⅬⅬⅬⅬⅬⅬⅬⅬⅬⅬⅬⅬⅬⅬⅬⅬⅬⅬⅬⅬⅬⅬⅬⅬ

Career Diplomat is the phrase to remember about Nelson Trusler Johnson. Born in Washington 52 years ago, he studied at Friends School and George Washington University. He was such a whiz at Latin, Greek and German that one of his professors casually said he ought to get a language appointment in the foreign service. He liked the idea, got a list of required subjects for the diplomatic exams, borrowed some books, read without instruction, passed in a walk, and before he knew it was at the end of the world.

He loved China. He was like a blotter for the language, and soon he was reading both newspapers and classics. His early changes of post gave him a habit of restlessness from which he has never relaxed: from Peking to bleak Mukden, Russified Harbin, hilly Hankow, busy Shanghai, river-girt Chungking, remote Changsha.

At 24 he was made judge in a Shanghai court. He was lenient to a fault. One day he freed a coolie accused of having stolen four ducks because evidence was insufficient—and the next day found four ducks missing from his own duck pond.

In 1918 he was called back to F. E. (as State Department officials call the Far Eastern Division). Here he learned for the first time what the State Department really is: not a policy-making machine, not a stable of thoroughbred cutaway-horses, not a mess of pigeon-holes, but an extremely expert research body for the use of one man, the President. He found it full of extraordinarily well-informed men, was delighted to learn that State's Far Eastern representatives, both at home and in the field, are traditionally among the best. And he learned how heart-breakingly slow the action of U. S. foreign policy is.

After expertizing at the Washington Conference on the Limi-

From *Time*, December 11, 1939, by permission of *Time*, Inc., publishers.

tation of Armaments and after a grand tour of the East as
Consul-General-at-Large, Nelson Johnson was called home again.
On his way he stopped in Japan, just after the great Yokohama
earthquake of 1923. Cardinal requisite of any foreign service
diplomat is that he shall be able to write clearly, vividly, movingly. Of the earthquake Nelson Johnson reported: "I found
Yokohama in ruins. I left it busy removing the last vestiges of the
confused masses of brick, a city of small galvanized iron shops
and houses looking for all the world like a crude mining town in
Alaska or a boom town of the prairies, and no longer the oriental
city of Kipling and the whaler. I shall go back presently. But
whatever Yokohama becomes I shall always see in it and behind
it the ruined city, the piles of confused brick and heat-twisted
iron, the china doll's head lying beside the whitened incinerated
bones of the child, here where two were killed, there where two
hundred were roasted alive, and it will always be a city of ghosts."

His new Washington appointment was as Chief of F. E.—
most important link in the chain of policy, the agent who boils
down for President and Secretary of State the mass of reports
from the field. Here Nelson Johnson was so useful that in 1927,
at 40, he was made Assistant Secretary of State, and, two years
later, Minister to China.

JOHNSON ON THE SPOT

The occasion on which he was welcomed to China as Minister was a landmark in the course of U. S.-Chinese relations. At
a vast, formal tea at the Grand Hotel in beautiful Tsing-tao, the
city's acting mayor rose, rustled his black silk gown, made a
pretty, set speech in Chinese. An interpreter laboriously translated. Then Mr. Johnson got up, paused, bowed to hosts and
guests. The audience set itself for a weary, long-winded speech
which most of them would not understand. With a grin, Nelson
Johnson proposed a toast and made a short speech in perfect
Mandarin. From then on, he had no need of paper airplanes to
make friends. Here was a white man who treated his yellow hosts
as equals—as superiors, sometimes.

Through trying times—civil war, Japan's invasion of Man-
churia, the Shanghai warfare of 1932—he was Johnson on the
Spot. He watched the Shanghai bombings from the roof of a
cotton mill. He liked to call himself the Commuting Minister,
and preferred the hinterland to Westernized coastal cities; only
went to Shanghai, he said, when he thought it was time to change

his shirt. Almost everywhere he went, his favorite book, *Alice in Wonderland*, went with him.

Until he was 43, he lived alone. In 1931, a tall, pretty, quiet, 30-year-old school-teacher from Cody, Wyo., named Jane Beck arrived in Peking with her brother on a round-the-world tour. The Becks and the Johnsons had been friends for three generations, so Jane and her brother stayed at the Embassy mansion. The guests stayed on and on, but since that is the way of Peking, no one was surprised—till one day the bachelor diplomat quietly told his friends that he and Jane Beck would be married the next day at six.

On September 17, 1935, Nelson Johnson was graduated from Minister to Ambassador, his salary raised from $10,000 to $17,500. All the while Japan was becoming more and more threatening, and by July 1937, when North China hostilities began, Ambassador Johnson had a really big job on his hands. It then took four hours for a cable to get to Washington, and considerably longer for an answer to return; and so he usually made decisions and consulted afterward.

At 52, Nelson Johnson is a regular Old King Cole. He is plump as a pillow. He has thinning pale-gold hair, with lashes and brows to match, a face all shades of pink, from salmon to sunset, big enough nose, strong chin, mouth with a chronic smile. In ricksha, cutaway or gas mask he looks more like a tire salesman than an Ambassador.

He is 100% American. He is apt to receive reporters in his underwear, reading a mystery novel. At various times he has played a ukulele, guitar, saxophone. The golf-bug has bitten him. Nothing is more fun for him than to roar out a lusty song (favorite: *My Name Is Jon Jonson, I Come From Wisconsin*), especially at formal dinners. At parties he sits on the floor if he can. When he drinks, it is not much; when he smokes, it is a Hatamen cigaret—cheap brand the coolies use.

The quality which above all others makes Nelson Johnson a really good diplomat is the ease with which he translates his corny U. S. traits into polished Chinese formulas. When he sits down at an important conference with Chinese statesmen, he begins by saying (in Chinese): "Well, boys, have I told you the one about the traveling salesman and the old farmer?" He can sing Chinese songs, too, and play the *pipa* (lute).

The U. S. Embassy in China now does business at three stands. The fancy establishment is at Peking, the working one at

Chungking, the routine one at Shanghai. When the Embassy set up offices in Chungking last year, it was housed on the top floor of a U. S. Navy canteen, and the staff had to use packing cases for desks and sit on bamboo chairs.

In his Chungking home, across the Yangtze from the city proper, Nelson Johnson rises at seven, eats a hearty breakfast (Sundays he has the staff in for waffles and chicken). He rides to the Embassy Office in a four-coolie sedan with specially strong bamboo lift-poles. There he reads and answers 40-odd telegrams from China sore-spots each day. If there is a big rush on, he helps decode messages. Some errand may take him to the Foreign Minister, less frequently to the Finance Minister, very seldom to Generalissimo Chiang Kai-shek. In the evening he occasionally gives a stag dinner (his wife and two children live in Peking), otherwise reads something light and goes to bed—sometimes to be wakened in the middle of the night by an air raid alarm. The Embassy has a stout dugout, but a direct hit would demolish it, Nelson Johnson, and U. S.-Japanese relations.

WHAT TO DO?

Fortnight ago Nelson Johnson left Chungking for the Shanghai establishment. There he hastily conferred with Commander in Chief of the Asiatic Fleet Admiral Thomas C. Hart and Shanghai Consul General Clarence E. Gauss, who were about to leave on Admiral Hart's Flagship U. S. S. *Augusta* for Manila for talks with Commissioner Sayre. The subject: what should the U. S. do?

Britain and France had just reduced their China garrisons. Japan was fulminating against the U. S. in its role of watchdog. The conferees went off to Manila with their boss's judgment (coinciding with their own): if Japan takes the present war as an occasion to move in on French and British interests, the U. S. must do everything short of war to resist. If you live in a firetrap, Nelson Johnson might say, and the apartment of the two people across the hall catches fire, you don't go on reading that romantic novel; you get busy. Occidentals want to go on hearing the sweet music of trade in the orient. For the time being, Nelson Trusler Johnson must bear the White Man's baton.

From Shanghai and business, Ambassador Johnson went to Peking and pleasure. In Peking with the Ambassador's wife are her son, Nelson Beck ("Nubby"), 6, and daughter, Betty Jane, for whose fourth birthday this week he made the trip north. He had not seen his family since last May (in the U. S., after a trip out of China via the then brand new 2,100-mile Burma Road, over which the Ambassador was the first civilian to drive).

When he arrived home last week, Nubby cocked a sleepy eye at his father's new-grown, straw-colored mustache and said: "That's got to come off." Next morning Nubby, Betty Jane and mother rigged a barber chair, forced the Ambassador into it, and hacked the thing off themselves—occasionally bringing the U. S. Ambassador closer to death than Japanese bombs ever have.

Thus ticks a prime foreign servant of the U. S. He may seem happy-go-lucky, too casual to force a grave issue, too apt to wait and see. But no legate could be a better Bearer of Good Will to the gentle people of China. Nelson Trusler Johnson is the sort of roly-poly man a Chinese can respect, love, even fear far more deeply than the man with bayonet, dollar, or arrogance.

DEWEY AT 80

STAFF OF *Time*

One Indian summery evening last week 1,000 people gathered
in Manhattan to praise "America's greatest philosopher." It was
John Dewey's 80th birthday, and many distinguished men and
women—among them Chinese Ambassador Hu Shih, Charles
Beard, Mrs. Eugene Meyer, Fiorello LaGuardia—had come to
his party. Nine organizations, including the Progressive Education Association and American Philosophical Association, had
arranged to honor him. Honor him they did, with oratory and
applause. But Dr. Dewey heard them not. He was not in Manhattan, not in Chicago, not in any of a dozen other places where
Dewey birthday meetings were held. Painfully modest Dr. Dewey
had hidden himself on a daughter's ranch in Greencastle, Mo.

Although he is one of the most famed modern philosophers
and has soapboxed for innumerable causes, few people know John
Dewey. To his intimate friends he is a sweet and lovable character. His absent-mindedness is fabulous. He sometimes shows up
a week late for appointments, goes to the wrong room to meet
his classes, has been known to wander into ladies' washrooms.
He often goes out into the snow without rubbers or muffler, but
rarely catches cold. Despite his absent-mindedness, he is scrupulous about fulfilling obligations, never breaks a promise. He used
to make it a rule never to read manuscripts submitted to him
for criticism by budding philosophers. But applicants learned
how to get around his rule: they brought manuscripts to his
office. Dewey peeked at them through a crack in the door, invariably melted and let them in. Having promised to read and
criticize a manuscript, he always did so—even if he sent it back
to the wrong address.

Dr. Dewey now spends his summers in Nova Scotia, his winters in a Manhattan apartment with his youngest daughter. His

From *Time*, October 30, 1939, by permission of *Time*, Inc., publishers.

favorite hobby is solving acrostic puzzles with his family. He also likes to read detective stories, fancies himself as a farmer. But John Dewey spends most of his time thinking. Father of six children (two died young and he adopted another), he early learned to concentrate on his work amidst domestic bustle. To his classes he lectured in a monotonous voice, made no rhetorical effort whatever to interest his audience. Once, after droning on to graduate students for three solid hours on the meaning of the word "this," he concluded: "I think this is a little clearer to me now."

Born in Burlington, Vt., where his father kept a general store displaying a sign: "Ham and Segars, Smoked and Unsmoked," John Dewey raised Yankee common sense to the status of a full-fledged philosophical system. Essence of his philosophy is indicated in the proverb: "The proof of the pudding is in the eating." Truth, to John Dewey, is not fixed or absolute, changes as conditions change. And he believes that the highest virtue is intelligence, that intelligence means resolving a problem with the answer that (1) is most workable, (2) makes the most people happy. Moral basis of Dr. Dewey's philosophy is a firm belief in democracy.

Dr. Dewey's philosophy was called pragmatism, naturalism, experimentalism, instrumentalism, other hard names. As an undergraduate at University of Vermont, a graduate student at Johns Hopkins, a professor at Michigan, Minnesota, Chicago and Columbia, he busied himself refining his philosophy, applying it, defending it. Dr. Dewey became known as a "philosopher of the plain man." But no one accused him of speaking plainly. Sample Dewey jargon: "The biological-anthropological method of approach to experience provides the way out of mentalistic into behavioral interpretation of experiencing, both in general and in its detailed manifestations. With equal necessity and pertinency, it points the way out of the belief that experience as such is inherently cognitional and that cognition is the sole path that leads into the natural world."

Despite his bad writing, Dewey had a profound influence on modern U. S. political theory, religion, especially education. No armchair philosopher, Dewey put his theories to the test of practice. He conducted a laboratory progressive school at Chicago, led a People's Lobby at Washington, campaigned for perennial Socialist Presidential Candidate Norman Thomas, tried to organize a third party in the U. S. Two years ago, at 78, he got into a fierce fight by trying and exonerating Leon Trotsky of Stalinist charges.

Today many a plain man reckons John Dewey an old dodo, his ideas a dusty commonplace. But there is no dust yet on old Dr. Dewey. Still able to write 5,000 to 7,000 words a day, throw it all in the waste basket and start afresh next morning, in the past 18 months John Dewey has written three major books, the greatest output of his career. Still dewey fresh at 80, Dr. Dewey last week had the strongest liberal voice in the U. S. On his birthday was published *Freedom and Culture*, an appeal for faith in the slow, hard process of intelligence. Whatever may be the state of younger liberals, John Dewey is not demoralized.

Dr. Dewey admitted certain disillusionments, however: disillusionment in the effectiveness of schooling (Germany is the world's most literate nation); disillusionment in Thomas Jefferson's faith in the corrective value of a free press (a politically free press may still not be free); disillusionment in Marxism (pretending to be scientific, it has become "thoroughly anti-scientific," an inflexible dogma); disillusionment in war (a supporter of the first war to "save democracy," Dr. Dewey now says: "Resort to military force is a first sure sign that we are giving up the struggle for the democratic way of life, and that the Old World has conquered morally as well as geographically").

To these disillusionments, Dr. Dewey has a hopeful but not a simple answer. He still believes that mankind's best chance is to go on solving its problems one by one, gaining increased intelligence, as it solves each problem, to solve the next one. He believes also that the method of solution is as important as the solution itself: a bad means cannot produce a good end. His creed:

"We have every right to appeal to the long and slow process of time to protect ourselves from the pessimism that comes from a short-span temporal view of events—under one condition. We must know that the dependence of ends upon means is such that the only ultimate result is the result that is attained today, tomorrow, the next day, and day after day, in the succession of years and generations. . . . At the end as at the beginning the democratic method is as fundamentally simple and as immensely difficult as is the energetic, unflagging, unceasing creation of an ever-present new road upon which we can walk together."

DARROW, FRIENDLY ENEMY

CLARENCE TRUE WILSON

Prejudice is one of the meanest traits of human nature; religious prejudice is worst of all. An honest confession, they say, is good for the soul. If so, it ought to be a good beginning for a tribute.

If there was any man in the United States whom I abhorred it was Clarence Darrow. His views and mine always differed. All the criminals whom I knew ought to be hanged he had cleared or got off with long prison terms. The folk I thought a menace to society he championed. I was deeply prejudiced against him.

One day a wire came from the temperance forces of Ohio, asking if I would meet Clarence Darrow in a debate on prohibition. I wanted to get at him and accepted at once.

We met in a hotel. I recognized Darrow by his pictures. Unintroduced, I accosted him and gave him my name. We at once walked into the dining room to breakfast together. I saw no horns. I saw instead the face of one of the most genial, lovable, friendly, frank men our nation ever produced. We did not conceal any of our differences, but each listened tolerantly to the other's views. We spent nearly three hours at that table, and before the debate came that night I dreaded having to attack my opponent, for I was learning to admire him.

All my prejudice against him for defending men's lives melted away when I heard him discuss capital punishment. I did not agree with him on the futility of hanging. But he believed that hanging is wrong, that the state has no more right to take a human life than you or I. Therefore, he was not inconsistent when he made a fight for even the worst criminal—not to clear him, not to circumvent the law, but to save a human life.

That night before a vast throng the battle royal was waged. I saw the other side of Darrow: the fighter. I took his personal thrusts. I was classified among the reformers who had never done

From *The Forum and Century*, July, 1938, by permission of the publishers.

any good but "curse the earth." The modest Methodist Building
where I lived and had my office he referred to as the Methodist
Vatican. The prohibitionists became "the long-haired men and
the short-haired women." I found that Darrow in action was one
man and Darrow in friendly intercourse another. I liked him in
both—heart-warming in friendship and interesting in fight.

The debate over, I introduced him to my wife. He said to her,
"Your husband debates like a gentleman. If I had known you
were here, I wouldn't have been such a ruffian."

When the time came to settle fees and expenses, my share
proved small, and Darrow came to my rescue as if he had been
a partisan of mine, insisting that I should have as much as he.
I explained to the manager that I was on a salary and really did
not deserve the fees, that expense was all I could justly claim;
but the generous Darrow insisted that I ought to have a greater
amount. I didn't take it or get it but I had a glimpse of Darrow's
generosity toward his opponents. He has won many a law case by
that trait.

After that memorable night, Darrow and I were opponents in
46 debates in as many cities and in about 30 States. We crossed
the continent together and returned as good friends as when we
started.

Once, at Portland, Oregon, after a heated two-hour set-to, we
left to board a night train. Portland was the home of my wife's
relatives, and they all came down with their children to see us
off. I thought it would be nice to introduce Darrow to our family
group. When I did so, he looked up in a quizzical way and
remarked, "I knew you packed the house on me tonight."

A CHRISTIAN GENTLEMAN

Debates such as those between Darrow and me are broadening
to the debaters and equally salutary for the hearers. The American nation is governed by a comparison of opinions. The acid
test of real culture and patriotism is the ability to think and let
think. We must get away from the notion that you have to
agree with me to be agreeable. A gentleman can be agreeable to
people with whom he differs. We haven't an American citizen
more agreeable to his opponents than was Clarence Darrow. If
kindliness and brotherliness, square dealing, fair treatment, doing
unto others as you would have them do to you are Christian
traits, then Darrow had the Christian characteristics without a
Christian creed.

One evening he and I were members of a party of sixteen who met in the home of the Editor of *The Forum* to discuss religion and morality—whether religion is necessary for the promotion of morality.

At a fairly late hour, the writer became quite aggressive in his insistence on the notion that without the fatherhood of Go there is no brotherhood of man, without the sense of brotherhood, no morality that will hold up in the stress of temptation or personal interest. As I recall it, I was attempting to show the reasonableness of Christian doctrine by illustrating the Trinity as a law of the universe: Man is a trinity—body, soul, and spirit; his mind is a trinity—intellect, sensibility, and will; the world is a trinity—mineral, vegetable, and animal. The sunshine is a daily sermon on the trinity; and all that the sun does for us it does through light and heat, so that the sun (the source), the light forever streaming from it, and the heat proceeding from it are a trinity in unity. I went on in this vein at some length.

Suddenly Darrow broke in on the whole company and said, "This man is going to invite us all up to the penitent form if we let him run on like this; I move we adjourn"—and the whole argument ended with a laugh.

Darrow always knew how to take care of his cause, sometimes with an argument, sometimes a bit of philosophy, sometimes a witticism; but he was lovable as a friend, affable as an acquaintance, open-minded as a student, and sincere in all his convictions. The people who hated him were those who did not know him; the people who loved him were those who knew him best.

In addressing a Methodist conference before his death, I let my heart speak about my acquaintance with the man and said, "I'd like to know that in the House of Many Mansions I could spend my first million years living right next door to the Darrows; with my mother and father on one side, I'd like to know the Darrows were to be on the other."

When Darrow saw a reference to this, he remarked, "Well, I guess Wilson hasn't any more information on that than I, but it would be pleasant, and I hope he is a better guesser than I am."

DARROW AND RELIGION

Most people who heard Darrow denouncing religion imagined him prejudiced and narrow. They were mistaken.

One morning we were taking breakfast on the train from

Baltimore to Philadelphia, having debated the night before, bound for another debate that evening.

Darrow ordered his breakfast and, pushing the card back, inquired, "Dr. Wilson, what do you think of the first chapter of Genesis?"

I replied: "I think Genesis, the first chapter, is the greatest poem that was ever written in any language on the earth. It lodges its main thought in the human mind better than any poem ever registered a thought. It is a series of seven pictures of how things came to be; it puts God at the head of His creation. Its central thought, 'In the beginning, God,' has been written more indelibly upon the human mind than any other poem ever wrote a thought. If our translation had put those parallel statements into lines, as the Psalms and some of the prophetic passages have been printed in the Revised Version, we would have saved all that silly controversy about whether that chapter is a geological treatise."

Surprisingly, Darrow, instead of being shocked or amused by this statement, agreed with me and added, "Yes, and it is perfectly amazing how nearly complete the parallel is between this chapter and the latest findings of geologists. There is scarcely any difference in the order of development traced by geology and the order of creation stated by Moses. As far as I know, there is only one slip in it—where it puts light before the sun. That, of course, is a slip, but it is not to be wondered at—written in that early age."

"Mr. Darrow," I said, "isn't it amazing that you and I read the same chapter and admire its poetry and its pictures but you select a statement as an error or a slip and I have fixed upon that as the supreme stroke of genius in the entire poem? Go to any astronomer and ask him to turn his telescope upon that most luminous patch of light in the Milky Way, and the lens will not resolve it into an orb but into a luminous patch of fire mist in the process of cooling and making an orb. There it is, a world in the building, but the light came first, and the body, which is to be an orb by process of cooling, was second. And there we have demonstrated before our eyes that that old prophet was right. The light comes first. It was light before the sun was formed."

Darrow declared: "I believe you are right about that. I'll never make that mistake again." He had his mind open for light from any source.

This open-mindedness I have learned greatly to admire—but, knowing him as I did, I can imagine what he might have said if in answer to his question I had replied, "That chapter is the inspired and inerrant word of God on the subject of world building."

He would probably have said in disgust, "It's all d—— nonsense."

Darrow's creed and mine differed. He was an agnostic, while I am a believer; but I have never known any human being with whom I loved to discuss religion more than with Clarence Darrow.

One of the most interesting conversations I ever had with him on this subject took place one night at his home. I was having such a good time that I wanted to spend the entire evening there but finally said, "I must go now; I am due to address a holiness convention."

Darrow looked up and inquired, "Doctor, just what do you mean by a holiness convention?"

"Well," I said, "down here in South Chicago there is an evangelistic institute that trains missionaries and Christian workers, and they invited into their school for this week's convention the holiness people of the country. Holiness is simply the word wholeness contracted. These people believe that the great fault of Christians is not that they fail to hit the mark every time but that they do not even put their standards high enough and that we ought to teach and preach and try to live up to the highest New Testament standard of experience and life; that Christianity ought to be nothing with us or all; that, if it is as important as we say it is, we ought to give everything we are and have to it, we ought to love God with all our heart, soul, mind, and strength and our neighbor as ourselves—in other words, a whole consecration and not a partial one. And this wholeness or completeness is contracted into holiness. It is insistence on a completely given-up life to the service of Christ."

"Well," said Mr. Darrow, "if I were a Christian at all, that's the kind of Christian I would want to be."

THE BLESSED SENSE OF HUMOR

When we were in Canada and happened to drive through a really prosperous town, with paved streets and beautiful homes and thriving business places, Darrow would turn to me and exclaim with mock seriousness, "Now, here is a prohibition town! Look, it's prosperous!"

The next building we passed would generally be the government liquor store, flanked by bootleg establishments underselling it and selling after hours, proving to me, if not to Mr. Darrow, that the prosperity was in spite of the liquor.

He enjoyed a joke on me.

Once traveling from Ottawa to Toronto, we drove through a number of quiet settlements, and I remarked that there didn't seem to be much business going on.

The Darrows remembered what I had strangely forgotten: it was Sunday. Mr. Darrow said he thought he would sing me some hymns to refresh my memory.

One of the things I always noted in my association with Darrow was his restraint in eating. I think he despised a gourmand fully as much as I do a drunkard or a drunkard-maker, and one of the things he never could forgive in a certain statesman was his rather excessive eating habits. Incidentally, Darrow himself, making no profession of temperance, was throughout his life very abstemious in drinking as well as in eating.

A mystery to me, who had never worked out a crossword puzzle in my life and wondered what there was to it, was the way Darrow could forget the scenery and the conversation as we traveled in our car. He sat at the right on the front seat working crossword puzzles day after day and getting a great kick out of it. Once he needed a four-letter word meaing a place of damnation. He looked at me with a quizzical expression and remarked, "Now, Doctor, here is a word you never would have been able to think of—h-e-l-l."

There are lots of purely imaginary characteristics which people somehow come to attribute to prominent persons. For example, it used to be said that Mr. Darrow dressed slouchily. The fact is that I have gone on a platform in ready-made clothes that cost $39, while beside me stood Darrow in a tailor-made suit, from the best tailor in Chicago, that cost him $100 or more (its selection supervised by his particular and painstaking wife)—and yet the newspapers next day reported:

Dr. Wilson appeared spic and span as if just from the tailor and Mr. Darrow came with hair disheveled and trousers bagging at the knee.

I had never thought of such a thing, but Mrs. Darrow had had her husband's clothes pressed to perfection just before that appearance.

When the Loeb-Leopold trial was in progress the newspapers ran this sort of thing about Darrow day by day until they brought Mrs. Darrow to tears. Finally she insisted he must do something about it.

So he called the whole group of newspapermen together and lectured them: "Now, boys, you are annoying Mrs. Darrow about this matter of my clothes. I have got a better suit on than any of you fellows wear or can afford. The difference is that you fellows take your clothes off before you go to bed at night."

Of course, this left them free to make plain their earnest belief that he slept in his—which, delighted, they did. Once get a good story started, and it cannot be stopped. It doesn't require any facts back of it.

A Life of Service

When Darrow went to Detroit to take the case of Dr. Sweet— a Negro who had moved into a white neighborhood and, compelled to defend his home from a mob, was now scheduled to die for killing a white man—Darrow believed so much in the righteousness of his cause that he was as irresistible as a prophet of old.

When he defended in the Loeb-Leopold case in Chicago and the facts were all against him, he had the two boys change their plea from *not guilty* to *guilty*. This was one of the most critical situations of his life. The defendants' parents were overwhelmed at the suggestion; the boys were rebellious; but Darrow insisted there was nothing else for them to do but throw themselves on the mercy of the court, while he stated the case against capital punishment. He won their lives against the most fearful odds and showed himself to be a master strategist and the greatest pleader that has stood before an American court in the annals of the Republic.

Irresistible in his appeals, Darrow never had a client hanged in all the terrible list of desperate cases he tried and never really lost a case in 50 years as a trial lawyer. I believe this record was compiled through consummate professional ability, utmost concentration on each task, giving heart and soul to every client. Before Darrow was through with a case, he spread the contagion of sympathy (even love) for his client to the judge, to the jury, to the witnesses, and to the mob that always crowded the courtroom. He created an atmosphere in which his man could not be convicted.

Most men who serve others are misunderstood (even as Jesus was) by those they help and envied and hated by those who look on. Darrow was an exception. For example, he always served the Negro. His father had one of the "underground" stations in the days of slavery. John Brown stopped there once with some runaway slaves and said to the little boy who helped feed them, "My son, always help the colored man; he has so few friends he can't afford to lose two; so let him count on you and me." Darrow remembered that, and was eternally rewarded for remembering it with the gratitude of the colored people.

Visiting Darrow in his home, I noticed that the best and latest books were strewn around his table and packed in every available space. Among them would always be a good sprinkling of religious books, not forgetting the Bible. There was, indeed, no great difference between the appearance of his workroom and that of a Methodist bishop I used to call on.

Darrow had a wife's devotion, a son's loyalty, and unmixed adoration from his grandchildren. These testified to his character as clearly as his winning celebrated cases for 50 years, drawing public acclaim, and gaining the love of a downtrodden race. The home test is best. If a man has a happy home where love abounds, he can close the door, shut out the universe, and never miss it. Darrow could have.

In the course of my debates with Darrow, no one ever accused me of picking an easy man to contend with. He had convictions and defended them strongly against all comers. No cause that was committed to his hands ever suffered from betrayal, neglect, or poor sponsorship.

In our prohibition fight, his cause won—mine lost. But he later wrote me a letter in which he said:

This rain of rum is not what I was contending for. I didn't want the government to try to make men moral or sober by law. But I am just as much opposed to making all the population drunk by social pressure. It seems to me that everybody is drinking now. Liquor is everywhere.

Where he was wrong, he acknowledged it. That is the acid test of sincerity.

Now Clarence Darrow is dead. The world is lonesome. I loved him as I did my father and brothers. My close association with him taught me to respect him, admire his personality, and enjoy his companionship. He was the greatest criminal lawyer of our age, the most colorful personality we have known since Theodore Roosevelt and William Jennings Bryan have gone. More than that, he was a true man.

BOY MEETS BULLFINCH

Geoffrey T. Hellman

⎍⎍⎍⎍⎍⎍⎍⎍⎍⎍⎍⎍⎍⎍⎍⎍⎍⎍⎍⎍⎍⎍⎍⎍⎍⎍⎍⎍

Dr. Frank M. Chapman, who has been Curator of Ornithology at the American Museum of Natural History since 1908, has probably spent more time in the society of birds than any other man alive. For over sixty years he has patiently concealed himself in bushes and blinds all over North and South America in order to study at close range the habits of everything from the blue jay and the pelican to the vulture and the dusky-tailed ant tanager. He has reported his findings in some two hundred scientific papers, in *Bird-Lore*, an ornithological magazine which he founded in 1899 and edited for thirty-six years, and in fifteen books, which have sold, all told, over a quarter of a million copies. His *Handbook of Birds of Eastern North America*, first published in 1895, still sells around 800 copies a year. Since going to work at the Museum in 1888, Dr. Chapman has helped build up its collection of bird specimens from about 10,000 to over 750,000 and to make its bird department the best in the world.

With the exception of a few species which he dislikes, like starlings and English sparrows, Chapman has a whole-souled admiration for birds. His approach to his subject is aesthetic and social rather than physiological, and he is more concerned with a bird's appearance, song, and way of life than with its underlying bone structure. His book *The Warblers of North America*, for example, carefully classifies warblers into such groups as Warblers Which Have Loud, Whistled Songs; Warblers Which Have Not Loud, Whistled Songs; Warblers Which Have Songs of the Wee-Chee or Cher-Wee Type, with a Whistled Quality; Warblers Whose Songs Possess Pebbly, Twittering Notes or Which Suggest a Song of the Chipping Sparrow or Junco Type; and Warblers in Whose Songs There Is a Pronounced Zee Quality. This book contains plenty of the sort of prose which has made

From *The New Yorker*, March 4, 1939, by permission of the author and publishers.

Dr. Chapman the most influential man since Audubon in interesting people in birds, prose which in its way tells a good deal about Dr. Chapman himself:

All the sweetness and promise of spring seems stored in Parula's little sizzling gurgle; there is good cheer and sunshine in Yellow Warbler's lay; peace and rest in the quaint *zeeing* of the Black-throated Green . . . If, however, you would see the [Yellow-Breasted] Chat satisfactorily, fight him with his own fire. Seat yourself in the thicket where as pursuer you are at the bird's mercy, and with pursed lips *squeak* gently but persistently. Soon there will be an answering *chut*, and with due patience and discretion you may induce this elusive creature to appear before you. I do not recall a more suspicious bird than the Chat. . . . The song of the Redstart can be readily recognized by those who know it but like so many Warblers' songs of what may be called the *weechy* type, loses all character when it is reduced to syllables.

Dr. Chapman's idea of a tremendous compliment is to compare a person to a bird, and he recently said of the late Lord Grey, bird-loving statesman, "Grey was the most charming host and companion, just like a bird." Dr. Chapman likes to think that birds are fond of him, too, and enjoys telling friends of the time an English wild eider duck permitted him to stroke her as she sat on her eggs. "She turned and pecked my finger gently, almost caressingly, I thought," he says. A good many birds have come to tolerate Dr. Chapman during his long career, and this pleases him immensely. One winter in Florida he spent the better part of three days forty-five feet up in a cypress tree, in a blind consisting of a green umbrella and a lot of Spanish moss, in order to observe herons and egrets. The birds in the vicinity kept their distance for a while, but toward the end of the third afternoon a spoonbill and two snowy egrets came and roosted in the same tree with him. Dr. Chapman, then a young man, felt he had arrived. "Surely," he later wrote in the first of several autobiographical books, *Camps and Cruises of an Ornithologist*, "this was an honor these rarest of American birds have accorded few ornithologists." He did not allow the experience to turn his head, however, and went on to report in a matter-of-fact way that the adult egret says "Cuk-cuk-cuk," while young egrets say "Kek-kek-kek."

For the last thirty-five years, Dr. Chapman, along with most North American birds, has migrated South in the winter, usually going to Florida, South America, or Panama. In the spring he comes North again with the first robin. He is able to reproduce

the songs of any number of birds by whistling and likes nothing
better than to fool a bird into thinking he is another bird. By
answering their songs in the woods, he has astonished many
varieties of birds, who have come up within a few feet of him
and looked at him closely. Since some of them sing only to
attract mates, Dr. Chapman's replies have led to a certain amount
of disappointment, misunderstanding, and bad feeling among
birds. He often used to imitate an owl's cry while walking in
the country, in order to get a flock of crows, who despise owls,
to fly up and caw at him. He once played this trick when a real
owl was around. Crows flew up and attacked the owl, which
was quietly taking a nap. The owl was amazed. Dr. Chapman,
who likes an owl as well as the next bird, has not done this
since. He did, however, in the interests of science, play a rather
elaborate trick not long ago on some blue jays. He wanted to
see, at close range, the jays feed their young, and after spending
several fruitless hours near a blue-jay nest, while concealed in
a canvas affair painted to resemble tree bark and liberally draped
with poison-ivy vines, he hit on the idea of wiring a mounted
blue jay to a limb below the nest. He thought the parent jays,
who were frightened away by his blind, would come back to
evict the stranger loitering near their home. Instead, the mother
at once returned and fed her young, apparently reassured by the
mounted bird, whom she took for an old friend of the family's.
Dr. Chapman next removed the dummy jay and replaced it with
a mounted screech owl, which is a great enemy of the jay.
The parent jays screamed in horror and attacked the owl, which
they knocked over so that it hung upside down, still wired to
the tree. Even in this position it continued to terrify the jays,
and Dr. Chapman, who thought the thing had gone far enough,
finally removed it.

Dr. Chapman has on several occasions occupied the nests of
some of the larger birds himself. Some years ago, marooned by
a storm on a small island in a Canadian lake, he moved three
pelican eggs from one nest to another and climbed into the
vacant nest, which was made of heaped-up sand and pebbles and
was well above water level. He sat there in comparative snugness
until the downpour was over, feeling exactly like a pelican. Another time, on a beach in the Bahamas, he passed several days in
an unoccupied nest in the middle of a settlement of two thousand
flamingos, making notes and taking photographs. The flamingos
accepted Dr. Chapman as one of themselves and poked about

right under his nose. "Seated on the deserted nest," he reported, "I myself seemed to have become a flamingo." For all this, Dr. Chapman realizes that he is actually neither a flamingo nor a pelican. He deplores the fact that there is no real communication between men and birds and that consequently he is unable to let certain birds know how much he enjoys their singing. "I often wish there were some way of assuring vireolanius that he is doing more than his duty," he once said.

Most of the time when he has not been directly fraternizing with birds, Dr. Chapman has spent classifying them, skinning them, writing about them, agitating to get them off women's hats, helping establish sanctuaries for them, and lecturing on them. He began to lecture in the eighteen-nineties in order to supplement the modest salary he was then getting as associate curator of the Museum's Department of Ornithology and Mammalogy. He made his first talk at the Ogontz School, a girls' institution near Philadelphia. Dr. Chapman, who in those days felt more at home in a cypress tree than on a lecture platform, pretended to himself that he was talking to a group of birds, and everything went smoothly. He soon became known as the most articulate ornithologist in the country and was invited to give lecture courses at places ranging all the way from the University of Indiana to the Lowell Institute in Boston. In 1901 he got a letter from the New York Farmers, an organization he had never heard of, asking him to speak on farm birds at their annual dinner. Dr. Chapman, then a rising young ornithologist of thirty-seven, was reluctant to waste an evening before a group of agriculturalists and rather offhandedly recommended another speaker, pleading a prior engagement. The next year the Farmers invited him again. Not wishing to be rude, he accepted and found himself at a dinner at the Metropolitan Club, surrounded by such farmers as J. P. Morgan, George F. Baker, Cleveland H. Dodge, and Adrian Iselin. The New York Farmers turned out to be a group of part-time country gentlemen who met once a year to eat an enormous meal and discuss the problems of Long Island and Westchester estates. The private dining room where Dr. Chapman addressed them was embellished with moss, plants, a small log cabin, and dozens of mounted birds. Dr. Chapman was torn between pleasure at the company and dismay at the arrangement of the stuffed birds. "Without regard to haunt or habit, 100 or more of these specimens were distributed where they could be most easily attached or seemed to produce the best effect," he wrote in his autobiography. "It was a Habitat group such as never was seen before or since. There were Terns in the evergreeens and Swallows on the forest floor, while birds of the Temperate and Tropic Zones met in a hitherto unheard-of association."

Dr. Chapman will be seventy-five in June. In recent years he has had to give up lecturing, but he still likes to talk about birds by the hour to friends and visitors at the Museum, and he is writing his sixteenth book about the subject with which he has been in love all his life. He was born in 1864 on his family's forty-acre farm in Englewood, N. J. The place was full of birds and he was conscious of the songs of wrens, bluebirds, and red-winged blackbirds from the start. He was the first birdman in the Chapman line. His father, a lawyer associated with Joseph H. Choate's firm, paid no particular attention to birds. Frank thinks he may have inherited from his grandfather the patience which has enabled him to set down long, detailed classifications of birds. His grandfather was Lebbeus Chapman, a banker who between July 1, 1846, and May 25, 1847, copied the entire Bible in longhand, averaging four hours a day at this work.

Dr. Chapman recalls seeing his first cardinal at the age of eight while visiting his grandparents in Georgia. This visit also brought him into contact with a European bullfinch, owned by a neighbor of his grandparents, which made a deep impression on him. He memorized the song of this bird and still whistles it occasionally. It takes twenty-three seconds, which is long for a birdcall. An uncle to whom he whistled the bullfinch song was so favorably affected that he gave Frank his first book about birds, Johnson's *Natural History*, and later sent him some pelican feathers. These became the nucleus of a rather large accumulation of feathers. Frank got his mother's cook to give him wings of prairie hens, then common in butcher shops, and enlarged his collection of feathers by shooting robins, blue jays, Carolina parakeets, and cedar waxwings, and by trapping bobolinks. Today he wouldn't think of trapping a bobolink. He has followed the bobolink to its winter quarters in the Argentine and has pronounced it his favorite American bird. "I like it for its sweet song," he wrote in one of his books, "for its high character, for its habits, and for its extraordinary migrations." He feels different about ducks, and has been an active duck-shooter most of his life, pursuing this sport somewhat surreptitiously in later years out of deference to an anti-duck-shooting bloc in the Audubon Society.

Dr. Chapman graduated from Englewood Academy in 1880 and then went to work for the American Exchange National Bank in New York. He had an independent income of around $2,000 a year, left to him by his father, and although he had no particular desire for more money, he thought he should find some sort of conventional career. He commuted every day and on the train fell in with a couple of Hackensack bird-lovers, who lent him ornithological books, showed him their collections of mounted birds, and introduced him to other birdmen. Dr. Chapman toiled faithfully at the bank, but his heart was in the woods and he frequently stimulated his colleagues by whistling bird songs as he worked. He became a faithful reader of *Forest & Stream* and in 1884 answered an appeal in this publication, issued by Dr. C. Hart Merriam, chairman of the committee on bird migration of the recently organized American Ornithologists' Union, calling for volunteers to observe and report on the seasonal movements of birds. In the line of duty, Dr. Chapman rose at dawn every morning from March 10th through May 23rd and went into the woods to shoot birds. He followed a route which got him to the West Englewood station at 7:30, where he checked the birds, changed from rough clothes to a double-breasted blue suit, and boarded the 7:39 train to business. In the evening he would pick up the birds at the station and usually shoot more specimens before dinner. After dinner he skinned the day's haul and took notes. During this period he turned up at the bank every day except May 15th, when he got so excited after getting a Brewster's warbler that he took the day off. His report was pronounced the best in the Atlantic Division and he was invited to join the Linnæan Society of New York, a natural-history group which specializes in birds. Through this organization he got to meet still more birdmen. In 1885 he was elected an associate member of the Ornithologists' Union. His passion for birds made him dissatisfied with his work at the bank but didn't interfere with his business progress, and in the fall of 1886 he was placed in charge of the city collecting department. He saw ahead long years of steady advancement and this discouraged him. He resigned at once. He had decided to become a full-time birdman.

He spent the next year studying water birds in Florida and helping Dr. J. A. Allen, Curator of Ornithology and Mammalogy at the American Museum of Natural History, assort, catalogue, label, and arrange a collection of 8,000 birds which had been given to the Museum. Dr. Chapman claims his previous experience in sorting checks at the bank was good training for this. He worked at first as a volunteer, living on his small income, but in the winter of 1888 Dr. Allen took him on as an assistant at $50 a month. Dr. Allen was more concerned with research than exhibition, and Dr. Chapman concentrated on building up ornithological showcases. One of the first things he did was to arrange a collection of all birds found nesting within fifty miles of City Hall. He later enlarged this to include migratory birds, which he placed on view at the time they were passing through the metropolitan district. Boys would come in from the Park to identify birds they had seen and Dr. Chapman's office became a centre for informal ornithological discussion.

During the eighteen-nineties, Dr. Chapman became recognized as one of the country's leading birdmen. His famous *Handbook* came out in 1895. Around this time he wrote a popular series on the birds of Central Park for the *Evening Post*, was elected president of the Linnæan Society, served on the council and committee on bird protection of the American Ornithologists' Union, and helped edit the Union's official magazine, the *Auk*. He wrote original papers on subjects like the origin of Bahaman bird life and the habits of grackles. He once tried to get permission to shoot a grackle in Central Park, but the Parks Department politely discouraged him. In 1897 he arranged the first meeting of the New York Audubon Society. Morris K. Jesup, president of the Society and of the Museum, spoke on bird conservation. "The audience . . . was doubtless the largest that had ever gathered in this country to urge recognition of Citizen Bird," Dr. Chapman wrote of the meeting. A few years later he was asked for his opinion of the eagles on the new $10 and $20 gold pieces designed by Augustus St. Gaudens. Dr. Chapman said the eagles were incorrect in pose and structure, but approved of the coins on aesthetic grounds.

Dr. Chapman's formal education stopped with high school. He owes his title of Doctor to an honorary scientific degree which Brown awarded him in 1913. He holds evolutionary theories which most scientists today feel are old-fashioned and incorrect, to the effect that environment can cause germinal changes. Younger curators on his staff, like Ernst Mayr, James P. Chapin, and Robert Cushman Murphy, have a command of morphology which Dr. Chapman lacks, but these men admire Dr. Chapman for making ornithology, once an almost esoteric affair, an enormously popular subject and for creating a good will which has been worth millions to the Museum. When Dr. Chapman first came to the Museum, the bird department consisted of a single room on the top floor of the original Museum building on Seventy-seventh Street. Today it has a $1,500,000 wing of its own, presented jointly by the late Harry Payne Whitney and the city of New York. The department overflows onto three additional floors, one of which is devoted to the Rothschild collection of 280,000 birds. Mrs. Whitney bought the Rothschild specimens for the Museum a few years ago from the late Lord Rothschild. Like ninety-nine per cent of the Museum's birds, they constitute a study collection and are not on public view. The skins, unmounted, repose in filing cabinets, where students may inspect them. The publicity which accompanied this gift brought hundreds of people to the Museum, who were indignant at not being able to see the birds. Some of them angrily told Dr. Chapman that they would report him to the Mayor. The British Museum was indignant, too, because Lord Rothschild, although a trustee, had never even offered to sell it his collection. Dr. Chapman has mollified the London Museum by giving it a lot of British birds which are of greater interest in England than here.

Dr. Chapman's greatest contribution to museology has been the introduction of the habitat idea in exhibitions. Fifty years ago an American museum's concept of a bird exhibit consisted of a lot of stuffed specimens arranged in a manner reminiscent of the grill of a college club. Around 1900, John L. Cadwalader, an early patron of the Museum, gave Dr. Chapman $1,200 and asked him to get up a bird group with a background that would make sense. Dr. Chapman produced a Cobb's Island, Virginia, group which contained black skimmers and other indigenous birds against a setting of beach composed of actual sand and artificial seaweed, which merged with a painted background of ocean, sky, and birds. Nesting birds were placed on the beach. A good many of the people in the Museum thought this was too informal and that the painted background verged on the sensational, but President Jesup proclaimed it beautiful and the Cobb's Island group, which is still there, is now part of a gallery of habitat groups of North American birds. The habitat idea has been applied to all the other departments in the Museum and has been taken up by museums all over the world.

In getting material for habitat groups, Dr. Chapman has travelled extensively in this country, Canada, the West Indies, and Central and South America. In order to facilitate expeditions through oil or mining territory that is closed to foreigners, he fortifies himself with letters from Museum trustees, which he does up with gold ribbon and calls his dago-dazzlers. He is inclined to minimize the occasional hardships of these trips and in his autobiography refers to being "interrupted" on one excursion when actually he had developed a fever two weeks from the nearest railhead and was blind for ten days. He is a pioneer photographer of wild life, never going on a trip without half a dozen cameras, and his pictures of tropical birds were the first photographs the Century Magazine ever published. He has written two 700-page volumes on the distribution of bird life in Colombia and Ecuador and has had a number of South American birds named after him—among them what was thought to be a new genus of parrots. A Brazilian naturalist named it Chapmania. Dr. Chapman is a little disparaging about Chapmania. "It wasn't really a separable genus," he says.

About fifteen years ago Dr. Chapman made his first visit to Barro Colorado Island, which is in Gatun Lake, a part of the Panama Canal. The island, once a mountain top, is a complete faunal unit, which means it has all the birds and animals it ought to have, with no depredations at the hands of man. Dr. Chapman built a house on Barro Colorado and has spent eight or nine winters there, surrounded by over 230 species of birds, including guans, parrots, wood hewers, purple gallinules, crested tinamous, wood quails, and short-keeled toucans. He has installed a Barro Colorado habitat case in the Museum, and he has also observed and taken flashlight pictures of ocelots, tapirs, peccaries, agoutis, crocodiles, and pumas. Most of these photographs were taken at night by camera traps sprung by trip wires, which set off the flash when an animal touched them. Dr. Chapman is the last man in the world to hurt the feelings of a peccary or a puma and has refused to install a second camera to get the animal's reaction to the flashlight of the first. "It is bad enough to give an animal the scare of its life," he says. "To photograph its uncontrollable response to the impulse of fear is adding insult to injury." Dr. Chapman has often lured animals to the trap by tying a ripe banana to the wire. The first time he got a tapir this way, he left a banana, unwired, as a gift the next day. While at Barro Colorado he got to like four-footed animals almost as much as birds. "Indeed, there were moments," he writes, "when I felt that I was an agouti."

After fifty years in the same office, Dr. Chapman moved to the new Whitney wing a year ago, but he still keeps his old rolltop desk. He seems to be more sensitive to electricity than most people and to keep from getting shocks he wears crêpe-soled shoes and has had his doorknobs covered with rubber. He used to encourage pigeons to come into his office, feeding them lavishly with seeds, but the Museum eventually discouraged this. He lunches with the other curators in a special room off the main restaurant in the Museum and at mealtimes he and Dr. Chapin often exchange whistling sounds, challenging each other to identify the bird whose song is being imitated. "It's near the genus Myiagra" is the kind of thing they say to each other on these occasions. Dr. Frank Lutz, the Museum's Curator of Entomology, sits opposite Dr. Chapman at lunch and the two men bandy remarks about the merits of their respective departments. New insect species turn up much more often than new birds, so Dr. Chapman is at a disadvantage in this respect, but his department naturally occupies more space than Dr. Lutz's, and Dr. Chapman is gratified by Lutz's charges that the Museum houses far too many birds. Everyone envies Dr. Barnum Brown, who is in charge of dinosaurs.

Forty-one years ago, Dr. Chapman married Mrs. Fannie Bates Embury, who had divorced her first husband, a lawyer. Dr. Chapman was delighted to find that his wife was a competent bird-skinner. He tried her out on their honeymoon in Florida with a long-billed marsh wren that had been badly shot, and she did so well that he next gave her a dusky seaside sparrow, a bird so rare, he says, that "I handle it myself with caution." Dr. Chapman has two stepdaughters and two stepsons, including Aymar Embury, the architect. He also has a son, Frank, Jr., who is married to Gladys Swarthout, the singer. Frank, Jr., is a singer, too, and attributes his vocal prowess to the wind power he developed blowing up air mattresses on early bird expeditions with his father in the Andes, where the 7,000- to 13,000-foot altitudes make blowing up mattresses very taxing. Dr. Chapman and his wife live at Ninety-seventh Street and Fifth Avenue in an apartment overlooking the Park. Their dining room is full of paintings of birds. The junior Chapmans frequently attend musi-

cal parties given by their parents, and on these occasions the
guests sing, play the piano, the violin, and the flute, and Dr.
Chapman whistles birdcalls he has brought back from South
America.

Mrs. Chapman has accompanied her husband on most of his
trips, although she rather surprised her son Aymar once by
sending him a special-delivery letter asking him to wire her to
come back from the Florida swamps. Aymar thought the marriage, which was then in its infancy, had gone on the rocks,
but it turned out that Dr. Chapman had merely promised his
bride there were no snakes in the swamps and that she had
seen twenty-three on the first day. Dr. Chapman used to play a
lot of golf, which he liked because there were birds on the
course, and for years played two or three brisk five-hole games
with the late John D. Rockefeller in Florida every winter, teaching Mr. Rockefeller a good deal about sandpipers and other birds.
During the war, Dr. Chapman was Red Cross Commissioner to
Latin America, and while in Washington awaiting orders spent
Sundays watching birds on the Chevy Chase links. He has given
the game up now. When thinking back over his long career, he
takes especial pride in the fact that in 1899 he started the
Christmas Bird Census, which today inspires several thousand
bird-lovers all over the country to send reports to the Audubon
Society of birds seen on Christmas Day walks. He is also proud
of his conservation work. He got into a bitter conservational row
several years ago with the late Dr. William T. Hornaday, director of the Bronx Zoo. Dr. Hornaday, whose eyesight was failing,
got the idea that American birds were rapidly disappearing and
declined to be reassured by Dr. Chapman, who said there were
plenty of birds around. Dr. Hornaday said the entire avifauna
of the continent was dying out and talked and wrote sarcastically
of Dr. Chapman's beautiful faith in the future of birds. His
attack was pronounced unfair by the scientific world. Dr. Chapman's position was strengthened by the fact that it was he who
started the whole system of bird sanctuaries in this country by
persuading Theodore Roosevelt to declare Pelican Island in Florida a bird reservation in 1903. At first the pelicans failed to
appreciate this, owing to the circumstance that the Audubon
Society erected an enormous white sign on Pelican Island with
"No Trespass" on it in black letters. This frightened the pelicans
so that they went to other islands, but after the sign was removed
the next year, they came back. Dr. Chapman corresponded about

birds with Roosevelt over a period of twenty years. He was a frequent visitor at the White House during the Roosevelt administration and was, with several other scientists, dining with the President at Sagamore Hill in 1910 when Roosevelt was called to the telephone to be informed of Taft's first public attack on him. Dr. Chapman recalls with admiration that when the President returned to the table, his first words were "Now, where did you say the Hudsonian form intergraded with the Alaskan?"

THE POPE

FREDERIC SONDERN, JR.

One night in December 1918, a squad of the Proletariat Red
Guard broke into the papal nunciature in Munich to kill Eugenio
Pacelli. Revolt and terror were running riot on the streets of the
hungry city. The Spartacus rising under Karl Liebknecht and
Rosa Luxemburg was reaching its height and Communist gun-
men roamed the Bavarian capital. Their strongest enemy was the
Italian Archbishop who, unmoved by threats, continued to thun-
der against them from the pulpit of the Munich cathedral and
managed to keep the masses of the faithful in hand. His assassination was finally decreed and a Kommando dispatched to the
nunciature. The Spartacides forced their way in, pistols drawn.

Down the broad staircase to meet them came a tall, spare
figure in scarlet and purple, calm and unflinching, a gold cross
gleaming on his breast. Revolvers were raised. Eugenio Pacelli
stood, looked and smiled quietly. "You will gain nothing by
killing me," he said, his musical voice low and even. "I am only
trying to help Germany." He went on, sympathizing with them
and their troubles, analyzing, explaining. Under the ban of those
compelling eyes, no one pulled a trigger. Sheepishly, the would-
be murderers let their arms drop to their sides and, one by one,
made for the door. Pacelli was left standing alone.

This man, as Pope Pius XII, is now spiritual ruler over 330,-
000,000 souls in a war-torn world and is faced with the task of
leading the Catholic Church through one of the most difficult
periods of its history. The Church holds colossal stakes in the
struggle between the atheist Red Dictator and his semi-pagan
Brown partner on the one side and Britain and France on the
other. Poland, Czechoslovakia and Austria, all traditional citadels
of the Catholic Church, have already fallen under the heel of
the Führer. In the Red Bolshevism of Russia and the Brown

From *Life*, December 4, 1939, by permission of the author and
Time, Inc., publishers.

Bolshevism of the Nazis, the Vatican sees an equal menace. The "pernicious error" which the Pope singled out for condemnation (along with the doctrine of Racism) in his first Encyclical was totalitarianism, crushing out not only Christianity but all religion and civilization as well. But the Church does not take sides in the war. For the military defeat of Germany might bring even worse things—bloody revolution, chaos and communism over all Europe. Pope Pius XII has set himself the task of preventing any catastrophe to the Christian religion, whatever the war's outcome. Fortunately for Christianity, the Holy See is in strong and able hands. Of all the successors of Saint Peter, none was ever more fitted, by training, character, energy, experience and faith, to help humanity than the great man who now wears the Fisherman's Ring.

Eugenio Pacelli was born in the shadow of the Vatican on March 2, 1876, of an old Roman family which had served the Popes for generations. His great-grandfather was Minister to Gregory XVI; his grandfather, Undersecretary of the Interior of the Papal States under Pius IX; and his father, dean of the College of Consistorial Advocates, an intimate of both Leo XIII and Pius X. Growing up in this tradition, the young Eugenio's interest centered on the Church at an early age. Vatican affairs and gossip were almost the exclusive subject of conversation in the Pacelli household. The other children at the public school that he attended with his brother even made fun of him. "Eugenio is always praying," they said, "and reading instead of playing games." When he was 10, he volunteered as an acolyte at the Chiesa Nuova and at 15, decided to study for the priesthood.

The Pacelli name opened all doors to Eugenio. He went through the Royal Lyceum with honors and then to the Capranica College, reserved for the cream of the Church's recruits. The tall, slim, pale student, Eugenio Pacelli, was brilliant. When he was only 22, he had his doctorates of philosophy, theology and civil law and, after his ordination as priest, he became professor of law at the famous Pontifical Institute of Apollinare. The Catholic University of America, in Washington, D. C., offered him a chair, which he regretfully refused.

At this time the young priest caught the eye of a man who was to be his teacher and friend for many years—Monsignor Pietro Gasparri, later to become the famous Cardinal and Secretary of State. While Pope Leo XIII lived and Gasparri was a rising

power in the Church, Pacelli advanced rapidly. Under Pope
Pius X, when Gasparri's great rival, Cardinal Merry del Val,
became the master of the Vatican, Gasparri and Pacelli were
relegated to tedious labor in the Vatican Library. But Pacelli
gained far more than advancement from the great Gasparri. The
older man was a brilliant philosopher, a charming raconteur, a
Papal diplomat of wide experience and he imparted freely of
his wisdom to the young priest.

The special ability which Eugenio Pacelli brought to the Papacy
last summer is that of the superb diplomat. The experience giving him this ability began in 1914 when Pope Benedict XV
made Cardinal Gasparri his Secretary of State, and Pacelli moved
into the front line of Vatican diplomacy. It meant working far
into the night to keep Gasparri and the Pope abreast of political
problems in the War. Pacelli made good and in the summer of
1917, he was given his first great task. The papal nuncio in
Munich had died and Gasparri decided to send his "young man"
to the Bavarian court. He was to try, from this inconspicuous
vantage point, to persuade Kaiser Wilhelm to accept a reason-
able peace. Munich was amazed when the slim, bespectacled,
ascetic 42-year-old scholar appeared in the maelstrom of Wartime diplomacy. No less was Kaiser Wilhelm surprised when the
young papal legate first visited him at his General Headquarters
at Kreuznach to present the peace plan which the Pope had
worked out with the Allies. His Imperial Majesty's surprise
quickly turned to admiration, however, and he afterwards wrote
in his memoirs: "Pacelli is a distinguished, likable man of high
intellect and excellent manners. The perfect pattern of an eminent prelate of the Catholic Church." The peace plan fell
through, but Pacelli grew in stature.

For twelve years he remained in Germany, making friends
from bootblacks to Ministers, sending back reports that were
classics of accurate reporting. He accomplished the impossible
by concluding, in the face of violent Lutheran and radical opposition, a Concordat with Prussia. In 1929 he was recalled to
Rome and a grateful Pope made him Cardinal.

Pius XI had come to the throne and the Church was having
plenty of trouble right in Rome. Mussolini wished to take the
youth of the nation away from the influence of the Vatican.
That must be fought with every legitimate weapon and Pacelli,
thought the Holy Father, was the man to do it. In February
1930, Gasparri, with tears of affection in his eyes, handed over

the Secretariat of State to the man he had loved and taught since boyhood.

The unsuspecting, swaggering Duce, already sure of his victory, against "the aged Vatican," suddenly found himself in the path of a tornado by the name of Pacelli, a master of quick political strategy to whose skill even Mussolini had to bow. To get a Papal Encyclical—against Mussolini's suppression of the Catholic Action—past the Italian censorship into the world press without the Duce's foreknowledge, Pacelli had it smuggled to Paris by two young Monsignori (one of whom was Francis J. Spellman, now Archbishop of New York). Pacelli's method was unheard of for the Vatican but it worked. The progressive Cardinal-Secretary, to escape censorship for all time, promptly persuaded Pope Pius to build a radio station. Most observers at the time failed to realize its significance. Mussolini did. The Vatican could no longer be gagged.

Of the many difficult problems with which Pacelli had to deal in the succeeding years, one of the knottiest was Father Coughlin. The far-flung network of the Vatican's Intelligence reported that the "radio priest" was seriously endangering Catholic prestige in the United States. Pacelli, characteristically, decided to see for himself. He took a boat, arrived in New York in October 1936 and began a triumphal tour such as few churchmen have ever had. With his unfailing tact and graciousness, he made friends wherever he went. New York fascinated him. Three times he left his automobile to inspect the Triborough Bridge. He marveled at Radio City. At the National Press Club in Washington, he thoroughly intrigued the newspapermen. Then in an 8,000-mile plane trip, he saw and consulted with 79 bishops in twelve of the 16 American Church provinces. And the day after President Roosevelt's re-election, he lunched and conferred with the President at Hyde Park. It was pathetic to see the newspapermen afterwards trying to cross-examine a story out of perhaps the world's shrewdest diplomat. Back in Rome, he reported his findings to the Pope. If Coughlin were left alone, he would hang himself with his own rope. Catholicism in the United States was strong enough to take care of its own problems without help.

On Feb. 10, 1939, Pope Pius XI died. When, as custom demands, Pacelli had to tap the dead Pope twice on the forehead with a silver mallet, calling him three times by his first name— "Achille! Achille! Achille!"—his voice trailed off and he almost broke down. It taught the Vatican that the man, generally so controlled and unemotional, was very human indeed. Two weeks later the Princes of the Church elected Cardinal Pacelli to be the 262nd Pope.

The Vatican adores its master. In the memory of even the oldest functionaries, there has been no one so universally beloved and respected. The man who, with his thin, ascetic face, looks so cold and unapproachable from a distance, has a smile and a manner so compelling on closer contact that few can resist them. He is a hero even to his valet. Giovanni Stefanori has been with him for years, but every afternoon about 5 they go through a ceremony. "Giovanni," says the Pope, "have you had your wine?" (Giovanni always drinks his afternoon *quarto di vino* in a little bar next to the Vatican.) "Yes, Holy Father." "Was it good?" "Yes, Holy Father," answers Giovanni. And both smile.

The Pope has an incredible memory. He used to demonstrate it by reading 20 verses of Homer over just twice and then reciting them out of his head. He applies that knack to names and faces. And though he dislikes chatting with gardeners and Swiss Guards, which his predecessor did by the hour, he always has a kindly word for the Vatican retainers whose family problems he always seems to know about.

A Lesson in How to Salute

He scrupulously returns the halberd salute of the Swiss Guards with a formal military gesture. Not long ago a new Guardsman was so surprised at suddenly seeing the Holy Father that he gave his salute rather clumsily. The Pope stopped. "Give me your halberd," he said. The Guard handed it over. "So!" said the Pope, saluting smartly. Then, grinning, he handed the weapon back. "I have always wanted to do that," he said. "And you see, I can do it as well as you."

In his office, he has brought with him all the efficiency that he learned so thoroughly in the Secretariat of State. He is a stickler for punctuality, and tardiness of anyone brings up one of his rare frowns and a few sharp words—delivered with icy calm—which his subalterns fear more than the worst tirade. The volume of work that crosses his desk is colossal. Not only does he carry the usual burden of decisions on everything from finance to the appointment of a Bishop in Java, but he insists on being kept up to the minute on every foreign political development anywhere in the world.

His day begins at 6 A.M. After rising, he scrupulously does his half-hour of gymnastic exercises and shaves himself, using an electric razor. At 7, he reads mass in his private chapel and goes to confess to his father-confessor, Father Caragnani. The Pope, according to dogma, is infallible only *dum ex cathedra loquitur* when he speaks from his throne or pulpit as head of the Church and is never impeccable. He must confess his sins and beg for absolution as every other Catholic.

At 8, after a Roman breakfast of black coffee, bread and butter, he starts work. First come the newspaper excerpts which have been prepared for him. Like Mussolini, the Pope is an avid newspaper reader and places great importance on the press. Then come conferences with the closest of his advisers. He has very few, preferring to have most of his officials submit written reports, upon which he acts in his own way. Cardinal Maglione, the Papal Secretary of State, the Monsignori Montini and Tardini, the chiefs of the divisions for "Ordinary Affairs" and "Extraordinary Affairs," are exceptions. They have free entry to the Pope at all times. Other members of his unofficial cabinet are the Cardinals Fumasoni-Biondi, Caccia-Dominioni, Canali and Monsignor Di Sant' Elia. But they carry little weight. They and Della Torre, editor of the powerful Vatican newspaper, *Osservatore Romano*, get their orders—and that's that.

Punctually at 9:30 the Pope goes down to the second floor, where the official reception rooms are, to begin his audiences. Often the shrewd-eyed, heavy-jowled Cardinal Maglione accompanies him. The office of Secretary of State, first adviser to the Pope, has always been the most important in the Vatican hierarchy. But with Pope Pius his own arbiter of foreign policy, there is little left except executive details for Maglione, a brilliant diplomat in his own right, to do. After Maglione come the others of the "cabinet" who have business. And after that comes the unending stream of foreign diplomats, and the bishops and other prelates who come from all over the globe to make their compulsory periodic calls on the Holy Father. Pope Pius always makes it his business to know about their problems in advance—a tremendous task in itself.

He Talks to Visitors in Eight Languages

Twice a week there are public audiences. These are of various grades, according to the prominence of the pilgrims. The Holy Father proceeds through a series of smaller rooms, where the

elite of the Faithful are gathered in small groups, to the large
Sala Clementina. There sometimes hundreds of pilgrims are
crowded together. After the general blessing and usually a short
speech, the Pope insists, to the horror of the Swiss Guards and
other attendants, on getting into the middle of the crush. He
likes talking to strangers and, since he commands not only Italian but English, French, German, Spanish, Hungarian and two
Slavic languages as well, there are few that he cannot talk to in
their own tongue. He recently even lost his Fisherman's Ring
to a lady who clutched his slim fingers too enthusiastically. She
was almost arrested while trying to return it. On several occasions
ecstatic women, clutching and kissing the skirt of his white gown,
have left red-lipstick marks all over it. In fact once an officer of
the Noble Guard, spying a blotch of red on the Holy Father's
sleeve, thought that he had been attacked and called for rein-
forcements. But despite the entreaties of his guards, the Pope
refuses to change his custom.

By 1:30, the audiences must be over. The Holy Father has his
lunch on the dot. The three Franciscan monks who serve him
are very strict about it. Always alone, as tradition requires, he
eats a very simple meal and drinks a glass of watered wine. After
lunch, he sleeps until 4, then drives the quarter-mile to the
Vatican garden for an hour's walk, generally taking a sheaf of
documents to study on the way.

He is always driven in his favorite car, a 1927 Graham-Paige,
which has a very comfortable thronelike single seat in the back.
There are four other automobiles in the Papal Garage—an Isotta-
Fraschini, a Fiat, a Mercédès and a Citroën, all gifts of the manufacturers—but he prefers the American car. During his walk
through the gardens which look down over Rome from the
highest point of the Vatican City, he is always accompanied by
an officer of the Noble Guard, a chamberlain and a servant.
They follow him at a respectful distance. Sometimes he likes to
sit in one of the charming flower-clad loggias and look at the
superb view. But generally, he walks quickly—too quickly for
the panting Monsignori in the rear.

By 5, he is back at his desk in the third-floor library of the
Palace. And with a short interruption for dinner, he generally
works until one or two in the morning. All his instructions for
papal legates, and they are many, are taken directly to the radio
station on the hill behind the Vatican and flashed by short wave
to nunciatures all over the world. The diplomat-Pope works very

quickly. His private secretary, Monsignor Rossignani, has been with him for years and anticipates every move. The Holy Father is an impatient executive and, though he is seldom brusque with his people, who cannot answer back, he keeps them all on their toes—an unusual state for the Vatican where life has long been unhurried and complacent.

Pius XI had telephones installed in the Vatican by the International Tel. & Tel. His own instrument was of gold, engraved with the Papal Arms. But he rarely used it. It made him nervous, he never could understand, and he shouted unintelligibly into the mouthpiece. His successor uses it continuously and with effect, to the horror of many of the oldtimers who dislike its abrupt contact. The Pope's number is Citta del Vaticano 101, but it is never rung without the Pope's permission.

One of the most annoying but necessary interruptions to his tight-packed schedule has been the insistence of the Vatican officials on pictures and statues of His Holiness. He finally agreed to sit for Canonica and Maag, the famous Italian and Swiss sculptors. But they would have to model him in his study as he worked. He could not just sit, doing nothing, no matter how important his face would be to posterity. Thus it was decreed, and the sculptors had to work while the Pope dictated, listened to reports and wrote on his own typewriter, as he frequently does.

He Enjoys Forbidden Chocolates

On Sunday evening, the Pope generally breaks his routine of work to see his friends. He has few who are close but with those he is intimate. His older brother and two young nephews are particularly welcome. Francesco Pacelli, the brother, followed in his father's footsteps to become a consistorial lawyer. Young Marcantonio Pacelli, his nephew, enjoys great favor. When he comes to visit, the Holy Father—with conspiratorial air—unearths a box of the chocolates, forbidden by doctor's orders, that both of them like so much.

His doctors are very severe with him. He suffers from liver trouble. And neuralgic headaches cause him great discomfort, particularly during long ceremonies when the heavy triple tiara, encrusted with gold and jewels, presses heavily on his forehead.

The Holy Father, unlike his predecessor, likes the comforts of modern equipment and, while he was away at his Castel Gandolfo residence this summer, had the Papal suite in the Vatican completely remodeled. His simply furnished but large corner bed-

room on the third floor overlooking St. Peter's square had its
cold stone floor covered with linoleum. A modern bathroom was
put in and a small gymnasium. Next to them are three book-
lined studies where he works and receives his closest officials,
and, beyond, the private chapel and a new small throne room
which saves him the trouble of going downstairs for the more
intimate private audiences. All is now heated by a brand new
central plant of which he is very proud.

But the bearer of the triple tiara leads a lonely life. Hemmed
in at every step by the maze of the Vatican's ceremonial traditions, he is set apart. The genuflections, the kissing of the ring,
the meticulously organized pomp, create a barrier between him
and his vistors which even the Pacelli charm finds difficult to
overcome. He was very unhappy when Monsignor Sant' Elia, on
the first day of his Papacy, told him that he must not as Pope
accompany his departing visitors to the door. But he had to obey
his stern chamberlain's command. It was the tradition.

In matters of state the Pope's sure feel is abundantly evident.
It shows in the close relations between the Vatican and Mussolini's Government. Hitler's pact with Russia, which sadly disillusioned Mussolini, gave Pius the chance he needed to strengthen
the Church in Italy. Very often now the Jesuit Father, Tacchi-
Venturi, makes his way between Vatican and Palazzo Venetia.
Tacchi-Venturi, a Gray Eminence of the Vatican, close friend
of the Pope and of Mussolini, recently refused a Cardinal's hat
for his great services to the Church in making the Duce see
reason on various important occasions. Little known, except to
the insiders, this small, modest, elderly man moves silently without provoking the curiosity of watchful correspondents. Both the
Pope and Mussolini trust him implicitly. And the Pope's coun-
sels now carry great weight in the Palazzo Venetia, as they do
also at the Royal Palace. The diplomat who is now Holy Father
has proved to the arrogant Dictator that his advice is well worth
listening to.

The whole of the vast Catholic system is working at top speed
under the Pope's relentless drive. Every parish priest is an important cog in the machine. He must report fully on the feeling
in his parish to his Bishop. Every Bishop reports to Rome. Along
with the reports come daily dispatches from the nuncios in every
capital on the activities of the government to which they are
accredited. As a result, the Secretariat of State is by far the best-
informed foreign-policy department in the world. Through this

mass of material, the Holy Father is searching for a solution that will bring the war to a speedy close. Not a week passes without the Papal Legates', in London, Paris and Rome, trying to start a new plan which has sprung from their master's mind. So far, without success. But Pope Pius XII will never cease fighting.

HICK ON BROADWAY

ALICE LEONE MOATS

In the popular, synthetic American definition, a big Broadway theatrical producer is a tough-talking, foreign-looking exhibitionist, with a diamond ring, fat hands and a lecherous expression. He dresses like the Duke of Windsor and smokes big cigars. Water makes him sick so he drinks nothing but champagne, preferably from pink ballet slippers. He lives in a penthouse and is driven about in patent-leather-and-chromium automobiles. He never sleeps, but divides his time between the theatre and the night clubs, where he gives lavish parties and moves with a convoy of eminently seductive young women. It is obvious that he will come to no good end, but somehow he never seems to get there.

This popular definition of a big Broadway producer does not apply to 50-year-old George Abbott, undoubtedly the most amazing producer currently practicing in New York. Last season, Abbott had three hits running on Broadway at the same time— *What a Life, The Boys from Syracuse* and *Primrose Path.* Abbott is the only man on Broadway connected with six shows which have run more than 500 performances each. Out of the 34 plays with which he has been connected since 1925 as author or producer, 15 have been hits. Before he became a producer, Abbott was a Broadway success in the comparatively menial capacities of actor, author and play-doctor.

A threatened actors' strike, the World's Fair disappointment and uncertainty over the effect of the European war on the American public, have combined to get the New York theatrical season off to a slow start. Most producers have been busy doing some watchful waiting. George Abbott is the outstanding exception. Early in August he announced four productions for the 1939-40 season—*See My Lawyer, Too Many Girls, Ring Two,*

From *Life,* October 23, 1939, by permission of the author and *Time,* Inc., publishers.

We, the Living—and they are going through exactly as scheduled. This is the heaviest program planned by any producing firm except the Playwrights Company, which after all is made up of four men. *See My Lawyer* is already on Broadway as a moderate hit. *Too Many Girls* was fortnight ago being rapturously cheered by Boston critics in a tryout run. The other two will be on by the first part of January. If they also succeed, and *See My Lawyer* lasts, there will be four Abbott productions playing simultaneously to full houses, a record, even for George Abbott.

These statistics, impressive as they may be, are not what make Abbott a unique figure in his line. His claim to an enduring place in Broadway history rests upon the fact that he is a living contradiction of all that the world has been taught to think that a producer should be. An unphenomenal phenomenon, a genius with no lunatic streak, Abbott might be considered colorless if he were a small-town druggist. As a member of the world's most colorful profession, he stands out in high relief. Other producers are more or less famous for their eccentricities. Abbott's complete normality, even more than his success, has made him a Times Square legend.

Tall, broad-shouldered, with blond hair cut short and cold china-blue eyes, Abbott looks like the vice president of a branch bank. He dresses soberly in plain shirts and dark suits. He seldom swears, never smokes and he drinks only in emergencies, disliking even wine unless "it tastes like orangeade." Last summer, at a dance on Long Island, Abbott astonished his companions by downing a glass of champagne. "I drank it," he later honestly explained, "so I wouldn't smell the liquor on my partner's breath."

Abbott's professional technique is as remarkable as, and in keeping with, his manners. Not only has he created no great stars, he rarely even employs one. Few of his most-profitable shows have had *succès d'estime*. Critics indeed have rated him as the Broadway equivalent of a Hollywood specialist in B-pictures and suggested that he was a kind of minor-league theatrical Dumas. While it is true that Abbott's plays rarely contain poetry, high comedy or fine flights of histrionic art, this objection is scarcely more valid than the equally familiar one that Abbott's first nights lack chic. Shakespeare, from whom Abbott stole *The Boys from Syracuse*, was a kleptomaniac himself and, like his celebrated predecessor, Abbott borrows shrewdly. The hallmarks of an Abbott show are pace and homely humor. He specializes in plays so packed with business, uproar and activity that the audience has no time to exercise its critical faculties. Many people along Broadway have tried to dissect the Abbott method, but none so far have succeeded. The fact is, of course, that the secret of Abbott's success lies in his temperament. Abbott senses intuitively what will appeal to the hickishness which metropolitanites try so hard to hide. Practically a walking barometer of public taste, it is not surprising that he is as successful in the theater as he is puzzling to his less appropriately constituted rivals.

Abbott's most worldly characteristic is undoubtedly his fondness, amounting almost to passion, for dancing, but this enthusiasm does not betoken a weakness for the surroundings or the company which, for a man in his position, might well accompany it. Instead of Monte Carlo or El Morocco, New York's smartest cafés, Abbott likes cabarets which specialize in big dance floors and hot bands and feels at home in Roseland, the city's most famous public dance hall.

Among Abbott's other behavioristic distinctions from his colleagues is the plane on which he conducts his relations with the opposite sex. In Abbott's mind, business and friendship have no relation to one another. Girls who hope to skip a couple of steps up the Broadway ladder by making an impression on him are destined for disappointment. At a first outing with a budding actress, Abbott will say, as they are stepping into the taxi, "Look. We can go out together often and have a good time but don't think it will help you in any way to get along on the stage."

Broadway's busiest producer is anything but a dashing beau. While able calmly to accept the loss of $20,000 on a poor show as an occupational hazard, Abbott, who was frugally reared, hates throwing money around. He puts the giving of flowers and presents to lady friends under the heading of extravagance, saying earnestly, "I don't want to buy their favors." A man whose advice Abbott often follows in such matters once told him that he must give Christmas presents to his lady friends. Convinced, Abbott sent several of them a pair of silk stockings each.

He Forces Himself to Splurge

Among the other things Abbott spends little money on is travel. When he says, "I wish that I could get away," all he really means is that he has been overworking and needs a rest.

In 1936, Abbott went to London to put on *Boy Meets Girl,* which failed, and to collect the profits of *Three Men on a Horse,* which had been a great London hit. Taking his money out of England would have meant paying such a huge tax that it scarcely seemed worthwhile so, motivated by prudence, he forced himself to splurge. He bought an entire wardrobe, gave parties and stayed in style at the Savoy, from which he wrote back to a friend: "This hotel is expensive but I must say that they give you your money's worth. The shower baths are even equipped with sprays that come up and wash one's feet!"

Abbott is really happy only when working; rehearsals may be tiring but they make him wide-awake, alert, gay and interested. He doesn't want to think or talk of anything else and is carried away by excitement. Lunching at Lindy's while *Too Many Girls* was in rehearsal, he said to his companion, "It's a swell show. And the best music Rodgers and Hart have ever written. Do you want to hear some of it?" He then sang all the tunes he liked best, completely unaware of his surroundings.

Neither heredity nor environment can account for Abbott's consuming passion for the theater. He comes of pre-Revolutionary, Scotch-English stock. His ancestors were solid New Englanders who moved west when things went badly in New England and settled in upper New York State. His father, Mayor of Salamanca, N. Y., when George was born on June 25, 1889, later became a government land agent with headquarters at Cheyenne, Wyo. When he was in his teens, the family moved to Hamburg, N. Y. After finishing high school, George went to the University of Rochester and it was there that he decided to become a playwright. Asked how he learned to write plays, Abbott says: "I decided the best way to write a play was to write it." The only producers he had ever heard of were the Shuberts and he sent his scripts to them. They came back with clocklike regularity. Later on when he had graduated from the University and enrolled in George Pierce Baker's '47 Workshop at Harvard, the Harvard Dramatic Club put on an Abbott one-act play. Another, *Man in the Manhole,* won the $100 prize offered by Keith's Theatre. Through that connection, George became superintendent of the theater at $15 a week.

In 1913, he arrived in New York. Of this period in his career he says: "I gave myself 30 days in which to get a job as an actor. If I didn't get one in that time, I was going to become a reporter in order to support myself while writing plays. On the 30th day

I went to the William Harris office but having taken such a beating at the hands of telephone girls and office boys, I walked past, deciding it was hopeless. Then I forced myself to return and found that Harris had a part waiting for me."

THE OFFICE BOY WRITES THE LINES

In 1917 Abbott went to work for John Golden as a glorified office boy. He was to read the plays that came in, make suggestions about them and could use all the office paper he liked for his own scribblings. He was always a fast worker and whenever an author hit a snag in a play, Golden would tell George to write the scene, knowing he would be back with it in a few hours. Abbott's cubby-hole office was called the "Abbottoir" and he was used as a sort of spur to lazy authors who would get to work immediately "rather than run the risk of having Golden use that lousy little office boy's lines."

One of his jobs with Golden was assistant stage manager and call boy in the tryout of *Three Wise Fools*. Helen Menken, who was the leading lady, remembers him sitting on the stage, chair tilted back, big feet stuck out before him, muttering, "When I run things they'll be run better than this." On another occasion, in his role of call boy, he knocked at her dressing-room door, and said, "Curtain going up, Miss Menken."

"Hold it just a minute," she answered, "I'm not quite ready."

"My job is to ring up that curtain on time," George told her, "and, it's going up on time." Miss Menken scrambled on the stage.

Playing in a road company around 1918, Abbott met James Gleason, who had thought up the plot of *The Fall Guy*. Abbott helped him write it. It opened in 1925, with Ernest Truex in the lead, but Abbott missed opening night because he was giving what he considers the best performance of his career in *Processional*. *The Fall Guy* was a hit. So were *Broadway* and *Love 'Em and Leave 'Em* produced by Jed Harris, on both of which Abbott collaborated as an author. Then came *Coquette* by Ann Preston Bridges. *Coquette* entered the Harris office as a comedy and came out again as a tragedy after a three-week rewrite by Abbott. It established Helen Hayes as one of the major luminaries on the American stage, and established Abbott's reputation as rewrite-man.

In addition to the 36 plays written, produced, or both, by George Abbott and a number of others, including *Chicago* and

Gentlemen of the Press, which he directed, there have been nine Abbott movies. In 1914 Abbott married Ednah Levis. Before her death in 1930, he worked two years for Paramount. Alice Duer Miller's *Manslaughter* with Fredric March and Claudette Colbert was his best effort but Abbott didn't like working in pictures because there was "too much interference." By 1930 he was back on Broadway and in 1932 he became a producer on his own.

Teamed with Philip Dunning, Abbott launched his new firm with the production of a flop titled *Lilly Turner*, followed by *Twentieth Century* by Ben Hecht and Charles MacArthur which fetched a good price in Hollywood and might have had a long Broadway run except for the bank closings in '33. Dunning dropped out of the firm, amicably, in 1934. Two years later Abbott, operating alone as a producer, cleared $500,000 on *Boy Meets Girl* and, operating in collaboration with John Cecil Holm as a playwright, netted a considerable sum from Alex Yokel's production, *Three Men on a Horse*.

Brother Rat, a schoolboy play by schoolboys which had been rejected by 31 producers before Abbott picked it up, grossed over a million between Broadway and the road. Similarly lucky was Abbott's encounter with *Room Service*. This incredible farce died during its opening in Philadelphia and lost $23,000 for Metro-Goldwyn-Mayer, backing Producer Sam Harris. The deflated authors took the *Room Service* script to Abbott. After making a few changes he produced it again. It ran for two years and sold to RKO pictures for $255,000, the highest price ever paid by Hollywood for a play.

The Abbott offices, consisting of a large main room and five offices for George and the staff, are in Radio City. Until last year, they were in a dingy building on West 42nd. His employes persuaded him to move, pointing out that the difference in the rent between Radio City and 42nd Street was so slight as to make it worthwhile. Having taken the step, he is now delighted and very proud of his pleasant surroundings but has firmly vetoed the suggestion that "International Building" be put on the letter-heads, thinking it might look pretentious.

Making the Show Business Efficient

Abbott loathes detail and considers that his staff is there to take it off his hands. He gives an order and expects it to be carried out with no further following up or interference on his part. When he tells a stage manager to get some furniture he may say, "We need a sofa, two chairs and a desk." After that the stage manager is on his own. In the Abbott shop, no time, no money are wasted. Scripts are read promptly. The plant runs year in and year out with no interruptions. This is unusual in the theater where many producers, after a flop, spend years getting backing for another show. The methodical boss likes to keep people on season after season and has worked out a system whereby in summer, the slack is taken up by working his units in shifts.

Most producers unintentionally run kindergartens for Hollywood and lose actors as soon as they have trained them. Abbott, however, has never yet lost one to the movies if he didn't want to and his regulars often return to him from Hollywood on demand. Actors who have worked for him are likely to adore him; Eugenie Leontovich describes him as an island in turbulent waters of Broadway and says that he is the one person she has met in America who lives up to her idea of what the hundred percent American should be.

He may get angry at stupidity but he rarely shows it because he does not want to frighten an actor. For the theater's characteristic vice of unpunctuality, however, he has no sympathy. Once, arriving early at a rehearsal, Abbott said, "Where is so and so? We're supposed to start at three." "It's only two minutes of three, Mr. Abbott," his assistant pointed out. Abbott looked at his wrist watch. "O. K.," he said, "I'll wait two minutes."

Having been on the stage himself Abbott understands players and their problems and knows exactly how to handle them. No one remembers ever having seen him faced with temperament. He takes actors into his confidence and won't hesitate to say, "This scene is wrong but let's leave it until we try the show on the road." With playwrights, Abbott is inclined to be less gentle. An author who had stayed up all night to rewrite a scene and early next morning showed it to Abbott, once said playfully, "Well, the mountain labored and I hope it brought forth a mouse." Abbott read the scene without changing expression and remarked, "The mountain labored and brought forth a louse. Let's go to the theater!"

Mr. Abbott Likes to Rumba

From the first of September to the middle of January, Abbott is in New York staging plays. Then he goes to Palm Beach where he takes an apartment for two or three months' rest where he sees a good deal of such socialites as Margaret Emerson, the Jay O'Briens and the Harrison Williams, but he would rather go dancing with a girl. He fancies himself a rumba artist. In the spring, he puts on another play, or drills companies for the road and attends to office affairs. Most of his scripts are read during the summer which he spends as a perennial guest with Neysa McMein, the illustrator, and her husband, John Baragwanath, at their place on Long Island. He gets up at eight, reads all morning or sits under a tree, thinking. The afternoons are devoted to his favorite outdoor sports—swimming, badminton, croquet. In the evenings, he follows the Baragwanaths' social program, even going manfully to dinner parties. But his idea of a really pleasant way to spend an evening in the country is playing hearts or Chinese checkers or backgammon or, if there is a larger party, games like twenty questions or competitive charades called "The Game."

Once or twice in the summer he will round up all the actors working for him and take them down to the hospitable Baragwanaths' in specially chartered buses and cars for a party. The regimentation is impressive. "Now, we will go walking," he will say. Or, "Now, we'll have a treasure hunt," or "Now, we will go swimming." Every winter, Abbott gives two or three parties at the Coffee House, also for his actors. On these occasions, re- garded by connoisseurs as some of the better parties of the season, the principal entertainment is a series of skits acted out by the guests, taking off their host's little peculiarities.

Abbott's ability to take the ribbing which his curious behavior naturally occasions is noteworthy and he is able to look at himself quite dispassionately. "I had to stop working with so and so," he once said, "because he wanted me to be too obvious. I have enough of a tendency that way myself without being egged on." His two best friends outside the theater are Baragwanath, noted for his wit, and William Rhinelander Stewart, noted for his polish. Abbott however has not been infected by either the tendency toward worldly repartee or metropolitan sophistication. Alexander Woollcott in a heated croquet game once turned on him and cried, "You tiresome hick!" "I know I'm a hick," George told someone later, "but I don't like to be called one."

In all probability, Abbott didn't really mind. In essentials he has not only remained the same upstate boy who came to the city 26 years ago but while making his mark on Broadway has resolutely refused to let Broadway make its mark on him. One day last summer George Kaufman, driving up Broadway, saw Abbott at Times Square, surveying what is, after all, his king- dom. He was standing with one foot on the curb, dreamily munching peanuts out of a paper bag.

HITLER

John Gunther

⊔⊓⊔⊓⊔⊓⊔⊓⊔⊓⊔⊓⊔⊓⊔⊓⊔⊓⊔⊓⊔⊓⊔⊓⊔⊓⊔⊓⊔⊓⊔⊓⊔⊓⊏

*The union of theorizer, organizer, and leader in one man
is the rarest phenomenon on earth; therein lies greatness.—*
ADOLF HITLER

Adolf Hitler, irrational, contradictory, complex, is an unpre-
dictable character; therein lie his power and his menace. To
millions of honest Germans he is sublime, a figure of adoration;
he fills them with love, fear, and nationalist ecstasy. To many
other Germans he is meager and ridiculous—a charlatan, a lucky
hysteric, and a lying demagogue. What are the reasons for this
paradox? What are the sources of his extraordinary power?

This paunchy, Charlie-Chaplin-mustached man, given to in-
somnia and emotionalism, who is the head of the Nazi party,
commander-in-chief of the German army and navy, Leader of
the German nation, creator, President, and chancellor of the
Third Reich, was born in Austria in 1889. He was not a German
by birth. This was a highly important point inflaming his early
nationalism. He developed the implacable patriotism of the frontiersman, the exile. Only an Austrian could take Germanism so
seriously.

The inside story of Hitler includes many extraordinary and
bizarre episodes. Before discussing his birth and childhood and
outlining his career, it may be well to present a broad detailed
picture of his character and his daily routine and his attitudes
and habits, his personal characteristics and limitations.

Hitler the Human Being

His imagination is purely political. I have seen his early paintings, those which he submitted to the Vienna art academy as a
boy. They are prosaic, utterly devoid of rhythm, color, feeling,

From John Gunther, *Inside Europe*, Harper & Brothers. Copyright
1933, 1934, 1935, 1936, 1937, 1938, 1940 by John Gunther.

or spiritual imagination. They are architect's sketches: painful and precise draftsmanship; nothing more. No wonder the Vienna professors told him to go to an architectural school and give up pure art as hopeless. Yet he still wants deeply to be an artist. In 1939, during the crisis leading to the Polish war, he told Sir Nevile Henderson, the British Ambassador, that his only ambition was to retire to the Berchtesgaden hills and paint.

He went only to elementary school, and by no stretch of generosity could he be called a person of genuine culture. He is not nearly so cultivated, so sophisticatedly interested in intellectual affairs as is, say, Mussolini. He reads almost nothing. The Treaty of Versailles was, probably, the most concrete single influence on his life; but it is doubtful if he ever read it in full. He dislikes intellectuals. He has never been outside Germany since his youth in Austria (if you except his War experiences in Flanders and two brief visits to Mussolini) and he speaks no foreign language, except a few words of French.

To many who meet him, Hitler seems awkward and ill at ease. This is because visitors, even among his subordinates, obtrude personal realities which interfere with his incessant fantasies. He has no poise. He finds it difficult to make quick decisions: capacity for quick decisions derives from inner harmony, which he lacks. He is no "strong, silent man."

Foreigners, especially interviewers from British or American papers, may find him cordial and even candid but they seldom have opportunity to question him, to participate in a give-and-take discussion. Hitler rants. He orates. He is extremely emotional.[1] He seldom answers questions. He talks to you as if you were a public meeting, and nothing can stop the gush of words.

Years ago, before signing his short-lived friendship pact with Poland, he received a well-known American publicist and editor. He did ask a question: What the American would think if, for example, Mexico were Poland and Texas were cut off from the United States by a "corridor" in Mexico. The American replied, "The answer to that is that Canada is not France." Hitler had intended the question rhetorically, and he was so shocked and upset by the little interruption that it took him some time to get in full voice again—on another point.

For a time it was said commonly that Hitler's best trait was loyalty. He would never, the sardonic joke put it, give up three

[1] He told one astonished group of interviewers that they could "crucify" him if he did not keep his promises.

things: the Jews, his friends, and Austria. Nobody would make that joke to-day, now that Captain Roehm is dead. Nor would anyone of knowledge and discernment have made it even before June 30, 1934, because the scroll of Hitler's disloyalties was written in giant words.

One after another he eliminated those who helped him to his career: Drexler, Feder, Gregor Strasser. It is true that he has been loyal to some colleagues—those who never disagreed with him, who gave him absolute obedience. This loyalty is not an unmixed virtue, considering the unsavoriness of such men as Streicher, the Nuremberg Jew-baiter. Nothing can persuade Hitler to give up Streicher and some other comrades. Unsavoriness alone is not enough to provoke his Draconian ingratitude.

His physical courage is doubtful. When his men were fired on in the Munich *Putsch* of 1923, he flung himself to the street with such violence that his shoulder was broken. Nazi explanations of this are two: (1) linked arm in arm with a man on his right who was shot and killed, he was jerked unwittingly to the pavement; (2) he behaved with the reflex action of the veteran front-line soldier, viz., sensibly fell flat when the bullets came.

Hitler has told an acquaintance his own story of the somewhat mysterious circumstances in which he won the Iron Cross. He was a dispatch-bearer. He was carrying messages across a part of No-Man's-Land which was believed to be clear of enemy troops, when he heard French voices. He was alone, armed only with a revolver; so with great presence of mind he shouted imaginary orders to an imaginary column of men. The Frenchmen tumbled out of a deserted dugout, seven in all, hands up. Hitler alone delivered all seven to the German lines. Recounting this story privately, he told his interlocutor that he knew the feat would have been impossible, had the seven men been American or English instead of French.[2]

Like that of all fanatics, his capacity for self-belief, his ability to delude himself, is enormous. Thus he is quite "sincere"—he really believes it—when in a preposterous interview with the *Daily Mail* he says that the Nazi revolution cost only twenty-six lives. He believes absolutely in what he says—at the moment.

But his lies have been notorious. Heiden[3] mentions some of

[2] This story is not the official version, which is more grandiloquent. Some mystery attaches to the exact circumstances. Cf. *Heli*, a bright anonymous British book about Germany, p. 9.

[3] *History of National Socialism*, by Konrad Heiden, a book indispensable for the study of the new Germany.

the more recondite untruths, and others are known to every student. Hitler promised the authorities of Bavaria not to make a *Putsch*; and promptly made one. He promised to tolerate the Papen government; then fought it. He promised not to change the composition of his first cabinet; then changed it. He promised to kill himself if the Munich coup failed; it failed, and he is still alive.

The Man Without Habits

Hitler, nearing fifty-one, is not in first-rate physical condition. He has gained about twelve pounds in the past few years, and his neck and midriff show it. His physical presence has always been indifferent; the sloppiness with which he salutes is, for instance, notorious. The forearm barely moves above the elbow. He had lung trouble as a boy, and was blinded by poison gas in the War.

In August, 1935, it was suddenly revealed that the Leader had suffered a minor operation some months before to remove a polyp on his vocal cords—penalty of years of tub-thumping. The operation was successful. The next month Hitler shocked his adherents at Nuremberg by alluding, in emotional and circumlocutory terms, to the possibility of his death. "I do not know when I shall finally close my eyes," he said, "but I do know that the party will continue and will rule. Leaders will come and Leaders will die, but Germany will live. . . . The army must preserve the power given to Germany and watch over it." The speech led to rumors (quite unconfirmed) that the growth in Hitler's throat was malignant, and that he had cancer.

Nowadays Hitler broods and talks about death a good deal. One reason for his prodigious expansionist efforts in 1938 and 1939 was fear of death before his work was complete.

He takes no exercise, and his only important relaxation—though lately he began to like battleship cruises in the Baltic or North Sea—is music. He is deeply musical. Wagner is one of the cardinal influences on his life; he is obsessed by Wagner. He goes to opera as often as he can, and he was attending the Bayreuth Festival when, on July 25, 1934, Nazi putschists murdered Chancellor Dollfuss of Austria. Sessions of the Reichstag, which take place in the Kroll Opera House, sometimes end with whole performances of Wagner operas—to the boredom of non-musical deputies!

When fatigued at night in the old days, his friend and court jester Hanfstaengl was sometimes summoned to play him to sleep, occasionally with Schumann or Verdi, more often with Beethoven and Wagner, for Hitler needs music like dope. Hanfstaengl is a demoniac pianist. I have heard him thump the keys at the Kaiserhof with such resonance that the walls shook. When Hanfstaengl plays, he keeps time to his own music by puffing out his cheeks and bellowing like a trumpet. The effect is amazing. You cannot but believe that a trumpeter is hidden somewhere in the room.

Hitler cares nothing for books; nothing for clothes (he seldom wears anything but an ordinary brown-shirt uniform, or a double-breasted blue serge suit, with the inevitable raincoat and slouch hat); very little for friends; and nothing for food and drink. He neither smokes nor drinks, and he will not allow anyone to smoke near him. He is practically a vegetarian. At the banquet tendered him by Mussolini he would eat only a double portion of scrambled eggs. He drinks coffee occasionally, but not often. Once or twice a week he crosses from the Chancellery to the Kaiserhof Hotel (the G. H. Q. of the Nazi party before he came to power), and sits there and sips—chocolate.

This has led many people to speak of Hitler's "asceticism" but asceticism is not quite the proper word. He is limited in aesthetic interests, but he is no flagellant or anchorite. There is very little of the *austere* in Hitler. He eats only vegetables—but they are prepared by an exquisitely competent chef. He lives "simply"—but his house in Berchtesgaden is the last word in modern sumptuousness.

He works, when in Berlin, in the palace of the Reichskanzler on the Wilhelmstrasse. He seldom uses the president's palace a hundred yards away on the same street, because when Hindenburg died he wanted to eliminate as much as possible the memory of Presidential Germany. The building is new, furnished in modern glass and metal, and Hitler helped design it. Murals of the life of Wotan adorn the walls. An improvised balcony has been built over the street, from which, on public occasions, the Leader may review his men. Beneath the hall—according to reports—is a comfortable bomb-proof cellar.

Hitler dislikes Berlin. He leaves the capital at any opportunity, preferring Munich or Berchtesgaden, a village in southern Bavaria, where he has an alpine establishment, Haus Wachenfeld. Perched on the side of a mountain, this retreat, dear to his heart, is not far from the former Austrian frontier, a psychological fact of great significance.. From his front porch he could almost see the homeland which repudiated him, and for which he yearned for many years.

Above the Berchtesgaden house—where he came in 1938 and 1939 to spend more and more time, often neglecting Berlin for weeks on end—is an amazing lookout or aerie his engineers have built on a mountain top, near Kehlstein. A special, heavily guarded, looping road leads to bronze gates cut into a sheer wall of rock; inside the solid mountain, an elevator shaft rises four hundred feet. Here, on top, is a large circular room walled with windows. And here, when he really wants to be alone, Hitler comes.

Another peculiar point about Hitler is his passionate interest in astrology. It is widely believed that he set the date for the Sudeten crisis by advice of astrologers.

FRIENDS

By a man's friends may ye know him. But Hitler has very few.

For years his most intimate associate, beyond all doubt, was Capt. Ernst Roehm, chief of staff of the SA (*Sturm Abteilung*— storm troops—Brown Shirts), who was executed on June 30, 1934. From one of the half dozen men in Germany indisputably most qualified to know, I have heard it that Roehm was the only man in Germany, the single German out of 65,000,000 Germans, with whom Hitler was on *Du-Fuss* (thee and thou) terms. Now that Roehm is dead, there is no single German who calls Hitler "Adolf." Roehm was a notorious homosexual, but one should not deduce from this that Hitler is homosexual also.

The man who is probably closest to Hitler since Roehm's death is his chief bodyguard, Lieut. Brückner. Another close associate is Max Amman, who was his top sergeant in the Great War. For a time his former captain, Fritz Weidemann, now German consul-general in San Francisco, was also close. Politically his most intimate adviser is certainly the foreign minister, Herr von Ribbentrop, who is one of the very few people who can see him at any time, without previous arrangement. He is bewitched by Ribbentrop's "wisdom." His chief permanent officials, like Dietrich, his Press secretary, may see him daily, and so may Hess, the deputy leader of the party; but even Hess is not an *intimate* friend. Neither Goering nor Goebbels may, as a rule, see Hitler without appointment.

He is almost oblivious of ordinary personal contacts. A colleague of mine traveled with him, in the same airplane, day after

day, for two months during the 1932 electoral campaigns. Hitler
never talked to a soul, not even to his secretaries, in the long
hours in the air; never stirred; never smiled. My friend remembers
most vividly that, in order to sneak a cigarette when the plane
stopped, he had to run out of sight of the *entourage*. He says
that he saw Hitler a steady five or six hours a day during his trip,
but that he is perfectly sure Hitler, meeting him by chance outside the airplane, would not have known his name or face.

He dams profession of emotion to the bursting point, then is
apt to break out in crying fits. A torrent of feminine tears com-
pensates for the months of uneasy struggle not to give himself
away. For instance, when he spent a whole night trying to persuade a dissident leader, Otto Strasser, from leaving the party, he
broke into tears three times. In the early days he often wept,
when other methods to carry a point failed.[4]

Hitler does not enjoy too great exposure of this weakness, and
he tends to keep all subordinates at a distance. They worship
him: but they do not know him well. They may see him every
day, year in year out; but they would never dare to be familiar.
Hanfstaengl told me once that in all the years of their association
he had never called Hitler anything except "Herr Hitler" or
"Herr Reichskanzler" after the Leader reached power; and that
Hitler had never called him by first name or his diminutive
(Putzi), but always "Hanfstaengl" or "Dr. Hanfstaengl." There
is an inhumanity about the inner circle of the Nazi party that is
scarcely credible.

An old-time party member, to-day, would address Hitler as
"Mein Führer"; others as "Herr Reichskanzler." When greeted
with the Nazi salute and the words "Heil Hitler," Hitler himself
replies with "Heil Hitler." Speechmaking, the Leader addresses
his followers as "My" German people. In posters for the plebiscites he asks, "Dost thou, German man, and thou, German
woman—etc." It is as if he feels closer to the German people in
bulk than to any individual German, and this is indeed true.
The German *people* are the chief emotional reality of his life.

Let us, now, examine Hitler's relation to the imperatives which
dominate the lives of most men.

Attitude Toward Women

He is totally uninterested in women from any personal sexual
point of view. He thinks of them as housewives and mothers or

---

[4] Compare with Stalin, for instance. Can one imagine Stalin bawling
after a hard day, or summoning a comrade to play him music?

potential mothers, to provide sons for the battlefield—other people's sons.

"The life of our people must be freed from the asphyxiating perfume of modern eroticism," he says in *Mein Kampf*, his autobiography.[5] His personal life embodies this precept to the fullest. He is not a woman-hater, but he avoids and evades women. His manners are those of the wary chevalier, given to hand-kissing— and nothing else. Many women are attracted to him sexually, but they have had to give up the chase. Frau Goebbels formerly had evening parties to which she asked pretty and distinguished women to meet him, but she was never able to arrange a match.[6] Occasional rumors of the engagement of the coy Leader to various ladies are nonsense. It is quite possible that Hitler has never had anything to do with a woman in his life.

Occasionally young English or American girls, ardent Aryans, come to see him, and sometimes they are received, like Miss Unity Mitford. But Hitler does little but harangue them. At the top of his voice he screeches politics, and after a time subsides, limp and exhausted. Even these occasions are not tête-à-tête. For Hitler is very fond of the little daughter of Dr. Goebbels, and, fantastic as it may seem, she is often in the room, sometimes on the Leader's knee.

Nor, as is so widely believed, is he homosexual. Several German journalists spent much time and energy, when such an investigation was possible, checking every lodging that Hitler, in Munich days, had slept in; they interviewed beer-hall proprietors, coffee-house waiters, landladies, porters. No evidence was discovered that Hitler had been intimate with anybody of any sex at any time. His sexual energies, at the beginning of his career, were obviously sublimated into oratory. The influence of his mother and childhood environment . . . contributed signally to his frustration. Most of those German writers and observers best equipped to know think that Hitler is a virgin.

Attitude Toward Money

Hitler has no use for money personally and therefore very little interest in it, except for political purposes. He has virtually

[5] Most of my quotations from *Mein Kampf* are from the English edition. (Hurst & Blackett, Ltd., 1933.)

[6] Frau Goebbels herself, before she married the propaganda minister, had designs on Hitler, it is said, but she gave up early.

no financial sophistication; his lack of knowledge of even the practical details of finance, as of economics, is profound.

Nowadays what would he need money for? The state furnishes him with servants, residences, motor-cars. One of his last personal purchases was a new raincoat for the visit to Mussolini in June, 1934. Incidentally, members of his staff got into trouble over this, because on their advice he carried only civilian clothes; when he stepped from his airplane and saw Mussolini and all the Italians in uniform, he was ashamed of his mufti nakedness; and even suspected his advisers of purposely embarrassing him.

Hitler takes no salary from the state; rather he donates it to a fund which supports workmen who have suffered from labor accidents; but his private fortune could be considerable, if he chose to save. He announced late in 1935 that he—alone among statesmen—had no bank account or stocks or shares. Previous to this, it had been thought that he was part-owner of Franz Eher & Co., Munich, the publishers of the chief Nazi organs, *Völkischer Beobachter*, *Angriff*, etc., one of the biggest publishing houses in Europe. Its director, Max Amman, Hitler's former sergeant, was for many years his business manager.

If Hitler has no personal fortune, he must have turned all his earnings from his autobiography, *Mein Kampf*, to the party. This book is obligatory reading for Germans and, at a high price (RM 7.20 or about $3.00), it has sold 5,200,000 copies since its publication in 1925, now being in its 494th edition. If his royalty is fifteen per cent, a moderate estimate, Hitler's total proceeds from this source at the end of 1939 should have been at least $3,000,000.

Nothing is more difficult in Europe than discovering the facts of the private fortunes of leading men. It is sacrosanct and thus forbidden ground to questioners in all countries. . . . Does any dictator, Hitler or Mussolini or Stalin, carry cash in his pocket, or make actual purchases in cash? It is unlikely.

ATTITUDE TOWARD RELIGION

Hitler was born and brought up a Roman Catholic. But he lost faith early and he attends no religious services of any kind. His Catholicism means nothing to him; he is impervious even to the solace of confession. On being formed his government almost immediately began a fierce religious war against Catholics, Protestants, and Jews alike.

Why? Perhaps the reason was not religion fundamentally, but politics. To Hitler the overwhelming first business of the Nazi revolution was the "unification," the *Gleichschaltung* (coördination) of Germany. He had one driving passion, the removal from the Reich of any competition, of whatever kind. The Vatican, like Judaism, was a profoundly international (thus non-German) organism. Therefore—out with it.

The basis of much of the early domestic madness of Hitlerism was his incredibly severe and drastic desire to purge Germany of non-German elements, to create a hundred per cent Germany for one hundred per cent Germans only. He disliked bankers and department stores—as Dorothy Thompson pointed out—because they represented non-German, international, financial and commercial forces. He detested socialists and communists because they were affiliated with world groups aiming to internationalize labor. He loathed, above all, pacifists, because pacifists, opposing war, were internationalists.

Catholicism he considered a particularly dangerous competitive force, because it demands two allegiances of a man, and double allegiance was something Hitler could not countenance. Thus the campaign against the "black moles," as Nazis call priests. Several times German relations with the Vatican have neared the breaking point. Protestantism was—theoretically—a simpler matter to deal with, because the Lutheran Church presumably was German and nationalist. Hitler thought that by the simple installation of an army chaplain, a ferocious Nazi named Mueller, as Reichsbishop, he could "coördinate" the Evangelical Church in Germany, and turn it to his service. The idea of a united Protestant Church appealed to his neat architect's mind. He was wrong. The church question has been an itching pot of trouble ever since. All through 1937 and 1938 it raged.

It was quite natural, following the confused failure to Nazify Protestantism, that some of Hitler's followers should have turned to Paganism. The Norse myths are a first-class nationalist substitute. Carried to its logical extreme. Nazism in fact demands the creation of a new and nationalist religion. Hitler indicated this in a speech at Nuremberg in September, 1935. "Christianity," he said, "succeeded for a time in uniting the old Teutonic tribes, but the Reformation destroyed this unity. Germany is now a united nation. National Socialism has succeeded where Christianity failed." And Heiden has quoted Hitler's remark, "We do not want any other God than Germany itself." This is a vital point. Germany is Hitler's religion.[7]

One of Hitler's grudges against God is the fact that Jesus was a Jew. He can't forgive either Christians or Jews for this. And many Nazis deny that Jesus was Jewish. Another grudge is nationalist in origin. The basis of the Nazi revolution was the defeat of Germany in the War. Thus religion had to be Nazified because no God who permitted the French and other "inferior" races to win the War could be a satisfactory God for Germany.

Hitler's attempt to unify religion in Germany may lead to one danger. He himself may become a god. And divinity entails difficulties. Gods have to perform miracles.

Vividly in *Mein Kampf* Hitler tells the story of his first encounter with a Jew. He was a boy of seventeen, alone in Vienna, and he had never seen a Jew in his life. The Jew, a visitor from Poland or the Ukraine, in native costume, outraged the tender susceptibilities of the youthful Hitler.

"Can this creature be a Jew?" he asked himself. Then, bursting on him, came a second question: "Can he possibly be a German?"

This early experience had a profound influence on him, forming the emotional base of his perfervid anti-Semitism. He was provincially mortified that any such creature could be one with himself, a sharer in German nationality. Later he "rationalized" his fury on economic and political grounds. Jews, he said, took jobs away from "Germans"; Jews controlled the Press of Berlin, the theater, the arts; there were too many Jewish lawyers, doctors, professors; the Jews were a "pestilence, worse than the Black Death."

No one can properly conceive the basic depth and breadth of Hitler's anti-Semitism who has not carefully read *Mein Kampf*. This book was written almost fifteen years ago. He has changed it as edition followed edition, in minor particulars, but in all editions his anti-Jewish prejudice remains implacable.

Long before he became chancellor, Hitler would not allow himself to speak to a Jew even on the telephone. A publicist as well known as Walter Lippmann, a statesman as eminent as Lord Reading, would not be received at the Brown House.

[7] In 1937 a special prayer was chanted over all German radio stations calling Hitler "God's revelation to the German people" and their "redeemer."

An interesting point arises. Has Hitler, in maturity, actually ever been in the company of a Jew, ever once talked to one? Possibly not.

"AM I MY BROTHER'S KEEPER?"

Extreme precautions are, naturally, taken to guard Hitler against assassination. When he rides out in Berlin, he travels in a Mercédès-Benz as big as a locomotive. Lieut. Brückner, his chief aide, usually sits beside him. Other bodyguards follow in another car, or in several cars. The principal chauffeur is named Schaub, who was an early comrade. SS men with rifles may stand on the running-boards. If the occasion is ceremonial and large crowds are present, the route is lined with SS men (black shirts) alternately facing inward and outward.

Brückner is of great importance politically because he serves to block Hitler off from normal contacts. The complaint frequently is heard that Hitler is badly informed on even vital matters, because Brückner so isolates him from wide acquaintance; even advisers with the best intentions may have little chance of seeing him.

Not long ago Hitler broke his new rule against social affairs by visiting informally a diplomat and his wife who had been useful to him in earlier days. The diplomat talked to Hitler frankly and told him some honest truths. Hitler was upset. Then, the story says, Brückner descended on the diplomat, warning him under no circumstances to dare talk frankly to Hitler again.

For years there was no authentic evidence of any attempt on Hitler's life. Rumors, however, dealt in several. On June 17, 1934, a fortnight before the June 30 clean-up, shots are supposed to have been fired at Hitler's car as he was returning from the burial in German soil of Goering's first wife. In the autumn of 1934 an SS bodyguard was allegedly shot in the finger in the Hotel Kaiserhof, by a bullet meant for Hitler. In March, 1937, General Goering surprised listeners by a veiled reference to possible dangers to Hitler and threats against a possible assassin. Then in November, 1939, came the unsuccessful bomb attempt in the Munich beer hall. Several people were killed; Hitler escaped by eleven minutes.

Insurance rates on his life are quoted in London. A man with important business in Germany, which might be ruined by the terror and revolution which would very likely follow Hitler's assassination, paid $52.50 per month for each $1,000 of insurance against Hitler's death.[8]

PERSONAL SOURCES OF POWER

Now we may proceed to summarize Hitler's very considerable positive qualities.

First, consider his single-mindedness, his intent fixity of purpose. His tactics may change; his strategy may change; his aim, never. His aim is to create a strong national Germany, with himself atop it. No opportunistic device, no zigzag in polemics, is too great for him; but the aim, the goal, never varies.

Associated with his single-mindedness is the quality of stamina. All dictators have stamina; all need it. Despite Hitler's flabbiness and lack of vigorous gesture, his physical endurance is considerable. I know interviewers who have talked to him on the eve of an election, after he has made several speeches a day, all over Germany, week on end; they found him fresh and even calm. "When I have a mission to fulfill, I will have the strength for it," he said.

Unlike most dictators, he has no great capacity for hard work, for industry; he is not the sloghorse for punishment that, for instance, Stalin is. He is not a good executive; his desk is usually high with documents requiring his decision which he neglects. He hates to make up his mind. His orders are often vague and contradictory.

Yet he gets a good deal of work done. "Industry" in a dictator or head of a state means, as a rule, ability to read and listen. The major part of the work of Hitler or Mussolini is perusal of reports and attention to the advice of experts and subordinates. Half their working time they are receiving information. Therefore it is necessary for a dictator (a) to choose men intelligently —many of Hitler's best men he inherited from the old civil service, (b) to instill faith in himself in them. Hitler has succeeded in this double task amply. And when his men fail him, he murders them.

Hitler's political sense is highly developed and acute. His calculations are shrewd and penetrating to the smallest detail. For instance, his first three major acts in foreign policy, Germany's departure from the League of Nations, the introduction of con-

[8] Cf. *News Chronicle*, London, May 21, 1935. The charge for similar insurance agaist Mussolini's assassination was $20 on $500 for three months.

scription, and the occupation of the Rhineland, were all set for Saturday afternoon, to ease the shock to opinion abroad. When he has something unpleasant to explain, the events of June 30 for instance, he usually speaks well after eight P.M., so that foreign newspapers can carry only a hurried and perhaps garbled account of his words.

He made good practical use of his anti-Semitism. The Jewish terror was, indeed, an excellent campaign maneuver. The Nazis surged into power in March, 1933, with an immense series of electoral pledges. They promised to end unemployment, rescind the Versailles Treaty, regain the Polish corridor, assimilate Austria, abolish department stores, socialize industry, eliminate interest on capital, give the people land. These aims were more easily talked about than achieved. One thing the Nazis could do. One pledge they could redeem—beat the Jews.

Hitler bases most decisions on intuition. Twice, on supreme occasions, it served him well. In the spring of 1932 his most powerful supporters, chiefly Roehm, pressed him to make a *Putsch*. Hitler refused, *feeling* absolute certainty that he could come to power in a legal manner. Again, in the autumn of 1932, after the Nazis had lost heavily in the November elections, a strong section of the party, led by Gregor Strasser, urged him to admit defeat and enter a coalition government on disadvantageous terms. Hitler, with consummate perspicacity, refused. And within three months he reached power such as the maddest of his followers had not dreamed of.

Another source of Hitler's power is his impersonality, as Frances Gunther has pointed out. His vanity is extreme, but in an odd way it is not personal. He has no peacockery. Mussolini must have given autographed photographs to thousands of admirers since 1922. Those which Hitler has bestowed on friends may be counted on the fingers of two hands. His vanity is the more effective because it expresses itself in non-personal terms. He is the vessel, the instrument, of the will of the German people; or so he pretends. Thus his famous statement, after the June 30 murders, that for twenty-four hours he had been the supreme court of Germany.

Heiden says that Hitler's power is based on intellect, and his intellect on logic. This would seem a dubious interpretation because Hitler's mind is not ratiocinative in the least: he is a man of passion, of instinct, not of reason. His "intellect" is that of a chameleon who knows when to change his color; his "logic" that of a panther who is hungry, and thus seeks food. He himself has said proudly that he is a "Somnambulist"—strange give-away!

His brain is small and vulgar, limited, sly, narrow, suspicious. But behind it is the lamp of passion, and this passion has such quality that it is immediately discernible and recognizable, like a diamond in the sand. The range of his interests is so slight that any sort of stimulus provokes the identical reflex: music, religion, economics, mean nothing to him except exercise in German nationalism.

Anthony Eden, when he visited Berlin in the spring of 1935, and talked with Hitler seven hours, was quoted as saying that he showed "complete mastery" of foreign affairs. This is, of course, nonsense. Hitler does not know one-tenth as much about foreign affairs as, say, H. R. Knickerbocker, or Vernon Bartlett, or Hamilton Fish Armstrong, or Dorothy Thompson, or Mr. Eden himself. What Eden meant was that Hitler showed unflagging mastery of *his own view* of foreign affairs.

DEMOSTHENES IN BROWN SHIRT

Then there is oratory. This is probably the chief external explanation of Hitler's rise. He talked himself to power. The strange thing is that Hitler is a bad speaker. He screeches; his mannerisms are awkward; his voice breaks at every peroration; he never knows when to stop. Goebbels is a far more subtle and accomplished orator. Yet Hitler, whose magnetism across the table is almost nil, can arouse an audience, especially a big audience, to frenzy.

He knows, of course, all the tricks. At one period he was accustomed to mention at great length the things that "We Germans" (wir) had, or did not have, or wanted to do, or could not do. The word *wir* drove into the audience with the rhythmic savagery of a pneumatic drill. Then Hitler would pause dramatically. That, he would say, was the whole trouble. In Germany the word *wir* had no meaning; the country was disunited; there was no "we."

Recently Hitler told a French interviewer about an early oratorical trick and triumph, eighteen years ago in a communist stronghold in Bavaria. He was savagely heckled. "At any moment they might have thrown me out of the window, especially when they produced a blind War invalid who began to speak against all the things that are sacred to me. Fortunately I had also been blind as the result of the War. So I said to these people, 'I know what this man feels. I was even more bewildered than he at one moment—but *I* have recovered my sight!' "

Hitler's first followers were converts in the literal sense of the term. They hit the sawdust trail. Hitler might have been Aimée Semple McPherson or Billy Sunday. Men listened to him once and were his for life—for instance, Goebbels, Brückner, Goering, Hess.

"RUIN SEIZE THEE, RUTHLESS KING"

Hitler never flinched from the use of terror, and terror played a powerful rôle in the creation of the Nazi state. From the beginning he encouraged terror. The only purely joyous passage in *Mein Kampf* is the description of his first big mass meeting, in which the newly organized SA pummeled hecklers bloody. The function of the SA was rough-house: first, rough-house with the aim of preserving "order" at public meetings; second, rough-house on the streets, to frighten, terrorize and murder communists.

He gave jobs, big jobs, to confessed and admitted terrorists like Killinger and Heines. When a communist was murdered at Potempa, in Silesia, in circumstances of peculiarly revolting brutality, Hitler announced publicly his spiritual unity with the murderers. When, in August, 1932, he thought that Hindenburg might appoint him chancellor, he asked for a three-day period during which the SA could run wild on the streets, and thus revenge themselves upon their enemies.

And we shall see presently what happened on the 30th June, 1934. To saying nothing of what happened to the Jews in 1938 and 1939.

FÜHRER PRINZIP

Hitler's chief contribution to political theory was the *Führer Prinzip* (Leader Principle). This means, briefly, authority from the top down, obedience from the bottom up, the reversal of the democratic theory of government. It was, as Heiden points out, a remarkably successful invention, since almost anybody could join the movement, no matter with what various aims, and yet feel spiritual cohesion through the personality of the leader. The Nazi movement gave wonderful play to diverse instincts and desires.

Then again, Germans love to be ruled. "The most blissful state a German can experience is that of being bossed," a friend of mine put it in Berlin. And Edgar Ansel Mowrer has recorded the shouts of Nazi youngsters on the streets, "We spit at freedom." A German feels undressed unless he is in uniform. The *Führer Prinzip* not only exploited this feeling by transforming the passive character of German docility, German obedience, into an active virtue; it gave expression also to the bipolar nature of obedience: namely, that most men—even Germans—associate with a desire to be governed a hidden will to govern. The *Führer Prinzip* created hundreds, thousands, of sub-*Führers*, little Hitlers, down to the lowest storm-troop leader. It combined dignified submission with opportunity for leadership.

Mein Kampf, for all its impersonality, reveals over and over again Hitler's faith in "the man." After race and nation, personality is his main preoccupation. It is easy to see that the *Führer Prinzip* is simply a rationalization of his own ambition; the theory is announced on the implicit understanding that the "man" is Hitler himself. "A majority," he says, "can never be a substitute for the Man."

Another Hitlerite doctrine is, of course, that of race. But Hitler did not invent the concept of Aryanism; he took it over from Gobineau and Houston Chamberlain. Most—if not all—neutral anthropologists think that Hitler's "racist doctrine" is nonsense. They do not believe that "pure" races exist.

OPPOSITION

Hitlerism in its first stages was the process of "unifying" Germany. Yet the Nazis struck at Protestants, Catholics, Jews; they mortally affronted the working classes; they could not put any serious program of economic amelioration into effect without offending the industrialists; they alienated, by brutality and terror, the republicans, democrats, socialists, communists.

Hitler has held three major plebiscites so far. One asked vindication of Germany's departure from the League, and he received a 92.3 per cent vote of confidence. The second sought acceptance of his combination of chancellorship and presidency after the death of Hindenburg; the affirmative vote was 38,-362,760 out of 43,529,710 ballots cast. The third followed the Rhineland crisis in March, 1936; his vote was no less than ninety-eight per cent. Of course none was a fair vote in the Anglo-Saxon sense of the term. The plebiscite in the Saar gave him ninety per cent but it probably would have been the same under any other chancellor. The last general election in Danzig, where

every effort was made to bring out the vote and which was a
better indication than the Saar of public feeling on a straight
for-or-against-Hitler issue, brought him 139,043 votes out of
234,956—good enough, but not the two-thirds majority he
hoped for.

The last reasonably fair German election, on March 5, 1933—
even though it took place under the shadow of the Reichstag
fire—gave Hitler thirty-seven per cent. I believe in an election
to-day he would better this considerably. Even so, the total Marx-
ist (communist-cum-socialist) vote in 1933 was 11,845,000. This
number has probably receded, but just the same there is still a
large opposition submerged in Germany. What has happened to
these millions of hidden voters?

They are terrified. They are hounded by the police and by
spies. They vote Yes in plebiscites because they are frightened of
their skins. Some few of them have sought cover actually by
joining the SA. Most simply swallow their opinions, their feelings,
their inward decency—and wait. They are waiting for their Day.
But are they an active political force? No.

The reason is that revolution is a profoundly difficult matter
in a police state like Germany, Russia, or Fascist Italy. It is
almost an axiom these days that no revolution can succeed until
the equipment in arms and ammunition of the revolutionaries is
equal or superior to that of the government. And this margin of
superiority is transcendently difficult to achieve.

The Nazis, to their own disadvantage, discovered the *essential*
necessity of arms in the Austrian civil war of July, 1934. They
neglected to arm their Austrian adherents, out of carelessness or
over-confidence; they assumed that once the signal for the revolt
was given the Austrian army and police would mutiny and turn
over their arms to the Nazis; this did not happen. The army and
police of Dr. Dollfuss remained, by and large, loyal. Therefore
we had the spectacle of thousands upon thousands of potentially
revolutionary Nazis inhibited from any decisive or direct action
simply because they did not possess arms. This lesson is cardinal. You cannot fight a machine-gun by saying "Boo" to it.

If the people riot, Hitler can simply shoot them down. He
has the Reichswehr (regular army) to do this, not merely the
SA and SS. The Reichswehr (the ranks are mostly peasant boys)
might not shoot at a rising in the agrarian districts, but the
farmers are the most tractable people in Hitler's Reich. An urban
population would get short shrift. But, one may say, no man, not

even Hitler, could shoot down tens of thousands of unarmed or roughly armed rebels. The answer to this is that it is not necessary to shoot down tens of thousands. A few hundreds will be enough.

What is more likely to happen than open rebellion is the slow pressure upward of mass discontent, grumbling, and passive resistance, sabotage caused by growing privation, until the morale of the government cracks, and the government, panicky, does foolish things. Discontent may corrosively simmer to the top, disorganizing the headship of state, causing new rivalries between sub-leaders, creating fissures between, say, Ribbentrop on the left and Goering on the right, so deep and so unbridgeable that Hitler is powerless to compose the conflict. But there are no signs that this is happening yet. The 1939 war, moreover, served to unify Germany, at least provisionally.

Succession to the Purple

If Hitler should die to-morrow his successor would certainly be Goering, bitterly as he is disliked and feared by many members of the party. The Leader might himself prefer Hess, his deputy, as successor, but in the rough-and-tumble that might follow his death, Hess would have small chance against such a doughty character as Goering. The general is the logical choice. Therefore when the Polish campaign began Hitler formally named Goering to the succession, with Hess as second choice. After Hess, the Nazi party is to choose the "strongest" man.

Goering has force, color, ambition; he is a figure of great popular appeal. The quality and quantity of his uniforms are highly attractive to Germans; his marriage may produce a dynasty. What is more important, the army likes him because he stands for the same thing as it stands for: a strong Germany. Moreover, in the SS and remnants of SA, Goering has a considerable armed force behind him. Finally, he has the courage to grab the job, if grabbing is necessary, which it probably won't be.

Goebbels would be impossible as successor to Hitler; he is the cleverest of all the Nazis, but everybody hates him. Frick is important, but too colorless; Ribbentrop too limited; Ley and Darré out of the running as "radicals"; Schacht is of the greatest importance in economics and finance, but impossible as a popular leader. In fact, the only alternative to Goering would seem to be a straight-out Reichswehr ministry formed by an army coup *d'état,* such as the one Schleicher might have headed. Or a dark horse.

Rumors, however, to the effect that Goering is *now* actively intriguing against Hitler are nonsense. There are many virtues that Goering lacks, but loyalty is not among them—at least not yet. Besides, Hitler could eliminate Goering to-day almost as easily as he eliminated Roehm. Hitler is all-powerful. Real rivals do not exist. Goering, Goebbels, and all the rest of them, as H. R. Knickerbocker once expressed it, are no more than moons to Hitler's sun. They shine—but only when the sun shines on them.[9]

[9] Sir Nevile Henderson, the British Ambassador in Berlin, stated in October, 1939, that Goering told him, "When a decision has to be taken, none of us counts more than the stones on which we are standing. It is the Führer alone who decides."

"THIS AGELESS SOUL"

Russell Maloney

⌐⌐⌐⌐⌐⌐⌐⌐⌐⌐⌐⌐⌐⌐⌐⌐⌐⌐⌐⌐⌐

The drama critics who attended the opening of young Orson Welles' revival of *Heartbreak House* last spring were practically unanimous in acclaiming it as a perfectly timed production. Shaw's gloomy prophecies about the decay of civilization, although written twenty-one years ago, were so pat and applicable to contemporary affairs, they exclaimed, that it was a stroke of genius for the Mercury Theatre to have decided to make them heard once again. This is probably no more than the truth, but it is nevertheless a thought-provoking fact that, up to the very moment *Heartbreak House* went into rehearsal, Welles had been leaning toward an alternative production—*Twelfth Night*, to be done in mid-Victorian costumes, with several scenes laid at a seaside bathing beach.

Looking for the essential qualities of a mind poised between *Heartbreak House* and a mid-Victorian *Twelfth Night*, the abashed biographer is forced to the conclusion that his subject is one of those characters who have served so many novelists so well—the actor whose world lies entirely behind the footlights, for whom the only realities are grease paint and tinsel. It is a simple fact that Welles has never been interested in anything outside the theatre and that he has experimented with everything in it—writing, directing, designing, acting, and producing. A biologist would call him an organism perfectly adapted to its surroundings. His spiritual makeup is a nice blend of optimism, good humor, and indomitable egotism. Because of his fortunate lack of formal education, his mind works with effortless originality and at surprising speed; he has already thought out enough productions, down to the last details of design, lighting, and direction, to keep him busy for the next decade. Although he is physically graceless offstage, pudgy and unathletic, his size and

From *The New Yorker*, October 8, 1938, by permission of the author and publishers.

booming voice give him an authoritative, if not actually overwhelming, stage presence; and some mysterious source of energy
enables him to get along with only two or three hours' sleep a
night during rehearsal weeks. It is hardly surprising that Welles
is a success. The fact that he is a success at twenty-three may
be ascribed to the operations of heredity, progressive education,
and the federal government.

Orson Welles was prenatally named by his father over a round
of drinks in Rio (George Orson Welles, for the humorist George
Ade and a man named Orson Wells, a friend but no relation of
the Welleses) and born, somewhat anticlimactically, in Kenosha,
Wisconsin. The date of his birth was May 6, 1915. Over and
over again, this date has been confirmed by the city fathers of
Kenosha for the benefit of Sunday-supplement journalists hopeful
of discovering that Welles is really thirty or thirty-five. This skepticism about his age has never angered Welles, but he cannot
restrain a sensation of gentle triumph whenever he hears that
another reporter has put himself to the useless expense of wiring
to Kenosha for a duplicate of the birth certificate.

Welles' mother was an Ives of Springfield, Illinois, which
meant a good finishing school and a dowry from the coal business. She was a talented amateur pianist, and had a number of
friends in the musical and operatic set of Chicago. When Orson
was two years old the family moved from Kenosha to Chicago.
Here, their house was constantly filled with musicians, and it
seemed understood that the child was to have a musical career.
He made an early début with the Chicago City Opera; a soprano
friend of the family borrowed him to play her illegitimate spawn
in *Madama Butterfly*. When Orson was six, his parents were
divorced and for two years he lived with his mother. Upon her
death, he was returned to the care of his father, surely one of the
oddest souls ever to come out of the Middle West.

If the name of Dick Welles seems familiar, it is because a restaurant, a race horse, and a cigar were named after him. (The
cigar may just possibly have been named after the race horse.)
Dick Welles had a substantial income from several wagon factories which belonged to his family, and was by profession an
inventor. He invented one of the first automobiles in America,
but never bothered about patents because the thing seemed impractical. He did, however, receive substantial royalties from an
improved type of bicycle lamp and from a picnic kit which the
government bought in quantities to issue to the troops during the

World War. In the intervals of invention, Dick Welles was what people used to call a *bon vivant*. He cut a wide swath on three continents, not to mention the island of Jamaica, where he maintained a winter home. Orson spent three years with his father, three years which might have got him down for good if he had not possessed a philosophic temperament and a strong constitution. Vicariously, as his father's travelling companion, he sampled the wine, women, and song of London, Paris, the Riviera, Singapore, Tokio, and Dixon, Illinois—the last-named place because Dick Welles unaccountably bought the local hotel and settled down to operate it. However, the building burned to the ground after a few weeks and the pair were off again, carrying with them nothing more than two bottles of fine Holland gin which Welles *père* had succeeded in saving from the holocaust. At one time or another they managed to look in on each of Welles' seven great-aunts, all women of pronounced individuality. One of them used to lope along the back roads of Missouri behind her limousine, to keep in condition; another used to bathe in ginger ale, because, she said, the price of champagne was exorbitant. Occasionally, when not en route, Orson stayed in Chicago with Dr. Maurice Bernstein, a friend of the family. It was Dr. Bernstein who administered the money left by Orson's mother and, in 1934, after the death of Dick Welles, became his son's legal guardian. This Dr. Bernstein, an orthopedist with cultured tastes, persuaded Dick Welles to enter his son, when the boy was eleven, in the Todd School at Woodstock, Illinois. Orson continued to travel with his father during summer vacations, but he had already found his vocation.

Todd is an expensive preparatory school of considerable antiquity, now run on severely progressive lines. The present headmaster, Roger Hill, a slim, white-haired tweed-wearing man, who looks as if he had been cast for his rôle by a motion-picture director, has never let the traditional preparatory-school curriculum stand in the way of creative work. All the boys spend as much time as they want in the machine shop, the printshop, the bookbindery, or the school theatre. Orson Welles was at Todd from 1926 to 1931. In those five years he completed eight years of academic work and qualified for admission to college, provided the college wasn't too particular about mathematics. Also, abetted by the delighted Mr. Hill, he gave himself a thorough course in the fundamentals of the theatre. It is probable that Welles, as a boy, wore more crêpe hair and putty noses than most actors do

in a lifetime. When he was thirteen, he began directing the
Todd Troupers, the school dramatic society. His first big job
that year was a production of *Julius Caesar*, played in togas but
nevertheless embodying many of the ideas he later used for the
Mercury's *Caesar*. This was the Todd School's entry in the annual Drama League contest for high schools and little-theatre
groups around Chicago. It didn't get the prize; the judges explained that, meritorious as the production was, the two lads
who played Cassius and Mark Antony were both too mature to
be bona-fide students. This was a severe disappointment for
Welles, who had cast himself in these two leading rôles to make
sure that they were played exactly right.

Welles directed about eight productions a year while he was at
Todd, usually playing one of the chief parts. He developed quite
a nice touch at scene-painting and even executed a mural for a
classroom. Fortunately, he was at a school which placed no emphasis on athletics. During his travels he learned to swim and to
ride a horse. That is today the extent of his physical accomplishments. If he attempts anything else even mildly athletic, he
sprains his ankle. Once he sprained his ankle while trying to chin
himself. Roger Hill is inclined to believe that there is some sort
of psychic slant to this infirmity, that Welles sprains his ankle
because he is worried or doubtful about something. It may be.

There would be no point to a recital of Welles' childish tri-
umphs if he had not turned up in New York a very few years
later and repeated some of them as commercial and artistic successes. For instance, his last big job before he graduated from
Todd was a mélange of Shakespeare's historical plays—edited
and directed by Orson Welles, starring Orson Welles. This was
the germ of the *Five Kings* chronicle play to be presented by the
Mercury this autumn to the Theatre Guild subscribers. Seven
years ago, if anybody had told the Guild directors that they were
going to buy an interest in a production then being whipped up
by a child in a progressive school, they wouldn't have believed it.
Welles, one imagines, would have been gratified but not particularly astonished.

After his graduation in 1931, Welles went to study drawing
at the Chicago Art Institute. A severe attack of hay fever put a
stop to this episode, so the youth got some money from his
father and set out for a tour of Scotland and Ireland in search of
pure air and things to sketch. While wandering about County
Donegal in a donkey cart, painting dubious water colors of the

local scenery, he fell in with a vactioning actor from the Gate Theatre in Dublin. A few weeks later he was passing through Dublin and went backstage to say hello to his friend. Before he left the theatre, he had agreed to make a series of appearances as guest star. He had been introduced to the director and had somehow allowed him to get the impression that he was a Theatre Guild star. It should be explained that Welles looked then, as he does today, like the sort of young man a suburban Gilbert-and-Sullivan society would cast as the Mikado. He is six feet two inches tall, weighs well over two hundred pounds, wears his hair long, and has a blunt-featured face with slanting brows. He said he was twenty-five, and got away with it. A splendid series of adult rôles was awarded him—Svengali, the Duke in *Jew Süss*, and the King in *Hamlet*—and he played them to frantic applause from the Gate audiences. "Strictly goons" is the way Welles describes these folk, meaning that they were given to intemperate enthusiasm. He stayed in Ireland until early in 1932, thus effectively scotching Roger Hill's plan to send him to Harvard. He was a great success. The Gate players generously lent him to the Abbey Players for a guest-guest-star appearance. He met all the Irish intelligentsia, and he even met Noel Coward, informally. Welles overheard Coward, in a café, making what he considered supercilious remarks about the British Empire. Being at the time in a violently Anglophile phase, Welles rose from his chair and shouted at Coward. Coward got up and shouted right back. "Neither of us said anything in the least brilliant," Welles says.

Tearing himself away from the doting Irish, he returned to Woodstock, Illinois, in March, 1932. He and Roger Hill had long had an idea for a historical play about the abolitionist John Brown. Welles worked out a scenario with his schoolmaster and went off to a lake in Wisconsin to spend the summer writing. The result was a practically interminable piece called *Marching Song*. Welles brought it to New York that autumn and showed it to all the producers, but without success. He seems to have accepted this defeat with an equanimity that would do credit to one of twice his years. "I am aware that disappointments, it matters not how many, should in no way affect my confidence, but they do," he wrote to Roger Hill, his Boswell. "Today, for example, it was not a shock nor a sense of failure, just the realization of a fact, the cementing of a profound conviction. I refer to Ben Boyar's returning the manuscript. I wasn't even surprised. He said, 'It's a swell show. It makes good reading. It would make a good book. I think maybe it's even a good play. But that don't matter. It won't make money. It isn't a commercial piece. At least that's what I think. Maybe I'm wrong.' He thanked me for letting him read it, nicely, I thought, repeated himself, and said goodbye. . . .

"I got an idea earlier this evening (it's now half after three) for a comedy, a comedy-drama let us say, on the subject of aphasia. That's the medical word, isn't it, for loss of memory? The idea, like so many others on ice, is merely embryonic."

Writing is the department of dramatics in which Welles has been the least successful. *Marching Song* never did get produced, nor did another play of this period called *Bright Lucifer*. This is a likely-sounding piece about a Hollywood horror actor, a sort of Boris Karloff, who eventually gets to the point of believing he is an honest-to-God menace. This delusion seizes him on an Indian reservation, and the Indians get him. Welles still thinks it might make a fine play.

Depressed by the fate of his plays and by his failure, after his Irish triumph, to land even a walk-on part in New York, Welles decided to get away from it all for a while. He sailed for Africa, one of the few places he had never been to, and disembarked in Morocco. Here he encountered The Glaoui, a Moroccan chieftain with an unaccountably Scotch-sounding title, whom he had known in Paris. The Glaoui (pronounced "The Glowie") was delighted to see Welles again. Welles told him that he was writing a travel book, and the chieftain asked him to be his guest. Welles had a fine time. Since he was nominally a Christian, he couldn't eat at table with the family, but delicious trays were sent to his room, and he had plenty of leisure to get on with his writing, which was not a travel book at all but a school edition of Shakespeare, another suggestion of Roger Hill's. This volume, called *Everybody's Shakespeare*, has stage directions and sketches for costume and set designs for *Twelfth Night, Julius Caesar*, and *The Merchant* of *Venice*; ninety thousand copies have already been sold. Many of Welles' close friends doubt the Glaoui episode, which annoys Welles no more than doubts about his age.

He was back in Chicago by the summer of 1933. Roger Hill introduced him to Thornton Wilder, who gave him a letter of introduction to Alexander Woollcott, who sent him around to Katharine Cornell. She had been looking for a convincingly young Marchbanks and hired Welles on the spot. This was for her famous tour with *Candida, The Barretts of Wimpole Street,* and *Romeo and Juliet*. Welles' other rôles were Mercutio and Octavius, the stuttering brother of Elizabeth Barrett. He set off on a thirty-week tour which took in some seventy-five cities. There is nothing to report about the tour except that, according to one of his companions in the troupe, Welles slept until noon every day, got into numerous tavern brawls, sprained his ankle several times, was publicly reproved by Miss Cornell for wearing a false beard in a San Francisco restaurant, and turned in two hundred-odd creditable performances. The tour wound up in the spring of 1934 and Welles hopped right back to Woodstock, where he and Roger Hill had planned to have a "summer theatre festival." This involved a coeducational dramatic school on the Todd campus, with the students supporting Welles and other guest stars in public performances. Welles courteously invited Micheál MacLiammóir and Hilton Edwards, two Gate Theatre players, to come over here and make guest appearances. These gentlemen, once they had recovered from their pardonable surprise at learning his true status, helped him to make a success of a nine-week repertory which included *Trilby*, *Tsar Paul*, and *Hamlet*. Welles, exercising almost incredible self-restraint, allowed MacLiammóir to play Hamlet and cast himself in his old rôle of the King.

Now, for the first time, love entered this busy life. One of the blondest and most beautiful of the girls at the dramatic school was Virginia Nicolson, the daughter of a well-to-do and socially impeccable Chicago family. Before the summer was over she and Welles were engaged. That Christmas he married her. At first the Nicolsons objected strongly to their baroque son-in-law, but their displeasure softened as the years passed, and melted away altogether last spring, with the birth of a granddaughter. The child, named Christopher because Welles had assumed that she would be a boy, was born quietly just before Welles started the intensive rehearsals of *Heartbreak House* and caused no interruption. His wife has made only one professional appearance, in *Horse Eats Hat*. Welles wants her to play Desdemona to his Othello when he gets around to it. She is an adoring wife and mother, and makes him comfortable in their eight-room house at Sneden's Landing. "You don't know what it means to me to have my own home," he sighs, looking back over the years.

The Mercury Theatre grew out of Welles' meeting with John Houseman. If Welles is the inspiration of the group, Houseman is the brains. He is thirteen years older than Welles, heavy-set, with receding hair and a weakness for checked suitings and suède shoes. He was educated in England and speaks with an English accent. Born in Bucharest of a French father and an English mother, he spent some time in the Argentine after he left England, arriving here just as the depression wiped out his wheat business. He then turned to the stage. He put on Gertrud Stein's *Four Saints in Three Acts* and was the co-director of the Theatre Guild's production of *Valley Forge*. He first saw Welles in the late autumn of 1934, when the latter was playing Tybalt in the New York run of Miss Cornell's *Romeo and Juliet*. Houseman went backstage, introduced himself and signed Welles up for a leading part in a two-performance run he planned for Archibald MacLeish's *Panic*, a poetic discussion of the current hard times.

About this time Welles broke into radio broadcasting. From a twenty-dollar engagement that paid a month's rent on a modest place in West Fourteenth Street, he worked up to the point where he played dozens of rôles a week and could afford the house at Sneden's Landing. He played innumerable current-history characters in the radio March of Time, whose officials hailed his rendition of the death of Sir Basil Zaharoff as a truly remarkable characterization. He got engagement after engagement and the problem of getting from one studio to another in time to broadcast became so acute that they used to keep an elevator waiting for him in the R.C.A. Building. He became the Great McCoy. He became the Voice of Chocolate Pudding. Finally he created The Shadow, a highly melodramatic character who becomes invisible and foils criminals over a coast-to-coast network. Rehearsals and performances of The Shadow used to take up almost all of Sunday; later he arranged to make recordings. The little pause which listeners may have noticed in The Shadow's fiendish and knowledgeable laugh used to be a signal to Mrs. Welles; meant he was thinking of her—or had been thinking of her when he made the recording. Somebody else is The Shadow these days. This summer Welles, assisted by a group of Mercury actors, presented a series of hour-long programs devoted to dramatizations of popular tales like *Treasure Island*, *Dracula*, and *The 39 Steps*. The program is to continue through the winter, on Sunday evenings, competing with Charlie McCarthy. Another Mercury activity was a complete recording of *Julius Caesar*, released last May by Columbia Records. Welles loyally includes the Mercury boys in whatever activity he embarks on; his reply to an attractive offer from Hollywood was that he would be satisfied with nothing less than his own production unit.

Panic was strictly an artistic experiment, which ran its scheduled two performances, was snarled at by the critics and then forgotten. It had, however, served to bring Houseman and Welles together. They decided to form a repertory company. Under the name of the Phoenix Theatre, they took an office in the Sardi Building, announced that they were going to produce Ford's *'Tis Pity She's a Whore*, and set out in search of backers. Nobody responded to their lure but a solitary eccentric, who said he wouldn't invest a nickel in any play going but was willing to back them to the extent of ten thousand dollars in remodelling the façade of the Bijou Theatre. Discouraged, Houseman drifted off and took a job with the Federal Theatre, while Welles continued to mutter and chuckle into the National Broadcasting Company's microphones.

A year later, Houseman again brought up the question of a partnership. He pointed out to Welles that it was not very often that two ambitious young producers got hold of an angel like the federal government. A flop produced with private funds might mean no more chances for five years, while in the WPA project a man might produce an unbroken series of flops. Welles saw the point and got right to work on an idea of Houseman's, a production of *Macbeth* to be done by the Harlem unit of the Federal Theatre. With its lush Haitian jungle peeping over the grim walls of the Scottish castle and its broad-shouldered black bucks playing out the drama of doomed ambition in scarlet and gold, it was probably the most effective presentation of this play ever put on. Just before the opening there was a brief moment when it looked as if Welles' throat was going to be cut by a delegation of Harlemites obscurely convinced that the play was going to make fun of them. He owes his present happy life to Canada Lee, the Banquo of the play, whose word carries a good deal of weight on upper Seventh Avenue.

After this success, Welles directed and acted in *Horse Eats Hat* for the WPA and played the lead in a WPA *Dr. Faustus*. Then came *The Cradle Will Rock*, which turned overnight from a WPA production into a Mercury play. You know the rest; in the Sunday dramatic sections you have read how Welles and Houseman, when the WPA cancelled the production, opened it under their somewhat scanty auspices, with no scenery, and the cast, to circumvent an Equity injunction, speaking their lines from seats in the orchestra. It is said that Marc Blitzstein, author of the show and the officiating pianist, bitterly resented the agreement with Equity which finally allowed the cast to join him on the stage.

Free of governmental regulation and with one successful play running, Welles and Houseman again set out to find backers. This time they got thirteen of them and a total of twenty thousand dollars. After six months of business, the Mercury paid back twenty-five per cent of its capital, as a gesture of solvency and good will. Now, with seventy per cent of the stock controlled by the partners, the Mercury is flourishing but not wealthy. *Julius Caesar* was so closely followed by *The Shoemaker's Holiday* and *Heartbreak House* that they got in each other's way and failed to earn as much money as they might have if handled in the conventional way. *Caesar*, Houseman says, would be running yet if *Shoemaker* hadn't been put on as an alternate bill. Similarly, *Shoemaker* was crowded out of the public's mind by *Heartbreak House*, which the Mercury put on just to keep everyone active. In effect, the Mercury was paying for three productions at a time and never drawing revenue from more than two. The Mercury paid its actors a total of $150,000 last season. Everybody except Welles works on a minimum-guarantee-and-percentage basis. An actor who could reasonably ask around four hundred a week makes something over two hundred with the Mercury. The attraction offered him is uninterrupted work all season and the privilege of leaving on two weeks' notice if he gets a better-paying part. Welles pays himself two hundred dollars a week, less than the earnings of many of his supporting actors.

Welles has no very definite political sympathies. He has been known to exclaim, "I love great big organizations!" and occasionally, in conversation, he manifests liberal tendencies. He says the political and sociological effectiveness of *Caesar* and *Heartbreak House* would not have justified their production if they had not also been what people used to call "good theatre." When his friend Burgess Meredith was president of Actors' Equity, Welles obligingly helped him in his campaign for the Pepper-Coffee Bill, which sponsored a permanent Federal Theatre, speaking at luncheons and occasionally flying down to Washington to testify at hearings. When Meredith's term was over, Welles stopped this activity.

A vague cheerfulness on the part of Welles when discussing

plays and plans for the future makes it difficult to find out what he is really up to. Whenever a play is mentioned in his presence he is more likely than not to exclaim, with absent-minded enthusiasm, "That's my favorite play!" Just now Welles is getting the Mercury Theatre's new season launched, with productions in repertory of *Danton's Death* and *Too Much Johnson*, making a series of educational recordings of Shakespearean plays for schoolroom use, and trying to work in a trip abroad, or a vacation of some sort, before he appears in *Five Kings*, which he will direct for the Guild subscribers later on. He thinks he'd like to do *The Duchess of Malfi*—"my favorite play!" He thinks he'd like to do *Liliom* with a cast of Negroes, an intimate and rather decadent Sunday-night revue, a Mozart operetta. Then, of course, there's the mid-Victorian *Twelfth Night*. There's even the unwritten play about aphasia. Houseman and Welles frown on only two types of play: Restoration comedy, which Houseman says is unsuited to the modern tempo; and plays by young and unknown playwrights, which Welles says the Mercury can't afford to undertake.

Martinelli, the singer, once called Welles "this ageless soul." If he meant his accomplishments in the theatre, about which critics are so very careful not to use the word "genius," O.K. If he meant Welles outside the theatre, Welles in his private life, Welles in his reaction to the realization of what he is accomplishing, he was wrong. That Welles is exactly twenty-three years old.

ADMIRAL BYRD

Charles J. V. Murphy

Since the death of the great Roald Amundsen in 1928, Rear Admiral Richard E. Byrd, U. S. N. (Retired), has been the world's No. 1 explorer. As early as 1925, while still an unknown naval officer, Byrd dabbled with aircraft as an exploring weapon on the Greenland ice cap. In 1926 he nosed out the veteran Amundsen in an aerial race to the North Pole. The following year, though a test-flight crash robbed him of a chance to beat Lindbergh to Paris, Byrd made a transatlantic flight which was one of the most hair-raising epics in aerial annals. Two years later he added the South Pole to his bag.

In the course of two Antarctic expeditions the Admiral has explored some 450,000 square miles of previously unknown lands. No explorer of Byrd's generation has looked upon so much virgin ice and snow. None has named so many nameless bights, peaks and headlands for grateful friends and backers. Furthermore, while most explorers are unadjudicated bankrupts, the Admiral has emerged from *terra incognita* a wealthy man.

One of the remarkable facts about Admiral Byrd's success is that it has been accomplished in a dying profession. The professional explorer is an anachronistic fragment, caught, like the kangaroo, behind the evolutionary eight-ball. A romanticist, he is suspect in a materialistic world. Doomed by a shrinking geography to comb comparatively worthless vacancies, he may even be ashamed to justify exploring for exploring's sake. A nonprofessional like Lincoln Ellsworth, who inherited a fortune (from a capitalist father), or a museum explorer who has monographs to write and specimen cases to fill, can obviously justify his escapist motives. Others, being dependent upon public handouts to buy ships and planes and supplies, and upon lectures

From *Life*, October 30, 1939, by permission of *Time*, Inc., publishers.

and books for a wage, are likely to find that all the endurance and resourcefulness developed by their Spartan travels are inadequate to solve the problem of earning a living between times at home. Byrd, however, has passed with flying colors the tests of the explorer's life both at the Poles and in the U. S. A. He is now not only the greatest living explorer but the only one still plying his trade on the grand scale. Byrd is now plying it on a grander scale than ever.

Next month Admiral Byrd is scheduled to depart f.om Boston on his third Antarctic expedition. All Byrd expeditions are fabulously expensive and this one will cost over $1,000,000 but, while the previous trips were Byrd's own private shows, financed by his admirers, the new expedition is being largely underwritten by the U. S. Treasury. In addition to providing $340,000 in cash, the Government is also providing a Department of Interior ship (the *North Star*), Department of Agriculture meteorologists, Navy photographers, and other experts.

There is a certain irony in the fact that, at the moment when what explorers wistfully call "civilization" is in the throes of a new war, the Admiral and 100-odd companions should be headed excitedly for the one continent that has never known one. Byrd himself is a serious student of international relations, and for the last three years has been working prodigiously on an international peace movement of his own.

Byrd's peace plan, which included a scheme for round-table chats between Hitler, Chamberlain and their peers, was the consequence of a promise he made at a testimonial dinner given to him at the Waldorf-Astoria on his return from the second Antarctic expedition. Before a distinguished group of educators, scientists and industrialists, the Admiral announced that henceforth he would devote himself to "international amity." Nonetheless, when reports reached the State Department that the Germans, on the basis of a preliminary reconnaissance last spring, were planning an extensive expedition to the Antarctic in the near future, the Admiral adjusted himself to the situation at once and volunteered to clinch for the U. S. the claims to the lands which he had previously discovered as an individual. President Roosevelt, his warm friend for years, approved the idea, and the necessary appropriation was put through a somewhat flabbergasted Congress.

To an ordinary, stay-at-home taxpayer, accustomed to seeing his money spent on battleships and on WPA leaf-raking, the

Government's sudden enthusiasm for the Antarctic may seem bewildering. It may even seem surprising to unimaginative students of the subject, who know that the Antarctic continent, though larger than the U. S. and Mexico combined, is little more than a monstrous icebox, inhabited mostly by the seals, penguins, gulls and petrels which invade the coastal fringes during the brief, squawking, young-rearing months. Admiral Byrd, however, takes an almost geologically long view. Traces of minerals and immense deposits of coal have, as the Admiral pointed out to a Congressional committee this year, been found. Although the coal is of poor quality to start with and lies 500 miles from the sea, past dangerous crevasses, in a region of gigantic glaciers, where the winter night is unbroken for five months, the cold is estimated at 90° below zero, and the blizzard blows with the persistence of a trade wind, it may come in handy some day. Mindful of the Pacific Islands that were allowed to slip out of our grasp through failure to perceive their future strategic value, Byrd is resolved that we shall not miss any bets in the Antarctic. What he envisages is nothing less than the extension of the Monroe Doctrine from Tierra del Fuego to the South Pole.

Strangers, when Byrd is pointed out to them, sometimes express surprise that this could be the famous explorer. What they expect, evidently, is the craggy, weather-beaten face of an Amundsen, and the bracing, physical power of a Captain Bartlett. Byrd is on the short side, and only by exercising over weight-lifting apparatus at home has he kept his waistline within reach of an Admiral's ideal. His wavy hair has turned quite gray, but his features, feminine in their delicacy, give him a young look. Born in Winchester, Va., in 1888, Byrd has spent most of his adult domestic life in the North; his only Southern mannerism is a certain softness of speech. But a latent imperiousness, a pride of family, what Byrd himself calls "my Virginian manhood," identifies the James River aristocrat.

TOM, DICK & HARRY

The first Byrd in the U. S. was Colonel William Byrd, according to one historian, "the first Gentleman in America." His son was President of the Virginia Council. Long before the arrival of Richard Evelyn Byrd, fourth in the line to bear the name, financial reversals had removed Westover and other great estates from the family. Byrd's father, now dead, was the U. S. District

Attorney, a leisurely old-school gentleman, schooled in the classics. His mother is descended from the Lords of Delaware. Now in her 70's, she is one of the great ladies of Virginia, with a debutante's energy and a mind sharp as a steel trap, the terror of the horsey Northern women who invade the Shenandoah Valley during the hunting season.

From this union issued the classic three sons—Tom, Dick and Harry. The eldest, Harry, after serving as Governor of Virginia, is now a U. S. Senator and, as a member of the economy bloc, a thorn in Roosevelt's side. Thomas, the youngest, studied law. During Harry's absences in Washington and Dick's elsewhere, he looks after the family's apple orchards, which are among the biggest east of the Mississippi. Of the trio, Dick is easily the most celebrated. He became a celebrity at 12 when, as the consequence of visiting a friend in the Philippines, he traveled around the world alone, supplying the Winchester *Star* with thrilling accounts of his experiences with Insurrectos, a typhoon and a cholera epidemic. With his brothers set upon the law and politics, it was inevitable that Dick, following Virginian tradition, should choose a career in the Service. He studied at the Shenandoah Valley Military Academy and V.M.I., spent a year at the University of Virginia and entered the Naval Academy, graduating in 1912, 63rd in a class of 165.

At Annapolis Byrd went in strenuously for football, but a slight physique kept him from ever being more than a third-string quarterback. Within two years after reporting to the Fleet, he won a medal for saving drowning seamen from the shark-infested waters of the Caribbean. In 1916 a foot injury, which left a slight limp, forced his retirement. Rather than quit the Navy entirely, Byrd took a job mobilizing the Rhode Island State Militia. Recalled to active duty on the declaration of War in 1917, he was detailed to assist Raymond B. Fosdick in organizing community singing, libraries and other recreational pursuits for the Navy's recruits. This seemed mild stuff to Byrd, who was itching for the front lines, but he endured it until he was finally assigned to Pensacola, where he was trained as a pilot. Given the impressive title of Commanding Officer of the U. S. Naval Aviation Force in Canada, Lieut. Byrd was sent to Halifax with a squadron, charged with patrolling the "Corner" against German 'raiders. No raiders appeared but this excursion was the climax of his war record. Yet it was apparent by this time that the third-string quarterback and the disappointed sea-dog was.

if sheer persistence meant anything, destined for great things. Instead of simply "covering his number" and waiting for the slow lift of seniority, Byrd thereafter constituted himself a one-man suicide squad for any project within the Navy's scope. Even before the Armistice he was badgering his superiors for permission to make a solo flight across the Atlantic. That the plane he had picked out would probably have fallen 200 miles short of the Irish coast without a boosting tail wind did not alarm him, his argument was that the flight would stimulate the Allies' morale. In 1919, when the NC flying boats were dispatched across the ocean, Byrd managed to hop a ride as far as Trepassey, Newfoundland. Two years later in 1921, he managed to get an assignment to cross the Atlantic in the ZR-2, which the Navy had just purchased from the British, only to have the dirigible blow up a few days after he landed in England. Finally in 1925, though he had done little flying since the War, Byrd was given command of the Navy flight unit detailed to collaborate with Commander Donald B. MacMillan in explorations around Etah, Greenland.

Had Byrd, who has 22 citations for, among other things, initiative, loyalty and devotion to duty, remained in the Navy, the chances are that, like most of his classmates, he would today rate only a Commander's three stripes. After the MacMillan expedition, however, he again abandoned active duty at his own request and within five years, on the strength of his expeditions, he became a Rear Admiral at 39 by act of Congress. His private reasons for quitting the service so opportunely were not only plausible but praiseworthy. He had married Marie Ames, a charming Boston girl, a Junior League member and a talented violinist, shortly after graduating from Annapolis. By 1925 they had three children. To Byrd the problem of raising a family on a Lieut. Commander's salary appeared insurmountable and his obligation clear.

"I Put Exploration into Big Business"

The talents which Byrd brought to the backward profession of exploration have never been properly evaluated. An explorer's worst hazards are not crevasses and frostbite, but poverty. Peary scraped and pinched pennies for years to finance his dash to the North Pole and most of his confreres were economic ne'er-do-wells. Possibly Byrd's greatest contribution to science was the proof, encouraging to explorers yet unborn, that their line of work, if carefully managed, will bring in a profit. Shrewdly taking advantage of lush conditions in the 1920's, Byrd had established himself by 1928 as the financial genius of the ice caps. He once truly remarked, "I've put exploration into Big Business."

It is doubtful whether the world will ever see another expedition like the Byrd Antarctic Expedition I (1928-30) which put out at the height of good times and returned the summer following the Crash. Charles V. Bob, the mining impresario, gave $108,000. John D. Rockefeller Jr. and Edsel Ford were big contributors and even schoolchildren joyfully sent in their pennies. The total cash contributions have been estimated at between $800,000 and $900,000, while the food, clothing, fuel and other material supplied gratis by manufacturers have been valued at $600,000. The Biltmore Hotel in New York was so delighted to have such a glamorous celebrity as guest of the house that it also put up his entire retinue free of charge. With characteristic if somewhat dramatic foresight, Byrd even had the expedition equipped with half a dozen straitjackets which, with the sleeves cut out, were later used as windproofs.

Perceiving the human desire for even a small measure of immortality, Byrd tapped an entirely new stratum of polar patrons by offering to name ships, airplanes, and still-to-be-discovered mountains and harbors for them. On the last Antarctic expedition, the late Col. Jacob Ruppert put up $25,000 and had the flagship (leased from the U. S. Shipping Board at $1 a year) named after him. The main exploring plane went to William Horlick, the malted-milk man, for a net of $30,000. For $5,000 the name Blue Blade was plastered on a worn-out Fokker. These are the basic economics of modern exploration. Columbus—who incidentally returned from his third voyage in chains—was financed by the Spanish sovereigns whose reimbursement was a major share of the expected treasure. In a modern democracy, Byrd is properly financed by the public which is paid off in vicarious thrills and by manufacturers who received the equivalent of the "Crown's Share" in advertising themselves as exclusive purveyors to an exacting expedition.

HERO OF THE LECTURE PLATFORMS

The cry of "terrific deficit" which often follows a Byrd expedition is at once a tribute to Byrd's business acumen in laying groundwork for a new campaign, and a reminder that an explorer's work is never done. Although he makes nothing out of his trips, directly, they supply the raw material for lecture tours to whose profits he is obviously entitled. The Admiral, among other things, is the most successful lecturer of his time. His 1935-36 tours netted him close to $190,000; the tour after the first expedition was even more successful. Byrd's usual fee is 60% of the box-office gross, with a $1,500 guarantee. For a one-day stand at Los Angeles, in 1935, he was paid $6,100. Last year the Admiral could have had any number of dates at $500, but his roly-poly manager, Leo McDonald, who once managed Krishnamurti, the Theosophist, turned them down as unworthy of Byrd's attention. McDonald permitted Krishna-murti, who was billed as a divinity, to sleep in upper berths but he sees to it that Byrd's explorations of the U. S. hinterland are conducted in a drawing room.

As an author of travel books, Byrd ranks with Lindbergh, the late Richard Halliburton or even the Abbe children. There are already five books under his name—*Skyward, Little America, Discovery, Alone* and *Exploring with Byrd*. With the exception of the last, which was for younger readers, all have been best-sellers. *Little America* sold 100,000 copies; *Alone*, his most recent book, is not far behind. The total sales of his books have been around $1,000,000. Even allowing for a collaborator's fee, his earnings as an author must be close to $130,000. In addition, the New York *Times* paid him $150,000 for the news rights to his first expedition, and Grape Nuts put up $145,000 for the broadcasting rights of the second.

Lectures and literature by no means exhaust the Admiral's potentialities as a money-maker. He is also a shrewd stockmarket investor, trading through Kidder, Peabody & Co. In advancing the profit motive to high latitudes, Byrd has even had a go at importing penguins. The scrawny creatures exhibited in zoos come either from Africa or the Galapagos, and Byrd decided there was a fortune to be made if he could bring back alive the majestic Emperors and the comical Adelies peculiar to the Antarctic. With characteristic thoroughness, he caused 40 of these flightless birds to be rounded up by his biologists. Few inhabitants of Little America will forget the morning they escaped their pen. "Damn it," the Admiral shouted, "there's $25,000 worth of assets vanished overnight. What kind of efficiency is that?" Another batch was captured and a half-dozen survived the voyage north. The mutual devotion between Byrd and these creatures was such that they all died soon after being separated from him, when sold to the Chicago Zoological Society.

Daring in the Air and on the Ice

Admiral Byrd has lived as dangerously as any modern man. On the North Pole flight he and Floyd Bennett sat and watched a slow oil leak. It finally plugged itself up, but not before they had reconciled themselves to a forced landing from which there was little hope of escape. And while his wisdom for taking the risk may be questioned, there can be no doubting the punishment Byrd endured during his famous self-imposed isolation on the Ross Shelf Ice, and the courageous manner in which he endured it.

His transatlantic flight makes even the Hollywood air epics seem pallid by contrast. After hours in fog, in which Byrd and his three companions caught only glimpses of the ocean, they finally reached the French coast. The second night was coming on, gas was low and nerves were raw. At this juncture, the ill-starred Bert Acosta, who had been at the controls for nearly 38 hours, momentarily lost control of his nerves. Muttering about a mysterious fifth man aboard, he wheeled the plane around hard and started back across the Atlantic. Whether it was Byrd himself or Bernt Balchen who knocked Acosta from the controls, and whether the weapon used was a flashlight or a wrench, no one but the four men in the *America* can say; and they have seldom discussed the episode. In his official log of the flight, Byrd, who has a deep respect and liking for Acosta, never mentioned it. As a Virginian, Byrd esteems loyalty above all other qualities and many of the men who have served him know that they can count on his help in any emergency "on the beach."

The Admiral has few of the iron attitudes and mannerisms of the quarterdeck. In the field, he seldom gives orders, only suggestions. This is in keeping with his philosophy that "the polar regions are best won by patience." Byrd is quick to praise, slow to criticize. At Little America he dealt with the troublemakers, the soreheads and the disappointed by taking them on long, exercising walks, while he discoursed on philosophy, politics, people, or whatever else might be in his mind. After he had chilled and generalized the recalcitrants into submission, he would then approach their faults in the manner of an understanding schoolmaster.

The most serious internal situation to vex any of his expeditions came out of the destruction of the whisky on the last. Winter darkness had fallen, the stores were still scattered over the Barrier, and much work remained to be done. But it was hard to keep men slaving in the cold and drift as long as the songs and laughter of good fellowship welled up through the crust from the celebrants in the shacks underneath. And because there was no safe place to hide liquor in that congested village, the second in command, himself a teetotaler, one night quietly gathered up the available supply, some 20 cases of rye and bourbon, and poured it, bottle by bottle, down a hole bored in the floor of his shack. Then he smashed the bottles inside a burlap sack, to deaden the sound, and scattered the fragments over the Barrier, so as to leave no trace. All winter long, supposing that the liquor had been moved to a new hiding place, Byrd's men spent their spare time prodding the Barrier with long brass rods, chanting:

> "Little Rod, won't you call
> When you've found the alcohol?"

Of this tragic decision, Byrd knew nothing. He was at Advance Base when it happened. Nevertheless he caught the brunt of the after-effects on his return to Little America in the spring, for his hardier explorers, after draining the compasses of alcohol, were then running mouth wash and a patent medicine called Dr. Baxter's Lung Preserver through a home-made still. The by-products, while producing a desirable numbness, left tempers vile.

Despite such distractions, a polar camp is hardly a gay, inspiring place. For every hour of excitement and mental stimulation, there are two haunted with emptiness or hungry memories. And because the Admiral is a gregarious soul, it puzzles his friends that he should want to return to the Antarctic again. The paradox is accentuated by his family life, which is no different from that of any successful man of good family. In Boston, the Byrds occupy an old-fashioned, five-story brick house, on the "water side" of Beacon Hill. They summer in Maine, either at South West Harbor, where the Admiral owns a small cove, or on the mainland at East Sullivan, where he recently purchased a 1,000-acre tract, surrounding a baronial clubhouse, from a group of sportsmen. His son, Dickie, is a sophomore at Harvard; his three daughters, still in their teens, attend the fashionable Winsor School in Boston. The Admiral himself is a member of such a Boston club as the late George Apley would have approved, the

Somerset, and there are few Americans of importance, from the Roosevelts (both branches), the Fords, the Rockefellers and on down, whom this lonely and intrepid wanderer does not know.

With the hero, as with the politician, the point is academic as to whether the office sought the man, or the man the office. The press is given to casting men into stereotyped roles, and Byrd has long been labelled HERO in the public mind. That he is, with Col. Lindbergh, an international symbol of the undaunted man of action is not to be denied; neither is the fact that many people, for reasons they find hard to define, do not altogether like him. As to that, one explanation may be that no man could possibly be the hero the public would like him to be. The Admiral is not unaware of the frailties of his role, and has constantly sought to widen his life.

Byrd looks upon himself as something of a mystic. He has peered at Christian Science and for a while he flirted with the Oxford Group. The desire to *believe*, to find "some replenishing philosophy," that persuaded him to go off by himself on the Shelf Ice, made it possible for him to ignore the opposition of his expedition. And the ambition to shape a universal peace movement had its inspiration in a similar desire to take root in some universal substance. When that came to nothing, there remained the Antarctic. And as Byrd once said at Little America: "You can forget the world here. There are no temptations. The only littleness is the littleness of man's mind."

AUTOBIOGRAPHY

THE EDUCATION OF AN AMERICAN

MARK SULLIVAN

Summer evenings, after supper, with the chores all done, we, with the youths from four or five neighboring farms, would gather at the bridge by the crossroads. Too tired for any kind of play, infected by the mood of the descending dusk, we would sit, some on the railings of the bridge, some on the fence, observing who was "going the road," and quietly talking. The talk was of girls and sex; of murders described in papers that came to us from the cities, and of the one ancient murder in our own neighborhood—it provided conversation for a decade (we Irish knew that merit lies not so much in a new tale as in an old tale well told); of local minor crimes; of the tricks of thieves, the one who reversed the shoes on a stolen horse so that pursuers tracking him would think he was going in the opposite direction. Some talk there was of baseball, though the irregularity of our access to daily papers kept us unfamiliar with the scores of professional games. One time or another most of us had seen a game between two locally celebrated teams, the respective prides of two larger towns near by, the Mohicans of Kennett Square and the Brandywines of West Chester. Very much talk there was of prize fights—the one in which John L. Sullivan won the championship from Jake Kilrain was to us a much more vital event than the victory of Cleveland over Harrison. We Sullivan boys, bearing the new champion's name, had by that fortuitous fact an elevation above our fellows.

So far as our crossroads evenings dealt with our ambitions, most of our talk was of "the West"; in that time and place "going West" was the most alluring of anticipations, at once an adventure and a career. Of the dozen farm youths who used to sit by that roadside bridge, half went West. One slipped away without telling his parents, and they never heard from him; two others also disappeared into death or silence—years later, after I had gone into the world and returned for visits, the parents of the lost sons would ask me had I, in my travels, heard anything of Johnny, or Gene, or Will. One youth of the neighborhood, older than I, who had gone West some years before, used to come back once a year, bringing with him a carload of Western horses to sell to the farmers. His little cavalcade, moving up the country road, was a stimulant to our ambitions. One youth who had gone West some years before was a cowboy on a ranch along the Little Missouri River, owned by a dude from New York. Years later, when the cowboy had returned to live a quiet life in the neighborhood that was his old home and mine, and when the dude ranch owner had become President Theodore Roosevelt, I helped to bring it about that Roosevelt should make his former cowboy postmaster of one of our neighborhood villages.

II

The contour of the land about my home could be compared to a shallow saucer, a mile or two in diameter. On the little rise in the middle of the saucer stood our house; from there the land sloped down very gently to a belt of meadows, in which quiet little streams meandered. Beyond the meadows the land sloped gently upward again, to the rim of the saucer, which was the horizon of my boyhood. That a boy should wonder what went on beyond that rise of land was a natural result of that kind of environment. That he should contemplate someday crossing the rise to see the scenes beyond was the most boyish of traits.

The condition was accentuated by the relation of the railroads to our home. There was no railroad in sight of the house, but just over the horizon were two branch lines, both so near that the passing of the train was always heard. The sounds of the engine bell and the rumble of the cars were a perpetual allurement. On one of the railroads the train, though out of sight on the other side of the horizon, passed at one point so close that by going to one of the upstairs windows I could almost, yet not quite, see the top of the locomotive stack. I was able to see the upward surging of the smoke as it came from the stack, in winter curling crisply.

One railroad, somewhat farther off, had a definite psychological effect on me. The main line of the Baltimore & Ohio was about nine miles away. Ordinarily the whistle of its locomotive could not be heard; but on frosty winter nights it came faint yet plain through the cold, clear air. The B. & O. trains, unlike those on the branch railroads nearer home, were expresses. They went with a thundering dash, and the whistle of them, heard across the hills as I stood on our porch on winter evenings, had a kind of rushing impetuousness, a headlong imperativeness, a summons to adventure; a call to Carcassonne—they were going to distant places, and sometime I must go too.

All of us, as we reached adolescence or a little later, left the farm; first to boarding school and then to jobs in the city. We never came back. The passage of the seven sons down that farm lane was as inexorable as an operation of nature. Our parents put no impediment in the way; on the contrary, the going to boarding school was encouraged, would have been insisted upon had insistence been necessary. They had come to know that the packing of the trunk for school was a ceremonial of permanent parting; after finishing school we would be off to the cities, and we would not return except for visits. They did not repine; or if ever they did, they did not let us know; they put no plea of sentiment in the way. My father occasionally, when one of us was looking forward to the city, would say that farming was a good life, that no city occupation could be better, but he said it in the spirit of what he thought was best for us. If in his mind there was ever any wish to keep us with him, any concern about being alone when he should come to old age and the farm work would be too much for him, he never let us see it. I, the youngest, was the last to go. I was not yet fourteen. As my father drove me to the station, my trunk in the back of the wagon, he gave me parental advice, with emphasis that I should "take care of my soul." He knew that he was launching the last of his brood from the nest, and forever. Excepting summer vacations from boarding school, and occasionally for a few weeks or months between jobs, none of us came back to live.

Our visits home were frequent; all but one of us were within one to three hours' distance; one or the other of us would be back, perhaps one Sunday out of four; and on Fourth of July and Christmas all of us together. The gathering on Christmas Eve, the table heaped by my mother with turkey, oysters, vegetables and pies, was a true festival, a spontaneous jollity. There comes to my mind a jest that I had not thought of for many a year. My mother had two or three kinds of pie, among which each son had his liking. The preference of one of my brothers was mince. When my mother, happy and hurried, cut into the crust and found it was raisin, the incident was occasion for laughter and teasing. My brother had a quip for the occasion: my mother, when she baked, ought to put distinguishing marks on the pie crust while it was yet soft—on the mince "T. M." for " 'tis mince"; on the others "T. M." for " 'tain't mince." After dinner there was playing the fiddle and dancing, my mother the only woman, and later, talking, long talking until after midnight, and finally the Rosary, all kneeling, my father leading, the rest of the family responding.

The following day, late in the afternoon, all would leave, usually walking to the station. I can remember them, on occasions when I was young and remained behind, going down the porch steps, crossing the yard, laughing as they raced with each other, and in their young vitality leaping the fence of the field they crossed. I lived to see them on visits years later, very willing to open the gate and walk with the staidness of men beginning to age.

That my father and mother were lonely when we were gone I knew very well. Age crept upon them. Coming back, I would find my father spending longer and longer afternoon hours on the settee near the warm kitchen stove. I knew they wished we would come oftener, though they never said so. Usually I did not tell them to expect me, but would appear, as a rule on Sunday morning, coming afoot by the path that led from the village across the fields. The path arrived at the farm at a point between the barn and the corncrib, so that the buildings concealed my approach until I was within a few score yards of the house. Once as I rounded the corner of the barn I saw, through the kitchen window, my mother. She was leaning, her hands resting on the window sill, peering out over her spectacles toward the opening between the barn and corncrib. She knew when the one Sunday morning train was due at the village, could hear it arrive and could calculate the time it would take for one of her sons, if he came, to reach the point at which she could see him. I reflected that many a Sunday morning she had leaned and peered without seeing any of her sons, and turned and sighed and resigned herself to another week of waiting, hoping nothing was wrong with her boys.

On another occasion I had ridden my bicycle to visit my brother, who at the time lived in a village some four or five miles from the farm. I counted on staying with my brother until Sunday afternoon, when I would ride my bicycle to the farm, visit my parents for an hour or so, and then take the train back to my work. But after I set out from my brother's this day something went wrong with my bicycle, requiring about an hour to fix before I could go on. The road by which I came approached the farm in such a way that I could see the house when I came within half a mile of it. As I rounded a turn and looked at the house I could see my father sitting on the porch. He had placed his chair far out on the end, where he could see farthest down the road upon which any of his sons, if they came, might arrive. On his lap he had his little fox terrier, which he was stroking. He looked lonely and old. I realized it all; but I had lost the hour I intended to spend with him, and if I was to catch the train back to my work I must hurry on to the station, keeping to the road, which at its nearest point to the house was a field away. I thought that merely to call out to him without going on up to see him would mystify and disturb him. At the crossroads at the corner of the farm I took the turn to the railroad station. I have had my share of experiences I would rather not have had, and memories I would prefer to forget; of them, that Sunday afternoon when I chose work and duty above pleasure to a lonely old man is the most poignant.

I, PATIENCE

PATIENCE, RICHARD, AND JOHN ABBE

กฎกฎกฎกฎกฎกฎกฎกฎกฎกฎกฎกฎกฎกฎกฎกฎกฎ

I

Richard, Johnny and I were born in Paris. I, Patience, was born in a hospital and so was Richard on the Boulevard de la Saussaye. Johnny the littlest was born in the Rue de Val de Grace in a Studio. Johnny has red hair, I have blond hair and Richard has brown hair. Our servant Antoinette carried me, Patience, on a pillow, to Monsieur le Curé so I could get my name, Patience.

Now the reason why I am called Patience is this. When Mamma was in the hospital waiting for me, and that was quite a while, her nurse told her she must have patience and so did the doctor. She tried her best, so when I did come Mamma looked in my basket and said to herself, "Well, there is my patience" and so that is why I am called Patience. But Mamma told me that Monsieur le Curé said there wasn't any such name as Patience in France. It was a word.

Mamma took us to see the first house that I, Patience, ever lived in after I got born. Mamma called it a "hut." She brought me from the hospital wrapped up in a long red Italian shawl to this hut. It was all hidden behind a tall stone wall, and you had to walk up a long, long lane to it, and the walls were covered with vines and honeysuckle. Then you came suddenly to a door like in "Hansel and Gretel" and this was the hut. You couldn't take a bath in that place when you had company because the bathtub was right at the head of the stairs which went up to the two bedrooms, and there was a dining salon and little kitchen which opened up right into a lovely garden and all hidden away. Papa got this hut from a Russian lady who escaped from the Revolution and next door lived a Baronne and Baron

From The Atlantic Monthly, March, 1936, also Around the World in Eleven Years, F. A. Stokes Co., by permission of Polly Shorrocks Abbe.

and they had all the pictures of the Czar's family hanging up because the Baron had been an officer of the Czar. He was working in a bank and could speak every language, and she was saleslady at Patou's. Her brother spent all his day teaching tennis and he was very unhappy because he could do better than this. They lived on their pearls and by now they must be all gone because when they were escaping from Russia the Baronne sold one pearl after another of her long string so they could get bread, and she lost all her three children from the pest, because sometimes in Turkey they had to work burying dead bodies that died of the pest. But they were very valiant.

Mamma's femme de ménage used to clean up the house and cook the lunch and then when she was leaving she would collect all the snails on the garden wall for her own lunch. The Russian lady whom we got this hut from died and her little daughter was taken in by the Baronne. She was very pitiful.

Then Mamma showed me the second house I ever lived in and this was a little pavilion behind Madame Darzans' house This was also in a beautiful garden and flowers were all around. But Mamma said Madame Darzans said she thought Mamma was either a very cruel woman or else insane because Mamma used to leave me out in the garden all day long in my berceau. And when it rained then Mamma said she wrapped me up in the lovely Italian shawl and left me in the berceau only she put an umbrella over me. And Mamma said the nice wet air made my cheeks as red as the shawl, but Madame Darzans used to come and argue with Mamma when it rained even though Mamma said I loved the umbrella. But Mamma said I stayed out in the rain with my umbrella no matter what Madame Darzans said.

Mamma said I, Patience, was supposed to be born, because while I was waiting to be born, Mamma fainted and fell off a bus on the Champs-Elysées. When Mamma woke up a crowd was standing around her and arguing, and she couldn't understand one word they were saying. Then suddenly a voice said in an American accent, "My husband is a doctor and we live right around here." So this lady took Mamma to her husband, and he made Mamma walk up and down for twenty minutes, and I didn't get born then, so this man said Mamma was all right.

This was the time Mamma didn't have any place to live. She and Papa were living at the Hotel de la Grande Bretagne on the

Rue Caumartin but one day the clerk cashed a check for 35 pounds for Papa into francs and when they collected they found that they had made a mistake in the exchange from pounds to francs and the hotel had given too many francs, and Papa didn't have the money to make up the difference, because he and Mamma had spent the 35 pounds. So since it is a crime to make a Frenchman lose anything, they thought it was a crime about this, and locked Papa's and Mamma's luggage in their rooms, and Papa and Mamma were on the street without even a toothbrush and not one sou in their pockets. And it was Easter and all the English were on holiday in Paris and all the small hotels were full, and you couldn't go into a big hotel without any luggage without paying in advance. So Mamma and Papa were on the streets. So Papa finally got his lawyer and borrowed fifty francs, and they went to two hotels, one each night, but they were rented after that. Then Mamma fell off the bus. So this lady said, "I shall put you in a taxi. What is your address?" Mamma didn't want to go in the taxi because she didn't have a sou. So Mamma said, "Oh, I live over there," but she couldn't thing of the name of any hotel. So then Mamma said, "Well, send me to the Café de la Paix," and Mamma was sweating all the way for fear Papa wouldn't be there to pay for the taxi, if he had the money. But luckily he was there watching the world go by and he rescued Mamma and then took Mamma down and bought her an ice-cream soda with the last three francs he had.

So then Mamma and Papa went over to a hotel in the Rue de Seine, and Mamma looked up at the little window in the ceiling and said, "If I am dead when I wake up, all will be well." Then the lady at this hotel stopped Mamma and Papa in the morning, and Mamma and Papa hadn't had any dinner the night before, and this lady said, "You don't look as though you are accustomed to coming to a hotel like this," and she gave Papa 100 francs, and Papa and Mamma went to the Deux Maggots and ate ten croissants apiece and four café au lait, and then after three days Papa paid this lady the 100 francs, and all this happened just before I was born.

But Papa had a good time before Johnny was born because he discovered how to stop all the traffic in Paris. He would take Mamma out in our Citroën and yell to the agents de police, "Femme enceinte," which means, "Woman with child," and the agent de police would stop all the trolley-cars and autos until Papa got by. Once Papa ran into a trolley-car and Mamma was on the trolley-car side and our Citroën went up, up in the air, but it didn't tip over, and then Papa and Mamma and all the agents de police and all the people began arguing, and then Papa said, "Femme enceinte," and everybody stopped arguing and the agent de police raised his stick and made way for Papa and Mamma, and everybody was saying, "Pardon, pardon!"

Mamma and we the children could get on all the buses and trolley-cars first because she had children with her, no matter how long the people on line had to wait and no matter how first their numbers were. The conductor would push everybody aside to let ladies with children on first and no one ever argued about it. Because you can go to jail for hitting anyone in Paris, that is why the French people argued so. You can't do anything to the French for arguing.

When Johnny was about to be born Lindbergh flew right over our studio at Val de Grace, so Mamma and Papa got into the Citroën with Aigner his secretary and they went racing out to Le Bourget to see Lindbergh land. And Papa said on the way a lot of other people in Paris had thought of the same thing so that the road was full of cars and no one could move an inch backwards or forwards. And all the French were arguing and talking. Then Mamma suddenly got some pains in her belly and Papa and Aigner got sweat on their heads because they couldn't get out of the car with Mamma, and even if Papa yelled "Femme enceinte" it wouldn't do any good, because all the cars were packed in like sardines. So while they waited to get somewhere they picked out the house they thought it would be nice to have Johnny born in on the side of the road, but Mamma then didn't get Johnny that night, but she nearly did, Papa said. Then suddenly down the line of buses and cars the French began, "Il a arrivé, Fantastique!" etc. And everyone was talking very excited. Then, Papa said, suddenly they were all very quiet thinking about this nice little fellow who flew over the ocean like an eagle, then suddenly one man said to the crowd, "Well, Messieurs, how do you think he—" And everybody laughed until they were hysterical. Of course, the French would think of a thing like that.

When Johnny came into the world Mamma had a new carriage because the one she had for Richard and me was like a gondola with big high wheels and the part you sat in was like a boat. But every time we moved in this carriage it tipped over, so Mamma said to save our skulls she had to buy a new carriage which had little tiny wheels and a big high box which you couldn't fall out of even when you stood up. But Mamma loved the gondola and we did too. Mémé, who was Mamma's Mamma, pushed Richard and me all over Paris in that gondola.

II

We lived in lots of places in France besides Paris. We lived in Normandie, Cannes, Juan Les Pins, St. Cloud and Neuilly. Whenever we moved we moved in two taxicabs, and once when we were moving to Le Touquet we had four taxicabs and just as we were getting into the gare our pot-de-chambre fell out of our luggage and rolled all over the gare. Aunt Hope Williams who was J. D. Williams' wife, and they were lovely people, came with us, and when we got into the train Aunt Hope said, "If we hadn't caught this train after I got up at five this morning to help you get off, I would not have gone with you." And Mamma said, "Well, you don't have to go even yet; the train isn't going very fast yet," and Aunt Hope said, "That's right, I didn't have to come, but I'll see it through."

When we lived at Val de Grace, Mahonri Young and Paul Manship lived in the court by us. This was a marvelous rich place. The best thing about it was that you could go in through three doors. You could go in through the kitchen, or a door into the dining-room. Then there was a winding staircase that went around and around made of iron, and on the second floor was Mémé's rooms, then you went up the winding staircase to the third floor and there was the maid's room and a bathroom and another room and a cabinet, then Mamma's room which had blue carpet on the floor which your feet sank into. The walls were all yellow silk and the bed, which didn't have any top to it, had a yellow satin thick cover on it and there was a golden mirror behind the bed on the wall. And there was a fireplace. Then you opened the door of Mamma's room and went down three steps into an entrée which the staircase of the studio came into and then there was the studio all glass with a balcony inside and out. And there was a large piano and a round table with benches which Harry Lachman found on the floor of a castle and made into this table and benches. It had designs on it. You didn't have to go out the same door you went in at if you didn't want to in that house, just like our house in St. Cloud. Harry

Lachman was an artist who rented us the studio, and now he is a director in Hollywood.

M. Perrin one day got the Nobel prize and M. Clemenceau came in our garden and saw me, Patience, and said, "What is your name, little cauliflower?" And I said, "Patience." And he said, "Tiens, tiens." And then he said, "How is your papa called?" And I said, "Abbe." So he said, "What a family."

Lélé and her husband lived next door. Her husband was a professor in the Sorbonne. Lélé was very nice and she and Mémé our grandma used to take us out in the Luxembourg gardens every day. Lélé couldn't speak English and Grandma couldn't speak French, so I, Patience, explained things to them.

We played with three children in the court and Jacqueline wrote a note to Lélé and said, "Paquit est très gentille quand elle dort. Richard est très gentil. Il est plus gentil que Paquit."

Downstairs under our studio lived a sick lady whom no one knew what was the matter with. After she died Mahonri Young came to live there. But this sick lady looked like a queen and came from Tennessee. One day she came in to Mémé because she loved Mémé and said that Ambassador Herrick had come to see her that afternoon and she was mortified because our bonne had all the diapers out in our garden. But she was only imagining this because our diapers were hung in the drying-room and no Ambassador had come to see her. Gardens in France are to sit in and no one EVER hangs clothes in them.

This lady loved Mamma sometimes and sometimes didn't. One night she screamed and broke all her windows and Mamma ran in to her, but she said, "I don't want you. I want Mémé." So Mémé went in and sat with her all night. And this lady lay in her bed all night and stared at the ceiling and said to Mémé, "If I could only die so that my husband would not have a scandal." This lady then went out on a stretcher one day, and she died and no one knew how she did it.

I had a birthday at Val de Grace, and Aunt Henriette Metcalf and Aunt Thelma Colman, Ronald Colman's wife, brought us dishes and books. We liked Val de Grace. L'Hôpital Militaire was on the corner and there were lots of soldiers' funerals. Once a soldier took out an avion and drove it right under the Tour Eiffel. He hit a telegraph wire and was killed. We saw the funeral.

One evening at Val de Grace Mamma was coming in and she saw a little old lady hunting in the garbage pail for food for her fifty cats. She lived on the Rue St. Jacques around the corner in an attic with another poor lady who was crazy. Her name was Anna. Mamma said to Anna, "If you will come to our kitchen every night we shall give you food so you won't have to go in the garbage can." Anna was good to us and insisted upon washing our dishes for us instead of the femme de ménage. Mémé always saved our coffee for her and eggs. One day when we came back from Paris Plage Anna was dead. They found her sitting so quiet in her attic with her fifty cats crying, and because she was so good everybody all around went to her funeral.

Mamma took us to the Louvre in Paris when we were very little. I remember a picture of a Prince with a collar around his neck and a lady was painting him.

We went to the circus often in Paris. It was much better than the American circus because they show one show at a time and we sat in a circle and could see everything. We were frightened of the Fratellinis because they had their faces painted white. We liked Grock because he was quiet. The Fratellinis had sixteen children, but Papa said they didn't own all of them. They took some in off the streets, and made clowns of them.

We liked the agents de police because they were kind to you. Once Mamma had to get an agent de police because Tina our cook was giving all her money to the boys in the bistrot. I remember she used to sit in the bistrot with the boys and let us play outside on the street. Mamma thought she had us in the park. We all cried when Tina went away with the agent de police because Tina used to read stories to us.

But once the agents de police took Papa to jail. Mamma didn't like Michelle, the Italian who attended to our chauffage Central. So one day Michelle didn't do right and Mamma hit him with a broom and beat him real hard, and Michelle ran out and got an agent de police. Then Mamma put her fist in Michelle's face and Michelle jumped and then Michelle and the agent de police began to argue, then Mamma argued and it was a big argument. Then Papa came rushing down from the studio and there was a terrible argument. Then the agent de police took Papa and Michelle to jail, and Mamma said she was going to go around and fight all the agents de police and Michelle and everybody. Papa said, "You are acting like a fishwife." And Mamma said, "Well, I don't care." And she wanted to go and hit Michelle again. But in Paris you go to jail if you hit anybody, so that is why the agent de police took Papa and Michelle to jail. And

Mémé said, "Imagine acting like that to Mamma," and Antoinette looked very scared. But then Mamma kept saying, "I don't care, I don't care, I wanted to hit Michelle for two years, and now I have done it." And Michelle was very big and fat too, but he ran away from Mamma. Then Mamma ran up the studio stairs and pretty soon we heard her arguing in the studio and soon Aigner, Papa's Hungarian secretary, came rushing down and said, "Madame is very angry." So then pretty soon we heard Mamma taking a bath and the shower going very hard. After awhile I, Patience, went up to her yellow silk room and there was Mamma sitting in bed putting pretty pink on her nails and in her black nightgown you could see through and the yellow satin cover over her. When she saw me she said, "Bon jour, Madame," and I said, "Bon jour, Madame, will you have your tea now?" So Mamma said, "Please, Madame, tell Antoinette to send it up on a tray." Mamma always apologizes when she loses her temper with us, but she never did apologize to anyone for Michelle. Then Papa came back from the jail, but he nor anybody else bothered Mamma again all that day.

Mamma is very excitable. Once when Tina was dressing us in the morning Mamma came in and left her bedroom door open and Papa was naked taking his exercises and Papa slammed the door after Mamma, and Mamma opened the door and was mad, and Papa slammed the door, and then Mamma kicked the door and then went out to school with us instead of Tina, and wouldn't have breakfast with Papa. Of course, I, Patience, would never live with a man who slammed a door in MY face.

Of course Mamma is always mad at Papa. And she always says she made a mistake to take up with a photographer. We asked her why, once, and she said, "Oh, photographers think you can live on air." Papa is a very poor business man, but he does no one any harm. He just doesn't understand about money. He is always spending a lot of money and when Mamma says, "Where is some money?" he says, "What money?" Then he gives Mamma all the money and then after a while she saves it, then he says, "Mamma, have you any money?" So then Mamma groans.

Of course when Mamma gets VERY mad Papa says, "Well, you still think you are a showgirl. You just won't forget that. You didn't get anywhere on the stage." Then Mamma says, "Is that so! Well, if I hadn't had the MISFORTUNE to meet you and you hadn't run all over the place after me and I just couldn't shake you, maybe I'd have got somewhere. Besides, if you hadn't been in the way I might have married that Ambassador." And Papa laughs and says, "Poor Mamma!"

And Papa says, "You mustn't mind Mamma, children. She's Irish." Then Mamma says, "And if it were not for the Irish, where would you be?" Then Papa says, "Well, look at my scrapbooks," and Mamma says, "Yes, look at them. But I don't see any money in the bank. What I want is money in the bank. And the next trip you go on don't think you are going to leave me holding any more bags." But then these fights don't last only a little while and then everything is all right again, and we go on a trip. And Papa says, "I'd rather have this Mamma for your Mamma than any other one," and we think the same.

III

Once Papa went off on a trip to Mexico for Uncle Szafranski. So we moved to Hennequeville which is in Normandie. Our house was a very rich house and we had Denise and Antoinette and Emil and later a cook working for us. The people who owned this house were our laundry people. Her sister was Madame Thereau who lived next door. She had been a femme de chambre for thirty-four years to a marquise, so now she was rich and owned her house and some other houses around and was "bourgeoisie." She didn't speak to everyone in the village. Only to special people. And when she went to church every Sunday she wore a black silk dress, ten petticoats, a hat that sat way up on her head, and black gloves. She used to come to our barrière and say, "Are you ready?" and we would come out all dressed up very chic and march behind her up to the church and sit in her pew which was the richest in the church.

Madame Thereau was 74 years old and very tall and had a mustache. She had a big breast and always walked with her hands on her belly. She adored Johnny because Johnny was singing the whole day long. And she used to take the three of us into her kitchen and divide one apple in equal parts between us.

Monsieur Thereau was 74 years old and never had been twenty miles away from home in all his life. He could cook. So when Mamma didn't have a cook, he bought Mamma's lapin and chicken and roasts and cooked them for her, because he said to eat is an art and to cook a religion.

But finally we got a cook. She was a woman as old as Mémé

and when Mémé got sick she was very good to Mémé because Mémé couldn't have salt in her food, so she used to set Mémé's place with leaves and flowers and make it look nicer than it tasted.

We never ate at table with Mémé and Mamma and Papa. We had our own table, and we were very polite then. We are not so polite in America now.

Our cook was very strict and used to say to Mamma, "Madame, I do not care if lunch is at four o'clock, so long as thè family is here to eat it at the hour you say they will be here." So Mamma had to worry all the time we were at the Deauville Plage to get us home in time for the cook. Because this cook made good food and considered it a sin not to be respected.

Our house in Hennequeville was called Le Clos Fleuri because we had lots of flowers in our garden. We had a donkey cart. Emil used to drive us in it to the marché at Deauville. The fishwives would say, "Eh, voilà, Madame. When you see the ear of the fish dripping purple and splendid then you know you do not offend God by eating the stale fish that the English eat." And she would pull up the ear of the fish and have Mamma look good and hard and then sell Mamma the fish. The butcher would say, "Eh, voilà, Madame. Do you need a lovely new fresh beautiful heart to-day? Renew your heart, Madame. Cannot you refresh yourself with a new set of brains? Delicious cooked in golden butter. I have also new kidneys to sell, and creamy, juicy magnificent tripe." This market was very gay.

We used to go to Deauville every morning at eleven and bathe, and there we saw Mistinguett and Von Dongen and all the people people know. Mistinguett took pictures of us for the cinema because Johnny would never wear his culotte on the beach. Gilda Gray and Gil Boag came to see us and took us up to Saint Simeon where we had tea, and played croquet on the lawn. Aunt Gilda became very angry at the English people because they played too much croquet during tea-time, and we almost had a fight.

Once we met an artist, and so he invited us all up to his villa for tea. When we got there the next day his wife was Scotch and had eight children, six hers and two his. They had a pool in their garden and had lots of funny people from England "dropping in," and this Frenchman would say about some of them, "Such bounders. All puffed up and bragging about knowing Augustus Johns, the painter." "No real dignity in life." But he liked us, and his French children had a nurse who was very old because she had been their mother's nurse too, and once this nurse went on holiday and she got sick and came running right back because she thought she might die away from her folks.

Sylvia Chen came to see us in Hennequeville. We were rich then. We had twelve rooms in our house. Her father Eugene Chen came also but he didn't live with us like Sylvia. He wore light silk suits and because he was Chinese wanted to live in peace in a hotel by himself.

Sylvia Chen went with Mamma to baccara. She wore a black Chinese pajama, very soft and silky and her hair was all black and hanging down and her eyes were black. But she said she was a Communist and wouldn't stay in the baccara room even after paying 150 francs to get in because she said the air was polluted with Capitalism. These people in the baccara spend lots of money, so I suppose they were Capitalists. But Mamma said lots of them were there trying to be Capitalists. Then we went to the cinema at the Casino and saw our pictures on the plage and Mistinguett showed us the ones she took too. She just loved me, Patience, and said Richard looked like a Prince and Johnny was "droll" because he walked up and down the plage without a stitch on, and no one could make him keep his culotte on.

Once Johnny caused some excitement at Hennequeville. The boy from the bistrot on the corner came running and said Johnnie was walking on the cliff down below our villa. Everybody in the two bistrots came running with Mamma, and we found Johnny walking along just as they said, so he came home with us, but after that we tied him up with a rope to a tree, and he didn't walk on any more cliffs after that.

When we went to the Bal d'Enfant, Mamma put a smoking on Richard and dressed me in my baptism dress with real lace from Malta and it trailed on the ground. Then when we got to the Casino Mamma sent us marching across the dance hall, my arm in Richard's and the orchestra played and everybody was having tea and said, "Regarde! Regarde!" and right then Richard had to go and slip on the floor which was very slippery and fell on his derrière. But then we went in and walked up to the judges at the Bal d'Enfant, my hand in Richard's arm. Then we danced and then suddenly they rang a bell, and the judges said, "Le Petit Marquis Abbe et son épouse, le premier prix," and we got a gold snake bracelet and a satin handkerchief case with perfume, which is still in Mamma's trunk in Paris with her African blankets, Mexican blankets, sheets and everything and the hat that the Spanish Count took off his head and gave Mamma. Some day we shall get these things again.

Once Mamma and I, Patience, went on the little schooner over the channel to Le Havre. All the French were very seasick, but there was one man who was English and he sat himself down and put a robe over him, placed a vomiting pan under his chin and then began to read his paper. He wasn't a bit excited, but the French were groaning and saying, "Mon Dieu! Mon Dieu!" and they were all green. Mamma and I stayed well.

Madame Thereau always took us to church on Sundays. Monsieur l'Abbé had many funerals in his church and weddings. His church was two hundred and fifty years old and he never asked the people to come to church.

Emil made cider in our garage from apples. He had a machine, but he used to walk on the apples. The cider was very good. All the people in Normandie had rotten teeth from drinking cider and Mamma wouldn't let us have any.

Monsieur and Madame Jeanne who were our laundry people were very careful like all the French and money was very good to them. So when they built this house we lived in they put rich furniture in it and had lovely curtains and a kitchen with a brick floor. But they forgot about being careful about the water pipes and so to save money built all the water pipes on the outside of the house and so saved a lot of money.

But one night it was very cold in the winter and all the French were groaning with the cold and the highway was all icy from the cold rain, and suddenly about two o'clock in the morning Mémé called out and said we were all drowning. We all had our own bedrooms and slept alone in them in our own beds. So Mamma came out in her slippers and dressing-gown and we all stood up in bed and our beds were floating in a river and the water was rushing down the stairs from the attic. So Mamma rushed out, Papa was in Mexico, and yelled up to Emil next door, and she yelled for twenty minutes or so and then threw stones up on the shutters. In France everyone shuts themselves in with shutters at night and shut their windows too and then pull down their curtains, so that is why it is hard for anyone to hear you on the outside. So then Emil put his head out the window and wanted to know what was the matter. And Mamma said, "Where is the robinet to shut off the water? We are drowning in Le Clos Fleuri!" So finally after another fifteen or twenty minutes Emil came down all dressed and went into the garden by the barrière and dug up a big stone, then shoveled out some straw and then turned off the robinet, but by that time our house was drowned and Mémé couldn't get out of her bed and we couldn't get out of ours because if we had we would have drowned. So Mamma and Emil took brooms and swept the water down the stairs and it ran like a dam, and the Jeannes didn't save any money at all by putting their pipes outside, because the house was ruined.

IV

Mémé we loved and she loved us. One day Mamma said to Mémé, "We shall all go to the cinema at Trouville." So Mamma got a little carriage and took Mémé down to a café and gave her Eau gaseuse. Then we went to the cinema and all the time Mémé was very quiet. But when we wanted to go Mémé could not get up from her seat and three men carried her out into a taxicab and we were all crying and Mémé's mouth was hanging down funny and she couldn't speak. Then Madame Thereau and Mamma helped Mémé to her room and our old doctor came up. He was 70 years old and very strict but good. He said, "Stroke." So that night Mamma took the car out, Papa was in Mexico. Mamma went down to Deauville and woke up the Pharmacy and got a bottle of leeches. Then Mamma tried to put these leeches on Mémé's leg because we couldn't get a sister from the hospital. But the leeches crawled all over the floor. So Mamma got these leeches again into the bottle and one by one made them bite Mémé by holding them on Mémé's leg with a piece of cotton. We were all crying because Mémé was maybe going to disappear soon.

But Mémé's mouth got better the next day and pretty soon she could walk, so she sat all day in the garden and was very sick and looked sad. Then Papa came home from Mexico because we couldn't go to Mexico because of Mémé's heart and took Mémé to Paris and we went on the train. Then Mémé got all purple in our room at the Hotel Excelsior, and Madame Pages owned this hotel and loved Mémé and made Mémé lovely rice. Papa said, "Let me persuade Mémé to go to the American Hospital," because Mémé was afraid of hospitals. So then Mémé said, "Yes." So then Papa put Mémé in our car and we went to the door with her and Madame Pages and Mémé looked back and smiled so sad like as though she would never see us again, and she said, "Goodbye, little loves, goodbye." But the next day we went to the American Hospital in Neuilly and Mémé said, "I thought you were not coming." So we went every day to see Mémé and she was in a lovely white bed and she wanted all our pictures which she kept in a big bag for herself.

Then one day Mémé saw Richard whom she loved more than anyone else in the world and she called him Johnny. Mémé was out of her mind. We said, "This is little Johnny, Mémé. Here is Richard." And Mémé looked at Richard and said, "How are you, little Johnny my love?" And she always kept calling Richard Johnny.

Then one day Madame Guignard whom we called Lele because Richard couldn't pronounce her name and called her "lady" and pronounced it "lele" was there and crying and Mémé got out of bed and sat on a chair and said, "It is beautiful, the sun." Then Mémé disappeared. But Mamma said she waited even though she was dead for Mamma to come once again to see her. After that she was really dead. But we saw Mémé in an avion riding on top of the sky and an angel was driving it. So we never saw Mémé again, and she was the only grandma we ever had. We did not know Mémé disappeared until after the funeral, and Mamma should have let us walk in the procession behind Mémé because she was our Mémé and no one else's. And no one ever had a better Mémé than we had and we shall never forget her. But anyway Mémé is sitting on a golden chair with God in God's house and has no pain and sees that we come to no harm and still loves us. It was only her body that went in the box.

So we didn't go back to our house in Hennequeville. But we remembered how we could see the great ships that went to America from Le Havre from our windows. We could hear the sea from our villa and see it from all our windows. And the great ships would go BOOM, BOOM, BOOM and then go off and we wouldn't see them any more. So then Madame Thereau must have heard us when finally we went to America because the Europa went also BOOM, BOOM, BOOM.

v

We went to live in St. Cloud then and Richard and I went to school. We had to say our prayers every morning in that school. We all got a prize in that school. Everybody in the school, no matter whether you were good or bad. My prize was for recitation and reading. Richard's was for "tranquillité."

Our house was small and lovely and it had a garden. We had a garden party at St. Cloud and it was also a birthday party. Murray Anderson who hadn't seen Mamma since she'd been in his show brought Mamma twelve red roses with long, long stems and some beautiful candy. Marc Connelly came with his Mamma. Irene Franklin also came with her Papa. And there were lots of other people. Doc Hunt was also there. He was working in the Pasteur Institute and stayed with us a month. When he came our cook left and so he cooked our meals for us. Doc Hunt was very nice. He even found some bread on the top of the shelf in our kitchen which our cook had left there and he said it was the most beautiful mould he had ever seen in his life, and he never could have hoped to get anything like that in his life for the Pasteur Institute. Doc Hunt was a very tall man whose head reached up to the top of the door, and he was too thin because he drank cognac every twenty minutes for his health. He used to go around our house in St. Cloud and say, "This is stunning, simply stunning! The whole idea is stunning. These Abbes!"

One day Dr. Poe who is professor in Boulder was at our house for tea with his people and Eugene Chen who is a Chinaman and nearly had his head cut off once and escaped on the Gobi Desert from a General who also is a Chinaman was also at our house for tea and Doc Hunt and us were having lunch in the dining-room while Mr. Chen and the Poes had tea in the salon. Doc Hunt kept still saying, "These Abbes are stunning. They have such stunning ideas."

Doc Hunt could make wonderful spaghetti and always bought the meat and if it smelled he said it was tender, and it tasted all right. He should have been with us in Russia. He would have known what to do with our Russian meat when it smelled. He knew about germs.

When we lived at St. Cloud Pavlova danced at the Théâtre des Champs-Elysées. She saw me and liked me. Pavlova was a beautiful lady with beautiful thin legs and eyes that looked as though they had a lamp in them. She spoke to me also at the Théâtre de Deauville when we were in Normandie, and from that day on I have chosen to be a dancer, because Pavlova was like a flower and her legs danced so beautiful and so like music

and she was a great lady, so I am going to be the second Pavlova.
We all cried when she went to God's house.

One day in our garden in St. Cloud Mamma found a dog. She
was a police dog. She had St. Vitus dance, but Mamma got a dog
specialist. He said, "If I were you I'd kill that dog." But Mamma
said, "No."

So he took the dog, which we had by now called "Waif" and
kept her for eight days and Waif came home then and had two
sets of pups and not one of those pups had St. Vitus dance.

Jimmy Abbe stayed with us in St. Cloud. Jimmy Abbe is
Papa's son. One day we were on the beach at Mr. Frank Gould's
house at Cap d'Antibes. We decided we'd go up to have tea
with them. After tea we went on his motorboat. Johnny was
very afraid when the motorboat started. Johnny wanted to come,
so he got on and we went off. Jimmy Abbe and Richard sat in
the back. Mr. Gould was driving the boat. I was sitting in front
with him all alone. Johnny and the steward sat in the second
seat. Richard and Jimmy Abbe were very wet in the back seat
because the water was splashing on them. Johnny fell asleep. All
this time Mamma was in the hospital because that day they carried her out on a stretcher. We were all waiting outside, and
when they carried Mamma out Richard said, "Mamma's dead,"
but she wasn't. She had a pain in her stomach. In our garden at
Juan Les Pins there were many fig trees. We went to the house
of Jean Gabriel Doumergue at Cannes and he had a marble
table in his dining-room. He also had a Russian wolfhound,
beige color.

Bedford was Papa's valet. Papa found him on the road in
England and brought him to St. Cloud. He was always trying to
kiss our bonne, so she left because the English and French don't
get along. But that was all right because Doc Hunt came then.
He said he was only going to stay the week-end, but he stayed
a month.

Bedford went away one morning very early before we went
downstairs because he said the house was haunted. He said he
shut the cellar door and went to fix the garden and when he
came back the cellar door was open. And this kept right on
happening. And our house had a service entrance with a service
gate and a master's gate and a staircase ran right up the service
entrance through our bedrooms and down the master entrance.
Bedford said he heard a man in boots thumping up, over and
down this staircase. Doc Hunt said he acted like that because

everything was too stunning for him. So Bedford walked to Boulogne from Paris and is now safe in England.

When we left St. Cloud we have never been back to France since. We went in our car to Salzburg and left Mamma to finish the packing.

FOSSIL REMNANTS OF THE FRONTIER

Notes on a Utah Boyhood

BERNARD DE VOTO

She was going, she said, to summon Bat Masterson. We had
been tormenting her with the ingenious deviltries of childhood
and, one small blonde girl against a half-dozen boys, she now
proposed to stop it. The invocation brought us to an uneasy
pause. Thirty-odd years later, I remember the rustle of cotton-
woods while triumph glinted in her eyes and a light buggy came
up the road. It drew abreast, and manliness restrained us from
bolting but was not capable of a jeer. Two booted men in flannel
shirts and wide tan Stetsons sat in that buggy, and a shotgun
stuck out from under the seat. They were probably no more than
a couple of neighbors bound up "the canyon road" for quail, but
a dreadful name lent them awe. They passed. The blonde child
said, "That's Bat Masterson and I know him," then stuck out
her tongue and disdainfully walked away. The killer-sheriff was
not within a thousand miles at the moment, probably, but in
Ogden, Utah, at about 1904, his name was a sufficient dissuader
of boys.

One of my mother's stories dealt with a friend of hers who
married and went to some Wyoming town. There, after some
years, her husband was murdered, "on the very steps of the court-
house." The misdemeanor may not have been sanctioned but
there was no thought of arresting the misdemeanant. The widow
was acquainted with the usages: before the corpse was carried
away she dipped a token in the thickening blood. She would
save it until her son grew up; then, my mother said, she would
give it to him and bid him "wash the stain from your mother's
handkerchief." The tale sounds a theme from the border ballads

From *Forays and Rebuttals*, by Bernard De Voto. Reprinted by permission of Little, Brown, & Company.

of all ages but it is quite true. To a boy growing up in that culture it had solemnity but nothing of the inappropriate.

The last loose confederacies of rustlers and train robbers were not much later than my birth. In interior Utah and Wyoming there was still much gunfire and such galloping below the skyline as the movies were soon to reproduce, but it was done by individuals, not gangs, by remnants of an outmoded lodge, in a tradition now formalized and obsolete. It was as far as the moon from Ogden. We were Butch Cassidy or Tom Horn. We held up the U. P. at Tipton; we rode down fanning our guns at Laramie; at Winnemucca or Castlegate we robbed banks and turned in our saddles to deal with citizens reckless enough to level rifles at us; we rode back to Robbers' Roost or Hole in the Wall for the orgies that convention demanded. But there was no feeling that such romance was related to our time and place: we were as ritualistic as the boys I see to-day in Cambridge, Massachusetts, firing machine guns from automobiles at government agents who had had the effrontery to pursue John Dillinger.

Utah has little history of Indian trouble. This is due in part to Brigham Young's enlightened policy—he believed, soundly, that it was cheaper to feed Indians than to kill them off—but in greater part to the fact that the Indians of Utah were a degenerate race. The bellicose Utes belonged to the eastward, the Bannocks ranged far to the north, the Apaches seldom came up as far as the Grand Canyon, and the Navajos, who reached our border in greater numbers, were not warlike. The resident tribes were mostly Gosh-Utes and Diggers, technological unemployed, victims of the competitive Indian society which had forced them to the badlands, where such culture as they possessed decayed, sometimes below the use of fire. Thus it was that in the stories of the elders the red slayer was commonly just a beggar and a thief. They had been sufficiently sophisticated to trade on the reputation of their race, so that, finding a woman alone in a farmhouse, they might sometimes frighten her into largesse. But they could not often do even that; my grandmother, startled by the apparition of a blanketed and painted buck singing Injun in her dooryard, simply picked up the weapon known to her generation as a horse pistol. At sight of it the brave forsook the dooryard and the warpath in one stride. The air was full of Indian stories, located elsewhere, of course. Neighbors had ridden to Sand Creek or had campaigned with Custer or Connor or Crook; had fought off Ogallala attacks on wagon trains or stage stations;

had galloped to distant settlements and found the naked, scalped, and raped bodies of women, and children curiously dismembered and hung up. Distance was on all these tales, however, and the closest we boys came to them was in the distinction of one playmate. An uncle of his had been captured by Apaches, who cut off his eyelids and the soles of his feet and then tied him to a stake in an ant-bed and left him to the desert sun.

But we inherited the frontier's sentiments about Indians. The ones we saw, to be sure, were just grunting, dour, and mostly drunken grotesques, without terror, whom it was desirable not to approach too closely lest your mother be obliged to wash your hair with kerosene. But the Indian as an image of thought was a savage whose extermination was dictated by the necessities of civilization. The attitude survived long enough to immunize me against one sentimentality of my literary generation. As a historian, I have been able to understand the Indian's side of extermination and to master his strategy, but as a literary critic, I have been withheld from mysticism about the Amerind. I have not found him a beauty-lover, the creator of a deeply spiritual religion, or an accomplished metaphysician who plumbed eternal secrets which his brutish conqueror could never understand. Sibylline women and rapt men from megalopolis have been unable to persuade me that his neolithic culture was anything but a neolithic culture. Remembering the scalp-dance, I have found the Amerind on the whole less likely to civilize the American continent than the Nordic; on Amerind art and religion, I hold, the frontier had a sounder criticism than Greenwich Village.

In such ways, remembered violence tinged life in Ogden during that pause between frontier society and industrialism in which I grew up. I cannot say how it affected our libido and personæ. Outwardly, combined with the tradition of the migratory hunter, it did no more than give us a familiarity with firearms earlier than boys were getting it to the eastward. I owned several sub-caliber rifles before I was twelve. By fifteen I was a good offhand shot and had owned not only twenty-twos but a really formidable arsenal as well. By inheritance, appropriation, and the trafficking of boyhood I had acquired at various times a high-powered rifle, a shotgun, an automatic pistol, and at least three revolvers. My friends were similarly armed, and the gulches above Ogden endlessly echoed with our gunfire. Firearms were our cult, as automobiles and radios became the cult of our successors. We were competent. I knew no boy who did not regularly strap a revolver on his belt, balance a rifle on his shoulder, and disappear with his gang into the hills; but I knew only one boy who was injured in all that time. Early as we came to them, we used our guns with skill. It was a formalized skill without survival value, so that we consciously practiced it as an art, but it was a frontier inheritance.

The quality of all this scarlet was its irrelevance. And that is precisely my point: the West's scarlet, the frontier's violence, was episodic and irrelevant. Our elders and their elders had been lifelong addicts of civilization and community building. The cowboys arriving at Trail's End, who liquored up and shot one another, were an inconvenience, like the breaking of a water main, and had nothing to do with the life of Dodge City. The schoolmarm took the children out to look for mayflowers through that intermittent barrage. Bat Masterson, on the prowl for a kill, stepped out of the way of matrons of the Eastern Star carrying crullers and chicken patties to a church supper. Just across the Weber River (a very small stream) from my grandfather's south field, the Morrisite war produced three days of rifle and artillery fire. Civil revolt and its suppression get one line in his journal, being subordinated to the record of his plowing. A cattle war, a battle of miners, the rape of a bank or a stage coach was just what it is to-day, a violent interruption of a peaceful process, and was met in the same way, with the same despatch. Only, the frontier, being a large country and insufficiently policed, had few community safeguards for life and property. That fact put such safeguards up to the individual: if his safety and his property were threatened he had to defend them himself. "The law west of the Pecos" was what one wore on one's hip or carried on one's shoulder. When someone stole your horse or dynamited your ditches you could not send east of the Pecos for a cop. The frontiersman sighed, dropped his plow, went for his arsenal, attended to the horsethief, and then came back, got his crop in, and became a private citizen. He gladly made a peace officer his vicar as soon as one was available, and if he sometimes showed a preference for one who had got his training among the outlawed, megalopolis shows the same preference to-day. Organization achieved, he promptly forgot his earlier phase. It is not in the West where a tradition of personal responsibility and violence persists. I have seen more pocket pistols at a single party in Georgia than in any ten years' travel in the entire West.

II

Ogden had seen a deeper violence than casual outlawry. From its first settlement on, Utah was constantly rocked by the deadliest of all warfare, economic and religious. The Church of Jesus Christ of Latter-Day Saints was a semi-co-operative society governed by an oligarchy who claimed divine sanction and exercised absolute power. It had reached Utah after a series of expulsions which proved that the American social system could not adjust itself to it. Once in the mountains, the Church did its best to establish its system in defiance of experience. Fifty years of economic war between Mormons and Gentiles, intensified and made picturesque by the religious idiom of its expression, ensued before the compromises which finally permitted the adjustment. In the course of that campaign the national government once sent an expeditionary force against the Church and at another time, in flagrant violation of the Constitution, confiscated the Church's property, dissolved its corporations, proscribed some hundreds of its leaders, and attached a test-oath to the franchise. On its part, the Church expropriated the property of many Gentiles, with and without process of law, maintained a Gay-pay-oo for the immemorial purposes of dictatorships, and ruled by terrorism such of its own members as it had to and such Gentiles as it could. If the principles of the warfare were economic and if its strategy was political, the actual front-line tactics necessitated a long series of murders and one massacre in the grand manner.

Yet this gaudy era too was over in that transition period during which I grew up. Ogden, as the railroad center of the State, had an actual majority of Gentiles and so had achieved a working compromise, a forced equilibrium, long before the rest of Mormonry. The violence of neighbors at one another's throats, calling upon God, morality, and the national sovereignty for vindication, had subsided, and very little strife found its way to children. Mormon and Gentile, we grew up together with little awareness that our fathers fought in hostile armies. The child of a Catholic father and a Mormon mother, I myself was evidence of the adjustment. One of my earliest memories is of a little girl's prophecy that the Wasatch mountains would be shaken down upon the plain in the imminent Last Days, and that I, as a Gentile, would be destroyed whereas she, as a Saint, would be saved for glory. Her prediction showed the smug self-righteousness as the Lord's chosen that characterizes all Mormons. Children had, even at four or five, a vivid feeling of membership in a unity, a secret and exotic way of life which entitled them to privileges denied the rest of us. They had also an array of duties, organizations, and badges that set them off, but, being children, frequently found them a bore and could be as skeptical of "primary" as we of St. Joseph's parish were of communion class. But this exclusiveness was less marked in Ogden than in other Utah towns, and far less marked than in the farming country where Mormonry was unalloyed.

The Irish priests of my own communion never preached against the heretics. Protestant ministers were less amiable, but it was only an occasional Gantry in the evangelical sects who bellowed excerpts from the filthy and preposterous anti-Mormon literature of the earlier age. We even mingled in Sunday School without shock. A Mormon meeting house was the place of worship nearest my home, and I was sometimes sent there for instruction until I was about seven, when Rome idly exercised its claim. (Somewhat to my relief. No Puritan divine in the Bay colony ever equalled the long-windedness of any Mormon bishop.) As we grew toward high-school age the lines tightened a little—surprisingly, by the formation of castes. The rudimentary aristocracy of Ogden tended to be Gentile, and a good many people began to feel superior on the simple ground that they had been baptized or married not for eternity but only for this world. As we grew still older, as the efficient Mormon system began to select its missionaries among the boys and point the girls toward marriage in the faith, the cleavage grew distinct. But even then it was unimportant and often humorous. I remember a debate when my high-school class selected a baccalaureate speaker. The Mormon contingent, a minority, proposed one of the Twelve Apostles. An opponent solemnly put Jesus Christ in nomination, and Catholic, Presbyterian, and Baptist united to vote down the Saints.

Polygamy, the sole symbol of Mormonism in the outside world, meant almost nothing to us. The truth of history, which historians have not yet understood, is that to the Mormons themselves it was only a religious symbol, lacked the coercion of economic logic, and was slowly and insensibly found to be a mistake. More briefly still, Mormon polygamy was a caste privilege. "The hierarchy" is the Mormon term for the governing class, the hagiocracy or plutocracy as distinguished from the body of the Church. In general only the hierarchy was permitted to practice polygamy; only the hierarchy could afford to practice it. Thus there were never enough polygamists to establish the tone of any community; there were fewer of them in Ogden than in other towns, and the institution had been driven underground by the persecutions of the 'Nineties. Some of our playmates were known to be polygamous children and the number was increased as we grew up and learned the open secrets of the town. So far as I can remember, that fact meant absolutely nothing to us except as it gave them a certain distinction. By the time we were adolescents some of them, especially the girls, felt, I believe, a kind of embarrassment or social inferiority which the training of the Church did not always transform to fervent superiority. It was, however, frequently compensated by the fact of plutocracy: a polygamist's child was likely to be a well-to-do child. Adolescence also informed us about the furtive practice of polygamy. We saw conspicuously monogamous Mormons paying regular parochial visits to conspicuously unmarried women. But there was no persecution to make such secrecy romantic and, unhappily, they were dreadfully ordinary people. We were just ribald about them. They were easily associated with the folklore that clustered about Brigham Young.

The way in which Mormonism did influence our daily life was to spice it with miracle. In few societies are angels as common as policemen and heaven rather more familiar than a city park: I have had a lifelong tenderness for the world's delusions because I grew up amid prophecy and the glories of the Lord. The whole aim of Brigham Young's policy, after one disastrous experiment, and that of his successors was to abandon the supernatural. The leaders tried to repress the impulses of their people, but the Church had been founded during the Apocalypse by a prophet of God and had always been recruited from the naturally ecstatic. Miracle might be officially denounced but it was a fundamental condition of daily life. Hired girls in my mother's kitchen looked into heaven. God spoke to ditch-diggers and garbage-collectors. On any day, at any corner, any Saint might meet an angel on his way. Patriarchs, prophets, and even deities nightly visited each block in Ogden when the Saints slept. The conversation of all Mormons was predominantly theological, and exegesis might at any moment change to prophecy—and when I say prophecy I mean not only the hosannas of the chosen but literal, detailed soothsaying by qualified seers and revelators under immediate inspiration of God.

Miraculous healing, of course, was commonest. The Lord sustained his people in all ailments from cancer to the common cold, from snakebite to St. Vitus dance. The Mormon elders had their sacred oils and liturgical pantomime, like all priests, but it was extempore miracles by individual Mormons that impressed us. In time of epidemic these were intensified to the classic symptoms of mass hysteria till terror and ecstasy walked the Ogden streets. But other miracles were more picturesque. The widow's cruse had an exact parallel in a miraculous flour sack owned by a widow in my block. All but empty in the fall, it fed her family through a hard winter and when spring came was fuller than it had been in October. The Three Nephites are the Mormon variation of the Wandering Jew, three survivors of the earlier church doomed to wander the earth till the Last Days. Rumor of their presence sometimes spread through the back lots; there were omens and queer sequels of their passing, and I knew several Saints who had seen them. Piety was rewarded by a legacy which paid the mortgage, by the miraculous provision of clothes or horseflesh or quails or manna. Sin received equally direct action: an accident that removed a "bad Mormon" was the judgment of an angry God, and drouth, plagues of grasshoppers and disastrous forest fires meant that the Saints were not living their religion— usually by skimping their tithes. The destruction of one village by cloudburst and of another by a snowslide was incontrovertible evidence of communal sin.

Deliverance from the plots of the Gentiles was common. The missionaries went forth without purse or scrip throughout the world and they were not always loved. But God's providence went with them. Sandy P., for instance, had been persecuted by the Austrians. One night a mysterious stranger, bearded and dressed in shining white, woke him from sleep and told him that Satan had prompted the villagers to take his life. Sandy rose and fled, the pursuit swiftly gathering behind him. It grew nearer as he labored through the night, and at last he came to a river too wide and rapid for him to cross. With the Mormon readiness for martyrdom, Sandy commended himself to the Lord. But a deep sleep came upon him. When he waked he was on the far side of the river and the frustrated lynchers were cursing him from the other bank.

That miraculous slumber and that white-clad stranger were

constantly with us in Mormonry. Portentous words thundered out of silence. The skies above Twelfth Street opened and Olaf Olafson, teamster or swineherd, saw unfolded the future course of his life. In the deep night Granny Gudmanson heard a sonorous, semi-Biblical apostrophe telling her how to improve a granddaughter's morals, how to treat an ailing cow, or how to build an extension on the chicken house. Celestial messengers overtook wayfarers and told them to turn back or armed them against danger on the route. Angels snatched one back from a train fated to be wrecked or came at night to bid one withdraw money from a shaky bank. And anything might be an omen or a portent. Dreams and visions made all the neighbors rapt. A configuration of the clouds, an egg with two yolks, a blight on the radish bed, even a nightmare had been inspired above and could either be interpreted at home or taken to some neighborhood seer for explanation. The Sandy P. I have mentioned was greatly gifted in divination. He kept his large family in a continual tension of miracle—and of terror; for do not suppose that communications from God are always conducive to a peaceful life. At about the age of five one of his grandchildren was repeatedly visited in dreams by another one who was dead. Through Sandy's interpretation the dead child's message was seen to be a warning that a third child was soon to die; and before long they took that third child to an asylum for the insane, which showed that Sandy hadn't missed it far. Sandy's youngest daughter was a classmate of mine at high school, and it was once my privilege to console her when a Mormon swain took some other maiden to a dance. She wept on my shoulder, most enjoyably to us both, but that night an angel visited her in a dream, and she laid the apparition before her prophet-father. Sandy interpreted and Sally sought me out. The Lord, Sandy decided, had pronounced her swain unworthy and had then given her a warning. "The Lord says," Sally told me, "that I must not let a Gentile kiss me any more."

Childhood on the Mormon frontier seems to me a rich heritage. It prepared me for the economic and governmental miracles of these days. It gave me a good many yardsticks for the behavior of the race. It dissuaded me from asking much rationality in human affairs, and it made my faculty of surprise abnormally inactive. It gave me laboratory experience in dictatorship. . . . And there was also my Mormon grandfather's revelation. The Bishop of Uinta once came to Grandfather's house and told him that the Lord had revealed an intention to bestow his daughter on the bishop as a plural wife. Grandfather was a devout man, a man who had lived his religion, followed the priesthood, and built up the kingdom. So now his piety was rewarded, in miracle. The skies were opened to him and he said, "I prophesy that if you don't get out of here, Brother L., and if you ever mention the revelation to anyone, I will shoot hell out of you."

III

The greatest influence on childhood of the vanished frontier was the freedom we enjoyed. It was an all-inclusive freedom that touched every aspect of our lives. Perhaps I can best suggest it by the relations of the sexes in adolescence, and of this the most vivid symbol I have is a memory from my last year at high school. Toward noon one day a girl and I were coming back toward Ogden over the foothills when we reached a barbed-wire fence. Helen stopped and modestly bade me look the other way lest I glimpse her calf when she climbed the fence. It was a request absolutely in accord with the Ogden folkways—and yet she and I had been alone in the mountains since one o'clock that morning, had climbed a peak and cooked our breakfast on the top. This, in 1914. It was the privilege of young people, in groups or in couples, to wander in the mountains unchaperoned and unsuspected of misbehavior—and, let me say, rightly unsuspected. At a time when elsewhere in America stringent restrictions were put on all such intercourse outside the home, we were quite free to go where we liked at any hours that pleased us. The form which the convention took is amusing: if we went into the mountains to cook supper we must be back before dawn, and if we wanted to cook breakfast we must be careful not to start till after midnight—otherwise we should spend the night together, which was unthinkable.

The mountains were a force in our freedom. By the time we were eight we went on day-long explorations of the foothills, miles from home, unsupervised by older people. Two or three years later we were beginning to climb the peaks, and by the time we were fourteen we were camping out for days at a time, with or without tents, in canyons a hundred miles up the range. I remember, at fifteen, spending a Christmas vacation in a deserted log cabin deep among the peaks and, with several companions, practicing the not inconsiderable skill that such a stay implies. The frontier had left this impress on us, and when the Boy Scout movement reached Utah just as we grew too old for it, we were contemptuous of its sterilized and evangelized woodscraft. Toward the supervised outdoor-life of the Boy Scouts and of the summer-camp movement which followed we felt a frontiersman's disdain for the counterfeit. At fourteen we were able to take care of ourselves in the wilderness. We wanted no lectures on the hazards of cliffs, poison ivy, and rattlesnakes, and no exhortations about the beauties and purities of nature. As for nature, we were realists—and that, I think, is one of the deepest values we experienced.

But be sure we also paid a tax. This was a time, let me repeat, between two ages. The frontier organization had collapsed and the organization of the industrial order had not taken its place. In this very matter of outdoor skills we suffered. We were practicing a frontier craft but practicing it as an art—survival value had gone from it and so nothing vital depended on it. For instance, I have deeply regretted my ignorance of the native botany and natural history. A generation earlier I should have learned the seasons, qualities, and uses of all native plants and woods, the habits of birds and animals, the use of traps, and the crafts of taxidermy and tanning quite as naturally as I did learn camping and mountain climbing and marksmanship. A few years later I should have learned them from the paid instructors supplied by a community grown suddenly solicitous about its young. I would rather have had the first training than the second certainly, but the second rather than none at all.

Frontier society disciplined children within its necessities; the industrial order taught them from a new sentiment of humanitarian responsibility. Our order granted them the frontier freedom and then, omitting discipline, disregarded them. In some ways it was not a bad system. Psychology approves its impersonality, and it taught children a practical Darwinism—they learned, earlier than children elsewhere, immediate implications of the struggle for existence. But it was a handicap in many ways, since the terms of that struggle were changing and we were not equipped for the new phase. Also, it had its immediate pangs. A regret that has lasted to my thirty-eighth year springs from my inability to become a really good swimmer. I never saw the crawl stroke till boys just older than I began coming home from college —the first generation of college men in Ogden. Now the crawl stroke is probably not universal in Utah even to-day (no river there has more than a thirty-yard stretch deep enough for swimming and there are only a half-dozen lakes in the whole State), but at least the new order teaches it. There was no one to teach me, and that fact has, I think, its significance. A boy who was not born with a knack for boys' skills was simply out of luck. To-day playgrounds and schools swarm with specialists who teach the awkward the approved technics of all games, sports, crafts, skills, and arts. In the Ogden of my time one had them or one never got them. No doubt the preferential treatment of to-day has been carried too far; but one would like to ask analysts and social pathologists how much maladjustment, inadequacy, and frustration they have traced to the wounds inflicted by its lack. Whole areas of experience, whole classes of social adjustment, may well have been thrown out of balance. Certainly it showed in the experience of my generation when we ventured away from Ogden. We had the rituals of our own society, but when we got away from it we had an ineptness that proper supervision of children would have prevented. The elders had brought us into the tribal house, but they had not fitted us to deal with the outlanders.

But one will have to go still deeper into the mind to appraise the basic fact of that frontier remnant. We learned as children, I say, implications of the struggle of existence. Frontier children always learned them, but the industrial order, at even its most squalid levels, delays that instruction and, above those levels, delays it perhaps too long. Among frontiersmen and those who succeeded to their heritage, such a realization has conditioned the entire climate and physiology of thought. The significance of that fundamental has been insufficiently realized and so has been grotesquely distorted by students of American society. Make of it what you will, to the despair of the hopeful or the apprehension of the merely liberal, one whole division of the Americans was conditioned by it. To that people the struggle of existence is not something that can be repealed by Act of Congress or demolished by rainmakers, philosophers, or the community meeting in prayer.

IV

There remains one frontier-fossil which I touch on with reluctance because, though one of the ideas which students of American life have been most voluble about, it cannot be clearly phrased or adequately defined here. It relates to that cliché of editorial writers—individualism, and its implications in the action of the frontier on the national history.

If as a critic of historical writing I have challenged the simplicities of certain historians about the American frontier, it is because I know of my own experience that frontier life was infinitely complex and not reducible to formula. Consider: I was the child of an apostate Mormon and an apostate Catholic, which suggested that the religious culture of the frontier was far from simple. Across the street from me lived a prosperous miner who made his cross on all documents because he could not write, whose wife could not read, and who did not send his children to school till the town forced him to. He was the type-frontiersman of many thinkers. Yet the book in which I was taught to read was a Pope's *Iliad* of 1781 and, chanting the couplets while I played with the miner's children, I was a laboratory specimen of frontier relationships which no literary or academic formula could express. One of my grandfathers was an English mechanic turned farmer, another was an Italian cavalry officer turned commission merchant. I played with the sons and grandsons of Hawaiian princes, Scandinavian murderers, German geologists with duelling scars, English poets, Spanish mathematicians, French gamblers, Virginia slave-owners, Yankee metaphysicians—of men who came from everywhere, who had every conceivable tradition, education, and canon of taste and behavior. On Memorial Day one ancient hung the Stars and Bars on his front door and mounted guard on it in butternut; the King's birthday was celebrated three doors away; a pastry cook made a Dauphinist of me at ten; down the street Kriss Kringle was venerated instead of Santa Claus; in the next block manuscript letters of Emerson created a whole ritual of behavior; beyond that house a fiercely silent dignity protected a national but locally unmentioned disgrace. Here, God knows, was none of that deadly uniformity of thought, habit, belief, and behavior which books about the frontier detect *in absentia*. I grew up in a culture much more various than I have found anywhere else.

Such a society could have no such coercive singleness of opinion, no such dictatorial and puritanical absolutism, as the books describe. Quite the contrary: it could survive only by the utmost latitude of thought, expression, and personal behavior. We learned to sing "What was your name in the States?" and we sang it in derision, but it had a meaning which the community taught us to respect. We learned that what a man thought about God, the government, the banks, the social revolution, women, sex, alcohol, or the Dauphin, Kriss Kringle, or separation for Ireland was most definitely his own business and not subject to our own views. More, we learned that what he did about them was, within the farthest possible limits of community elasticity, even more his business and not ours. We learned this from our parents and ourselves and from the daily practice of our community. The frontier had lapsed just so far that the lesson was not occasionally italicized by gunfire. We learned, in short, that the frontier had existed as a community, and could have existed, only by the constant exercise of the freedoms, individualisms, and eccentricities which the absentee critic finds it never had.

I may say too that we saw these conditions end. As my generation grew up, industrialism and megalopolis made us their benefactions. Luncheon clubs arrived, and Chautauqua, the Y.M.C.A., the syndicated press, booster movements, the hysterias and compulsions of wartime and prohibition, and the liberal point of view and national prosperity. We had been boys in the despotic uniformity of the intellectuals; we did not know what uniformity was till their Utopia gathered us in.

At the same time a boy who had once risen from bed at three of a spring morning with an arctic wind blowing out of the canyons, to irrigate his grandfather's fields with icy water at just such times as the community chose to allot—such a boy understood another widely denied quality of the frontier. For the books have struck the frontier paradox and solved it exactly wrong. They find that the frontier rigidly suppressed individualism in personal opinion and behavior, whereas frontiersmen could live together only by virtue of a greater latitude in such matters than any other part of America permitted. And they find that the frontier enforced an even greater individualism in economic and governmental affairs, whereas the very conditions of frontier life imposed co-operation. When glacial water seeped down my boots in a canyon wind at hours dictated by the water commissars, I was working in the earliest tradition of the pioneers, locally sixty-five years old and ninety years earlier than Mr. Ickes. Who but the economic individualist was the proverbial victim of frontier violence? It would be unfair to allude to the stage-robber and the horse-thief; but surely the rustler, the claim-jumper, and the fraudulent homesteader were lynched by co-operative effort; surely the stock-detective, the wolf-hunter, and the fence-rider were agents of a frontier economy in which the individualism of the critics had small part. How indeed did a frontier community exist at all except by means of a close-knit co-operation? Especially, how did a frontier community in the desert exist?

The first job I ever held for any length of time was in a land-title office and it took me deep into territorial organization. I found the intricate network of a co-operative system. Not the co-operative merely, for the frontier had its share of communistic experiments which went the way of all communisms and, it may be, left some skeptical deposit on the minds of Westerners. Even Mormonism, whose co-operative society ruled in the name of God by a superior hierarchy, a privileged class, is a practical answer to the enigma of government, had once quaintly investigated communism. There in the records I digested was the United Order of Enoch and its melancholy teachings, with the Prophet John Taylor instead of Stalin to change its alignment. But in the routine of business I had to master the water laws, the grazing laws, the mining code—I had to re-create the frontier's co-operative reduction of chaos. Do not wonder if I have, in print, sometimes suggested that metropolitan authorities on frontier life go and do likewise. Or if I commend to them such casual items from frontier journals as this: "To-day our water committee waited on Stark and Stevens and told them to close up their dams until they come into the agreement." With its entry of a week later that Messrs. Stark and Stevens, kulaks of rugged frontier individualism, have been liquidated.

Well, Ogden of those days was the damnedest place. We were really *fin de siècle*, we were the frontier's afterglow. We saw that glow fade out. We stood, as it were, on a watershed, and also we went down the other side. In the class of 1914 at the Ogden High School there were three girls each of whom had one pair of silk stockings. By the class of 1918 there was no girl who had ever worn cotton stockings to the school, and the town had broken out with something that looked like a bucolic variant of the Junior League. Children of parents who had been conceived in cottonwood lean-tos, with their older brothers looking on, had suddenly become a plutocracy with a mistaken belief that they were a fashionable caste. But the sagebrush debutante is without interest to history and is hereby abandoned to literature, which so far has left her out.

GET OUT AND HOE

As told to and written by CLAUDE V. DUNNAGAN

"No, I don't mind tellin' you about me and Morrison and the young-uns. Won't you sit down. Ollie! Bring out another chair. We got company. People don't come around so often. Sometime Uncle Hank comes from across the creek to see us. We get sort of lonesome. I'm mighty glad to have somebody to talk to. I use to tell Morrison our lives would make a good true story—like you read in the magazines and hear on the radio—Ma Perkins and the others. Oh, yes! We got a radio—a battery set. You see, we ain't got no electric power. We listen to all the good stories and string music. Sometimes we buy things they sell on the radio . . . medicine and other things.

"I guess we been hard luck renters all our lives, me and Morrison both. They was ten young-uns in my family, and I was next to the youngest. We had it awful hard—I reckon my father was about the meanest there ever was—he used to beat me and run me out of the house, but I'd come back when he cooled off. It was his hot-headedness that ruined us. They was a neighbor, Sam Hicklin, that lived near us. His farm run next to ours, and one day he come over to the house and told my father that he was plantin' corn all the way over on his land, and he had better put up a fence and watch out. My father told him to tend to his own business and this made Sam mad. Next day, when my father went out to work, he saw a big ditch cut right down through the middle of his cornfield. Old Sam was settin' on a fence watchin' him. They started cussin' and in a minute they was throwin' rocks at each other. Well, both of 'em got lawyers and took it to court. The judge divided the land halfway between the ditch and the end of the cornfield, but this didn't do any good, because

From *These Are Our Lives*, Federal Writers' Project, Works Progress Administration, by permission of The University of North Carolina Press, sponsors and publishers.

when the case was settled, the lawyers' bills was so big they couldn't pay it. The lawyers got the farms and left Sam Hicklin and us without anything. The lawyers sold our farm and we had to move out. That was when I was nineteen.

"We went to Yadkin County and rented an old rundown farm for a share of what we could raise. The crops wasn't any good that year, the landlord came and got what we had raised and had the auctioneers come and sell our tools and furniture. They was a bunch of people at the sale that day from all around. I was standin' there watchin' the man sell the things when I saw a good lookin' man in overalls lookin' toward me. He watched me all during the sale and I knew what he was thinkin'. That was the first time I ever saw Morrison. I reckon he fell in love with me right off, for we were married a few days later. Morrison didn't have no true father. His mother wasn't married, and he was raised up by his kin folks. Then we moved to a little farm near Shortridge, about ten miles away. The owner said we could have three-fourths of what we raised. The first two years the crops turned out pretty good so we could pay off the landlord and buy a little furniture . . . a bed and table and some chairs. Then the first baby came on. That was Bernhard. He's out in the field workin' now, suckerin' tobacco. By that time, we was able to get a cow, and that came in good, for the baby was awful thin and weak.

"After that, things didn't go so good. Another baby come on and we had our hands full takin' care of the two children and lookin' after the farm work. When the second baby was four years old, he started gettin' pale and thin. We put him to bed one day because he looked so sick we thought he was goin' to die. We didn't call a doctor for a long while. You see, we didn't have any money then, and we'd heard that the doctor up in town wouldn't come unless you had the money ready. But Morrison said he didn't care, so one night after dark he started walkin' through the woods toward the highway. He caught a ride into town and about two hours later, him and the doctor drove up in the yard.

"When the doctor finished lookin' at the baby, he turned around with a worried look on his face and said he had meningitis. That was some kind of ailment that got in his back. The next, he got awful and sick and when the doctor come again, my little boy had a stroke of infantile paralysis. He died the next day. After we had buried him up at the church cemetery, we went on with our work. There wasn't much we could do but try to forget little Sammy. But we did love him so much. I go to his grave and put flowers on it every Sunday.

"The crops was comin' in and we had to work hard to get the tobacco suckered and cured before the market opened, or else we couldn't pay the landlord his share, come fall.

"Bernhard was only six, but he could help a lot, pullin' and tyin' the tobacco, and helpin' hand it in the barn. We got out more tobacco that year than any other, but when we took it to market in Winston, they wasn't payin' but about twelve cents a pound for the best grade, so when we give the landlord his share and paid the fertilizer bill, we didn't have enough left to pay the doctor and store bill. We didn't know what we was goin' to do durin' the winter. Morrison had raised a few vegetables and apples, so we canned what we could and traded the rest for some cotton cloth up at the store so the children would have something to wear that winter. Morrison got a job helpin' build a barn for a neighbor, but it didn't last but two days. The neighbor gave him two second hand pairs of overalls for the work.

"That was one of the hardest years we come to. Next spring another baby was born. That made four. You see, we'd already had another one, a girl, before little Sammy died. This one was a boy. He was the strongest and healthiest one we'd had yet. I loved him so much, because I thought he would take the place of little Sammy. Just before he was one year old, Morrison said we ought to bake a cake for his birthday. I was in the kitchen bakin' the cake and some pies, when I heard little Tom start cryin'. I ran to see what was the matter, and he was layin' on the floor, all pale and sick lookin'. I put him in bed and ran out toward the field and called Morrison . . . he was hoein' corn. When Morrison looked at Tom, he said: 'It looks like a bad spell. I'm goin' after the doctor.' I'll never forget how scared I was while I waited for Morrison to come back. I sat there beside little Tom holding a wet rag on his head, and prayin' he'd get well. I recollect how I prayed that night. I said, 'Oh, God, please don't let him die like little Sammy. He's the only baby I've got.'

"Morrison and the doctor came; little Tom was awful hot. The doctor looked at him a minute and then turned around to me and Morrison.

" 'He's been dead half an hour.' I guess he must've died while I was prayin'.

"Next spring when we was plantin' tobacco, Morrison got to leavin' home every night, and comin' in about midnight. I didn't know what he was doin' till one of the neighbors that lived up the road tole me that he had seen Morrison goin' up to the Carson house every night. The Carsons didn't have any children but a girl named Amelia Carson lived with them. She was some kin to them. Amelia was sixteen years old and pretty, too, but she had a bad name. A month after Morrison started goin' up to her house, they ran off together. That was the first time I started gettin' relief from the government. They was a government woman that come around and gave orders for food and clothes, and sometimes we got a little money. I needed it awful bad, because with Morrison gone,' they wasn't any way to feed the two children. I had to do most of the work in the field that summer, and sometimes I would go to the neighbors' house and wash for them for a piece of meat.

"Then, about two months after Morrison and Amelia ran off, the sheriff down in the sandhills, in the eastern part of the State, found them livin' together. They brought Amelia back home but they didn't get Morrison. A month later, I was settin' in the kitchen sewin' when Morrison walked in. He looked kinda' bad like he'd been hungry for a long time. He sat down in a chair in front of the fire, like he was awful tired and said to me:

" 'I been a damn fool, Irma. That crazy woman didn't want nothin' but my money. You ain't mad at me, are you, Irma?'

"I said: 'I ain't got no right to be mad now, Morrison. You had your fling and done come home. We need you awful bad. We got to get out and hoe in the tobacco tomorrow. You better get some sleep.'

"About six months later, Amelia had a baby. Right off, she blamed it on Morrison. When she took it to court, Morrison denied it—said it was just as apt to be somebody else's baby. But the judge said he was guilty and told him to pay Amelia fifty dollars. Morrison didn't have any money then, so he went to jail and served twenty-one days. Accordin' to the law, he had paid his debt. That was the fourth baby Amelia had . . . all of 'em born out of wedlock. Only two of 'em are living now. She had two by one man. I still can't believe Morrison was the father of one of the children. Anyway, that's all in the past now, and today there's no better man than Morrison. This year he gave a week's labor on the Methodist Church at Center. That was when they built a new part to it. All the men in the neighborhood that can't give money help on it. Morrison had always give his share.

"Things are a lot better for the renter today than in the past. It used to be we couldn't get enough to eat and wear. Now we got a cow, a hog, and some chickens. Morrison bought a second-hand car and every Sunday afternoon we ride somewhere. It's the only time we ever get away from home.

"The landlord gives us five-sixths of what we raise, so we get along pretty good when the crops are fair. Of course we have to furnish the fertilizer and livestock. This year we had seven barns of tobacco and four acres of corn. Wheat turned out pretty good, too. We raised forty-three bushels, and I hear the price is going to be fair at the roller mill. I reckon we still got about a hundred cans in the pantry.

"We never owned any land, but Morrison and me just bought a house. It's the old school house down the road about two miles. We bought it from the county for $270. We only got $150 paid but we can pay the rest after next year's crop. They's only one thing bad about it though. It's right next door to where Amelia Carson lives—with her children. It's goin' to be hard to face her after what happened between her and Morrison. It'll take a lot of courage, I guess—more'n I've got. I don't think she'll attempt again, though. He's learned his lesson.

"Some day we hope to own our own land as well as the house. It might be a long time, but with the grace of God we'll get there. It seems like that man in Washington has got a real love for the poor people in his heart, and I believe it's due to him and his helpers that the poor renters are goin' to get a chance. We've got more hope now than we ever had before.

"I'm mighty glad you stopped to see us. Won't you come again? We'll be livin' in the new place then, I reckon."

THE HIDING GENERATION

James Thurber

ᒪ᠊ᒥ᠊ᒪᒥ᠊ᒪᒥ᠊ᒪᒥ᠊ᒪᒥ᠊ᒪᒥ᠊ᒪᒥ᠊ᒪᒥ᠊ᒪᒥ᠊ᒪᒥ᠊ᒪᒥ᠊ᒪᒥ᠊ᒪᒥ᠊ᒪᒥ

One afternoon almost two years ago, at a cocktail party (at least, this is the way I have been telling the story), an eager middle-aged woman said to me, "Do you belong to the Lost Generation, Mr. T.?" and I retorted, coldly and quick as a flash, "No, Madam, I belong to the Hiding Generation."

As a matter of fact, no woman ever asked me such a question at a cocktail party or anywhere else. I thought up the little dialogue one night when I couldn't sleep. At the time, my retort seemed pretty sharp and satirical to me, and I hoped that some day somebody *would* ask me if I belonged to the Lost Generation, so that I could say no, I belonged to the Hiding Generation. But nobody ever has. My retort, however, began working in the back of my mind. I decided that since I was apparently never going to get a chance to use it as repartee, I ought to do something else with it, if only to get it out of the back of my mind. About ten months ago I got around to the idea of writing a book called "The Hiding Generation," which would be the story of my own intellectual conflicts, emotional disturbances, spiritual adventures, and journalistic experiences, something in the manner of Malcolm Cowley's *Exile's Return* or Vincent Sheean's *Personal History*. The notion seemed to me a remarkably good one, and I was quite excited by it. I bought a new typewriter ribbon and a ream of fresh copy paper; I sharpened a dozen pencils; I got a pipe and tobacco. Then I sat down at the typewriter, lighted my pipe, and wrote on a sheet of paper "The Hiding Generation, by James Thurber." That was as far as I got, because I discovered that I could not think of anything else to say. I mean anything at all.

Thus passed the first five or six hours of my work on the book. In the late afternoon some people dropped in for cocktails, and

From James Thurber, *Let Your Mind Alone*, Harper & Brothers.

I didn't get around to the book again for two more days. Then I found that I still didn't have anything to say. I wondered if I had already said everything I had to say, but I decided, in looking over what I had said in the past, that I really hadn't ever said anything. This was an extremely depressing thought, and for a while I considered going into some other line of work. But I am not fitted for any other line of work, by inclination, experience, or aptitude. There was consequently nothing left for me but to go back to work on "The Hiding Generation." I decided to "write it in my mind," in the manner of Arnold Bennett (who did practically all of *The Old Wives' Tale* in his head), and this I devoted myself to for about seven months. At length I sat down at the typewriter once more, and there I was again, tapping my fingers on the table, lighting and relighting my pipe, getting up every now and then for a drink of water. I figured finally that maybe I had better make an outline of the book; probably all the writers I had in mind—and there was a pretty big list of them now, including Walter Duranty and Negley Farson—had made an outline of what they were going to say, using Roman numerals for the main divisions and small letters "a" and "b," etc., for the subdivisions. So I set down some Roman numerals and small letters on a sheet of paper. First I wrote "I. Early Youth." I could think of no subdivisions to go under that, so I put down "II. Young Manhood." All I could think of to go under that was "a. Studs Lonigan." Obviously that wouldn't do, so I tore up the sheet of paper and put the whole thing by for another week.

During that week I was tortured by the realization that I couldn't think of anything important that had happened to me up to the time I was thirty-three and began raising Scotch terriers. The conviction that nothing important had happened to me until I was thirty-three, that I had apparently had no intellectual conflicts or emotional disturbances, or anything, reduced me to such a state of dejection that I decided to go to Bridgeport for a few days and stay all alone in a hotel room. The motivation behind this decision is still a little vague in my mind, but I think it grew out of a feeling that I wasn't worthy of going away to Florida or Bermuda or Nassau or any other nice place. I had Bridgeport "coming to me," in a sense, as retribution for my blank youth and my blank young manhood. In the end, of course, I did not go to Bridgeport. I took a new sheet of paper and began another outline.

This time I started out with "I. University Life. a. Intellectual Conflicts." No other workable subdivisions occurred to me. The only Emotional Disturbance that came to my mind was unworthy of being incorporated in the book, for it had to do with the moment, during the Phi Psi May Dance of 1917, when I knocked a fruit salad onto the floor. The incident was as bald as that, and somehow I couldn't correlate it with anything. To start out with such an episode and then just leave it hanging in the air would not give the reader anything to get his teeth into. Therefore I concentrated on "Intellectual Conflicts," but I could not seem to call up any which had torn my mind asunder during my college days. Yet there must have been some. I made a lot of little squares and circles with a pencil for half an hour, and finally I remembered one intellectual conflict—if you could call it that. It was really only an argument I had had with a classmate at Ohio State University named Arthur Spencer, about *Tess of the D'Urbervilles*. I had taken the view that the hero of the book was not justified in running away to South America and abandoning Tess simply because she had been indiscreet in her youth. Spencer, on the other hand, contended the man was fully justified, and that he (Spencer) would have run away to South America and left Tess, or any other woman, under the circumstances—that is, if he had had the money. As a matter of fact, Spencer settled down in East Liverpool, Ohio, where he is partner in his father's hardware store, and married a very nice girl named Sarah Gammadinger, who had been a Kappa at Ohio State.

I came to the conclusion finally that I would have to leave my university life out of the book, along with my early youth and young manhood. Therefore, my next Roman numeral, which would normally have been IV, automatically became I. I placed it after the words "Paris: A New World. a. Thoughts at Sea." It happened that upon leaving the university, in 1918, I went to Paris as a clerk, Grade B, in the American Embassy. In those days I didn't call it clerk, Grade B, I called it attaché, but it seemed to me that the honest and forceful thing to do was to tell the truth. The book would have more power and persuasion if I told the truth—providing I could remember the truth. There was a lot I couldn't remember, I found out in trying to. For instance, I had put down "Thoughts at Sea" after "a" because I couldn't recall anything significant that had happened to me during the five months I spent in Washington, D. C., before sailing for France. (Furthermore, it didn't seem logical to put a subdivision called "Washington Days" under a general heading called "Paris: A New World.") Something, of course, must have happened to me in Washington, something provocative or instructive, something that added to my stature, but all that comes back to me is a series of paltry little memories. I remember there was a waitress in the Post Café, at the corner of Thirteenth and E Streets, whose last name was Rabbit. I've forgotten her first name and even what she looked like, but her last name was Rabbit. A Mrs. Rabbit. Then there was the flu epidemic, during which I gargled glycothymoline three times a day. All the rest has gone from me.

I found I could remember quite a lot about my days at sea on my way to Paris: A New World. In the first place, I had bought a box of San Felice cigars to take with me on the transport, but I was seasick all the way over and the cigars were smoked by a man named Ed Corcoran, who travelled with me. He was not sick a day. I believe he said he had never been sick a day in his life. Even some of the sailors were sick, but not Corcoran. No, sir. He was constantly in and out of our stateroom, singing, joking, smoking my cigars. The other thing I remembered about the voyage was that my trunk and suitcase failed to get on the ship; they were put by mistake on some other ship—the *Minnetonka*, perhaps, or the *Charles O. Sprague*, a coastwise fruit steamer. In any case, I didn't recover them until May, 1920, in Paris, and the Hershey bars my mother had packed here and there in both the trunk and the suitcase had melted and were all over everything. All my suits were brown, even the gray one. But I am anticipating myself. All this belongs under "Paris: A New World. b. Paris."

I was just twenty-five when I first saw Paris, and I was still a little sick. Unfortunately, when I try to remember my first impressions of Paris and the things that happened to me, I get them mixed up with my second trip to Paris, which was seven years later, when I was feeling much better and really got around more. On that first trip to Paris I was, naturally enough, without any clothes, except what I had on, and I had to outfit myself at once, which I did at the Galeries Lafayette. I paid $4.75 in American money for a pair of B.V.D.s. I remember that, all right. Nothing else comes back to me very clearly; everything comes back to me all jumbled up. I tried about five times to write down a comprehensive outline of my experiences in Paris:

A New World, but the thing remained sketchy and trivial. If there was any development in my character or change in my outlook on life during that phase, I forget just where it came in and why. So I cut out the Paris interlude.

I find, in looking over my accumulation of outlines, that my last attempt to get the volume started began with the heading "I. New York Again: An Old World." This was confusing, because it could have meaning and pertinence only if it followed the chapter outlined as "Paris: A New World," and that had all been eliminated along with my Early Youth, Young Manhood, and University Days. Moreover, while my life back in New York must have done a great deal to change my character, viewpoint, objectives, and political ideals, I forget just exactly how this happened. I am the kind of man who should keep notes about such things. If I do not keep notes, I simply cannot remember a thing. Oh, I remember odds and ends, as you have seen, but they certainly would not tie up into anything like a moving chronicle of a man's life, running to a hundred and fifty thousand words. If they ran to twenty-five hundred words, I would be going good. Now, it's a funny thing: catch me in a drawing-room, over the coffee and liqueurs, particularly the Scotch-and-sodas, and I could hold you, or at least keep talking to you, for five or six hours about my life, but somebody would have to take down what I said and organize it into a book. When I sit down to write the story of my life, all I can think of is Mrs. Rabbit, and the Hershey bars, and the B.V.D.s that came within two bits of costing five bucks. That is, of course, until I get up to the time when I was thirty-three and began raising Scotch terriers. I can put down all of that, completely and movingly, without even making an outline. Naturally, as complete and as moving as it might be, it would scarcely make a biography like, say Negley Farson's, and it certainly would not sustain so pretentious a title as "The Hiding Generation." I would have to publish it as a pamphlet entitled "The Care and Training of Scotch Terriers." I am very much afraid that that is what my long arduous struggle to write the story of my life is going to come down to, if it is going to come down to anything.

Well, all of us cannot write long autobiographies. But almost all of us can.

NOTES ON AUTHORS AND SELECTIONS

ᒐᒐᒐᒐᒐᒐᒐᒐᒐᒐᒐᒐᒐᒐᒐᒐᒐᒐᒐᒐᒐᒐᒐ

GAMALIEL BRADFORD, poet, biographer, essayist, and the only child of his parents to reach maturity, was born in Boston in 1863. His father, also named Gamaliel, was a banker and publicist, comfortably well-off and able to supply the background suitable to the tastes and development of a boy whose eagerness for literature and the other arts showed itself at a very early age. Bradford attended Harvard in 1882, but was forced by ill-health to leave without taking a degree. Financially able to ignore the struggle for survival which has handicapped many another young aspirant to literary fame, Bradford was able to pursue his interest single-heartedly and without haste. The gradual accession of skill and effectiveness in writing shows strongly in his work; his literary and intellectual progress was steady and consciously fostered.

The life of Bradford, therefore, is a list of published works of ascending quality rather than a series of institutional or personal positions held, or other outward events. Some of the development of Bradford's mind, theories of biography, attitude toward men, etc.,· is presented below. The reader who desires a more complete picture of Bradford's intellectual growth will want to refer to Van Wyck Brooks's one-volume edition of the *Journal*, which, if published in its entirety, would fill a shelf of volumes. Among the voluminous works of this author, the following will enable the reader to study Bradford's development of the craft of writing, especially of biography, from the beginning to end: *Lee, The American* (1912); *Union Portraits* (1916); *Damaged Souls* (1923); *Wives* (1925); *The Quick and the Dead* (1931), from which the life of Wilson is taken; and *Biography and the Human Heart* (1932), which contains much of the theory of biography that Bradford had taken fifty years to develop. Bradford died in 1932, surrounded by the books he loved—Latin, Greek, and French classics, and his own "psychographs."

Bradford's secure reputation in biographical writing rests upon his development of the "psychograph." Such biography neglects almost entirely the chronological sequence of events in a subject's life and concentrates on "what is essential, permanent, and vitally characteristic." The psychographer analyzes the character of his subject into its component parts, examines each in detail, gathers all the evidence he can, and synthesizes his conclusions into a finished biography or "psychograph." Of the one hundred and thirteen "psychographs" Bradford wrote, ranging in time from Xenophon and Pliny to Wilson, Lenin, and Mussolini, the one of Wilson included here is a good illustrative example.

Bradford's detailed and enlightening *Journal* is invaluable to the student of literature. It covers his entire literary life and is stimulating not only because of the insight it gives into his life, but also because of the revealing reflective passages concerning his writing—his methods and his choice of subjects. It is interesting to observe the daily change and growth of his first impression of a subject and the crystallization of his plan of development as the investigation advances.

The first mention of Wilson in the *Journal* is in November, 1918. Bradford here expresses his astonishment at Wilson's confidence and calm readiness to settle the future of the world. In January, 1919, he speculates on the "future and fortunes" of Wilson. Feeling that Wilson has undertaken an impossible task, Bradford wonders how he will explain his failure. He concludes that he will take the position "that he would have accomplished everything if it had not been for his ill-wishers." Also in this entry Bradford states that he is prejudiced against Wilson and wonders whether something in the man's character repels him.

On June 23, 1929, he mentions Wilson with several others as possible subjects for a series of contemporary character studies to be entitled *The Quick and the Dead*. By July, 1930, he is in the process of writing his biography of Wilson and is exasperated because Wilson talks so much about forgetting himself and about his disinterestedness. Bradford does not doubt his sincerity, but believes Wilson is deceiving himself. September 20, 1930, the material for Wilson is ready. Bradford feels that he has worked out a satisfactory method of portraying him. Although he is confident that the finished composition will suggest the "tangles" of Wilson's character "in due proportion and fit adjustment to each other," he doubts that it will satisfy either Wilson "worshippers or haters." September 26, he is still working on Wilson. He considers the material magnificent, but wonders whether he has erred in quoting too much. On the whole he is pleased with his treatment of Wilson's character. By September 28 Wilson's "psychograph" is finished, and Bradford's original repulsion has changed to admiration for Wilson's genius and power—equal, he considers, to those of Theodore Roosevelt.

JOHN (RODERIGO) DOS PASSOS was born in Chicago in 1896. He took a degree at Harvard in 1916 and immediately thereafter went overseas to serve in various ambulance units during the World War. Returning to America not long after the Armistice, he began to express some of his ideas in a novel about the American soldier's experiences in the war, *Three Soldiers* (1921). The book achieved a reasonably good reputation from the start, at least among critics, although the author's attempt at factual reality offended many readers who were still being nurtured in romantic traditions, not only about war but about experience of any sort. Dos Passos did not have to continue the fight alone, for many another writer, on returning from overseas service, began to make America conscious of what it called "the war generation." The violent shocking-power of what the public saw as brutal, disillusioning skepticism created a tempest of conflicting critical opinions. Thus, from the first, Dos Passos's work was regarded as ultra-liberal, even radical, in both content and form. His writings, novels, poems, plays, and essays have always shown a strong social consciousness and have aroused much discussion. He spent years wandering over much of the world and all parts of the United States as a newspaper correspondent and magazine free-lance writer, reporting social conflicts and political revolutions. He has been hailed as a sympathizer with the underdog, the champion of lost causes, a communist, an historian of class struggle, and the leader in writing proletarian novels.

Dos Passos is not primarily a biographer. "Meester Veelson" is one of a series of biographical portraits appearing in *U.S.A.*, a trilogy of novels affording a varied and comprehensive picture of the American scene in the first three decades of the twentieth century. Critics have judged these portraits to be the best part of his book.

BEVERLY SMITH was born in Baltimore in 1898. He graduated from Johns Hopkins University in 1919, after having served as a second lieutenant of artillery during the War. He subsequently studied law at Harvard and Oxford, and practiced in New York

City from 1922 to 1926. He was on the staff of the New York
Herald Tribune as reporter, foreign correspondent, and colum-
nist from 1926 to 1931. Since then he has been a free-lance writer
of magazine articles.

ELIZABETH SHEPLEY SERGEANT was born in Winchester, Massachusetts, in 1881. She graduated from Bryn Mawr in 1903 and
subsequently studied at the Sorbonne and the Collège de France.
She has done social work in Boston and New York, but has
been even more interested in writing. Her stay in France led
her to a preoccupation with French ideas and values, and of these
she has written understandingly in *French Perspectives* (1916).
She has also translated the work of the contemporary French
novelist, Jean Giraudoux.

Fire Under the Andes, from which the life of Holmes is taken,
is subtitled "A Group of North American Portraits" and includes,
also, pieces on Amy Lowell, Eugene O'Neill, Elinor Wylie, Paul
Robeson, and others. The unifying idea of the book is expressed
in the following quotation which appears on the title page of
the volume: "We must not only have hydrogen in balloons and
steel springs under coaches, but we must have fire under the
Andes at the core of the world." Characteristically, the life of
Holmes bears the subtitle "Justice Touched with Fire."

A comparison of this account of Holmes with its companion
piece by Beverly Smith will immediately bring out certain obvious differences. The key lies in the realization of the fact that
the two articles are addressed to entirely different audiences.
The American Magazine has a tremendous circulation. The
magazines which originally published the separate essays of *Fire
Under the Andes* (*The New Republic, Harper's Magazine, The
Nation*, etc.) have a more limited appeal, and to more highly
educated tastes. This, however, is no reason for supposing one
presentation inferior to the other. With this caution the reader
is left to make his own distinctions between the two selections.

SIGMUND SPAETH, widely known as the "tune detective," a popular writer and lecturer on musical subjects, was born in Philadelphia in 1885. Graduating from Haverford College in 1905,
he afterward took a Ph.D. at Princeton (1910). He has been a
teacher, a musical editor for various magazines (*McCall's, Es-*

quire, *Literary Digest*), and has written many popular books directed at non-specialist and lay audiences of people who are earnestly striving for musical literacy. In this way Spaeth has immeasurably helped the cause of musical education in America. Representative examples of such books are: *The Common Sense of Music* (1924), *American Mountain Songs* (1927), *The Art of Enjoying Music* (1933), *Great Symphonies* (1936), the titles of which indicate the non-professional character of the audience to which they are addressed. Spaeth has also had at least one successful radio program, *The Tune Detective*, which was built around the idea that modern popular music is melodically unoriginal, that it borrows snatches here and there from classical musical literature and puts them together in what appears to be, but is not, an original composition. Spaeth's interest in American popular music is further evinced by the life of Stephen Collins Foster of "Tin-Pan Alley," as are also his popular style and method of treatment.

A comparison of the three Foster pieces will bring out many ideas about each which could be apprehended only with difficulty—if at all—from the consideration of one piece alone. However, no attempt to interfere with the reader's own discrimination and judgment will be made here, except to suggest, as a starting point in the consideration of the three separate approaches of the individual authors, that one account appeared in a magazine called *Etude*, one in a series of radio broadcasts called *Pilgrimage of Poetry*, one in a book called *Pittsburgh Memoranda*.

TED MALONE (Frank Alden Russell) was born in 1908 in Colorado Springs, Colorado, where his father was a clergyman. He attended William Jewell College in Missouri, but did not graduate. He began his radio career as a ukulele player with KMBC in Kansas City over fifteen years ago. Since then he has been a writer of scripts for motion pictures, continuity editor for KMBC, and later production manager and program director of the same station. *Between the Book Ends*, a daily program begun locally in 1931, has been a coast-to-coast program since 1935. Malone wrote a monthly column on poetry for *Pictorial Review*, beginning November, 1937, and has since begun a similar one for *Good Housekeeping*. *The Pilgrimage of Poetry*, NBC, 1939-40, was a weekly fifteen-minute broadcast from the shrines of thirty-two American poets. Malone wrote to seven hundred United States colleges for a list of preferred figures, and out of these selected the most popular. Joseph Auslander, poetry consultant to the Library of Congress and an admirer of Malone, gave the send-off to the series, which began in the fall of 1939. Since then Malone has made a broadcasting tour of 10,000 miles— all the way from Boston, home of Oliver Wendell Holmes, to the Californian coast, the country of Joaquin Miller. The broadcasts combine biography with recitations of selected poems, and make considerable use of sound effects closely connected with the poet's life in the particular setting chosen. For instance, in the broadcast from Edgar Allan Poe's cottage in New York, the listener hears, first the closing of the front door, and then the knocking and tapping on the inner chamber door that suggests the recurrent theme of *The Raven*.

This type of biography is singularly effective because, recognizing the difficulty of attempting to draw near to a figure in *time*, it succeeds in getting close to it in *space*. The tone of the series is, of course, popular and non-academic, as one would expect a radio program to be. Its treatment of biography is affectionate and even sentimental, rather than critical, for the same reason. But just as radio has already succeeded in helping to create not only a wider but a more discriminating taste in music, so this type of program, though not of such long standing or such frequency, is perhaps helping to stimulate greater popular interest in poets and their work. Malone has already planned a new series of broadcasts on American literary classics and their authors for the season 1940-41.

HANIEL LONG was born in Burma in 1888, where his father was a missionary. However, his family belonged to Pittsburgh, and it was here that Long spent much of his life. He was educated at Exeter and at Harvard. His first position was on the staff of the New York *Globe*, but, finding this too strenuous, he began teaching at Carnegie Institute of Technology in Pittsburgh. Since 1929 Long and his family have lived in Santa Fe, New Mexico, where, in 1933, he helped to form a writers' publishing organization called Writers' Editions, Inc., which prints original work and arranges for its distribution and sale. Long has written several books of verse, one of which, *Pittsburgh Memoranda*, presents several personalities who had a significant connection with Pittsburgh.

The biography in verse, although uncommon, is not without precedent, even in American literature. For other contemporary examples the reader is referred to the Benéts' (Rosemary and Stephen Vincent) *A Book of Americans* (1933), and to the long biographical passages on Lincoln and General Beauregard in Stephen Vincent Benét's narrative poem of the Civil War, *John Brown's Body* (1928).

CARL SANDBURG, until recently, was mainly recognized for his poetry; now he is in a fair way to being regarded as a great biographer, especially since the publication of the final volumes of the life of Abraham Lincoln in 1939, a work that may never be superseded in completeness or wealth of authentic documentation. Sandburg was born in Galesburg, Illinois, in 1878. His parents were Swedish immigrants of the name of Johnson, a name so common and confusing in a Scandinavian community that Sandburg took for himself the name he is now known by. His school days were interrupted by periods of hard work. Much of his insight into the workaday world was the result of first-hand experience as a porter, scene-schifter, truck driver, painter—in all manner of skilled and unskilled labor in both rural and industrial areas. This period came to an end with the outbreak of the Spanish-American War, during which Sandburg served in an Illinois infantry regiment in Puerto Rico. On returning home after the war, he attended Lombard College from 1898 to 1902. After graduation he embarked upon a varied career of selling, political campaigning, reporting, editing, and writing poetry.

Encouraged by Harriet Monroe's publication of his early poems in *Poetry* in 1914 and the winning of a poetry prize, Sandburg issued the volume by which his reputation became established, *Chicago Poems* (1916), followed by other volumes of equal merit. With his career as a poet, however, we are only indirectly concerned. After 1920 Sandburg began to develop other interests—the collecting and editing of American ballads and folksongs, and the writing of prose. In 1926 appeared the first part of the life of Lincoln, *Abraham Lincoln, The Prairie Years*, in two volumes. Here he found an interest which was to last him throughout the many years of his later career. In 1932 appeared what was apparently an offshoot of his Lincoln research and a pendant to that work, *Mary Lincoln; Wife and Widow,* with a collection of letters edited by Paul Angle. Not until 1939 did Sandburg complete the tremendous task of accumulating and editing the vast amount of Lincolniana that went to the writing of the final four volumes: *The War Years.* Altogether, the six-volume biography is a major work which would alone confer on its author the status of a great writer, and indeed it is a question whether Sandburg the biographer or Sandburg the poet will be remembered longer. Actually, this question need not be decided, for Sandburg the biographer is still a poet. The imaginative vision which produced the interpretative poetry for which he is known is used to the full in the "life." It is a poet's work as well as an historian's chronicle. The idea of writing about Lincoln must primarily have appealed to the poet's sense of the cultural depth of Lincoln's prairie origins, his close kinship with the Illinois soil and the characteristic values of the middle-western frontier. Poetic as it is, however, the biography is not in the least unscholarly, rare as the combination may be; and it is this combination of qualities which may assure to Sandburg the honor of being Lincoln's greatest biographer. Some critics have found defects in the "life"; it is said to be too rich in meticulous detail, that the broader outlines are lost while through long chapters the author minutely explores hardly relevant events in all their complexity. But none has failed to admit the scope and power of the work, and none will in future be able to ignore it.

The life of Mrs. Lincoln appeared first in serial form in *Woman's Home Companion,* and was intended for a popular audience of housewives. It differs slightly in tone from the life of her husband, perhaps because it was not easy for the author to see a close relationship between the prairie soil and the woman who was primarily known as a Kentucky belle—a woman whose personality could more characteristically be set in a mid-century drawing room, where the transplanted values of a more urban culture tended to deny rather than support the homely, backwoods Lincoln tradition. But the story of the woman who has been sufficient of an enigma to confound most biographers from Herndon and Rankin down to Gamaliel Bradford is told understandingly and with sympathy.

CARL VAN DOREN was born in Hope, Illinois, in 1885. After graduating from the University of Illinois in 1907, and subsequently obtaining a Ph.D. from Columbia, he taught English, first at Illinois (1907-14), then at Columbia (1916-30). He was literary editor of *The Nation* (1919-22) and of *The Century* (1922-25), and editor of *The Literary Guild* (1926-34), as well as being a member of the committee of management of the *Dictionary of American Biography* (1926-36). His sizable list of works is mainly in the field of literary criticism and biography.

By reason of his connection with the *Dictionary of American Biography* (issued 1928-37), Van Doren is well fitted to write of the lives of American authors. Undoubtedly, he had much to do with the excellence of the *D.A.B.*, which is as scholarly as its British counterpart, *Dictionary of National Biography*, and much more readable. The reader is referred to the *D.A.B.* entry for the poet Elinor Wylie, written by Van Doren, not only as an example of the quality of the biographies in that series of volumes, but also as a comparison to the one presented in this text on the same subject by the same author. The two are worth comparing because they were written by the same man for two entirely different purposes, and will help to acquaint the reader with the problems of approach and method in biography. Noteworthy is the fact that the more personalized life here reprinted is a biography within an autobiography, an important part of *Three Worlds* (1936), wherein the author chronicles the several stages of his interesting career. This book should be read in its entirety by anyone who wishes to know more about Van Doren, and also about a large number of American notables whom he knew personally during his years as a journalist in New York in the nineteen-twenties. His most highly regarded recent biography is *Benjamin Franklin* (1938); elsewhere he combines literary criticism and biography in books on such widely different figures as Thomas Love Peacock, Jonathan Swift, and Sinclair Lewis.

ISHBEL ROSS (Mrs. Bruce Rae) was born in Scotland, but came to the New World at an early age. Like many Scotch immigrants, her family moved to the province of Ontario, Canada, where Mrs. Rae's career as a journalist began. After a year's experience in Toronto she removed to New York, where she has worked as a journalist for over fifteen years. Her husband was assistant managing editor of *The New York Times*.

Mrs. Rae has traveled extensively in her capacity as a journalist, has flown over the Victoria Falls in Africa and over Mt. Everest—exploits very similar to those of the earlier globe-trotter whose life she wrote. She is also the author of several novels of modern life, and other works of non-fiction besides *Ladies of the Press*, from which "Nellie Bly" is taken. Well qualified to write of women as journalists, Mrs. Rae treats in her book of the long line of distinguished newspaper women of America from the figure here presented down to such recent ones as Dorothy Thompson. Her accounts have, of course, the authenticity of an insider's.

FREDERICK LEWIS ALLEN is a prominent American journalist who has been on the editorial staffs of a half-dozen of America's foremost magazines. He was born in Boston, graduated from Harvard in 1912, and took his master's degree in the following year. He has been a member of the department of English of his own university, assistant editor of *The Atlantic Monthly* and *Harper's Magazine*, managing editor of *The Century*, and is now associate editor of *Harper's Magazine*.

His chief claim to the attention of the student is his having written one of the best informal histories of the nineteen-twenties, *Only Yesterday* (1931). Chapter IX of this book is a valuable, compact account of the intellectual and literary activities of the decade. Recently (1940) Mr. Allen has published a continuation of his chronicle called *Since Yesterday*, a book which deals with the period from the stock-market crash of October, 1929, to the early autumn of 1939 and the outbreak of the war in Europe.

The account of Horatio Alger was published in *The Saturday Review of Literature*, one of the few weekly publications in America devoted exclusively to literature. Similar articles, constituting something of a series, have appeared in this periodical, which, although mostly devoted to reviews of current books, frequently presents criticisms of well-known literary figures of the past. It is significant that the popular work of Alger, long considered beneath the notice of intellectuals, is here presented as having value to the searcher after popular aspects of American culture. It is equally significant that the man who in *Only Yesterday* was able to present such aspects should here deal with the man who wrote the most popular juvenile fiction of his day. The first part of the selection is rather strictly biographical, reasonably complete, factual, and supported by dates. The second part is a presentation of Alger's literary work in the light of the preceding biography. As a type, a work of the kind is frequently to be met with in periodicals devoted to book reviews.

THE STAFF OF *Time* is an association of writers gathered together for the express purpose of forming, developing, and perpetuating a "group style" by means of certain unifying mannerisms, devices, and editorial attitudes toward news. *Time* is, therefore, one of the most self-consciously "stylized" of the modern ventures in American journalism. Begun in 1923, it soon achieved a reputation for the lively, readable presentation of news that is implied in its slogan: "Curt, Clear, Complete"—a phrase which further illustrates an alliterative mannerism which it carries over into actual reporting.

By now, *Time's* style is easily recognizable to most magazine readers, even when it is met with in imitative or emulative writers not on *Time's* Staff, by several characteristic signs: inversion of the regular word order of subject and verb; omission of articles, conjunctions, and even the verb *to be*; formation of such "portmanteau" words (made popular by Lewis Carroll) as "cinemactor," "radiorator," etc.; inventive figures of speech of great vigor and originality; and finally, the use of the adjectival epithet similar to such "fixed epithets" of Homer as *"wine-dark seas"* and *"goodly* Odysseus." This last device has been used largely to give flavor to the description of personalities in the news, as in the alliterative epithet, *"bumbling* Mr. Baldwin." It was this habit which chiefly drew the criticism of "flippant" from conservative readers and journalists, since most of the epithets call attention to the physical, frequently grotesque, attributes of public figures, and thus introduce a note of caricature into the reporting technique. Though presumably not often libelous, such epithets do tend to make the person ridiculous rather than realistic.

A wealth of biographical material is to be found in *Time*, but only as the figure concerned, at the moment of the particular issue in which he appears, is for some reason or other in the public eye—unless, in short, he is newsworthy at that moment. Yet this is a very useful kind of biographical writing, and one which adds considerable value to the reporting of an event by making the history of the central figure support and underlie the event itself, which then achieves a deeper significance. This practice is one which gives *Time* a really distinctive approach to the presentation of the news. Note that the account of George S. Kaufman appeared when the production of a play in which he collaborated became news for the section entitled "The Theatre," that the one of Ambassador Johnson appeared when the Sino-Japanese War began to involve the nationals of the United States, that the one of Dr. John Dewey appeared when the celebration of his eightieth birthday became news for the section entitled "Education."

CLARENCE TRUE WILSON, perhaps the best known of American temperance workers, was born in Milton, Delaware, in 1872. He attended a small Maryland college, later graduated from the University of Southern California, and was afterward granted several honorary degrees by other institutions. He was ordained in the Methodist Episcopal Church, and held numerous pastorates. He became national secretary of the Temperance Society of the M. E. Church in 1910, a post which he held until his death. He was largely responsible for the erection of the temperance headquarters building in Washington, and wrote numerous books on temperance subjects (see *The Case for Prohibition*). He was even more widely known as a platform lecturer, and he participated in debates and symposia with the outstanding opponents of the prohibition movement—especially Clarence Darrow.

The uniqueness of the portrait of Darrow is that it was written, as the title suggests, by a man whose ideas were violently inimical to those of his subject. Yet, in an age when it is fashionable for biographers to "debunk" the lives of men with whom they are out of sympathy, this "friendly" approach to the "enemy" seems unusually acceptable. It is not merely the clergyman's professional tolerance toward a heretic or disbeliever; it has the more universal grace of ordinary human friendliness.

GEOFFREY THEODORE HELLMAN was born in New York in 1907, graduated from Yale in 1928, and since then has followed an active journalistic career. He was on the staff of *The New Yorker* from 1929 to 1936, with the exception of a year of association with *Fortune* (1931-32). He has also been associate editor of *Life*. Much of his original work has been in the form of the short biography, and he has contributed "close-ups" to *Life* and "profiles" to *The New Yorker*, from which latter magazine the life of Dr. Frank Chapman is taken.

The New Yorker, as might be supposed, tends toward a bright and debonair style of writing, even in its more serious "profiles." Humor is not out of place in the critical biography, provided it does not demean the subject or render him unrealistically undignified. Dr. Chapman's life is treated humorously at times, but also good-humoredly; and the reader is left in no doubt as to the author's respect and admiration for the colorful naturalist. Other portraits in *The New Yorker*, usually of figures within the specialized acquaintanceship of the well-educated urbanites of the country's largest metropolitan area, are more satiric and occasionally even biting—and, it may be added, seldom dull. For a more satiric use of humor and irony the reader is referred to the "profile" of Orson Welles.

FREDERIC SONDERN, JR., is of immigrant German parentage, the son of a well-known New York pathologist. He has very recently appeared as a prolific contributor of sound articles on contemporary affairs to the better-class magazines. Much of his writing centers around events and personalities related to the present conflict in Europe; and much of his interest, since he has written of King Victor Emmanuel and Mussolini as well as the Pope, apparently focuses on the Italian aspects of it.

The selection on the present Pope appeared as one of the series of "close-ups" which form a regular department of *Life*, photographic weekly newsmagazine, published by *Time*, Inc. Like *Time*, *Life* is one of the newer developments in American journalism, and was tremendously successful from the first issue. It aims at a pictorial and photographic presentation of people and events, and its "close-ups" are an attempt to treat biographical material from that point of view. However, recognizing the impossibility of being able to present a complete account by means of the camera alone, it unifies and supplies continuity to the pictures with explanatory captions and supplementary written material. It is hard to say whether the photography or the writing is primary. In the "close-ups," at least, though the latter is probably more able to stand alone, the former is by no means merely illustrative and visual support. The excellence of these biographies lies precisely in the combination of pictorial and literary elements. Good as the written account of the Pope is, it must lose something when deprived of the camera studies (twenty separate pictures in all); for the writer, who was partly relieved of the necessity of appealing to the visual imagination by means of physical description, is here deprived of at least some small element of his support. Some typical photographs: *Tomb of Pius XI, Vatican Radio Station* (interior), *Consecration of Bishops in St. Peter's at Rome,* etc. These not only tell us what the subject looked like at different periods of his career, but also supply other contemporary figures, and conjure up what is often called "background" or "atmosphere." The "close-ups" of *Life* are almost unique in the use of the camera as biographer; indeed, it may be recalled that the term "close-up" itself was borrowed from the vocabulary of motion-picture photographers.

ALICE LEONE MOATS was born of American parents in Mexico City in 1910. She was educated in the United States and abroad. Both she and her mother (Mrs. Wallace Payne Moats) have been regular contributors to such magazines as *Saturday Evening Post, Collier's, House and Garden, Country Life,* etc., and have collaborated on a very readable guide-book called *Off to Mexico* (1935). Miss Moats achieved public notice in 1933 by the publication of a liberal book of etiquette, *Nice Girls Don't Swear,* a title which indicates something of the author's approach to her subject. The range of the author's interests is wide—from international affairs to the humorous aspects of social manners, from short biography to the literature of travel and local color.

JOHN GUNTHER is one of that large fraternity of American newspaper correspondents which keeps this country the best informed in the world regarding international affairs in every political center of the globe. He was born in Chicago in 1901, graduated from the University of Chicago in 1922, was a reporter for the *Chicago Daily News* from 1924 to 1926, and began his career as a foreign correspondent in the latter year in London. Subsequently he was in Paris, Moscow, Berlin, Rome, Scandinavia, Geneva, and the Near East. He was Central European correspondent in Vienna from 1930 to 1936, returning to London for the years 1935 and 1936. During this time he interviewed a large number of foreign dictators, diplomats, political and financial celebrities, most of whom appear in his best work, *Inside Europe* (1936). He reported the Palestine riots (1929), the evacuation of the Rhineland (1930), the Spanish revolution (1932), as well as other important events. These widespread experiences formed the basis for the author's presentation of European power-politics in the above-mentioned book.

The numerous works of such foreign correspondents as Gunther, Vincent Sheean, Negley Farson, William Chamberlin, Webb Miller, etc., are not entirely unique in contemporary literature, but they are better defined as a type and much more plentiful than ever before. They combine exposition of political, economic, and social materials with personal experience, autobiography, and biography; and they use a journalistic, reportorial style that has been polished and otherwise modified for acceptance as permanent record. Such authors display a variety of literary skills—some exhibit a more consciously literary, some a more strictly reportorial, others a more formally expository, style.

The life of Hitler by Gunther is the first chapter of *Inside Europe*. Its genesis and development are illustrative of the type of writing to which it belongs. It was first published as "Hitler: An Unretouched Portrait" in the January, 1936, issue of *Harper's Magazine*, and appeared later in the year in the first edition of *Inside Europe*. But Europe did not stand still; neither did Hitler. Already in 1937 and more so in 1938 the biography was incomplete, and the political exegesis partly invalid. Gunther revised both the book and the included biography. The latest edition to date (War Edition, 1940) presents Hitler at "fifty-one," not "forty-six." Thus a biography or "profile" grows, and is expanded and amended as its subject gets older and the events of his life require a new set of generalizations concerning his essential character. Presumably, Gunther will keep on revising and become the author of a "progressive biography"—a unique type created by the opportunities and limitations inherent in the foreign correspondent's relation to his material. The reader will do well to trace not only additions to fact in the various "states" or "proofs" of this biographical "etching," but also the resultant reinterpretation of character and of the political significance of the events concerned.

RUSSELL MALONEY, like Thurber and Hellman, is a regular contributor of "profiles" to *The New Yorker*, and has, like them, achieved proficiency in this form of contemporary biography. For further information on this style of writing the reader is referred to the remarks on *The New Yorker* in the introductory note on Geoffrey Hellman.

CHARLES J(OHN) V(INCENT) MURPHY was born in Newton, Massachusetts, in 1904. From 1922 to 1924 he was a student at Harvard, which he left without graduating, to take up a journalistic career with the Associated Press. He worked on the staff of the New York *Sun* (1925), became advertising manager for a commercial company (1926), and returned to newspaper work for the New York *Evening Post* (1927). He was a political writer for the New York *World* (1929), and was placed in charge of that paper's relief-plane rescue of the Bremen flyers in Labrador (1928). In the same year he wrote a full-length biography of Admiral Byrd, *Struggle*, followed by a popular work on aviation, *Parachute* (1929). He has reported various important events, including the earthquake in Nicaragua (1931), and was in charge of the radio broadcasts of Byrd's Second Antarctic Expedition (1934). He has also written articles for *Harper's*, *Collier's*, and *The American*.

The account of Byrd here reprinted from *Life* exhibits the characteristics already discussed in connection with Frederic Sondern's account of the Pope. Its publication was occasioned by the news interest of Byrd's 1939 expedition to the Antarctic, and the popular public interest in the strange-looking vehicle especially designed for polar transportation. It is informative and somewhat panegyrical, and reflects the experience of its author as advertiser and publicity agent rather than as critic. Its readable presentation of factual information is closer, for instance, to Beverly Smith's treatment of Holmes than Sergeant's, and it suffers perhaps even more from the absence of photographs than Sondern's life of the Pope. To get the best out of Murphy's biography the reader should refer to its original publication in *Life*. However, the very fact of the biography's slight lack of completeness without photographic aid enables the reader to isolate the *literary* characteristics of the type.

MARK SULLIVAN, like another prominent journalist of the muckraking era—Lincoln Steffens—has at last written the story of his ˜eer. He calls it *The Education of an American*, a title which

significantly recalls that another American writer called his autobiography *The Education of Henry Adams*. Sullivan's account of
his life is much more compact, more simple, and considerably
less self-important than Steffens's. As a matter of fact, Sullivan
knew Steffens well, met him countless times as their paths crossed
in the days when *Collier's* and *McClure's* magazines were conducting their vigorous social and political campaigns against graft.
Sullivan did not think highly of his contemporary, considering
him a poseur and an indifferent reporter.

Sullivan's career reads like a typical success story of the period.
At nineteen he had saved $300.00 which he invested in a small
Pennsylvania newspaper. Three years later he sold a half interest for $5,500.00. He took a law degree but never practiced law.
Instead he embarked upon a journalistic career, campaigning
with *The Ladies' Home Journal*, editing *Collier's*, writing political columns for the New York *Evening Post*, the New York
Tribune (now the *Herald Tribune*), attending press conferences
at the White House, and acting as confidant to Republican
Presidents, especially Herbert Hoover. During these years of
activity Sullivan nevertheless had energy enough to produce a
six-volume history of the nation from 1900 to the present—
Our Times.

The Education of an American is the story of the first part of
Sullivan's life. It stops in mid-career with the stock market crash
of 1929. The rest of the chronicle has not been written, but is
vaguely promised at the close of the book. Chapter IX does not
deal with the public life of its author. Rather it is the affectionate, nostalgic, even poetic reminiscence of an aging man on the
values of a lost youth spent in the household of an immigrant
farmer in rural Pennsylvania. It is an elegiac recalling of the
characteristic background of so many urban dwellers who were
drawn from the farming districts of America to the large industrial, financial, and political centers. The mood is one of sentiment; it is even lyrical. The chronological and narrative aspects
of biography are here restrained, almost non-existent. Short as
the selection is, it is complete in itself and needs no supporting
context.

PATIENCE, RICHARD, and JOHN ABBE are the children of James
and Polly Shorrocks Abbe. Their father, an international press
photographer, was stationed in Paris at the time of their several

births, covering assignments for British and American news-papers. The family traveled about Europe—to Moscow, to Berlin (where the children attended a German public school), and finally back to America. Patience, the eldest child, and eleven years old in 1936 when "I, Patience" appeared in *The Atlantic Monthly*, wrote the story of herself and her interesting family with, as she says, "the occasional collaboration of Richard and Johnny." Richard was then nine, and Johnny only eight. The whole autobiography, complete in two issues of the magazine, was published in book form under the title *Around the World in Eleven Years*. Since their return home to America the three youthful collaborators have produced another book, *No Place Like Home* (1940). They spend much time on the Abbe Ranch in Colorado, of which they are themselves the proprietors.

Since most autobiographies are written by adults, that part of them which deals with childhood experiences is likely to receive elegiac, idealized, or merely synoptic treatment. It is one thing to *remember* one's childhood, to look back at it with the eyes of an adult; it is another to record it at the very moment of childhood itself, and with a child's perception. The very lack of an adult's education, experience, and acquaintance with the financial and other problems of a grown-up stamps a child's expression with a peculiar identity. The very limitation of his outlook is the source of compensatory powers. He sees and thinks and feels things which in grown-ups' lives are submerged by what to them are more important matters. Whenever children, gifted above ordinary with the ability to express themselves, are able to record their ideas and feelings, they contribute to literature something immeasurably better than a mere circus-like precocity.

BERNARD DE VOTO, at present one of the editorial staff of *Harper's Magazine*, was born at Ogden, Utah, in 1897. He left this Mormon community of his boyhood to attend Harvard, but his career there was interrupted in 1917 while he served as a second lieutenant in the infantry. Nevertheless he was elected to Phi Beta Kappa and returned to receive his degree (as of 1918) in 1920. He taught English at Northwestern University from 1922 to 1927, at Harvard from 1935 to 1936. In the meantime he had begun to write stories for the more popular magazines, such as the *Saturday Evening Post*, and had also achieved a critical reputation with the publishing of *Mark Twain's America*, a finely interpretative account of both Twain and the American scene which he mirrored. In 1936 various essays and narratives were collected out of magazines and published in book form as *Forays and Rebuttals*. At this time De Voto was on the staff of *The Saturday Review of Literature* (1936-38); he now writes "The Easy Chair" for *Harper's Magazine*.

De Voto is at his best as a chronicler and interpreter of the frontier—its history, its political and social philosophy, its folk customs, and especially its relation to the men and women who created it. As the picture of a frontier Utah boyhood, it is as typical as it is individualistic—at once the affectionate chronicle of its author's youth and that of thousands of others. Except for the regional character of religious custom and some slight geographical details, it is representative of a widespread phase of American culture.

CLAUDE V. DUNNAGAN was one of a number of southern writers employed under the Works Progress Administration on a Federal Writers' Project sponsored by the University of North Carolina. W. T. Couch, Regional Director of the Writers' Project, explains the purpose of the volume *These Are Our Lives* in the preface:

> Several months ago the writing of life histories of tenant farmers, farm owners, textile and other factory workers, persons in service occupations in towns and cities (such as bell hops, waitresses, messenger boy, clerks in five and ten cent stores, soda jerks), and persons in miscellaneous occupations such as lumbering, mining, turpentining, and fishing was begun by the Federal Writers' Project in North Carolina. This work has recently been extended to six other states, and a large number of stories have already been written.
>
> The idea is to get life histories which are readable and faithful representations of living persons, and which, taken together, will give a fair picture of the structure and working of society. So far as I know, this method of portraying the quality of life of a people, of revealing the real workings of institutions, customs, habits, has never before been used for the people of any region or country. It seems to me that the method here used has certain possibilities and advantages which should no longer be ignored.

Equally informative are Mr. Couch's instructions to writers employed in the compiling of data and the writing of the lives. The following are a few specific directions:

1. Materials are to be collected on tenant farmers and their families, farm owners and their families, cotton mill villagers and their families, persons and their families in service occupations in towns and cities, and persons and their families in miscellaneous occupations such as lumbering, mining, fishing, turpentining.

2. The life histories may range from approximately two thousand words to ten or fifteen thousand words, depending upon the interest of the material.

3. It is immaterial whether the stories are written in the first, second, or third person. Insofar as possible, the stories should be told in the words of the persons who are consulted. The effort should be made to get definite information. Avoid generalities such as "those who are industrious and ambitious can do well," "had not made good use of opportunities"—wherever possible expand such wording to give detail, that is, exactly what industry and ambition might have done or what the opportunities were that could have been used. In general avoid the expression of judgment. The writer will, of course, have to exercise judgment in determining the course of a conversation through which he gains information, but aside from this, he should keep his own opinions and feelings in the background as much as possible. For instance, if he sees people living under conditions which he thinks are terrible, he should be most careful not to express his opinion in any way and thus possibly affect the opinion of the person to whom he is talking. He must try to discover the real feeling of the person consulted and must record this feeling regardless of his own attitude toward it. Any story in which this principle is violated will be worthless.

4. The purpose of this work is to secure material which will give an accurate, honest, interesting, and fairly comprehensive view of the kind of life that is lived by the majority of the people in the South. It is extremely important that families be fairly selected for stories as well as those that make a less favorable impression. The sub-normal, the normal, the above normal, all should have stories written about them.

Following the instructions appears an outline for life histories prepared by Ida Moore, who wrote the first sample lives under the plan. The main topics suggested are:

    I. FAMILY
    II. EDUCATION
    III. INCOME
    IV. ATTITUDE TOWARD OCCUPATION AND KIND OF
        LIFE
    V. POLITICS
    VI. RELIGION AND MORALS
    VII. MEDICAL NEEDS
   VIII. DIET

IX. MISCELLANEOUS OBSERVATIONS
X. USE OF TIME

Although these life histories are written by professional writers, they are in a very real sense autobiographies. For the most part they are told in the first person, the writer really acting as amanuensis for people who, though by no means inarticulate, are frequently illiterate. The general significance implicit in the publication of the lives of such people is that a wealth of experience and expression fails to reach the public, autobiographically at least, as long as the means of communication is beyond the reach of the persons involved; unless, of course, such admirable attempts as this book can continue to overcome the inherent difficulties. The editors of the present text feel that the above materials are well worth this space, since they are so pertinent to the whole matter of biography and may lead to a better understanding of it.

JAMES THURBER—illustrator, essayist, and playwright—was born at Columbus, Ohio. He attended Ohio State University, but left in mid-career to serve during the War as a code clerk, first at Washington and then at the Paris Embassy. He had been rendered unfit for military service by the loss of an eye in childhood while playing with bows and arrows with other boys. On returning to civilian life he worked for the Columbus *Dispatch*, later for *The Paris Tribune*, and also the New York *Evening Post*. While still at college he had contributed numerous original drawings and cartoons to the student magazine, *Sun Dial*. Even while writing for the various newspapers, and later while a staff member of *The New Yorker*, he used to make drawings of the inimitable people and animals the public admires so much today. At first done on scraps of paper and the margins of manuscripts, they were noticed by colleagues, and eventually and yet hesitantly presented to the public. Since then Thurber's popularity as an illustrator has been phenomenal. In 1939 appeared the latest of his books of pictures with their characteristic captions, *The Lost Flower*, a tender yet bitter commentary on the stupidity of war. Recently, in collaboration with an old acquaintance, Elliot Nugent, Thurber has written a play which gives Thurberism a new and dramatic heightening—*The Male Animal*.

As an essayist Thurber is most usually associated with *The*

New Yorker, to which he has contributed some of its most characteristic writing. Thurber is neither a biographer nor an autobiographer, even in a less strict sense of the words; yet a study of his essays will show that without the autobiographical element they would lose most of their savor. Humorous though the typical familiar essay of Thurber is, the facts of the author's life there presented are true except for a humorist's license. The selection chosen for this volume was mainly intended to point to the fact that, although biography and autobiography today are legitimately large in volume, there is also a natural tendency for them to be merely fashionable, and consequently a prey to indiscriminate exploitation by anyone who wishes to ride on the wave of what is popular and financially profitable. Thurber's delightful reduction to absurdity of the mannerisms of the autobiographical fad may have a healthful, tonic effect. It will do no harm for the student of biography to laugh at a too intense, too serious, too complete preoccupation with the subject of this volume.

A READER'S GUIDE TO FACTS AND INTERPRETATIONS

⊔⊓⊔⊓⊔⊓⊔⊓⊔⊓⊔⊓⊔⊓⊔⊓⊔⊓⊔⊓⊔⊓⊔⊓⊔⊓⊔⊓⊔⊓⊔⊓⊓

BRAINS WIN AND LOSE	MEESTER VEELSON
Gamaliel Bradford	John Dos Passos

Reading Questions: Synthesis

Compare the two biographies, considering the following:

1. The significance of the titles
2. The style of the two authors (Note particularly the effect of Dos Passos's short sentences.)
3. The interpretations of Wilson's character
4. The selections of facts
5. The methods of development

Reading Questions: Analysis

(Bradford)

1. Why is the biography preceded by a chronology of Wilson's life?
2. What was Wilson's knowledge of the limitations and defects of intellectual life?
3. How much did Wilson owe to education?
4. What is Bradford's judgment of Wilson's intellectual versatility?
5. What evidence is presented to prove that Wilson was not lacking in nerves and sensibility?
6. What did Wilson believe the ideal form of government?
7. How successful was Wilson in dealing with men?
8. What was Wilson's own view of his career?

(Dos Passos)

9. How does Wilson's childhood choice of a favorite book and hero reveal his character?
10. Why was the slogan used in Wilson's reelection to the Presidency ironical?
11. In what way was Wilson's trip to Europe unique for United States Presidents?
12. How was Wilson received in Europe?
13. What comparison makes the deliberations of the Council of Four vivid?

326

14. What country's representative withdrew from the Council of Four?

Vocabulary Study

What is the meaning of the following terms: (Bradford) (1) indolent, (2) lucidity, (3) pedantry, (4) versatility, (5) orthodoxy, (6) clemency, (7) dénouement, (8) malevolence, (Dos Passos) (9) manse, (10) incontrovertible, (11) wardheeler, (12) "Merlin of politics," (13) ormolu, (14) protocols, (15) serried, (16) "wobblies"?

Correlated Reading

The library card catalog and *The Readers' Guide* list many items concerning Wilson. Recommended are:

1. Full-length biographies:
   Annin, Robert Edwards: *Woodrow Wilson; A Character Study*, Dodd, Mead, 1924
   Baker, Ray Stannard: *Woodrow Wilson, Life and Letters*, Doubleday, Doran, 1927
   Kerney, James: *The Political Education of Woodrow Wilson*, Appleton-Century, 1926
   Low, Alfred Maurice: *Woodrow Wilson, an Interpretation*, Little, Brown, 1918
   White, William Allen: *Woodrow Wilson, the Man, His Times, and His Task*, Houghton Mifflin, 1924
2. Short biographies:
   Bolitho, William: "Woodrow Wilson," *Twelve Against the Gods*, Simon and Schuster, 1929
   Brooks, W. E.: "Woodrow Wilson: Study in Personality," *The Century*, August, 1929
   Daniels, J.: "Wilson: Idealist and Statesman," *Saturday Review of Literature*, December 19, 1931
   Ludwig, Emil: "Woodrow Wilson," *Genius and Character*, Harcourt, 1927
   Williams, C. L.: "Woodrow Wilson as an Undergraduate," *Current History*, January, 1930
3. Miscellaneous items containing much information about Wilson:
   Baker, R. S., and Dodd, W. E.: *Public Papers of Woodrow Wilson*, Harper, 1925
   Lansing, Robert: *The Peace Negotiations, a Personal Narrative*, Houghton Mifflin, 1921
4. For additional biographies by Bradford see introductory note.
5. Other recommended short biographies from Dos Passos's *U.S.A.*:
   "The Plant Wizard" (Luther Burbank)

"The Electrical Wizard" (Thomas Edison)
"Tin Lizzie" (Henry Ford)
"The Campers at Kitty Hawk" (Wright brothers)
"Poor Little Rich Boy" (William Randolph Hearst)
"Art and Isadora" (Isadora Duncan)

Subjects for Writing

1. Woodrow Wilson and Democracy.
2. Woodrow Wilson's Famous Phrases.
3. Woodrow Wilson's Tragic Life. (Base this paper on Bolitho's biography.)
4. The Fourteen Points.
5. Woodrow Wilson, The Private Individual. (Base this paper on Edith Bolling Wilson's *My Memoir*, Bobbs-Merrill, 1938.)
6. Trace Bradford's growth of interest from his first mention of some individual in his *Journal* (see introductory note) until the biography of the individual is written.

JUSTICE HOLMES	OLIVER WENDELL HOLMES
Beverly Smith	Elizabeth Sergeant

Reading Questions: Synthesis

1. What motive inspired the writing of each of these biographies?
2. From the biographical details given make a chronological sketch of Holmes's life.
3. Compare the character of Holmes as revealed in the two biographies.
4. Summarize in one sentence the character of Holmes.
5. Compare the style of the two pieces.
6. Which narrative gave you the more pleasurable reading experience? Why?

Reading Questions: Analysis

(Smith)

1. Describe the environment in which Holmes grew up.
2. What purpose does the anecdote about the watchman and his dog serve?
3. Why was Holmes called the Great Dissenter?
4. What were some of the social and legal principles in which Holmes believed?
5. What was his opinion of wealth?
6. What new view of the common law did Holmes present in his book *The Common Law*?

(Sergeant)

7. What is the significance of the statement, "Here is a Yankee, strayed from Olympus"?

8. What other two fields of knowledge, besides law, interested Holmes?
9. Who was the "Bill James" with whom Holmes discussed philosophy?
10. Explain the meaning of the statement, "he has a spice of the Mephistophelean quality."
11. Select one anecdote and tell why you consider it biographically effective.

Vocabulary Study

What is the meaning of the following terms: (Smith) (1) aquiline, (2) debonair, (3) Brahmin, (4) voraciously, (5) liaison, (6) symposium, (Sergeant) (7) cryptic, (8) epigrammatic, (9) profundity, (10) divinations, (11) punctilio, (12) scintillating, (13) naïveté, (14) elixir, (15) aphorisms, (16) interstitial?

Correlated Reading

1. Consult the library card catalog and The Readers' Guide for additional works on Holmes. Recommended are:
   Beard, C. A.: "Justice Oliver Wendell Holmes," Current History, March, 1931
   Bent, Silas: Justice Oliver Wendell Holmes, Garden City, 1932
   Berle, Jr., A. A.: "Justice Holmes: Liberal," Survey Graphic, April, 1935
   Biddle, R.: "Mr. Justice Holmes," New Republic, September 7, 1932
   Cohen, M. R.: "Justice Holmes," New Republic, April 3, 1935
   Cottler, Joseph: "Judge Holmes and the Constitution," Champions of Democracy, Little, Brown, 1936
   Frankfurter, Felix: "Justice Holmes Defends the Constitution," The Atlantic Monthly, October, 1938
   Lief, Alfred: Dissenting Opinions of Mr. Justice Holmes, Vanguard, 1929
   Lerner, M.: "Justice Holmes: Flowering and Defeat," Nation, June 10, 1936
   Pollard, J. P.: "Justice Holmes Dissents," Scribner's Magazine, January, 1929
2. Consult The Readers' Guide for additional short biographies and portraits by Beverly Smith of such well-known figures as Winold Reiss, Fritz Kreisler, William E. Borah, Jay N. Darling, John L. Lewis, Cordell Hull, Eamon de Valera.
3. See the introductory note for other biographies by Sergeant, and consult The Readers' Guide for additional ones.

Subjects for Writing

1. Compare the legal careers of Holmes and Clarence Darrow.
2. Holmes's Supreme Court Career.
3. Develop an exposition of one of Holmes's famous interpretations.

STEVE FOSTER OF "TIN PAN ALLEY"
Sigmund Spaeth

STEPHEN FOSTER	STEPHEN FOSTER
Ted Malone	Haniel Long

Reading Questions: Synthesis

1. Compare the three biographies in approach, form, style, unifying element.
2. Did class discussion change your mind about which essay you preferred?

Reading Questions: Analysis

(Spaeth)

1. What characteristics did Foster have in common with most composers of popular "hits"?
2. What was Foster's physical appearance?
3. What "useful" occupation did Foster follow before he devoted himself to music?
4. How did Foster first bring his songs to public attention?
5. Why does Spaeth retell the story of Foster's selection of the Swanee River when composing *Old Folks at Home*?
6. What habit caused Foster to lose control of the income of his best sellers?
7. What is Spaeth's opinion of Foster's originality?

(Malone)

8. Why did Malone select Federal Hill for his broadcast of Foster?
9. What directed the attention of Foster's father on Stephen's birthday?
10. Why isn't "Oh Susanna" typical of Foster life?
11. Why do people who delight in pointing out how Foster chose the Swanee River for his song miss the secret of Stephen Foster?
12. Account for the simplicity of the vocabulary of this piece.

(Long)

13. What phrase in Walt Whitman's *Song of Myself* (Section XL) is echoed in Long's poem on Foster?
14. What is the context of the quotation at the end of Long's

poem in its original source, Keat's *Hyperion: A Fragment,*
and what is the significance of the analogy?

Vocabulary Study

What is the meaning of the following terms: (Spaeth) (1)
hauteur, (2) saccharine, (3) nostalgia, (4) effervescent?

Correlated Reading

1. Recommended full-length biographies:
Foster, Morrison: *My Brother Stephen,* Private printing,
1932
Howard, John Tasker: *Stephen Foster, America's Trouba-
dour,* Crowell, 1934
Milligan, Harold Vincent: *Stephen Collins Foster,* G.
Shirmer, 1920
Walters, Raymond: *Stephen Foster, Youth's Golden
Dream,* Princeton University Press, 1936
2. Short biographies and articles:
Bowman, John E.: "A Singer to Pioneers," *The Atlantic
Monthly,* July, 1935
Devine, E.: "Gentle Hearts," *Commonweal,* April 6, 1934
Graham, R. X.: "New Stephen Foster Memorial," *Etude,*
August, 1932
McCleary, A. L.: "My Old Kentucky Home," *Etude,* May,
1939
Palmer, Catherine W.: "Stephen Collins Foster," *Diction-
ary of American Biography,* Scribner's, 1928
Schmitt, G.: "Dusky Singing" (radio play), *Scholastic,*
April 30, 1938

Subjects for Writing

1. Universal Appeals in Foster Songs.
2. Select one of Foster's songs and find out all the facts you
can about it—its composition, geography, biography, popularity, significance, etc. Present your facts in the form of a
paper.
3. Folk Songs of America.
4. Compare the careers of Foster and Irving Berlin.
5. Compare the songs of Foster with those of Robert Burns.

MARY LINCOLN
Carl Sandburg

Reading Questions: Synthesis

1. To what extent do you consider Sandburg's treatment im-
partial?
2. Summarize in one sentence the character of Mary Todd
Lincoln.

Reading Questions: Analysis
1. Summarize Sandburg's judgment on each of the following attributes of Mary Lincoln's character: marital relationship, parental relationship, relationship to other people, temper, social interests, pride, jealousy, vanity.
2. Identify anecdotes or incidents used to illustrate any of the above characteristics.

Vocabulary Study
What is the meaning of the following terms: (1) audacious, (2) hallucinations, (3) poignantly, (4) charlatan, (5) palliate, (6) anathema, (7) self-abnegation, (8) penuriousness?

Correlated Reading
1. Other biographical works of Carl Sandburg:
Abe Lincoln Grows Up, Harcourt, 1938
Abraham Lincoln, the Prairie Years, Harcourt, 1926
Abraham Lincoln; the War Years, Harcourt, 1940
2. Other biographies of Mrs. Lincoln:
Barton, W. E.: *The Women Lincoln Loved*, Bobbs-Merrill, 1927
Barton, W. E.: "Mr. and Mrs. Lincoln," *Woman's Home Companion*, February, 1930
Bradford, Gamaliel: "Mrs. Abraham Lincoln," *Wives*, 1925
Carnegie, Dale: "The Woman in Lincoln's Life," *Reader's Digest*, January, 1937

Subjects for Writing
1. Compare Gamaliel Bradford's biography of Mrs. Lincoln with Sandburg's.
2. Compare Robert E. Sherwood's treatment of Mrs. Lincoln in the play *Abe Lincoln in Illinois* with that of Sandburg.

ELINOR WYLIE
Carl Van Doren

Reading Questions: Synthesis
1. What is Van Doren's point of view in this biography?
2. Summarize in one sentence the character of Elinor Wylie.
3. Make a chronology of Elinor Wylie's life.
4. What autobiographical purpose does the biography serve?

Reading Questions: Analysis
1. What one of Elinor Wylie's novels was inspired by her adulation of an English poet?
2. What was Elinor Wylie's early environment?
3. What anecdote does Van Doren use to illustrate Elinor Wylie's vanity?

4. What was Elinor Wylie's method of composition?
5. What is the meaning of the statement, "The document wanders, the work of art marches"?
6. What inspired the writing of Elinor Wylie's last sonnets?
7. What was Philip Hichborn's opinion of his mother?
8. What do you consider the most tragic element in Elinor Wylie's life?

Vocabulary Study

What is the meaning of the following terms: (1) obsessed, (2) precocious, (3) agile, (4) benign, (5) pillory, (6) chimaera, (7) damask, (8) reticent, (9) obdurate, (10) expatriates?

Correlated Reading

1. Other biographies of Elinor Wylie:
   Monroe, Harriet: "Comment," Poetry, February, 1929
   Sergeant, Elizabeth S. "Elinor Wylie," New Republic, December 1, 1926; also Fire Under the Andes, Knopf, 1927
2. Other biographies by Carl Van Doren:
   Benjamin Franklin, Viking, 1938
   James Branch Cabell, McBride, 1932
   Many Minds, Knopf, 1924 (contains short biographies of many 20th-century literary figures)
   "Mary Austin, Prophet and Poet of the Southwest," Scholastic, September 29, 1934
   Sinclair Lewis, Doubleday, Doran, 1933
   "Stephen Crane," American Mercury, January, 1924
   Swift, Viking, 1930
   "Thomas Hardy," Outlook, January 25, 1928

Subjects for Writing

1. Compare Van Doren's biography in the Dictionary of American Biography with the one here presented.
2. After reading the poems of Elinor Wylie mentioned in the biography and any others, write a paper telling to what extent biographical knowledge of Elinor Wylie aided in the appreciation of her poetry. (Consult The Readers' Guide for articles about the poetry of Elinor Wylie.)
3. Notable Friends of Carl Van Doren. (See Three Worlds.)

NELLIE BLY
Ishbel Ross

Reading Questions: Synthesis

1. What is Ishbel Ross's estimate of Nellie Bly?
2. To what degree did the style influence your appreciation?

Reading Questions: Analysis

1. What was Nellie Bly's great coup?
2. Where was Nellie Bly born and what was her childhood environment?
3. How did Nellie Bly obtain her pseudonym?
4. Why did Nellie Bly's physical appearance "fool" many of her victims?
5. What was Nellie Bly's first assignment with the *World*?
6. What were some of the reforms Nellie Bly worked for?
7. What was the talisman Nellie Bly considered lucky?
8. Why was the public at this time particularly interested in a trip around the world?

Vocabulary Study

What is the meaning of the following terms: (1) ghillie cap, (2) pseudonym, (3) histrionics, (4) percipient, (5) exposé, (6) garnitures, (7) talisman, (8) monsoon, (9) cataclysmic, (10) mitigate?

Correlated Reading

1. Consult the library card catalog and *The Readers' Guide* for biographies of other such notable newspaper women as Dorothy Thompson, Anna Eleanor Roosevelt, Sarah Josepha Hale, Inez Callaway Robb.
2. Many additional biographies of women famous in journalism are contained in Ishbel Ross's *Ladies of the Press*.

Subjects for Writing

1. Sob Sisters.
2. Women Editors (Sarah Josepha Hale, Eleanor Patterson).

HORATIO ALGER, JR.
Frederick Lewis Allen

Reading Questions: Synthesis

1. What is Allen's estimate of Alger's books?
2. Summarize in one sentence the impression you received from the biography of Alger the man.
3. How do you account for the popularity of Alger's books in 1895 as compared to their almost total neglect in, say, 1932?

Reading Questions: Analysis

1. Why is the career of Horatio Alger, Jr., a paradox?
2. How was Alger's own boyhood different from that of most of his heroes?
3. How does Allen account for Alger's unusual success in the writing of boys' stories?

Vocabulary Study

What is the meaning of the following terms: (1) paradox, (2) impostor, (3) frustration, (4) prerogatives, (5) padrone, (6) indefatigable, (7) abstemious, (8) clichés, (9) improvisation?

Correlated Reading

Consult the library card catalog and *The Readers' Guide* for additional biographies and articles by Allen and biographies and articles about Alger. Recommended are:

Allen, Frederick Lewis, *Only Yesterday* (particularly Chapter IX), Harper, 1931

Allen, Frederick Lewis, *Since Yesterday; the Nineteen-thirties in America*, Harper, 1940

Mayes, Herbert R., *Alger: A Biography Without a Hero*, Macy-Masius, 1928

Subjects for Writing

1. How Alger Books Reflect the Period of Their Popularity.
2. Read one of the Alger books mentioned in the biography, and write a review of it based on Allen's criticism.

PAST MASTER

EXCELLENCY IN A RICKSHA   DEWEY AT 80

Staff of *Time*

Reading Questions: Synthesis

1. To what extent do you consider that portraits like these increase comprehension of news stories?
2. What is *Time's* estimate of Kaufman's success?
3. What is *Time's* appraisal of Johnson as a diplomat?
4. Rename the portrait of Dewey with a title that will give some insight into his character and achievements.

Reading Questions: Analysis

("Kaufman")

1. In what way does the career of Kaufman refute the statement, "the creative spirit dwells celibate and solitary"?
2. Why has Kaufman been especially successful in the field of comedy and satire?
3. Why is Kaufman an ideal collaborator?
4. Describe Kaufman's working habits.
5. Sketch Kaufman's life before he began his theatrical career.
6. List some of Kaufman's idiosyncrasies.

("Johnson")

7. As a student, what ability did Johnson have that portended his success as a diplomat?

8. What trait of Johnson's character is vivified by the anecdote of the four ducks?
9. Why is Johnson's account of the earthquake in Yokohama in 1923 quoted?
10. Describe Johnson's appearance.

("Dewey")

11. Why wasn't Dewey present at any of the birthday meetings held in his honor?
12. What trait of Dewey's character is fabulous?
13. How does Dewey's favorite hobby reveal his character?
14. What proverb expresses the essence of Dewey's philosophy?
15. What is Dewey's answer to the disillusionments he admits?

Vocabulary Study

What is the meaning of the following terms: (Kaufman) (1) celibate, (2) emporium, (3) permeate, (4) amicably, (5) infallible, (6) ad-lib, (7) stodgy, (8) brusque, (Johnson) (9) cardinal, (10) incinerated, (11) mandarin, (12) chronic, (13) fulminating, (Dewey) (14) acrostic, (15) pragmatism, (16) anthropological, (17) cognition, (18) exonerating, (19) dodo, (20) demoralized?

Correlated Reading

1. Examine the current issue of some news periodical for biographical sketches of newsworthy figures. Examine past issues of *Time* for articles entitled "Man of the Year" published in the first issue in January each year.
2. Other portraits of George S. Kaufman:
   Carmer, C.: "George Kaufman, Playmaker to Broadway," *Theatre Arts*, October, 1932
   Corbin, J.: "George S. Kaufman," *Saturday Review of Literature*, January 21, 1933
   Moses, M. J.: "Satirist in the American Theatre," *North American*, January, 1934
3. Other portraits of Nelson Trusler Johnson:
   "Ambassador Johnson," *Newsweek*, December 27, 1937
   Palmer, W. F.: "Men of State," *New Outlook*, May, 1934
   "They Stand Out from the Crowd," *Literary Digest*, June 22, 1935
   "Up from the Ranks," *Scholastic*, October 2, 1937
4. Other portraits of John Dewey:
   Hook, Sidney: *John Dewey, an Intellectual Portrait*, John Day, 1939
   Schilpp, Paul Arthur: *The Philosophy of John Dewey* (introductory biography), Northwestern University, 1939

Slosson, Edwin Emery: *Six Major Prophets*, Little, Brown, 1917

5. *The Readers' Guide* lists many more articles by and about these three men—especially John Dewey, a prolific writer.

Subjects for Writing

1. *Time's* Style. (See analysis of *Time's* style in introductory note.)
2. Read one of Kaufman's plays and tell how a biographical knowledge increased your appreciation.
3. The Pulitzer Prize.
4. Famous American Diplomats.
5. Famous American Educators.

DARROW, FRIENDLY ENEMY
Clarence True Wilson

Reading Questions: Synthesis

1. What motivated the writing of this portrait?
2. How does the title indicate the unity of the portrait?
3. What is Wilson's final appraisal of Darrow?

Reading Questions: Analysis

1. What was the writer's original feeling toward Darrow?
2. Why does Wilson relate the incident in which Darrow demanded an equal fee for him?
3. What were Darrow's Christian traits?
4. What biographical purpose is served by the anecdote about Darrow's clothes and the reporters?
5. For what kind of cases was Darrow famous?

Vocabulary Study

What is the meaning of the following terms: (1) quizzical, (2) salutory, (3) agnostic, (4) gourmand?

Correlated Reading

1. Consult *The Readers' Guide* from 1920 to 1939 for articles by Clarence True Wilson. Note that many of these concern prohibition, the subject of his debates with Darrow.
2. Other biographies and portraits of Darrow:
   Darrow, Clarence S.: *The Story of My Life*, Scribner's, 1932 (autobiography)
   Eaton, W. P.: "Clarence Darrow: Crusader for Social Justice," *Current History*, March, 1932
   Garrison, W. E.: "Darrow the Tolerant," *Christian Century*, March 23, 1932

Steffens, Lincoln: "Attorney for the Damned," *Saturday Review of Literature*, February 27, 1932

Stolberg, B.: "Clarence Darrow," *Nation*, March 2, 1932

Subjects for Writing

1. Darrow and the Case of Big Bill Haywood. (See "Big Bill," Dos Passos, *U.S.A.*)
2. Famous American Temperance Workers.
3. Read Darrow's account in his autobiography of any incident mentioned in Wilson's biography or any other incident of Darrow's life that may interest you. Make a précis of your reading.

BOY MEETS BULLFINCH
Geoffrey T. Hellman

Reading Questions: Synthesis

1. What is Hellman's appraisal of Dr. Chapman?
2. Indicate the logical divisions of the profile.
3. In what way does the title indicate the unity of the entire profile?

Reading Questions: Analysis

1. Account for Dr. Chapman's dislike of some birds.
2. What is Dr. Chapman's approach to the study of birds?
3. From whom does Dr. Chapman think he inherited the patience required of an ornithologist?
4. What bird has Dr. Chapman pronounced his American favorite?
5. What work did Dr. Chapman do before he devoted all his time to birds?
6. What ability of his wife particularly delighted Dr. Chapman?
7. Point out several instances of the author's use of irony.
8. What formal education did Dr. Chapman have?

Vocabulary Study

What is the meaning of the following terms: (1) curator, (2) ornithology, (3) viveolanius, (4) surreptitiously, (5) esoteric, (6) museology, (7) faunal, (8) arifauna?

Correlated Reading

1. Other portraits by Hellman:
   "Human Firecracker," *Reader's Digest*, August, 1939
   "Mrs. Roosevelt," *Life*, February 5, 1940
   "Thinker in Hollywood," *New Yorker*, February 24, 1940
2. Autobiographical works of Dr. Chapman:
   Autobiography of a Bird Lover, Appleton-Century, 1933

Camps and Cruises of an Ornithologist, Appleton-Century, 1908

Life in an Air Castle; Nature Studies in the Tropics, Appleton-Century, 1938

My Tropical Air Castle; Nature Studies in Panama, Appleton-Century, 1929

3. Consult *The Readers' Guide* for the many articles about and by Dr. Chapman. Recommended is: "Naturalist, Artist, Author, Educator," *Bird Lore*, July, 1935

Subjects for Writing

1. In Dr. Chapman's autobiographical works read the full account of any incident mentioned in the biography. Make a précis of your reading.
2. Compare the careers and interests of Dr. Chapman and John James Audubon.
3. Some Famous American Naturalists.

THE POPE
Frederic Sondern, Jr.

Reading Questions: Synthesis

What is Sondern's estimate of the Pope as (1) a man, (2) a statesman, and (3) an ecclesiastic?

Reading Questions: Analysis

1. What attribute of the Pope's character does the opening anecdote illustrate?
2. Describe the Pope's background and education.
3. What special ability did Eugenio Pacelli bring to the Papacy?
4. Why did Pacelli visit the United States in 1936?
5. How does Sondern emphasize the fact that Pope Pius XII is "universally beloved and respected"?
6. How does Pacelli's "incredible memory" serve him in his work?
7. How does Sondern's account of the usual daily routine of the Pope develop his character?
8. Why is the Pope's life lonely?

Vocabulary Study

What is the meaning of the following terms: (1) nunciature, (2) raconteur, (3) nuncio, (4) ascetic, (5) tirade, (6) *dum ex cathedra loquitur*, (7) impeccable, (8) loggias, (9) consistorial, (10) genuflections?

Correlated Reading

1. Other portraits by Sondern:
   "Hitler's Himmler," *Current History*, June, 1940
   "Little King," *Life*, May 27, 1940
   "Mussolini Grows Old," *American Mercury*, March, 1940
   "Wilhelmina of Holland," *Reader's Digest*, April, 1940
2. Full-length biography of Pacelli:
   Dinneen, Joseph E.: *Pius XII, Pope of Peace*, McBride, 1939

Subjects for Writing

1. The Nature of the Vatican State.
2. Famous Ecclesiastical Statesmen (Richelieu, Wolsey, etc.).
3. Compare Sondern's biography of Mussolini with that of Gunther.

HICK ON BROADWAY
Alice Leone Moats

Reading Questions: Synthesis

1. How does the title indicate the unity of the portrait?
2. How does the closing sentence emphasize the unity of the portrait?

Reading Questions: Analysis

1. How does Abbott differ from the popular conception of a Broadway theatrical producer?
2. What is Abbott's physical appearance?
3. What is Abbott's most worldly characteristic?
4. What other work in addition to writing, producing, and acting in his plays has Abbott done?
5. How is Abbott regarded by his actors?
6. What is Abbott's attitude toward women, money, recreation?
7. What use does the portrait make of anecdotes?

Vocabulary Study

What is the meaning of the following terms: (1) menial, (2) succès d'estime, (3) chic, (4) kleptomaniac, (5) "abbattoir"?

Correlated Reading

1. Consult *The Readers' Guide* and the library card catalog for books and articles by Alice Leone Moats covering a wide range of interest.
2. Consult the library card catalog and *The Readers' Guide* for works by and about George Abbott.

Subjects for Writing

1. Read one of the "hit" plays of Abbott mentioned in the portrait. Write a paper concerning it based on the critical comments of the portrait.
2. What knowledge of theatrical organization can you gain from the three selections dealing with the theatre included in the text?

HITLER
John Gunther

Reading Questions: Synthesis

1. To what extent is Gunther's treatment of his subject sympathetic? Unsympathetic? Disinterested?
2. Why did Gunther select the quotation from Hitler with which he starts the biography?
3. Write a sentence of your own that would serve as a thesis sentence of the biography.
4. Make a chronology of Hitler's life.

Reading Questions: Analysis

1. Why is Hitler a paradox?
2. Analyze the character of Hitler into its component parts— love, ambition, religion, physical courage, loyalty, etc. Summarize briefly what Gunther has to say about each.
3. What positive qualities of character does Hitler possess that Gunther considers contribute to his power?
4. List some of the epithets that make the portrait vivid to you.
5. What significant purpose do Gunther's anecdotes serve?

Vocabulary Study

What is the meaning of the following terms: (1) bizarre, (2) draconian, (3) *Putsch*, (4) circumlocutory, (5) demoniac, (6) *Reichskanzler*, (7) eroticism, (8) sacrosanct, (9) somnambulist, (10) amelioration, (11) plebiscite?

Correlated Reading

1. Gunther's two popular books—*Inside Europe* and *Inside Asia*—contain portraits of many other contemporary statesmen. Recommended are:
   "Stalin," also in *Harper's Magazine*, December, 1935
   "Mussolini," also in *Harper's Magazine*, February, 1936
   "King of Kings," also in *Harper's Magazine*, December, 1938
   "The Emperor of Japan," also in *Harper's Magazine*, February, 1938

"Manuel Quezon," also in *The Atlantic Monthly*, January, 1939
2. Consult *The Readers' Guide* for other portraits of Hitler. Recommended is:
"Man of the Year," *Time*, January 2, 1939
3. Self-portraits are Hitler's *Mein Kampf* and his speeches— for example, "Address to the Reichstag, September 1, 1939," *Vital Speeches*, September, 1939

Subjects for Writing

1. Explain Gunther's statement that the theory of the *Führer Prinzip* is "the reversal of the democratic theory of government."
2. What was the Munich *Putsch* of 1923?
3. Compare and contrast the anti-Semitism in Germany with the treatment of racial minority groups in other countries —for example, the Irish in Great Britain, the Negro in America.
4. Goering: Hitler's Successor. (Consult *The Readers' Guide* for portraits of Goering.)
5. After reading Gunther's "Mussolini" (see also Frederic Sondern's portrait), write a paper comparing the two dictators.
6. Compare the 1936 and the 1940 portraits of Hitler by Gunther.

"THIS AGELESS SOUL"
Russell Maloney

Reading Questions: Synthesis

1. What is the author's opinion of Welles?
2. What characteristic of Welles does Maloney emphasize?

Reading Questions: Analysis

1. To what three things does Maloney ascribe Welles's success?
2. What is the extent of Welles's formal education?
3. Where did Welles make his first successful dramatic appearance?
4. In what department of dramatics has Welles been the least successful?
5. What book of Welles's has sold 90,000 copies?
6. What is Welles's physical appearance?
7. What elements in Welles's make-up adapt him perfectly to his surroundings?
8. What gives Welles an authoritative stage presence?

Vocabulary Study

What is the meaning of the following terms: (1) *bon vivant*, (2) vicariously, (3) mural, (4) mélange, (5) aphasia, (6) impeccable, (7) baroque?

Correlated Reading

1. Consult *The Readers' Guide* for other portraits by Russell Maloney. Recommended are:
   "Awful Bore," *New Yorker*, April 6, 1940
   "Reporter at Large," *New Yorker*, May 11, 1940
2. Consult *The Readers' Guide* for other articles by and about Orson Welles. Recommended are:
   "Marvelous Boy," *Time*, May 9, 1938
   "New Star in the American Theatre," *Newsweek*, January, 1937
   "Playboy," *American Magazine*, June, 1938
   Vernon, G.: "Age Twenty-two," *Commonweal*, August 27, 1937

Subjects for Writing

1. Listen to a radio performance presenting Orson Welles (if available), and from his preliminary conversation and his part in the play form your own opinion of his personality. Give a written account of this.
2. Outstanding Radio Personalities.

ADMIRAL BYRD

Charles J. V. Murphy

Reading Questions: Synthesis

1. To what degree is Murphy's treatment eulogistic?
2. What is his appraisal of Byrd as a man? As an explorer?

Reading Questions: Analysis

1. What is particularly remarkable about Byrd's success?
2. What places has Byrd explored in addition to the Antarctic?
3. What are Byrd's interests besides exploration?
4. What is Byrd's physical appearance?
5. What is the background of Byrd's career?
6. How has Byrd made exploration pay?

Vocabulary Study

What is the meaning of the following terms: (1) bights, (2) unadjudicated, (3) *terra incognita*, (4) anachronistic, (5) retinue, (6) acumen, (7) recalcitrants?

Correlated Reading

1. Other biographical works by Charles J. V. Murphy:
   "Conqueror of the White Plague" (Edward Livingstone
   Trudeau), *Reader's Digest*, April, 1940
   *Struggle; the Life and Exploits of Commander Richard E.
   Byrd*, Stokes, 1928
2. Autobiographical works by Richard E. Byrd:
   Alone, Putnam, 1938
   *Discovery; the Story of the Second Byrd Antarctic Ex-
   pedition*, Putnam, 1935
   Little America, Putnam, 1930

Subjects for Writing

1. Animal Life of the Antarctic.
2. The Geography of Little America.
3. With the help of Murphy's full-length biography and
   Byrd's autobiographies, expand any incident mentioned in
   the portrait into a detailed account.

THE EDUCATION OF AN AMERICAN

Mark Sullivan

Reading Questions: Synthesis

1. What is the mood of the selection?
2. What gives it universality of appeal?
3. Give a title to the essay that is interesting but that still
   suggests the unity and mood of the selection.

Reading Questions: Analysis

1. What were the subjects the boys talked about on summer
   evenings?
2. What was the most alluring of their ambitions?
3. What accentuated Sullivan's desire to see what was beyond
   the horizon?
4. What was the reaction of Sullivan's parents to their boys'
   leaving home?
5. Describe a typical visit home.
6. How did Sullivan know that his parents were lonely?

Vocabulary Study

What is the meaning of the following terms: (1) fortuitous,
(2) cavalcade, (3) contour, (4) accentuated, (5) impetuousness, (6) "a call to Carcassonne," (7) inexorable, (8) repine,
(9) staidness, (10) poignant?

Correlated Reading

1. Interesting articles about Sullivan:
   "Average American," *Time*, November 18, 1935

"Writer Turns Back to First Job for 50-Year Celebration,"
Newsweek, November 21, 1938

2. Sullivan, Mark: *Our Times*, Scribner's, 1936

Subjects for Writing

1. My "Call to Carcassonne."
2. Compare the boyhoods of Sullivan and De Voto.
3. Famous American Muckrakers.

I, PATIENCE
Patience Abbe

Reading Questions: Synthesis

1. To what extent is this selection subject to the usual suspicion attached to children's works of having been extensively revised by adults?
2. Why is a work like this interesting to adults ?
3. What do you learn indirectly about Patience's family?

Reading Questions: Analysis

1. If this autobiography had been written by an adult, what are some incidents you think would consciously have been left out?
2. What are some incidents that you think would unconsciously have been left out by the adult writer?

Correlated Reading

Consult the library card catalog and *The Readers' Guide* for other works written by children. Suggested are:

De La Mare, Walter John: *Early One Morning in the Spring*, Macmillan, 1935
Lin, Abet and Anor: *Our Family*, John Day, 1939
McMurray, Devon: *Hoosier Schoolboy on Hudson Bay*, Little, Brown, 1937
Mearns, Hughes: *Creative Power*, Doubleday, Doran, 1929

Subjects for Writing

1. Compare this autobiography of childhood with the two by adults included in the text.
2. Characterize the compositional devices used by children.

FOSSIL REMNANTS OF THE FRONTIER
Bernard De Voto

Reading Questions: Synthesis

1. What is the significance of the title?
2. In a word or phrase entitle each of the divisions of the narrative.

Reading Questions: Analysis

1. In what way is the opening incident relevant to the narrative?
2. List the "fossil remnants" De Voto discusses.
3. Why has Utah little history of Indian trouble?
4. What frontier attitude toward Indians did De Voto inherit?
5. What deeper violence than casual outlawry did Ogden experience?
6. In what ways does De Voto consider his childhood on the Mormon frontier a rich heritage?
7. What "fossil remnant" of the frontier had the greatest influence on De Voto's childhood?
8. What has De Voto to say about individualism and the frontier?

Vocabulary Study

What is the meaning of the following terms: (1) misdemeanor, (2) orgies, (3) effrontery, (4) bellicose, (5) technological unemployed, (6) largesse, (7) amerind, (8) sibylline, (9) megalopolis, (10) neolithic, (11) exotic, (12) excerpts, (13) furtive, (14) parochial, (15) apocalypse, (16) ecstatic, (17) exegesis, (18) liturgical, (19) frustrated, (20) apostate, (21) metaphysicians, (22) enigma, (23) kulaks, (24) fin de siècle, (25) bucolic?

Correlated Reading

Consult the library card catalog and *The Readers' Guide* for further fiction and non-fiction by De Voto. The following contain material relevant to the included autobiography:

Forays and Rebuttals, Little, Brown, 1936
Mark Twain's America, Little, Brown, 1932
"Real Frontier," *Harper's Magazine*, June, 1931
"West: A Plundered Province," *Harper's Magazine*, August, 1934

Subjects for Writing

1. My Childhood Environment.
2. Read several of De Voto's "Easy Chair" articles (see monthly numbers of *Harper's Magazine* from November, 1935) and write a critical essay on why they are so called.

GET OUT AND HOE

Claude V. Dunnagan

Reading Questions: Synthesis

1. Do you consider the title well chosen? Why?
2. What do you learn of the life of white sharecroppers?

Reading Questions: Analysis
1. To what extent does this autobiography fulfill the purpose of the volume in which it was published? (See introductory note.)
2. How closely does the writer follow his instructions?
3. Are all the topics of the outline included?

Vocabulary Study
To what degree does the language used improve the effectiveness of the piece?

Correlated Reading
1. Consult *The Readers' Guide* under "farm tenancy" for articles on sharecroppers. Recommended are:
Barry, D. L.: "Men Without Hope," *Catholic World*, August, 1938
Caldwell, E.: "You Have Seen Their Faces," *The Atlantic Monthly*, November, 1937
Wallace, H. A.: "Farm Tenancy," *Vital Speeches*, February, 1937
2. Consult the library card catalog for stories of sharecroppers by Erskine Caldwell and William Faulkner.

Subjects for Writing
1. Using the instructions and the outline given, write a biography of someone you can interview.
2. The Sharecropper in Fiction.
3. The Value of Ghost-writing.

THE HIDING GENERATION
James Thurber

Correlated Reading
1. Articles about Thurber:
Bacon, L.: "Humors and Careers," *Saturday Review of Literature*, April 29, 1939
"Early Thurber," *Life*, April 22, 1940
2. Articles by Thurber:
"Adverbial Advice," *Scholastic*, March 13, 1937
"Fables for Our Times," *New Yorker*, February 17, 1940
"Snapshot of a Dog," *Reader's Digest*, March, 1936
"Tempest in a Looking Glass," *Forum*, April, 1937
"Thinking Ourselves into Trouble," *Forum*, June, 1939
"Thurber Reports His Own Play," *Life*, January 29, 1940

Subjects for Writing
1. Thurber's Humor.
2. Vivid but Insignificant Incidents from My Own Life.
3. The Critical Value of Thurber's Autobiographical Essay.